IN THE ARENA

IN THE ARENA

The Care and Feeding of American Politics

Vernon F. Anderson
North Seattle Community College

Roger A. Van Winkle
Harford Community College

HARPER & ROW, PUBLISHERS
New York Hagerstown San Francisco London

It is not the Critic who counts, not the one who points out how the strong man stumbled or how the doer of deeds might have done them better.

The credit belongs to the man who is actually in the arena, whose face is marred with sweat and dust and blood; who strives valiantly; who errs and comes short again and again; who knows the great enthusiasms, the great devotions, and spends himself in a worthy cause; who, if he wins, knows the triumph of high achievement; and who, if he fails, at least fails while daring greatly, so that his place shall never be with those cold and timid souls who know neither victory nor defeat.

Theodore Roosevelt

Sponsoring Editor: Dale Tharp
Project Editor: Pamela Landau
Designer: Andrea C. Goodman
Production Supervisor: George Buckman
Compositor: University Graphics, Inc.
Printer and Binder: The Murray Printing Company
Art Studio: Edward Malsberg
Cover illustration: Edward Malsberg

IN THE ARENA THE CARE AND FEEDING OF AMERICAN POLITICS

Library of Congress Cataloging in Publication Data
Anderson, Vernon F
  In the arena.
  1. Electioneering—United States. 2. Politics,
Practical. I. Van Winkle, Roger, joint author.
II. Title.
JK2281.A62   329'.00973   76-2535
ISBN 0-06-046811-4

Contents

3 The Whys of Voting   *76*

4 Party Politics: Who Runs the Show?   *110*

5 Campaign Fever: What Are the Symptoms?   *157*

6   The Decision: Running for Public Office   226

7   Strategy, Technology, and Politics   254

8 Control: The Art of Campaign Management   *286*

9 The Image Builders   *342*

10   Challenge of Decision Making: A Serious Game of Politics   *394*

Preface

"I'm not going to vote for him; I'm voting against that other guy." How many times have all of us heard a similar comment? In America today an increasing percentage of voters seem to feel that there is little choice for the average citizen really to influence the outcome of the electoral process. Yet the opportunities for citizen participation have never been greater, nor the need for citizen involvement more acute.

This book, then, was developed both to introduce readers to the radical organizational and technological changes occurring in campaign politics and to help them realize their potential as participants in that system. We do not claim that instant political success awaits the eager reader of this work; but we do suggest that the reader be able, on completion, to comprehend, in a positive fashion, politics and its impact on the electorate.

Today's citizenry tends to be *turned off* by the whole concept of government. They would prefer to sit in front of their television sets and deride the "corrupt" system rather than to try to understand what has really taken place. The Watergate defendants were not alone in standing trail for betraying the republic. Each American who looked the other way when power was corrupted, or delegated by forfeiture his or her right to determine America's priorities, was also guilty. We as citizens must learn how the system works, how it is controlled, how we judge the validity of political causes and countercauses, and how we may most easily influence the political process.

This book, then, demands awareness—awareness of the political system and how it works. Recognizing, however, that the general reader has had little exposure to the political process, we have chosen a wide variety of materials for inclusion in these chapters. Politicians, academicians, journalists, campaign consultants, and advertising specialists, have lent their skills to the discussion. Some of the material is original, resulting from research, personal interviews, panel presentations, or taped discussions at the Center for the Study of Practical Politics, Seattle, Washington. Other inclusions will seem familiar but perhaps will be used in a different form. Ultimately our purpose is to inform the reader better about American politics.

In order to facilitate this goal, we have included a campaign simulation game at the end of the book. The game is designed to be used over a four-day period. At the option of the participants, it can be included at the end of the course or integrated as a "working" part of the assignment. Although participation in the game is not a necessity to successful use of the book, it expands the readers' knowledge by helping them to apply, under controlled circumstances, the principles delineated in the preceding chapters. Such a simulation can be the ideal conclusion to a study of the American political process.

Ideally the work is especially suited to be used in the standard courses in American government, political behavior, political parties, or public opinion and for the variety of programs using the internship concept.

In the preparation of this manuscript, we would like to especially thank the American Association of Political Consultants, Campaign Associates Inc., and the *Congressional Quarterly* for their assistance in the development of this work. In addition we would like to extend our appreciation to several individuals who have read and commented on the work while in progress, especially John Hempelmann, Seattle, Washington; Raymond L. Hazlet, Long Beach, California; Norman R. Luttbeg, Florida State University; Steve J. Mazurana, University of Northern Colorado; and E. H. Ferguson, Jr., San Jacinto College. Among the numerous politicians and political consultants who were particularly helpful, we would like to thank Christopher Bayley, King County prosecutor; Governor Daniel J. Evans; Senator Henry M. Jackson; Congressman Joel Pritchard; Allan Munro, political consultant; and Lee Bartlett, advertising executive, for their advice and assistance.

We also wish to express our sincere gratitude to Judi Marulla for her skillful assistance in typing and proofreading the manuscript. Acknowledgment is also due to the students who enthusiastically participated in the development of the campaign simulation that concludes this work. And, finally, we wish to acknowledge the graphic assistance provided by Keith Arsenaux.

V. F. A.
R. A. V.

IN THE ARENA

Like his contemporaries, Thomas Jefferson saw public office as being held in trust for the governed—a responsibility to be borne. The question of duty and ethical conduct was as natural as the *natural law* philosophy on which the Declaration of Independence and the Constitution were based. However, none among the founding fathers saw any incongruency with the need to guarantee the enforcement of this ethical standard. Jefferson's solution was "a little rebellion now and then," to "clear the atmosphere." But to the majority of the founding fathers, rebellion was but the exchange of one tyranny for another.

They had experienced oppression and the violation of governmental ethics during British rule and were determined to prevent similar abuses in the new nation. Thus, to the authors of the Constitution, the Aristotelian concept that "all power corrupts and absolute power corrupts absolutely" had been confirmed by the British and was to be prevented at all costs. Yet, as the Articles of Confederation proved their ineffectiveness, those same advocates recognized the clear and present need for a stronger government.

They were indeed fearful of *absolute power,* but the growing discord among the states and the even greater threat of mob rule convinced most of them that some adjustments in the Articles were necessary. The convention which met as a committee to modify and strengthen the confederation, adjourned after bringing forth the United States Constitution.

Morality and Politics: Whose Responsibility?

The people are the only censors of their governors.

THOMAS JEFFERSON

The goal was simple: to establish justice and maintain order. But although the goal was precise, the means of implementation were much more uncertain. It had been obvious to all, save the most outspoken supporters of individual rights,[1] that the rule of the mob was not a viable alternative to prevent the centralization of power and the growth of corruption. These men of wealth and integrity realized the need to regulate the power of government to prevent excesses; with equal conviction they abhored the concept that revolution was the ultimate check on government.

Thus after much debate and compromise a system of checks and balances was provided between two and potentially three equal branches of government,[2] each tending to restrain the excesses of the other. Yet even then the authors recognized that some ultimate weapon was needed to prevent individuals from assuming those excesses of power they so greatly feared.

Impeachment: An Institution for Preserving Government

It was therefore decided that the solution was to provide for an orderly procedure for removing officials from public office—that is, impeachment. The concept was not new, having evolved from English Common Law as an "institution for the preservation of government." Yet its application was to be somewhat broadened. Any individual could be removed from office for "conviction of treason, bribery, or other high crimes and misdemeanors."[3] In thus casting this warning into the Constitution, the founding fathers put all public officials on notice. Their offices were a sacred trust. The power exercised while in office was designed to secure liberty and justice for all *citizens*—not for the aggrandizement of the officeholder. The concept of stewardship, recognized among the framers, was to be guaranteed, even if none believed that removal through the impeachment process was a real likelihood.

Jefferson, in commenting from Paris on this "stern warning,"

[1]Jefferson, writing from France, did not support the idea of a strong centralized government, believing that the Articles of Confederation were the best form possible. Only after the Bill of Rights was added did he give the concept his qualified support. See Dumas Malone, *Jefferson and the Rights of Man* (Boston: Little, Brown, 1951), pp. 153–214.

[2]The Constitution clearly established the legislative and executive branches of government but was considerably briefer regarding the judiciary. The equality of the three branches came with the development of judicial review as a legitimate concept of government.

[3]U.S. Constitution, Article II, Section 4.

remarked that it did little more than remind officials of their responsibilities. In his belief it was "the scarecrow of the Constitution." Thus, the importance of impeachment as a deterrent was not in its elaborate procedure for removal of public officials but rather in the Constitutional declaration of its existence. As Hamilton noted, impeachment was "a method of national inquest into the conduct of public men." In other words, it was a demand for public morality, not a threat of retribution.

But, like many important provisions of the Constitution, the impeachment clause is very ambiguous. Though this makes the document flexible and dynamic, its actual development is dependent on the interplay of judicial interpretation and political forces.

The President

In the case of impeachment, this ultimate step has been used so rarely that its development suffers from severe atrophy. Thirteen federal officials have been impeached, but only four convicted. As far as a presidential impeachment is concerned, we must look back over a century for our only example.

Consequently, when Peter Rodino's House Judiciary Committee faced the question of considering the impeachment of Richard Nixon, it was forced into defining what was ethical conduct for public officials. Little legal precedent was available. The popular panacea that *all public officials were by nature crooked* would not suffice. In pursuing its assignment the Rodino

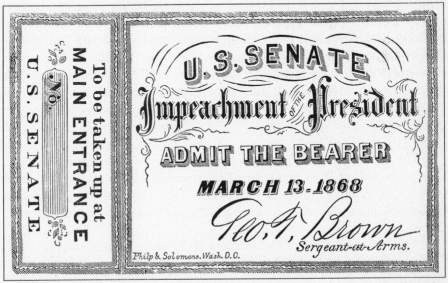

Herbert Goldberg in *Saturday Review*/WORLD, 20 April 1974. By permission.

"Remember how we all grew up wanting to be President?"

Committee, as well as the rest of the nation, quickly realized that Americans had been remiss in developing a comprehensive philosophy of public ethics, to say nothing of effective enforcement provisions.

The Hatch Acts (1887, 1939) and the Corrupt Practices Act (1925) remained as the principal guides for official public conduct, despite the recognition that their loopholes made a mockery of campaign financing regulations. As Congressman Lee Hamilton of Indiana observed, "the gaps in [these laws] . . . make a slice of Swiss cheese look like a brick wall."[4] Evading the outlandish campaign spending limitations of $25,000 for a U.S. Senate seat and $5,000 for House candidates was the rule, not the exception.

While the American people were concerned with the cavalier conduct of public officials during the 1940s and 1950s, they were nevertheless too involved in World War II and the subsequent Cold War to insist on compliance. However, in the 1960s, certain irregularities by congressmen were revealed, which rekindled an interest in ethical standards (for example, Congressman Adam Clayton Powell and Senator Thomas Dodd). Both the House and the Senate passed legislation establishing committees on ethical conduct in government. But "according to the public record . . . [the House] has never undertaken a formal investigation specifically directed toward a member of Congress,"[5] and the Senate record has been little better.

The fact is that, until the passage of the Federal Revenue and Election Campaign Acts of 1971, the public had generally been uninterested in close supervision of public officials. This is not to say that such organizations as Common Cause and other concerned citizens' groups were not abhored by

[4]"Political Fund-Raising: Methods and High Costs," *Congressional Quarterly: Weekly Report,* 14 August 1971, p. 1711.
[5]"Congressional Ethics: Need for Stricter Regulation," *Congressional Quarterly: Weekly Report,* 27 May 1972, p. 1182.

political excesses, but that the average citizen seemed to believe that whatever corruption there was represented *politics as usual*.

Watergate and the Citizens' Need to Know

However, after 1972, citizens were rudely reminded of their need to know. The Watergate affair awakened that basic distrust of power, recognized and feared over 200 years ago by the founding fathers, and led to the demand for political reforms. But the impetus for reform was not merely the tragedy that became known as the Watergate affair. The crises of confidence in government and politics that eventually led to the downfall of the Nixon administration had its roots in the preceding decade—a decade of domestic turmoil and an unpopular foreign war.

The optimism of the Kennedy years ended on a November day in Dallas, leaving the nation shocked, demoralized, and numbed. The civil rights upheaval reverberated throughout the land, as did the shots that struck down Martin Luther King and Robert Kennedy and left George Wallace an invalid. In the same decade the urban centers were torn by racial riots that fed the fires of fear, prejudice, and polarization.

In Asia, America's longest war spread from Vietnam and intensified into neighboring countries in a fashion similar to a reverse "domino theory." As hostilities dragged on, dissatisfaction at home increased, and President Johnson decided not to seek a second term. The onslaught of peace demonstrations were often marred by violence and further polarized American society. At Chicago in 1968, and two years later at Kent State University, the turmoil left wounded and dying in its wake. One mother, watching the evening news, saw her son killed in Vietnam.

While newspapers and magazines worked overtime to analyze the turmoil, television brought the upheaval into the living rooms of the nation, often in living color. The psychic impact of instant news is difficult to measure but probably cannot be underestimated. There is little doubt that the informational deluge that cascaded onto the general public was historically unprecedented.

Thus, as the citizenry watched the apparent inability of government to overcome the trials and tribulations of the republic, their confidence in governmental and political institutions steadily declined. Polls demonstrated that, while the President's popularity hit a record low, so did that of Congress. When the Watergate break-in occurred in June 1972, it served as a catalyst for action. The Senate set up the Select Committee on Presidential Campaign Activities (the Watergate Committee) to investigate not only the break-in but also the general decline in political morality apparently so widespread in the 1972 election. The Sam Ervin Committee ignited the public fuse. It seemed that the Aristotelian concept, acknowledged by the founding fathers, had indeed borne fruit. "Absolute power" had "corrupted absolutely." The murmuring public resentment grew to an outcry that eventually forced President Nixon's resignation. Once stirred, the usually lethargic beast of public indignation was not to be silenced. The citizenry demanded a "cleaning up" of politics.

Meanwhile, the Rodino Committee's impeachment proceedings, while steering a nonpartisan course through the foggy waters of presidential conduct, had set the tone for a new ethical political base in the 1970s. Forced to investigate what were *impeachable offenses,* the committee settled not only on a list of particulars but also established guidelines for all conduct in public office.

The Committee noted that the president, and indeed all elected officials, were "to take care that the laws be faithfully executed." They argued that the activities of subordinates were the responsibilities of that individual into whose hands the public had placed their trust. The executive branch of government was the responsibility of the president, and it was his charge to "take care that the Executive is so organized and operated that his duty is performed."[6]

The *New York Times* went a step further, noting that the excesses in public office, whose remedy is impeachment, "surely encompasses criminal felonies; but it extends well beyond them to include abuse of authority and misuse of official influence. In short, impeachment is a remedy designed to punish political crimes that would not be defined in statute since only a high officer of state would have the opportunity to commit them." The editorial went on to explain: "Where official authority is abused, where high officials profess to be ignorant of grave misconduct by their closest associates, and where conspiracies exist to perform diverse, illegal acts, it is not necessarily a single overt act, but the flagrant, persistent and widespread misconduct that may well be decisive. . . . There can be no doubt that the Constitution envisaged the exercise of the impeachment power in a broad context. . . . It is not merely an alternative to the local criminal court." As the *Times* alluded, impeachment of public officials extended beyond "gross crimes," to the domain of integrity in government and politics.[7]

But what does all the flapping of musty records and historical documents mean? In addition to demonstrating the tenacity of the constitutional

---

[6]"Grounds for Impeachment?" *Newsweek,* 5 November 1973, p. 32.
[7]"Impeachable Offenses . . . ," *New York Times,* 14 July 1974, E-16.

process, and that a "world cannot live without Richard Nixon" line of defense was wholesale bunk, it means that all politicians have been warned. The Constitution has proven capable of providing a viable tool to enforce a revitalized standard of ethics for public officials. The American people have demanded of their political leadership a new code of political ethics.

A Majority of Americans Are Alienated

Indeed, the gravity of this mood was documented by a recent and comprehensive analysis of public attitudes commissioned by Senator Edmund S. Muskie's SubCommittee on Intergovernmental Relations. This survey states that:

. . . A majority of Americans display a degree of alienation and discontent not felt since two popular leaders, the Reverend Martin Luther King and Senator Robert F. Kennedy, were assassinated in the early and late Spring of 1968.

For the first time since June 1968, the circumscribed minority of citizens who thought something was "deeply wrong" with their country had become a national majority, embracing men and women, from coast to coast and including most of the middle-range of working Americans. Only the most affluent, the best-educated, the youngest—*and the State and local office-holders surveyed*—preferred the view that the Nation "always has one crisis or another."

And for the first time in the 10 years of opinion sampling by the Harris Survey, the growing trend of public opinion toward disenchantment with government swept more than half of all Americans with it. Measured by agreement with four negative statements about social justice and the responsiveness of government, 55% of the people displayed profound cynicism and alienation toward their political leadership. The discontent was not limited to the traditionally discontented: the elderly, Southerners, skilled laborers and residents of rural communities all shared similar strong feelings of powerlessness and distress. . . .

This "crisis of confidence" spans the range of society's institutions, leaving only doctors and trash collectors in command of majority respect. But it is focused sharply on the institutions of government, and most tellingly on the Federal establishment, with the executive branch and the White House earning the trust of fewer than one American in five. . . .

With just two exceptions, the amount of confidence Americans display in every institution tested has decreased since 1966. Those two exceptions are the press—slightly up from its 1966 rating—and television news which enjoys the confidence of 41% of the people today compared to the 25% it enjoyed seven years ago. All other institutions from medicine to organized religions, from the Supreme Court to the Congress, from major companies to the military, more or less lost ground with the public. And the sharpest steadiest fall from grace was that of the executive branch. Significantly, State and local government services and institutions, like education, sanitation, law enforcement, and highway construction and maintenance . . . rate relatively high. . . .

Americans say they want and deeply believe they can have a government whose leaders are honest and open; whose performance is continually reviewed by an informed citizenry, the press and special-interest groups; and whose intrusion into their private behavior is firmly restricted. Above all, the report concludes, the public will respond to a government which, is itself, responsive to them within the traditional framework of existing political institutions and values. . . .[8]

Early Efforts at Reform

Movements were afoot to address at least some of these demands and expectations prior to the advent of the Watergate-inspired uproar. With the intent of preventing the purchase of political influence, and concurrently increasing public involvement in the electoral process, the Revenue Act of 1971 was passed. It provided an income tax check-off system, whereby taxpayers could designate $1 of their tax obligation to subsidize presidential election campaigns. Whatever the amount, these funds are to be divided equally among the two major political parties before campaigns. Minor parties will qualify for subsidies if they garner 5 percent of the votes cast.

All candidates receiving monies from the fund must limit campaign expenditures to an amount equal to 15¢ for each voter. They can solicit private contributions only if their funds do not equal this amount. Other sections of the same law provide tax incentives to encourage support of candidates at any level of government. Under the provisions of this statute, taxpayers can claim a tax deduction or claim a tax credit against their federal income tax.[9]

[8]From Subcommittee on Intergovernmental Relations of the Committee on Government Operations, United States Senate, "Confidence and Concern: Citizens View American Government—A Survey of Public Attitudes" (Washington, D.C. Government Printing Office, 3 December 1973), pp. VI–VII, XI.

[9]"$30 Million in the Kitty For the '76 Election," U.S. News & World Report, 30 September 1974, p. 58.

WHAT'S A GUY LIKE HIM DOING
IN A RACE LIKE THIS?*

Chicago—Most political candidates say they want to run high-class, ethical campaigns, based on the issues, but few of them are daring enough to try it.

But one man has. He is Tom Flynn, 34, a teacher and law student, who is running for the Illinois State Senate.

I've watched a lot of campaigns, but I've never seen one like this.

It is so ethical, high-minded, and noble that it is a disaster.

Flynn, a Democrat, is the only politician I know who managed to lose money at a fund-raising dinner.

He did this because he felt it would be wrong to sell people $7.50 tickets and then give them a skimpy meal. He told the restaurant to give everyone the very best. They cheered. Then Flynn had to borrow money from relatives to pay the dinner bill.

"I *guess* I'm not very good at raising funds," said Flynn.

He also tried to raise campaign money by sending out 10,000 letters.

It was a fine letter. It forthrightly explained why he was running and asked for a $1 contribution to his campaign.

Of the 10,000 people who received the letter, 174 sent dollars.

Since the printing and postage cost him $850, he lost almost $700 on that venture.

"I guess it could have been worse," Flynn says. "What if nobody had responded?"

Some of Flynn's supporters came to him recently and said they wanted to put up Flynn posters all over the suburbs. They wanted to stick thousands of them on light poles, trees, everywhere.

"They said I needed some recognition," he said.

But Flynn refused.

"Those kind of posters are visual pollution. They are an eyesore and I don't believe that is the way to run a campaign. All you get out of it is name recognition, but after the campaign, they are still there, a nuisance."

So Flynn sat down and wrote another position paper and sent it off to the newspapers, which didn't have time to read it. He has written 80 lengthy position papers. . . . One of them, dealing with the need for moderately priced housing, is 40 pages long.

While Flynn was writing his latest position paper, his opponent, John Nimrod, put up thousands of Nimrod posters on light poles and trees all over the suburbs.

"I *still* consider it visual pollution," says Flynn. "But I guess his name is now better known than mine."

*Mike Royko, "What's a Guy Like Him Doing in a Race Like This?" *Dispatch News Service International,* 5 November 1972.

People who run for local office must go to civic and community meetings and give speeches. Invitations to such gatherings are valuable.

Flynn was recently invited to speak at a Knights of Columbus meeting in a suburb. A big crowd was expected because awards were to be given to outstanding Boy Scouts.

Flynn agreed to speak. But he decided not to mention that he was running for office. He didn't think it would be proper to discuss politics in front of Boy Scouts and KCs. He said he would talk on consumer protection. . . .

[H]e made the speech . . . although he didn't mention he was running for office.

"I guess people think I'm a jerk," he said.

Flynn's campaign triumph was in helping persuade Senator Edward Kennedy to come to his district to stump for the local Democratic candidates. . . .

The trouble is, everybody forgot to tell Flynn when the rally was to be.

"A fireman mentioned the rally to me because he had to go to the high school, where it was going to be held, to turn off some sirens.

"When I got to the rally, they had not made any provisions for me to get up on the platform."

"When I tried to get up there, one of the Secret Service men gave me some kind of judo chop on my wrist."

So candidate Flynn, who was probably instrumental in getting Senator Kennedy to appear, sat in the audience.

"They didn't even introduce me so I could stand up and take a bow."

Flynn figured out his expenses and says he has spent $5,000—his savings—on the campaign. "And I can only account for $3,000 of it."

"I've had to manage everything myself. Jerry Skaja, one of the owners of the Skaja Funeral Home, was my campaign manager. He tried to help, but his hours at the funeral home are a little weird. He has to work a lot at night."

With a week to go before the election, I asked Flynn how it looks to him.

"It stinks. I'm getting the hell out of politics. If I win I'll run for reelection, but I doubt if I'll win."

That's what I mean about honesty. Try to find another candidate who will say that with a week to go.

The Federal Election Campaign Act, the other major financial legislation of 1971, provided for limitations on media expenditures, and comprehensive disclosure of political donations. Similar to the *open legislation* mandated by such states as Colorado and Washington, this law required the reporting of all transactions over $100 by committees involved in handling more than $1000 a year. The law also requires periodic reports on

'Alas, poor Agnew, Mitchell, Stans, Ehrlichman, Haldeman, Dean, Kalmbach, LaRue, Mardian, Strachan, McCord, Liddy, Chapin, Hunt, Colson, Krogh—I knew them ...'

all surpluses and debts and forbids any contributions by an individual in the name of another person. In addition, this reform act addressed the questions of post-campaign contributions, individual contributions to candidates and political committees, and contributions of candidates and their immediate families to their own campaign activities.[10] In the area of advertising restriction, this statute stipulated that not more than 60 percent of campaign expenditures may be spent on television and radio and that the total media outlay may not exceed 10¢ per person of voting age.[11] Yet before the close of the following year, the limitations of this legislation had begun to be exposed by the Watergate affair.

If there was any compensatory impact of the scandals of the early 1970s, it came in the form of rekindling the impetus for further reform. Proposals ranged from introducing a single six-year term for the presidency to that of publicly financing all federal elections. One of the legislative recommendations of the Senate Watergate Committee was the creation of

[10]"Interest Groups Bigger Spenders in '74 Races," *Congressional Quarterly: Weekly Report,* 28 September 1974, p. 2583.

[11]Herbert E. Alexander, *Political Financing* (Minneapolis: Burgess, 1972), p. 42. The media expenditure limitations imposed by this statute were repealed by the Federal Campaign Reform Act of 1974. See "Financing Elections: Law Under New Attack," *Congressional Quarterly: Weekly Report,* 14 June 1975, p. 1241.

a permanent and independent special prosecutor who would monitor executive branch agencies and conflict-of-interest cases. The committee also suggested the establishment of an independent elections commission to monitor and enforce federal election laws.[12]

But the impact of the Watergate investigations also caused many candidates to impose self-restrictions. In contrast to the past, it was not uncommon in the 1974 congressional races for incumbents to make serious efforts to distinguish between official government business expenses and campaign activities. Other candidates placed limits on the size of individual contributions they would accept and rebuffed cash donations. Edmond Brown, Jr., and Houston Flourney, gubernatorial contestants in California, agreed to limit spending even though the campaign reform law in that state did not go into effect until the following year.

State Response to Campaign Reform

However, in terms of legislative responsiveness, the states were more aggressive than Congress in dealing with those conditions which have undermined public confidence. The vanguard initiatives dealing with money and/or secrecy in government and politics passed by voters in Colorado and Washington were rapidly followed by significant initiatives or statutes in most other states. In 1973 and 1974 at least 40 states passed 67 measures that covered a broad gamut of problem areas: open-meeting laws, disclosure of lobbyist activities and expenditures, independent ethics commissions to review personal financial statements of public officials, tax incentives to encourage small campaign contributions, and imposition of spending limits on campaigning.[13]

Reform at the National Level

Major differences between the House and Senate versions of the federal campaign reform legislation forestalled final action at the national level until late 1974. What finally emerged was the tough new Federal Campaign Reform Act. For the first time in U.S. history there appeared to be realistic limitations on contributions and expenditures. It also required

[12]James R. Dickenson, "In the Senate Report, A Sense of Shock . . . ," *The National Observer*, 20 July 1974, p. 12. Also see "Watergate Committee Recommends Strong Laws to Prevent Future Election Process Abuses," *Campaign Practices Report*, 12 August 1974, p. 7.

[13]"Campaign Finance: States Push for Reform," *Congressional Quarterly: Weekly Report*, 31 August 1974, pp. 2360–2365.

the disclosure of contributions over $100. In addition to the creation of the Federal Elections Commission as a bi-partisan enforcement agency, the new law provided for the public financing of presidential campaigns and national party conventions.

The first testing ground for the new campaign controls was the U.S. Court of Appeals of the District of Columbia and eventually the U.S. Supreme Court. Within 48 hours of the statute's effective date, an unlikely political alliance filed a suite which contended that the law violated the freedom of speech, separation of powers and equal protection clauses of the Constitution.[14] The end result was a Supreme Court ruling which struck down the provisions of the statute that imposed spending limitations and the method for selecting the Federal Elections Commission. Left intact were the strict regulations on campaign contributions, reporting, and the public financing of presidential elections and national party conventions.

In a vote of 6-2, the high court rejected the argument that contribution limits interfere with the freedom of speech or discriminate against certain categories of candidates. Under this statute individual contributions may not exceed $1000 per race to any one candidate—a possible $3000 total for the primary, runoff, and general election. The total amount that an individual can donate to all federal elections is $25,000. Organizational contributions are limited to $5000 for each of these three elections. However, the court did rule that statutory limitations on the use of personal funds by candidates was unconstitutional.[15]

The meaningfulness of the campaign reform legislation can only be evaluated with the perspective of time. Nonetheless, the direction of the impact is already observable. Before the Federal Election Commission lost its power to distribute funds, the $12,618,241 of matching money maintained the financial solvency of several presidential hopefuls.[16] Organizational changes have also become evident. Planning and organization have become much more businesslike, for frugality is the new watchword of presidential campaigns. The distribution formula of matching only contributions to $250 or less, in conjunction with the qualification requirement

[14]The 34-count complaint that challenged every major provision of the Campaign Reform Act was filed jointly by Conservative Senator James Buckley, former Democratic Senator Eugene McCarthy, Republican Representative William Steiger, and the New York Civil Liberties Union.

[15]"Campaign Finance: Congress Weighing New Law," *Congressional Quarterly: Weekly Report,* 7 February 1976, pp. 267–274.

[16]"Senate Accepts Compromise Campaign Bill," *Congressional Quarterly: Weekly Report,* 27 March 1976, p. 657. At the time of this writing, the high court's stay on their ruling to disband the election guidelines has become a major issue in the second session of the 94th Congress. Hostility toward the commission and partisan wrangling has delayed any quick action on the campaign bill.

of raising $100,000 in at least 20 states in amounts of $250 or less, has mandated a broad-based fund raising effort in all presidential efforts. The fat cats, who have traditionally provided start-up money to initiate the campaigns of presidential aspirants, have become another endangered species.[17] "The fat cat who could give us $100,000 or $200,000 isn't important today," explained Richard Kline, finance chairman for Senator Henry Jackson. "Now the most important people are the fund raisers, the men who know where to tap $100 contributors. . . ."[18] Yet we are reminded that this legislation is no panacea by the charge of Associate Justice William H. Rehnquist in a dissenting opinion which charged that the "law enshrines the Republican and Democratic parties in permanently preferred positions."[19]

We see, then, that the reforms to this point in the 1970s have focused primarily on the problems of financing campaigns—and the sources of dollars to bankroll these perennial extravaganzas. Since the 1950s, the costs of getting the message out through the ever-more sophisticated medium of television to constitutents of ever-increasing mobility in a period of inflation have resulted in spiraling campaign costs. The following serves to illustrate: $140 million in 1952, $155 million in 1956, $175 million in 1960, $200 million in 1968, and $400 million in 1972.[20]

Are the Costs of Democracy Too High?

Though this pattern is evidence of the soaring costs of democracy, these costs are not necessarily *too high*. Herbert Alexander, among others, has offered an alternative view. He notes that, " . . . whether too much is spent on political campaigns depends on what measures of 'too high' or 'too much' is used. . . ."[21] Campaign expenditures are excessive only if they impose conditions that are incongruent with the purpose of elections, that is, deter free access of all serious candidates to the electorate. Given that the United States expends less on campaigning per capita than most other nations, it is quite plausible to argue that too little is expended to support our democratic system.[22]

Obviously there is no question that strict regulatory provisions will continue to be needed to prevent conflicts of interest. After all, politicians are human like the rest of us and are exposed to far more frequent and

[17]"They're Pinched," *Time* Magazine, 12 April 1976, p. 20.
[18]"Financing Elections: New Law Under Attack," op. cit., p. 1242.
[19]"Campaign Finance: Congress Weighing New Law," op. cit., p. 268.
[20]Tom Wicker, "The High Cost of Politics," *New York Times,* 3 January 1971, p. E-
[21]Alexander, op. cit., p. 38. Also see David Adamany, *Campaign Finance in America*
[22]Ibid., p. 39.

seductive temptations. However, if political reform is more than an attempt to pacify the post-Watergate public righteousness, negative legislative measures will not suffice.

We may discover that *ethical absolution* may be incompatible with the complexities of political finance. As Alexander Heard noted, the ineffectiveness of past "statutes has resulted basically from legislative intent out of harmony with the needs of the electoral system. . . ."[23] Perhaps the delicate balance will be found in part through the medium of financial disclosure measures monitored by independent ethics commissions and either greater public participation or more extensive public subsidy. Whatever the combination, the panacea will not be found in law alone.[24]

In focusing on the nation's efforts to establish a new standard of ethics, reform proposals and legislative actions have been discussed. But we have not pursued perhaps the most crucial problem of reestablishing the political health of our democratic process. What reform will salve the public fury? What caliber of public official must be created to rejuvenate the faith of the populace in the system? What will entice the citizen to become an active supporter and participant in the politics of the republic? Carcasses of the fallen lions of power have adorned the political landscape, and properly so. Yet, has the "vengeance is mine, sayeth the citizen" mood so whetted the nation's appetite that there has been an overreaction? Does the citizen's aloofness toward politics only recreate the atmosphere that led to the present problems?

How Can the Health of the Body Politic Be Restored?

The answer to these inquiries are somewhat elusive. Nonetheless, they are of central concern to any consideration of political reform because in politics there is no such thing as a free lunch. Perhaps the reaction of a student to the moaning complaints of a friend said it best: "If you don't pay your dues, don't bitch!" In other words, each individual has a responsibility to the political community. As columnist Carl Rowan noted during a lecture series at the University of Delaware, "You are never going to create a situation where you have a government or anything else you can have some confidence in if you don't get down to the nitty-gritty of caring about who's mayor of your town, or who your senator is, or who your vice president is. It's a little bit late to start complaining when they start firing special prosecutors and paying off vice presidents, and slipping money in nice,

[23]Alexander Heard, *The Cost of Democracy* (Chapel Hill: University of North Carolina Press, 1960), p. 9.

[24]Senator Sam Ervin, noting that "law merely deters some human beings from

unnamed envelopes to people in your government. . . . you didn't need a Watergate to know that we face a crisis in these United States. . . ."[25]

The solution to the problem of government and politics—be it the problem of integrity or inflation—cannot be discovered in the legislative halls or the White House, even if the incumbents are squeaky clean. As for laws, they can only create an atmosphere for a responsive political system. We, too, are the problem; we who are part of the majority of Americans who take no more than a perfunctory role in political life. Every time we conclude that "politics is dirty," we have shirked our responsibility to make the system work as we believe it should. Politics is as good as the people who participate.

Now that may sound like a quaint truism in the age of "future shock," but our sophisticated society may very well benefit by occasionally looking back to the roots of the nation. The founding fathers built a nation "conceived in liberty," and rather than banging our beer cans on the coffee table and yelling profanities at the television when we are told of the high cost of campaigning or corruption in government, we might ask ourselves, Why? The answer is that people are too busy following the path of upward mobility or groveling in their alienation to keep abreast of who is *your representative* and what he or she is saying.

Most Americans Are Unfamiliar with Politics

If you have any doubts, remember that 62 percent of Americans rated their familiarity on current political happenings as poor or worse. Consistently, only 41 percent of the voting age population correctly identify the name and party affiliation of their congressmen. In the same nationwide survey 60 percent of Americans gave themselves negative ratings on their knowledge of what's going on in the federal government, while 73 percent didn't understand their state government and 57 percent their local government.[26] Given the disinterest of the public, political information must be force-fed to potential voters through mass media. As pointed out in Chapter 9, the costs of television, radio, and direct mail have inflated 20 to 25 percent since 1972 alone. And then there are those who are "too pure" to contribute to a political campaign, yet are shocked by candidates who solicit large sums of money from "fat cats." Given the diminishing number of volunteers and the consequent need for dollars to communicate to the apathetic majority,

[25]Donald W. Howard, ed., *Crisis in Confidence: The Impact of Watergate* (Boston:
[26]"Confidence and Concern. . . ." *Intergovernmental Relations,* op. cit., pp. 238–241, 249.

what alternatives are available to the political aspirant? Appeals for broad-based financial contributions are expensive, because the return rate from a direct-mail solicitation is meager. Less than 8 percent contribute to political campaigns.

A similar case can be made in the legislative arena. Every time we fail to keep informed on current issues and do not advise our legislators of our feelings, we acquiesce the power of our numbers to those that pay their dues, that is, interest groups. Of course, there will be those who will ignore or rationalize these realities of political life by exclaiming that they just cannot bring themselves to being coopted by *establishment* politics. The system as it presently exists is overwhelmingly corrupt. The "fat cats" and vested interests—the military-industrial complex—have such a hold on the government and politics of America that is is beyond hope. Could it be that these cynics are the most serious victims of *idealist fallout?* By this we refer to the attitudinal condition that afflicts large numbers of American political observers, an affliction that has little to do with the integrity of public officials or political institutions. It is a disenchantment caused by exposure to contemporary political reality after having been unwittingly nurtured on a sugar-coated version of "America the Beautiful." Against this backdrop, noted one urban mayor, the shock is comparable "to that of the Victorian maiden who never quite recovers from the trauma of her wedding night."[27]

Americans Are Too Unsophisticated to Understand Politics

What is being advanced here is that the majority of Americans have not developed a sophisticated, critical capacity to evaluate public officials or the complexity of political interactions. The process begins with the political induction of children into the *American Dream.* The social studies curriculum of public education has often been closer to catechism sessions than to a candid examination of our history, government and politics. Public school texts never raised the issue of our treasonous forefathers who drafted the Declaration of Independence, though there may be mention of the Tory aristocracy that for some strange reason remained faithful to the British Crown. There was no conflict or political compromise at the Constitutional Convention. And, as we all know, George Washington wasn't political, for he made a speech against political parties (even though he happened to be a Federalist).

[27]Mayor of Seattle Wes Uhlman, speech to Washington Educational Association, Spokane, 16 October 1970.

The human frailties of past leaders are totally overlooked as they are cast bigger than life. In a similar vein, the Civil War was fought to free the slaves. Any remaining major problems of the blacks were constitutionally solved with the *Brown* vs. *Board of Education* decision of the Supreme Court in 1954.

Americans Don't Want to Understand
—Look at Civics and History

Equally antithetical to political reality is the pap taught in civics courses. The legislative description of the framework of government—"there are three branches of the federal government"—is presented as the appropriate, if not the natural, structure for any good government. Thus, description is integrated with prescription.

Rather than viewing the social and political problems of our nation as difficulties with which the citizen should grapple as a good and patriotic American, "the picture of unity, equality, and freedom that is so often presented is distorted, oversimplified and, to a degree, false. . . . The image of the United States . . . is one of a country which is an effective force for world peace, in which the laws are fair, justice prevails . . . and what goes on in government is all for the best."[28]

Yet the largest void in political education and the chief contributor to disillusionment is the failure to recognize that controversy, conflict, and compromise are integral components of the American system, past and present. The young are led to believe that American history and politics is a "cotton candy" world of consensus. The classes of secondary educational institutions are "ashamed of certain political facts of life . . . (1) people characteristically make use of power and influence in order to advance their particular and often competing interests; (2) conflict is therefore endemic to the system; (3) politics is an effort to resolve that conflict; (4) in resolving conflict, organized groups frequently have more effect upon political decision making than individuals. . . ."[29]

These facts of life are not sordid—much to the contrary. One of the attributes of any society that alleges to be free is the ability of individuals to hold a diversity of values and interests, including differing beliefs and expectations of their government. Without politics there would be no procedure through which the natural complexities of a diverse society could be resolved. All of these variations have a right to be heard in the

[28]Robert D. Hess, "Political Socialization in the Schools," *Harvard Educational Review* 38 (Summer 1968): 531.
[29]Uhlman, op. cit.

marketplace of ideas. Thus to understand the impact of people on the political process it is crucial that one recognize that there are in fact many publics, each with their own interests. In talking about the responsiveness of government to the public, one must first ask, Responsive to which public(s)? Government is usually responsive to those publics which are attentive to particular issues and organize in support or opposition to those issues.

The knowledge of American history and politics with which youth emerge from public education is a mixed bag of oversimplified and idealized facts. What they fail to gain is a realistic grasp of what public life and political decision making are all about. There is little wonder, if this is the cornerstone of their political education, that people are frustrated by today's politicians. Politicians are human, with all the frailties that the word implies. How can the citizenry be satisfied by contemporary public policy and political personalities when their reference point is

Franklin D. Roosevelt [who] personally rescued the nation from the depths of the Great Depression. Roosevelt, together with Harry Truman, brought World War II to a proud conclusion. Courageous Truman personally committed us to resist Communist aggression around the globe. General Dwight D. Eisenhower pledged that as President he would "go to Korea" and end that war—and he did. These are prevailing idealized images that most American students read and remember. . . .

Presidents are expected to perform as purposeful activists, who know what they want to accomplish and relish the challenges of the office. The student learns that the Presidency is "the great engine of democracy," the "American people's one authentic trumpet," "the central instrument of democracy," and "probably the most important government institution in the world." With the New Deal Presidency in mind, the textbook portrait states that Presidents must instruct the nation as national teacher and guide the nation as national preacher. . . .[30]

If these are the experiences that prepare a generation for their later political responsibilities, who can blame them for being isolated from the reality of what is *honest politics?*

As if to reinforce this belief, media aids us in our inflated expectations. A case in point is John Kennedy. After a decade and a half of eulogizing, we remember only his charismic style—the 1000 days of Camelot. The problem is that this quasi-religious concept of the presidency has implications

[30]Thomas E. Cronin, "The Textbook Presidency," in *Inside The System,* Charles Peters and John Rothchild, eds. (New York: Praeger, 1973), pp. 6–7.

"IT WASN'T MEANT TO HIDE BEHIND, BUDDY!"

for present and future occupants of the White House. Recall how, when Richard Nixon was under attack, he would wrap himself in the Great Seal of the Presidency of the United States. To many Americans the man was the office and therefore above criticism.

A World That Never Was

Americans cannot afford a false love of the president or any other political institution, a love that is faithful only if both the office and its incumbent remain on the pedestal with the other great leaders of our heritage. The American public approaches the political arena with a serious disadvantage. Their understanding of the conflict and the give-and-take of compromise that is involved in shaping, enacting, and applying public policy is, at best, limited. Their expectation of what government should and could do if the politicians were only honest is impossible. *Their model is a world that never was.*

Yet how does this serve to explain the present crisis of confidence? Has the political education in civics courses taken a significant decline in the last decade? Is today's citizen a unique phenomenon of the late 1960s and 1970s? The answer to these inquiries is a categorical "no."

Why Are Americans Disillusioned?

Much of the current disillusionment with government and politics can be attributed to the dramatic and tragic events of the 1960s and early 1970s, as noted above. But equally important was the radical technological changes in media, which brought the cold reality of these events into every home.

During the 1950s, media was a reflection of the American dream. It was the purveyor of middle-class viewpoint and reinforced the belief that *we have it made in America.* GNP soared upward and everybody liked Ike. There were also "commies" and "commie dupes," but Senator Joseph McCarthy was hot on their trail. The media were preoccupied with American invincibility and helping their government in the fight against communism. Edward R. Murrow's "Crusade for Freedom" series and the popular television counter spy drama, "I Led Three Lives" reflected this mood. The 1950s was the era before television documentaries focused on the sociopolitical problems and inequities of our society. Arthur Godfrey was still with us, and Ed Sullivan and "Father Knows Best" kept the nation amused.

And then came the 1960s with the growth of a new generation of journalists. Investigative reporting no longer considered government news releases adequate. Advocacy journalism disregarded the cozy government–media relationship that had characterized the post-World War II period. In the early 1960s a byline of David Halberstam, correspondent for the *New York Times,* contradicted the position of the government on the progress of the Vietnam conflict. Halberstam announced that the United States was losing the war. Whether this new style of journalism resulted from a change of attitudes in the news industry, new personnel filling the working journalists ranks, the onrush of events on the 1960s, or a combination of these factors, one can only speculate. Whatever the reasons, advocacy journalism became commonplace. When we add to this development the proliferation of television sets through the nation, the picture begins to focus more clearly. America was bombarded with information. Media no longer allowed them to hide in the *we are best* syndrome of America that characterized the 1950s.

Conditions that existed in the "good old days," like poverty and injustice, were exposed in documentaries: "Poverty in America," "Hunger in America," "Justice and the Poor." Other long-standing social problems literally exploded into the living rooms of Americans. The intensity, fears, and apprehensions of Watts and Newark were no longer removed. And, of course, the controversy and anxiety of Vietnam removed any illusion of a total political consensus. As the decade drew to a close, people were shocked and disenchanted by the barrage of instantaneous information. That Americans did not like what they saw and heard was indicated by the wave of antimedia criticism reflected by Agnew in Des Moines, a criticism of the "instant analysis and scurrulous criticism . . . [by] a tiny enclosed fraternity of privileged men elected by no one." . . .[31]

The citizen was overloaded, so to speak, by events and facts that were totally inconsistent with their political icons. The media were tenacious, and Carl Bernstein and Bob Woodward of the *Washington Post* exposed the Watergate affair. The gavel-to-gavel hearings of the Sam Ervin Show, the resignation of Richard Nixon, and finally, the overwhelming realization that we did not have all the answers brought the last optimist to his knees.

PUBLIC FINANCING

POINT

Moving away from the existing system of private campaign contributions to one of publicly supported campaigns was seen by many as the only way to avoid future Watergates—to remove the corrupting influence of vast sums of money in campaigns, the purchasing of influence by large contributors and special interest groups, the necessity for candidates or their agents to go begging for funds.

The existing system was government for sale to the highest bidder, "a national disgrace," said Sen. Edward M. Kennedy (D—Mass.). A number of large, influential organizations, such as Common Cause and the League of Women Voters, agreed and were lobbying hard for public financing.

COUNTERPOINT

. . . What advocates called a historic breakthrough could just as well be classified as the total destruction of the American political system as it had been known, they warned.

Public financing would not prevent special-interest groups or others from influencing office-holders or helping favored candidates in some way, opponents noted. Many felt that disclosure of campaign contributions, required since April 7, 1972, would be sufficient to avoid future Watergate-type abuses.

Among the critics were President[s] Nixon [and] . . . Ford, the U.S. Chamber of Commerce and, reportedly, most members of the Senate Watergate committee.

---

[31]"The Nixon Administration and the Media," *Congressional Quarterly: Weekly Report*, 1 January 1972, p. 4.

Public financing would equalize access to public office by all candidates, advocates contended, whereas the existing system favored incumbents, the wealthy or those with access to rich friends or special-interest groups.

Public financing for all federal elections could be had for $89-million a year, said the Senate Rules Committee. This could be more than adequately paid for if every taxpayer marked his $1 check-off on his income tax each year.

This would be a small price to pay for elected officials free to act in the public interest, beholden to no special interests, public financing advocates claimed. They said it would be a far smaller price than the billions already paid indirectly, in higher prices for milk, fuel and food, for example, as a result of government policies bought by special interests with huge contributions.

There would be safeguards in the legislation to ensure that candidates without significant grass-roots support could not get public money to run, advocates said. Over-all campaign spending limits would ensure that tax money was not wasted, and proportional funding to minor or new party candidates would prevent discrimination, they noted.

Like voter registration and polling places, campaigns are part of the electoral process and should be tax-funded.

It was wrong, possibly unconstitutional, opponents argued, to tax people to pay for campaigns of people they did not agree with or wish to support. It also could be a violation of the First Amendment to prevent people from giving money to candidates of their choice, critics said.

The success of some candidates in recent years in attracting large numbers of small contributions showed that people would give voluntarily to candidates they believed in, encouraging such broad-based contributions could lessen candidates' dependence on "fat cats," opponents said.

Limiting candidates to a given amount of public funds would give unfair advantage to incumbents, who already had ample means of keeping themselves in the public eye—and won more than 95 per cent of their elections, critics pointed out. They claimed that public funds also would encourage frivolous candidates to run for office. And public financing, said the critics, could discriminate against third-party or new-party candidates who actually might represent a sizable number of votes.

Public financing also would weaken the political parties, since candidates would be funded directly under public financing proposals, critics charged.*

*"Should Taxpayers Subsidize Federal Election Campaigns?" *Congressional Quarterly: Weekly Report*, 30 March 1974, p. 798.

Public Enemy Number One

Public enemy number one vacillated from government to politicians to politics in general. Symptomatic of our general indictment of government and politics was a bumper sticker that appeared during the 1974 election: VOTE AGAINST INCUMBENTS. Americans appeared to be looking for a political messiah to lead them from the corrupt desert of politics.

But to be elected with our full faith and confidence, an individual had to be not only a wholesome *nice guy,* but had to exhibit the wit of Dick Cavett and the articulateness of Walter Cronkite. What evolved was the pressure on the candidate to develop an *image* to satisfy the fantasies of an electorate that did not possess sufficient information or understanding to evaluate a politician by any other criteria.

Thus out of necessity the political aspirant attempts to build an image of perfection. "When elected I will" . . . "in a manner that is palatable to all my constituents" . . . "with the utmost of credibility." To do otherwise

(*Time,* 6 August 1973. By permission.)

would be to invite the bitter taste of defeat. Not that defeat is necessarily bad—except perhaps for the public when the political combatant has a contribution to make to public life.

As noted recently by historian Daniel Boostin, "developments in our society . . . have led us to put a premium on what's credible rather than on what's true, and what looks good rather than what are the facts of the case. . . . We have been led to assume by implication that it's good to be concerned with credibility—that it's good to be credible. That's the wrong way to put it. It's good to state the truth, but the ability to be credible is a dangerous ability—not a virtue."[32]

Is Campaign Reform the Real Answer?

Using this yardstick, perhaps our unquestioning belief in the credibility of campaign reform laws needs to be reexamined. In the post-Watergate furor to purify the system, the public has permitted little time to inquire into the long-range impact of reform legislation. Some of the questions that need consideration were posed by Governor Patrick Lucey at the National Governor's Conference: " . . . What should be a public official's right to privacy? What are the partisan implications of the various campaign finance reform proposals? What is the cost of requiring full disclosure of appointees to task forces and citizen boards? What is the value of requiring candidates to raise private campaign contributions? At what point do contribution and expenditure limits thwart the candidacy of a maverick, or encourage the re-election of an incumbent? When does interest group involvement stop being helpful and start being a hindrance to good government? Should important public interest groups, such as the press, be required to meet the same stringent disclosure standards as elected officials? . . . ."[33]

Nor do the questions raised by Governor Lucey address other perennial areas of concern in the electoral process. For example, there is the long recognized problem for all political challengers, for which there appears no legislative solution which is both equitable and constitutional, of incumbency. As commented by Democratic campaign consultant Matt Reese, "the incumbent has all the advantages. His job is a political action.

---

[32]"Historian Decries Watergate as 'Cult of Personality,'" *Congressional Quarterly: Weekly Report,* 7 July 1973, p. 1798.

[33]Remarks of Governor Patrick J. Lucey, National Governor's Conference, Seattle, 4 June 1974.

He does no non-political act."[34] The dollar value of this advantage, without consideration of matters such as prestige or name recognition, has been estimated at $375,000 a year.[35]

Not yet confronted are the potential abuses that may emerge with the resurrection of the fat cat as an independent political agent in electioneering *for* a candidate. As a result of the U.S. Supreme Court ruling on the Federal Campaign Reform Act of 1974, any citizen may expend unlimited funds in promoting a candidacy. The only legal stipulation is that the expenditures may not be made in collusion with a candidate. According to Democratic fund-raiser George Agree, the high court has "converted an incumbent's protection act into a millionaire's protection act."[36]

Although seriousness of these and other problems will vary in relation to specific geographical localities of the country and the level of office being sought, some insight may be gained by the results of one of the nation's first campaign reform laws, passed in the state of Washington. The initial response was an unprecedented resignation among lesser, non paid officials.

There were also the resignations of at least 10 legislators, among them some of the best in the state. However, the real irony came in the first primary election under a law that was praised as a model for the country. Voter participation dipped to a historical low, and not a single incumbent was defeated. In fact, the only real contest for federal office that year happened in the district where the retirement of Congresswoman Julia Butler Hansen left an "open seat."

The post-Watergate reform magic of full disclosure also had side effects in other states that few of its advocates anticipated. An account offered by columnist David Broder provides but one illustration.

" . . . I can recall last year hearing a Midwest Democratic governor of impeccable reformist credentials argue vainly that if 'total disclosure' of even the smallest contribution was required in this state, you'll never have another upset winner like me elected governor."

"You'll make it easy for me next year, . . . " he said. "You'll choke off my opposition. But the bill passed over his objections, and as predicted,

[34]"Financing Elections: New Law Under Attack," *Congressional Quarterly: Weekly Report,* 14 June 1975, p. 1243.

[35]The estimate was computed by Americans for Democratic Action, a liberal political organization. Included in the figure are the costs of ranking privilege, staff, travel allowances and office space. Ibid., p. 1244.

[36]"Campaign Finance: Congress Weighing New Law," *Congressional Quarterly: Weekly Report,* 7 February 1976, p. 267.

he is having a free ride for re-election against an ill-financed Republican. . . . "[37]

What, Then, If Not Campaign Reform?

Where will the answer be found? During the last 20 years we have passed the baton of responsibility for our problems. There were the "commie dupes" of the 1950s and then the civil rights activists, followed by the war resisters. More recently the "bad guys" have shifted from the news media to government and politics.

But we seem to forget that *participatory democracy* needs *participants*. This should not be interpreted as "you should register and vote in the next election." That is like righteously attending church on Christmas and hustling shoddy used cars to unwary buyers for the rest of the year. This does not mean that there is anything wrong with going to church or voting. It just so happens that the annual observation of either of these two rites is not sufficient to resolve the sociopolitical problems that confront the nation.

The founding fathers feared power, be it from corruption or the *mob*, and forged a government based on compromise and law. But while hailing the founding fathers for their genius of foresight, we seem to have overlooked the equal charge that the citizenry must be educated and willing to protect their own interests—we all have them. Democracy cannot function without a partnership between elected officials and citizens. Americans have revived the requirement that elected officials guard the "public trust" but have consequently chosen to ignore their own responsibilities. Morality in government is a two-way street. Laws governing elected officials are not enough.

[37]David S. Broder, "Campaign Finance Restrictions Lock in the Incumbents," *Seattle Times*, 6 October 1974.

Political Behavior, Some Socioeconomic Implications

In 1970 Richard Scammon and Ben Wattenberg authored a work which since has come to be regarded as a political classic—*The Real Majority.*[1] These two authors researched the activities and political behavior of the American electorate, basing their analytical conclusions on voter demographics. Using demographic profiles as well as election and preference polls, they created what they considered to be the average American voter. She (more women than men) is "middle aged," of "middle income," "Protestant," "middle educated," and white. She is generally concerned with crime in the streets and money, has mixed views of black civil rights, and is distressed over drug abuse. The authors go so far as to specify that "Middle Voter is a forty-seven-year-old housewife from the outskirts of Dayton, Ohio, whose husband is a machinist."[2]

Ms. "Middle American Voter"

After the combined efforts of a local Dayton newspaper, and the local machinists' union, Mrs. "Middle Voter" materialized in Fairborn, 12 miles north of Dayton. While occasionally voting a split ticket, she is a registered Democrat and turned forty-seven the year after the book was published. Her husband is a machinist. In an interview with *Life* magazine she was nearly an exact parallel to her profile as described in *The*

[1]Benjamin J. Wattenberg and Richard M. Scammon, *The Real Majority* (New York: Coward, McCann, 1970).
[2]Ibid., pp. 70–71.

Real Majority. Speaking like a conservative political candidate, she was well aware that she represented the "Middle American Voter."[3] But are her concerns and interests really those of the the average voter? What socioeconomic factors influence the majority of the electorate? Is ours a nation of Mrs. Lowreys, or rather a mixture that merely averages out to an occasional Mrs. Lowrey?

Perhaps, as was argued in *The American Voter,*[4] socioeconomic forces do play a major role in establishing voter behavior. Indeed, the Wattenberg-Scammon description of the "middle voter" relies heavily on such factors in determining what constitutes "the real majority." Thus, although social classes and group influences do not constitute the only explanation for voter behavior, we hasten to point out that they certainly are of major importance. Though sometimes broad and ill-defined, social forces nevertheless serve as valuable references for the average voter.[5]

Voters can usually be classified into four general groups: social classes, primary groups, secondary groups, and categoric groups. Of course these classifications are often blurred as the concept of pluralism interacts.[6] For example, social classes generally consist of broad aggregates of persons who base their association on certain mutually exclusive criteria. Upper class, for instance, generally denotes an individual whose income is in the upper 25 percent of the population. Additionally they are college educated and have certain social contacts which place them in situations of public notice and/or esteem (for example, leaders in charity, government, business, fashions). Whereas this description fluctuates, it tends to hold true. This class is found in both political parties, among independents, and in most religious denominations and ethnic groups.

Primary groups, on the other hand, consist of individuals who have an ongoing face-to-face relationship. Families, close friends, and frequently co-workers are found in this group. Secondary groups generally refer to organizations that exist midway between the more intimate primary group relationships and the rather ill-defined social class. Such organizations as labor unions, professional societies, and religious groups are found in this category. Lastly, categoric groups are most inclusive, overlapping the other groupings. Usually they consist of individuals who mutually occupy a

[3]*Life* magazine, 30 October 1970, pp. 30–31.

[4]Angus Campbell et al., *The American Voter* (New York: Wiley, 1960).

[5]Hugh A. Bone and Austin Ranney, *American Politics and the Party System* (New York: McGraw-Hill, 1971), p. 23.

[6]Pluralism portrays the sociopolitical community as consisting of a multitude of independent and diverse groups (for example, unions, churches, environmentalists, and military), which are in conflict. In the process of conflict these groups contribute to the values of their members and to the formulation of social norms and public policy.

particular category (for example, college graduates, women, ethnic groups, Catholics, Jews). As is evident, these categories exist not only within social classes; they are also found between primary and secondary groups.

Social Grouping

Particularly in the area of social classes the relationship between group activity and political activity is difficult to measure. Political scientists have often theorized on the importance of social classes in voting behavior. But in America, where most adults do not consider themselves members of any class (other than middle), this assumption may be unrealistic. In *The American Voter,* the authors demonstrated that the relationship between a particular candidate and the class whose vote he attracts is not so significant as the membership of partisans within that class.[7] This is not to say that social classes (middle, upper, lower) are divided, but rather that the numbers of partisans within the social groups influence how a class votes as an aggregate.[8] Thus, while social class standing occasionally influences the voter, little evidence indicates that Americans vote by class. We are not asserting that the economic factor of wealth is unimportant to voters, but apparently a self-realization of this class role cannot be found in voting behavior, at least in America.[9]

Primary Groups

Primary group political influences are as ill defined in many instances as those of social class. Individuals in primary groups generally experience very little overt pressure to conform to a certain generally accepted political standard. This is because political concerns are generally of only slight interest between members of, say, a family or club or between friends. [Table 2.1] Nonetheless, members of a group often reflect similar political views because of an unconscious desire to be socially acceptable. For instance, small children often designate themselves as "little Republicans" and "little Democrats." This is obviously not based on an overt decision on their part to support one party *vis-à-vis* another but is more a learned response; that is, a desire to conform to the political views held by their parents and/or older siblings. On the same note wives may vote identically

[7]Campbell et al., op. cit., p. 347, Figure 3.2.
[8]Ibid., particularly Chapter 13.
[9]For an exceptionally good account of the role of class in voting behavior, see David Butler and Donald E. Stokes, *Political Change in Britain* (New York: St. Martin's, 1969).

Table 2.1   No Generation Gap in Political Views

"In comparing your political viewpoints to those of your parents, would you say that your ideas are—identical; vary slightly; vary significantly; or vary considerably?"

	Overall	Student	Nonstudent
identical	12.1%	10.8%	12.5%
vary slightly	53.8	55.1	53.4
vary significantly	13.4	17.3	12.1
vary considerably	14.0	15.0	13.7
no answer	6.7	1.8	8.3

(Results taken from a nationwide survey of the nation's young. Copyright 1972, Unidex Corporation.)

to their husbands not necessarily because of a privately arrived-at decision but because of a desire to please.[10]

The American Voter demonstrated the high voting correlation between members of primary groups. It was found that approximately 90 percent of the spouses surveyed voted for the same candidates. Indeed, other members of the family conformed almost as completely, voting 80 to 92 percent of the time with their parents. The survey also indicated that, among friends and co-workers in the primary group category, the correlation at 76 to 85 percent was almost as high as for family members.[11]

This evidence does not mean to imply that primary groups are actively committed to social and political conformity. Actually it tends to be an unconscious act, arrived at after continual interaction with family, friends, and associates. It would be less than logical to expect that common economic, professional, and religious experiences would result in anything less than similar political orientations. Whereas more recent data indicate that the homogeneity among primary group participants is not quite so highly correlated as in *The American Voter,* significant evidence indicates that these relationships still exist throughout the voting population.[12]

[10]For a more complete discussion of parental influences, see M. Kent Jennings and Richard G. Niemi, "The Transmission of Political Values from Parent to Child," *American Political Science Review* 61 (March 1968): 169–184.

[11]Campbell et al., op. cit., p. 77, Table 4.3.

[12]Jennings and Niemi, op. cit., pp. 169–184. See also R. W. Connell, "Political Socialization in the American Family: The Evidence Reexamined," *Public Opinion Quarterly* 36 (Fall 1972): 323–333; M. Kent Jennings and Kenneth R. Langton, "Mothers vs. Fathers: The Formation of Political Orientations Among Young Americans," *Journal of Politics* (1969): 329–358; "Youth Opinion: No Generation Gap in Political Views," *Seattle Times,* 5 November 1972. In this article Daniel C. Beggs and Hanry A. Copeland, basing their information on a national survey of the Unidex Corporation, demonstrate the similarities between generations of voters.

Secondary Groups

Secondary groups are often more overtly concerned with political activity than are primary groups. Religious organizations, labor unions, and professional societies tend to require a certain conformity to basic principles. A commitment to these beliefs and the degree of that commitment are major factors in influencing voter behavior. *The American Voter* discovered an extremely high correlation between support of group aspirations/goals and voter behavior. That is, if an individual believes particularly in the activity of his union, for instance, he generally conforms to its political orientation.[13] This does not necessarily suggest coercion on the part of the organization. Members of labor groups are most likely involved in similar occupations, have similar incomes, belong to similar social and religious organizations, and have similar educational backgrounds. Because of this commonality a similar political point of view is understandable and predictable.

Categoric Groups

Categoric group membership is often more clearly defined than are secondary groups or social classes but is generally of less political impact. That is to say, the commonality of the members of categoric groups are of limited political scope. Generally speaking, categoric groups cover the four broad areas of age, sex, education, and ethnic origin.

As a case in point, let us consider the notoriety given to the youth vote of some 25 million that was supposed to materialize as a result of the 26th Amendment. Given the all-time high of voters in the 18-to-24 category, activists were joined by some political buffs in declaring the "liberal millenium" upon us. Yet such expectations were not based on facts. The liberal voice of youth came primarily from "student" youth, but not all students are liberal. Furthermore, the majority of these new voters—70 percent— were in the nonstudent category. Thus 17.5 million of these voters were separated by the same socioeconomic forces that influenced the remainder of the electorate. This category shared only age, and, as typical with all American youth, showed the lowest level of political interest.[14]

So the possibility exists that younger voters may have a significant impact on future elections, but 1972 and 1974 provide evidence to support the likelihood that politics will continue to be dominated by the middle-age category. Despite the declining number of middle-aged voters, the largest "block ballots" were still cast by this group, the traditional patterns.

[13]Campbell et al., op. cit., pp. 322–366.
[14]See Gallup Poll survey data in William Chapman, "Democrats Defeated in Droves," *Washington Post*, 13 December 1972.

Editorial cartoon by John Fischetti. Courtesy of Field Newspaper Syndicate.

'He has a new lease on life; he's transferred his anti-Roosevelt feelings to McGovern.'

Similarly the elderly do not vote the same on all issues. Any tendency to homogeneity in voting is limited to certain questions in which age is a pivotal factor—pensions, social security, medical care, and the like. As far as their partisanship, the Democratic or Republican affiliations established in earlier years are generally maintained. Thus the belief that the older one becomes, the more likely he is to become conservative, is not brought out by the evidence. Generally speaking, senior voters stay with their party but vote for the more conservative representatives (for example, Humphrey rather than McGovern).[15]

Sex of Voter
Generally Unimportant

Traditionally the sex role of the individual voter has generally been unimportant. Although women outnumber men, they have tended to vote less frequently, thus averaging out the total number of votes cast. In past years women were content to allow their husbands to dictate voting patterns for the family. Indeed the *American Voter* study demonstrated this. However,

[15]Herbert H. Hyman, *Political Socialization* (New York: Free Press, 1959), Chapter 6.

as the educational levels of women increase, their general willingness to become involved in all the "dirty" areas of business and politics also increase. Today, under *affirmative action* programs by both government and the private sector, women are becoming more involved in politics. A call to a new feminism has perhaps reawakened a spark of political interest. In the 1920s women successfully organized politically to gain the vote. In the 1970s women successfully organized politically to gain power, if the 1974 elections are to be a harbinger of the future. During that year some 3000 women were on the campaign trail speaking in behalf of their own candidacy. Compared with previous years, that was a 300 percent increase. The net result of this surge was a 27 percent increase in the number of women who hold elective office.[16] Though the U.S. Senate remains an all-male institution, the wins of 1974 increased the female contingent of the U.S. House of Representatives to 17 congresswomen. With the retirement of 4 congresswomen, this was a net gain of 1. In statewide races the victory of Ella Grasso as governor of Connecticut by a 20 percent margin attracted considerable attention. Other statewide gains in what *Newsweek* called a *psychic breakthrough* for women politicos occurred in sundry parts of the country—California, Alabama, New York, and North Carolina.[17]

Education Is a Major Determinant of Voting Behavior

Education has traditionally played a major role in the American political behavior. Between 1950 and 1970 the percentage of voters with a college education rose from 8 to nearly 25 percent, while that of those with a high school diploma increased from 47 to nearly 68 percent. In the past, voters with the most education have leaned toward the Republican party, but this trend is in a state of fluctuation. Watergate, questions of honesty in government, and other similar problems have lost the Republicans a larger percentage of the college-educated electorate. However, Democrats have not benefitted from this shift; the largest percentage of this category becoming Independents.

Economics Is an Important Ingredient

As important as social relationships are to the establishment of voting patterns, one must certainly include the influences of economics as a major

[16]"Womanpower at the Polls," *Newsweek* (18 November 1974), p. 39.
[17]"Women Increase by One in U.S. House," *Seattle Times*, 6 November 1974, p. D-2.

determinant of voting behavior. Few aspects have been as well documented as the economic impact on voting. As a result, a few accepted generalizations can be made. Persons of high income tend to vote more frequently than individuals of lower income. However, high- and middle-income groups vote at about the same frequency. Voter turnout varies with occupation. Professional and white-collar groups vote most frequently, followed by skilled and semiskilled workers and then farmers. Unskilled workers are the most unlikely to participate in the electoral process.

Generally speaking, individuals in the categories most likely to participate are of the highest socioeconomic status. That is, those factors discussed under social class tend to work in conjunction with economic factors to create an interest in the political process. These individuals, for a variety of economic and other considerations, are concerned with government policy and its impact on their own life styles. This may cause an individual to oppose a state income tax, because it will raise his share of the tax load, and at the same time commit himself to supporting bond issues for better schools.

Thus a complexity of issues, social and economic, come to the fore in establishing a demographic profile of the "average" American voter. Indeed, one wonders if the middle American voter is a statistical accident rather than a representative member of the electorate, regardless of Mrs. Lowrey of Fairborn, Ohio.

As America passes the midpoint in the 1970s, we see an ever-increasing breadth of diversity among voters. They are more willing to shed the old values and allegiances and to form new coalitions for mutual political benefit. Many of the social implications of the past no longer hold true as women organize to gain political power; racial minorities are elected to public office from heretofore antiminority constituencies; youth become more vocal, and the once proud and powerful WASP finds himself a minority among minorities. If we are to understand the socioeconomic implications of the changing face of politics in this decade, we must understand the attitudes of those groups bringing about these changes.

Race as an Issue

In 1972 Andrew Young, a black civil rights leader, a lieutenant of Martin Luther King and a leader of the Southern Christian Leadership Conference, ran for Congress in Georgia's 5th Congressional District (Atlanta). He was elected as the first black congressman from the South since 1901, a feat that is even more surprising because the 5th Congressional District is 62 percent white. Young represents the new wave of black politician. Since the late 1960s, blacks have been elected to mayoral and

congressional seats and even to the United States Senate. This new wave of minority power is hard to understand within the framework of traditional voting behavior, unless one closely listens to the message. It's not a cry for the new freedom but rather one of issues and candidates.

"Alabama's white politicians were frank," [Young said]. "They called us niggers. A year or two later, when blacks in a community got 30 per cent of the vote, we became nigras. Later on still, at about 40 per cent, we were either Nee-grows or colored people, and by the time we had gotten a clear majority of the vote, the pols had adopted us as their black brothers."

The line evoked laughter, as everywhere it does, whatever the complexion of the audience at hand. Yet a message is lurking amid the escalating statistics. It is Andy Young's way of getting over to people why a fervent and evangelical civil rights movement has suddenly moved among the money-changing denizens of politics—why unambiguous slogans such as "Freedom Now" are being abandoned these days in favor of close analyses of the issues.

The man at the lectern embodies that transition. A top comrade-in-arms of Dr. Martin Luther King, with credits at Selma and similar Southern fronts, Young has won election to the U.S. House of Representatives—and from a recently redistricted Atlanta constituency in which 62 per cent of the registered voters are white. . . .

If irony applies, it is lost upon Andy. Whether speaking before the crowds of conscientious students, or declaiming at a luncheon in Atlanta's black community, the first black Congressman from the South since post-Reconstruction sees no conflict whatever in the direction he has chosen.

"There just comes a time when *any* social movement has to come in off the street and enter politics," he contends. . . . "I've never been given to a lot of blacker-than-thou rhetoric and that will not be the style that I'll adopt in Washington. You cannot serve a black issue by approaching it as such—or not in *this* Congress. Instead, you must plug for jobs in legislation, or a day-care program, or some similar goal. Do it another way and you turn people off. In Atlanta, for example, I supported a new rapid transit construction. At least 30 percent of the construction workers are black people."

He is equally realistic on the subject of his constituency. The 5th Congressional District, the result of a recent rezoning, includes the greater part of metropolitan Atlanta plus a rural hinterland just north of the city. Included are the majority of Atlanta's black voters, but there are wards around the city's plush Buckhead area which are overwhelmingly white—and affluent as all get-out. Before the reapportionment, the percentage of black voters in the district was less than 30. Blacks now account for about 38 per cent, but the fact that the remainder of the electorate is white poses extraordinary problems for a former civil rights figure.

"Well, let's face it," says Young philosophically, "there is still a hard-core element of racists in the South. But there is also a growing new liberal white vote. In Atlanta, we like to call it our New South Coalition: black voters, liberal votes, white labor votes. Now the problem is to involve those new white voters without stirring up the dyed-in-the-wool racists in the process. It's difficult. In 1970, when I ran and lost, we sent white volunteers into certain white areas. It didn't work. Many of the whites were as resentful of those kids as they would have been of black people banging on their doors. In 1972, we did it a little differently: more low-key, I suppose, and apparently we succeeded. I have nothing but faith in Atlanta's white electorate. There are channels for racial communication down here which few other cities in America can match. The same constituency behind Massell and Jackson [white liberal mayor Sam Massell and black vice-mayor Maynard Jackson] supported my own candidacy. We hope to extend that base next year. . . ."

Andrew Young has just slipped behind the wheel of his 1970 pearl-grey Audi. He will speak this morning before Atlanta's Junior League, a society of well-to-do socialite women who are active in political and other affairs. He is a lean, handsome, youthful-looking man with something about him reflecting confidence and success. There is also a curious serenity about the man—the wordless assumption that whatever the calamity the Lord will provide: one must never lose faith. In his meticulously tailored, conservative-mode suit, there is little to recall the young civil rights activist who led racial demonstrations during the 1960's.

Optimism Is a Popular Ingredient

The speech goes well. A Congregationalist minister, and rather middle-class in life style, Andy is extraordinarily effective in suburbia where response is immediate to the set of values he projects: community awareness, a Christian way of life, concern for one's children and a faith in human nature. There's a heavy-handed boosterism in many of his talks: the projection of Atlanta as a "hopeful sort of place—capable of becoming the greatest community in America."

His schedule is far from over, however, and soon he has returned to his crowded suite of offices overlooking the remnants of the city's wretched Buttermilk Bottom. "I'm gonna be a *working* representative," he declares. "That's how we won—we got out and worked. I try to tell these young people: it's not always the good guy who wins the election, but the man who works harder. If the better man just happens to work a little harder, then he wins, but bad guys are usually up early in the morning. I intend to visit my district every weekend. Church on Sunday, a school every Monday. That's doubly important where black people are concerned. We're terribly cynical about people we don't see. We don't read too much about our men in the paper, so it's their physical presence and accessibility that counts.

"Blacks don't say, 'Go up there and do a good job.' They say, 'Don't you forget about us, hear?' We've been betrayed and used so much in the past that we must be constantly assured that our politicians are with us. Just look at Adam Clayton Powell, before his troubles with the courts."

There is a warmth and folksiness about Andrew Young which will make this aspect of his job seem child's play. And searching about for some kind of theme equating the three directions or phases of his life—clergyman, civil rights worker, public servant—it is probably this concern about people which best applies.

Young, 40, the son of a dentist, was raised in a middle-class environment in New Orleans. There is little to distinguish his adolescent years, but by his senior year at Howard University something curiously cathartic seems to have happened to the man. "Graduation, in particular, was traumatic," he recalls. "Even though I had been through college, I really began doubting that I had learned very much. I suppose I was just typical of your student in those days: you know, gym, girls, the fraternity house and stuff. I also did a lot of sleeping. Suddenly it started to dawn on me that here I was, a college graduate, supposedly, and just what did it all mean. I'd majored in biology, sort of a pre-dental program, but I knew I wasn't interested. Just where was I going?

"There was this fellow I knew, a clergyman of some kind, who was staying that summer at my parents' in New Orleans. What struck me as strange was not his work in the community but the fact that he appeared to be enjoying it so much. I mean really. I know it's a cliché, but he actually seemed to be living his work."

Andy eventually attended the Hartford (Conn.) Theological Seminary, earning a bachelor of divinity degree in 1955. He later took the pastorate of a church in Hartford before returning to the South to head churches in Alabama. It was there that he was introduced to Jean, his wife, now a curriculum research specialist with the Atlanta public schools.

He had eased into the life of a simple country preacher after Portuguese officials rejected his request to establish a mission in rural Angola. But the South was in turmoil, and Andy, as a recognized leader in his community, was soon up to his neck in assorted civil rights work.

"My wife, as it happened, was a friend of Coretta Scott King, and it was in this way that I was able to meet Martin Luther King—involved at the time in the Montgomery bus boycott. We talked a few times and I volunteered to help. But nothing much happened and when the National Council of Churches asked me to work in its youth department, we left Alabama and moved to New York."

By the '60s, however, Dr. King and his aides had formed the Southern Christian Leadership Conference and greatly expanded their operations. Andy then decided to return to the South.

Amid the voter registration drives and other activity that dominated the South in the early 1960s, the qualities of Andrew Young became apparent. He was known primarily as a rational sort of person whose cool analysis of complex issues was greatly valued in a movement in which zealots often ruled. It was said that whenever a mass arrest seemed likely, Dr. King would insist that young Andy leave the scene.

By 1964, Andy Young had been promoted to executive director of the SCLC, and it was in that assignment that he later took part in some of the major skirmishes of the civil rights war: Birmingham, Selma, St. Augustine. He was also a top strategist and theorist for the movement. He assisted in the drafting of both the Civil Rights Act of 1964 and the Voting Rights Act of 1965 and was one of a number of top tactical advisers who were present in Memphis when Dr. King was shot to death.

We Never Really
Talked About Death

Andy doesn't talk about the assassination much, but his memories of the movement and its leader are very vivid ones. "We never really talked about death," he recalls. "It just never came up—except, once or twice, in a joking sort of way. I remember one night during a Mississippi visit. Martin and I were driving to Natchez although officials had just warned us of an assassination threat. About an hour out of Jackson, this strange-looking car slowed down in front of us. It just sat there a while. Martin said, jokingly, 'Lord, they gonna blow us right off this highway.' Fortunately, I was the one who was sitting at the wheel. I stepped on the gas and passed that car at 90 miles an hour.

"Oh, the movement has been a vital one. All the protests of the '60s— the anti-war movement, even the women's lib crusade—were indirect spin-offs of the civil rights fight. Of course, it got to be the fashion to condemn nonviolence—but considering the South, what it was at that time, and the resources existing in the Southern black community, it was the only real approach. Any other handling of the problem would have been suicide."

Pressure? I Actually
Seem to Enjoy It

It is the following day. Andy Young, consistent with his philosophy, is up early in the morning. Later in the day he must fly to New York for a meeting of the board of the Field Foundation (the agenda: the allocation of philanthropic funds). It is one of a number of civic activities which he has since been forced to abandon for a while. The weather has turned badly. Billowing clouds blot the north Georgia skies sending cascading rain across the metropolitan area. Hardly the sort of weather to take an airplane trip. An hour or two later, on its approach to LaGuardia, the plane descends through a mile or so of fog, but the unperturbable Andy simply fastens his seat belt and calmly resumes his perusal of a magazine.

His schedule is crowded but before leaving town he visits for a while with Dr. Kenneth B. Clark, head of New York's Metropolitan Applied Research Center. They are chatting about the problems of a freshman in

Congress when Andy abruptly glances at his watch, remembering that the departure of his flight is drawing near. Another scramble for the airport. Sometime, in the pre-dawn hours of the morning, when saner men have been slumbering for hours, Andrew Young will be returning to his family. "Oh, I don't mind the pressure that much," he insists. "In fact, there comes a point when you actually seem to enjoy it. I go like this maybe four or five days then relax on Sunday and watch a football game. I really wasn't able to see one this week, so as a result I feel the pressure. . . ."

That kind of pressure resumed for Andrew Young in 1970, when he embarked upon the first of two Congressional campaigns. It had long been decided among Atlanta's black leaders that some black or other would seek the 5th District seat. The incumbent representative, Fletcher Thompson, was a conservative Republican who seldom even bothered to visit black wards. This despite the fact that blacks in the district accounted for 29 per cent of the registered vote. For a while it was expected that Julian Bond, another civil rights figure with a national reputation, would be the candidate. But when Bond begged off the assignment went to Andy—and to Lonnie King, a widely popular militant in the area.

Andy was a winner in the Democratic primary but the struggle with King and his supporters had been damaging. Despite massive voting in the city's black wards, Thompson prevailed, and the blacks went back to work. Within months of the election, the NAACP's Legal Defense Fund submitted litigation protesting the alignment of the district in light of recently issued federal census figures showing an increase in the proportion of blacks in Atlanta. The suit was successful and boundaries were redrawn so that 38 per cent of registered voters were black. Andy then decided to campaign again.

His opponent this time was Rodney Cook, a white moderate. In a drive perhaps typical of grass-roots politicking, Andy inundated the all-black wards with sound trucks, music and gala dancing in the street. His hundreds of volunteers fanned across the city with catchy slogans such as "Think Young," "Young Ideas for Atlanta," and the like. Despite a drenching rain on election day itself, turnout among blacks ran to 95 per cent and Andy sneaked in with an 8,000-vote margin. His percentage in some white wards: as high as 43 per cent.

On the night of the election a few well-meaning friends hired a consort of security guards to *protect* Andy's family. The precaution was unnecessary. "It just got to be sort of a joke," recalls his wife, "though we did appreciate it. I never worry about Andy. Even at the height of the civil rights stuff we never were concerned about safety as such. When you are involved in something, you are not as anxious about it as people who are merely spectators. As for his schedule, we've all gotten used to it by now.''

It is hurry time again. Andy is scuffling to catch a late flight into Huntsville, Ala., where he will address a group of students. At a boarding gate of Atlanta's Hartsfield Airport, a familiar-looking figure sits unnoticed among the passengers. He is Jim Brown, the famous football player turned B-rate movie star. An old friend, as it happens. Shoving through the crowd, Andy goes over to chat.

The late Alabama flight has just been delayed so Andy browses at a paperback book rack. He is an avid and admitted health food nut who is a dedicated reader of nutritionist Adelle Davis. He is sold on the value of a vitamin intake and swallows several pills daily—''mostly A's but occasionally the B-complex stuff which are nothing more, really, than yeast tablets.'' When his schedule will permit him, he also jogs a couple of miles near his ranch-style home in southwest Atlanta's comfortable Cascade Heights.

Plain Limitations
for the Freshman Congressman

Andy is aware of the many plain limitations which a freshman Congressman must bring to the Hill and he has no illusions as to what he can accomplish. But he has already taken stands supporting school decentralization (''schools must be more responsive and accountable to local communities''), tax reform, health care legislation and a federal day-care program. He also will attempt to introduce a bill declaring the wooded banks of the Chattahoochee River (which passes through Atlanta) as Georgia's first national park.

But there is much to be done on the *political* side of the fence. Andy isn't certain who his challenger will be but he assumes that the Republicans will field another white man. ''In a way, that's fortunate. All this political fighting pitting blacks against blacks runs a serious risk of turning off the voter. Blacks don't like it when you fight each other. They see it as divisive and as damaging to the cause.''

What worries him most is the terrifying prospect of having to share the state ticket with Lester Maddox, . . . recalling the colorful one-time governor of Georgia who rose to prominence as an arch-segrationist. ''But voters have been splitting their tickets these days, so maybe it isn't so serious as it seems.''

Lester Maddox or no Lester Maddox, however, Andy Young will be ready for the battle. And any would-be challenger for the seat had better be aware of it. During a thank-you tour through Atlanta's black precincts,

Andy was stopped at one point by a youthful supporter and asked if he figured on remaining in the House.

He stared at his inquisitor.

"Yes sir!" he replied.[18]

Like other minority politicians, Andrew Young has abandoned the rhetoric but not the goals of the civil rights movements. As a member of the *new politics* Young and other similar individuals are espousing social goals through political means. As he stated himself: "There just comes a time when any social movement has to come in off the street and enter politics."

In many respects the woman in politics must overcome the same kinds of problems as the minority office seeker. She is stereotyped as a sex object, not really capable of making decisions but good at licking envelopes and warming beds. She is refused entrance into the smoke-filled room, but many times it is her own fault.

**Many Times
It's Her Own Fault**

One politician remarked that "women aren't willing to fight hard enough." Indeed this may be part of the problem. Unlike their male counterparts, whose goals are power, money, and prestige, women in politics often limit their interests to social issues. Their drive is to achieve social reform or a reprioritizing of goals, rather than the power needed to bring about these changes. Andrew Young well stated the issue when he noted that, "It's not always the good guy who wins the election, but the man who works harder." Sometimes women seem to lack the ability to handle the *crude trade-offs of the political marketplace.* They show an *aloofness,* which ultimately perpetuates their exclusion from politics.

However, those women who have learned their political ABCs and have an ability to deflect the propositions and innuendos rampant in the male-dominated political arena are the insiders and members of the smoke-filled rooms, a fact that came across loud and clear in the electoral gains for women in 1974. But all too many women refuse to "get their hands dirty." The goal of power must be sought after; and the prize goes to the hardest fighter.

[18]From Hamilton Bims, "A Southern Activist Goes to the House," *Ebony,* February 1973, pp. 83–90. Reprinted by permission of *Ebony* magazine, copyright 1973 by Johnson Publishing Company, Inc. (All footnotes in this chapter have been consecutively renumbered for the convenience of the reader.)

The very texture of American politics—its folkways and byways—militates against women's entry into mainstream politics. The smoke-filled rooms, bourbon-and-branch-water rites and all-night poker games exclude women out of hand from the fellowship and cronyism that seal the bonds of power. Neither years of service nor party loyalty provides women with a passport to the sanctum sanctorum, where decisions are made, priorities set, and candidacies determined. Millicent Fenwick, an extraordinarily erudite and practical Republican who served in the New Jersey legislature before her present appointment as the state's Director of Consumer Affairs, says that "Women are on the outside when the door to the smoke-filled room is closed." . . .

Women Are Underrepresented in Government

Although women represent fifty-three percent of the national vote, they lack even token representation in the councils of government, particularly on the national level. There are no women in the Senate, and [few] . . . in the House. . . . No women hold cabinet posts, although President Nixon . . . more than doubled the number of women in high executive posts. The Supreme Court has never seated a woman justice. . . . In the state legislatures, however, the representation of women [has] increased significantly . . . ; and [several] . . . women mayors preside over small- to medium-sized cities. . . .

Perhaps the greatest strides toward increased representation were made by the Democrats and Republicans at their 1972 conventions. Women made up forty percent of the Democratic delegates, compared with thirteen percent in 1968, and thirty percent of the Republican delegates, compared with seventeen percent in 1968. But many women delegates complained that male delegates failed to grasp the historic aspects of the female presence, and treated the women as carnal convenience. "You have no conception of how gross some of the men were," recalls Lee Novick, a Connecticut Democrat describing her experiences at the Miami Beach convention. "They'd walk over to you on the floor of the convention and say, 'Hey, you want to get laid?' They were absolute Neanderthals." . . .

Men Think Women Are in Politics for Sex

Women who work in campaigns—especially single women—often find that the criterion for their acceptance rests on sexuality rather than on

© 1974 by NEA, Inc.

"... And if she's going into politics, we have
this lovely new scent called 'Clout'!"

intellect or ability. Esther Newberg, one of the "Boiler Room Girls" in
Senator Robert F. Kennedy's office, who served as Muskie's campaign
manager in New York State, says of the local politicians: "They told me I
had better legs than Crangle's. They relate to us sexually. It has to be
worse for a single woman. They assume that the reason you're in politics is
for sex. . . ."

The problem for many women in politics is how to keep the game
between the sexes from interfering with their own seriousness of purpose.
For if men continue to relate to political women as sex objects, it only
heightens the struggle of women politicians to coexist with men on an
equal basis. To avoid some of these problems, politically astute Margaret
Heckler conducted her first primary campaign wearing a grey flannel suit
at every appearance on her schedule. It was a costume, she says, designed
to allow her to blend into the grey Massachusetts sky and into the equally
grey male political arena, so that the voters would be forced unconsciously
to identify her with the issues and forget about the fact that she was a
woman. The strategy worked; after her victory, her opponent said he had

belatedly discovered some devastating material concerning her background, which he would have used against her during the campaign. "You're a mother," he said accusingly. "You have children." . . .

Women have ruefully come to realize, moreover, that their exclusion has helped to shape the character of the game—to their disadvantage. Although they have not responded to the traditional incentives offered male politicians—money, jobs and contracts—they have been energized by social issues long ignored by male politicians. Their rallying cries have focused on peace, women's rights, abortion reform, day-care centers, and greater sensitivity toward the disenfranchised—children, minorities and the poor. . . .

Women Could Become a Major Force for Social Change

If women constituted a significant input into its policy-making apparatus, would the Nixon Administration have been able to preside over a priority system than paid billions in cost overruns on the C-5A while at the same time cutting back school lunch programs and milk money in its budget? Would the same Administration have vetoed the day-care bill with such strong language—likening day care to the start of a communal life-style— if a woman lent her perspective to its cabinet? Defense contracts in the city of Charleston alone totaled $66,900,000 . . . while several hundred million dollars of Federal appropriations for day care have been withdrawn this year from the state of New York—an act that will force working mothers who are the sole support of their children to go on the welfare roles.

Nevertheless, many women, knowledgeable, compassionate and resourceful women who seek to change these priorities, find that they cannot surmount the obstacles to running for office or move from the periphery into the centers of power. . . .

Why this hostility toward women in politics? It is undoubtedly true that many men enter the time-consuming, all-engrossing world of politics to escape from their home lives, and for such men, the last thing in the world they would seem to want would be a meaningful relationship with a woman. Not merely on a romantic level, but also on a business or professional level.

For many politicians, politics provides male companionship from breakfast through a nightcap. Meade Esposito, the powerful Brooklyn Democratic leader, meets with his key male aides every weekday morning at a cafeteria and often ends his day with them in the wee hours of the morning with a nightcap at a Coney Island bar.

The big-time politician inhabits an unreal world, without clocks or geographic locations, families or outside interests. The unreality is heightened during political campaigns, when politicians wake up in unfamiliar cities, in unfamiliar hotel rooms, with unfamiliar bed partners. These campaigns exude an air of sexuality, reflecting the anxieties of those involved in the campaign, from anxious staffers to insecure candidates. The gratification received from a triumphant tour seems interchangeable with the gratification received from a sexual encounter. "The real definition of a politician is that if he wakes up happy in the morning, he can't remember if he's had a good crowd or a good lay the night before," says Robert Squier, a political television consultant.

Even when "protected" women take part in a campaign, they often find themselves in secondary and degraded roles, regardless of their role within the organization. Jane Squier, who is her husband's partner in the television consultant firm that worked for both Muskie and Humphrey, recalls that she has been an invisible person in the eyes of some politicians. "I was literally introduced to Hubert Humphrey twenty-six times, and he always reacted as if it was the first time," she says. As for the Muskie campaign, "I got shunted to Jane Muskie quite a bit." Senator Eagleton was an exception, she added. He accepted her creative contributions without assuming out of hand that she merely did her husband's secretarial work.

Parties Often Oppose Women Candidates

More often than not, the political parties discourage women—particularly young women—from seeking office. Bonnie Andrikopoulos, a member of the Colorado Women's Political Caucus who campaigned for Congresswoman Pat Schroeder, described how the party tried to dissuade her candidate from running. "The party was one of Pat's greatest obstacles. They told her, 'Don't do that this year—you haven't had the experience.' We've had a lot of qualified women who should have been running a long time ago, but they've gone to the [party] leadership and the leadership always said, 'Oh, it isn't time yet; don't ruffle the waters. We'll run a man.' I think that from the success that we had in Colorado women won't believe that anymore. You can do it without the backing of the party leadership. Pat didn't ever have strong support from the party."

When a woman does manage, through a primary fight, to win her party's nomination, the party often tries other strategies to block her success. It's almost as if they'd rather lose an election than see a woman win. In Pat Schroeder's case, according to Doris Meissner, the executive director of the National Women's Political Caucus, the Democratic Party of Denver deprived her of funds usually given the candidate who has won the primary. This was followed by cutoff of A.F.L.-C.I.O. funds that normally are given a Democratic candidate. As a result of the efforts of the Caucus, continued Ms. Meissner, "We were able to get a good chunk of money to her because we pushed the Democratic Study Group [in Congress] as well as some of those groups involved with the whole discrimination issue."

Like insurgents everywhere, women in politics find that the rules are sometimes changed by the party in midstream to affect them adversely. Ronnie Eldridge, who was Senator Robert Kennedy's liaison in New York City, learned this lesson when she tried to run for New York County leader in 1967. She won a majority of the votes among the district leaders—traditionally all that was needed to elect a leader—but a reform caucus changed the rules to require a two-thirds vote. With a tinge of bitterness in her voice, Ms. Eldridge recalled: "I remember one of the leaders standing up and saying—and this was a reform leader—'How could a woman be a county leader? She couldn't sit and talk with the other county leaders. We couldn't get any business done.'" The strategy worked and Ms. Eldridge withdrew from the race.

"I'm not trying to insinuate anything, but have you noticed that almost all of the Watergate characters are men?"

Women Are Expected
to Seek No Rewards

Another lesson in the double standard pointed out by Ronnie Eldridge's career in politics is that male politicians expect women to work endlessly without claiming rewards that would ordinarily be given to men who performed the same services. Those who used Ms. Eldgridge's clout with the Senator took her usefulness for granted, never expecting her to have ambitions of her own, and never expecting her to cash in on the IOU's that constitute the backbone of clubhouse politics. Several years later, after working in the super cabinet of John Lindsay and organizing women across the country for his abortive Presidential campaign, Ms. Eldridge found the same discriminatory treatment meted out by the Lindsay administration, indicating that the same patterns prevailed regardless of a politician's political ideology. "All I wanted was the job of First Deputy City Administrator," said Ms. Eldridge. "I was offered the job of Deputy City Administrator. The job paid $4000 less. I said I was offended. I wanted the title and the money. Ed Hamilton [the Deputy Mayor] called me and offered me part of the extra money, but not the title. I didn't take the job."

Liabilities Often Come
from Women Themselves

But women in politics are also the first to admit that many of the obstacles to their success come from women themselves. Mayor Sam Massell of Atlanta says that, "It is not at all popular, not only with the men but also with the women, to name a woman to anything. There's absolutely no political benefit whatever. Some women may be jealous. Some definitely feel that women should not play roles that compete with men. They feel a personal challenge in having to deal with another woman. I don't get any letters, any calls of support, other than from women's lib organizations. There's no goodwill in this at all."

Some women believe that a false sense of idealism holds political women back from demanding a quid pro quo for their votes, money and services. It is a familiar lament, professed by women from all parts of the country: a certain delicacy in handling the crude trade-offs of the political marketplace, an aloofness which ultimately perpetuates their exclusion from politics. Think of the potential to be gained if women could cross this barrier to claim their due: appointive and elective offices, rechanneled government funds and reordered priorities. Perhaps women will realize that they do not have to compromise their ideology to negotiate a political deal. Indeed, contributing their efforts to the woman candidate who works for day-care legislation does not constitute a sellout.

Other women do not see the necessity of electing women to replace good men, men who support women's issues. "What do you do when there are good women running against good men?" asks Ronnie Eldridge. "What do you do with women who have worked for a long time for Al Blumenthal, Herman Badillo, and Jerry Kretchmer?" Held back by the mechanics of this psychology, women political activists are beginning to organize through their state political caucuses to overcome it. Donna Brunstad, a Connecticut Democrat active in her state's political caucus, recalls that similar arguments were used to dissuade blacks from seeking political office. "They'd say, 'Look, you don't need a black candidate. This man speaks out on civil rights, he has more power to speak out, he has the rest of the white community, so you just stay down there and let the rest of us do your job.' That's not the way it's going to be, though."[19] . . .

In addition to minorities and sex, age is another important categorical group operative in American politics today. Yet, as we have observed, the greatest potential impact derived from this group will be found among the burgeoning ranks of the young adult. Not only is this group the fastest growing, but it is truly a *revolutionary generation*. That is, it has grown to adulthood during perhaps the most monumental "flux . . . in human history."

It represents a generation hell-bent on establishing the immediate relevancy of all activity. Even among the less vocal majority, the youth of the new generation moves at a rate their seniors find impossible to pace. Better educated, more widely traveled, concerned with not only economic security but also the immediacy of self-expression and individualism, this new generation may shake the American political system to its very foundations. Like those other groups that make up America's pluralistic society, this new generation represents a power source with which to be reckoned.

**Youth—
A Distinct Generation***

The potential public impact of all the young people coming of age in the 1970s lies not in just their numbers but in the distinctiveness of much about them. "This is not just a new generation," *Time* noted in naming the group a collective "Man of the Year" before it was even twenty-one years

[19]From Susan and Martin Tolchin, "Getting Clout," *Esquire,* July 1973, pp. 112–115, 181–183. First published in *Esquire* magazine.

*From *Changing Sources of Power: American Politics of the 1970's* by Frederick G. Dutton. Copyright © 1971 by Frederick G. Dutton. Used with permission of McGraw-Hill Book Co.

old, "but a new kind of generation." . . . In . . . fundamental ways, this generation has been built of revolutionary technologies and rapidly changing conditions in their immediate world.

These young people know the Depression, World War II, and most of the cold war only as episodes in history textbooks. They have been shaped instead by the greatest material outpouring for almost an entire society that the world has ever seen, capped . . . by the longest-sustained prosperity this country has yet had. And so the conditioning and the expectations they bring into the electorate are as different from the Depression-rooted attitudes and insecurities as the ICBM is from the Model T.

Compared to any past generation, a fairly small portion of this group had to do menial labor for long hours in the early and middle years of adolescence. The majority will become more pocketbook-minded as they move further into their working and family-rearing years. But in contrast to earlier generations, this one is significantly less economic and more social—with the accent on social conscience for some and social status for others. Over-all, they have primarily a "doing and using" rather than "working and saving" outlook.

A really precipitous downturn in the national economy could sharply temper the easy economic attitudes of many of these young people. This country has never been stoic about panics and depressions in the past, and the new group could react in an ugly way to a long and severe recession or an effort to curtail its living standards for other priorities. . . . Many members of the new generation feel that in some way they have a "right" to and a "guarantee" of good times. That outlook may be faulted by economic conservatives, but it is a political fact of life which politicians may disregard at their peril.

"The shagginess and chosen poverty of student communities have nuances that may be tremendously important to the future," Paul Goodman has commented. "We must remember that these are the young of the affluent society, used to a high standard of living and confident that if and when they want, they can fit in and make good money. Having suffered little pressure of insecurity, they have little need to climb, just as, coming from respectable homes, they feel no disgrace about sitting a few nights in jail. By confidence they are aristocrats—en masse." . . . What is happening beneath the beards and beads and all the other garb is a rearranging of preferences and purposes—and that still has to be sorted out in the American economy, value structure, and political system.

Nurtured by Television

Almost as important as the economic conditioning is the fact that these young people are, quite precisely, the first baby crop to be nurtured by television. TV went public just as the first of them arrived on the scene. In 1946 the U.S. had fewer than 17,000 sets; five years later it had well over 10 million. By the early 1960s, when this group was in adolescence, the nation had over 45 million sets. . . .

And it affected not just the *content* of their thought but *how* they think as well. As Marshall McLuhan and others have written, a child before a TV set is conditioned differently from a child undergoing the straight-line, tightly ordered, set mental discipline of the printed page. . . . The new generation cannot really be understood, much less communicated with, without taking into account the interior "participation" and nonverbal personal levels encouraged by television.

Accelerated Education

Still another important conditioning experience for this group has been its greatly accelerated education. The first of these young people were barely halfway through grammar school and the rest of them not yet even there when the Soviet launching of Sputnik I in 1957 suddenly triggered an unprecedented speedup and enrichment of almost the entire educational system in the United States. . . . Ironically, the intensified education of this group was largely a response to America's cold-war alarm over the Soviets being first to put a man into space. . . . Opinion surveys indicate that more and more young people are simply dismissing talk about a Communist threat as irrelevant. . . .

The overwhelming majority of the eligible new voters have been provided not only a greatly accelerated and enriched education but also more years of it than any previous group. The new generation on which the New Deal [was] built had the equivalent of an eighth-grade education; the group coming to maturity at the end of the sixties and in the . . . seventies . . . have received the equivalent of a little more than a high school education. . . .

A closer look is needed, however, to see the full effect of the rising educational achievement as it bears on the younger, middle, and older groups of voters. The heavy majority of senior citizens now voting have had a grammar school education. The clear majority of the rest of the voters have had a high school education. But a majority of the new voters of this decade will have had at least some education beyond high school.

What is happening at the upper level of the educational range, in fact, may be particularly relevant since this group is usually the most influential. . . . In the 1970s, well over half of high school graduates will go on for some college education. The actual number of university students jumped from less than three million to eight million during the last ten years alone, and almost half of all college freshmen now hope to continue their education beyond a four-year degree. . . .

The direct political impact of the general educational upgrading going on is nevertheless important and fairly immediate. For better-educated individuals vote and participate in public affairs much more than the less educated. . . . The higher educational level of the young generation should help assure its substantial political activity regardless of the staying power of its youthful activism.

Important but less measurable is the probable effect of more schooling on the quality of the public dialogue and candidates who run for public office. In-depth opinion studies show, predictably, that better-educated voters tend to have a sharper perception of immediate events and issues and a fuller understanding of the political system and the historical context into which they fit. Less educated voters usually give only the most general and passing attention to such matters, being moved more by personality, party label, and the mood of the period than by particular issues. The better-educated tend to be more specific, selective, systematic, and "ideologically oriented." More education thus tends to shift the grounds on which elections turn. This could have increasing effect on campaigns and eventually enhance the usually negligible leverage which election mandates have on the governing process. Of all the forces at work on the new politics, the educational dynamics and divisions are clearly among the more influential.

Civil Rights Movement —An Unknown Impact on Youth

Another basic conditioning aspect of the new generation of voters is that very clearly its members saw the civil rights struggle through television if not at first hand. Most, though certainly far from all, of the group came through that turmoil with attitudes at least several decades ahead of their parents. . . . The civil rights struggle, in fact, is almost certainly as significant for its politicalization of both the young whites and the young blacks as for such tangible progress as it has yet led to for most Negroes.

The Vietnam war further insistently shaped much of this generation. It provokes a grating mixture of disillusionment and compromising rationalizations in a heavy portion of the young. . . . The draft itself . . . [was] an immediate pressure on millions of young men already vaguely against war, [while] . . . frequent televising . . . of the mortal nightmares of Vietnam . . . probably contributed more directly to the hostility and unsettlement of this age group than any other single factor. . . .

(Jules Feiffer, Publishers-Hall Syndicate, 1970. By permission.)

Nuclear Generation

This is also the first generation which has grown up entirely within the setting of the nuclear age. . . . And many of the group have taken more seriously than their elders the idea, as expressed by journalist John Poppy, that a "situation in which a decision by a man can undo everything evolution has built over three billion years gives moral questions and questions of sanity a new vitality." . . .

The view of much of the younger group about more traditional politicians of the time-tested school of conventional convictions and reassuring homilies drops somewhere below contempt. Political analyst Haynes Johnson wrote after a coast-to-coast tour interviewing young people in 1968 that they bear "a political consciousness shaped by the New Frontier and shattered during the Great Society." . . . Quite predictably, a popular "campaign button" on many campuses has been *Harass Your Local Politician.*

Out of all the protean conditioning is coming a generation which . . . is far and away the most fiercely independent, perceptive, and self-motivated they have ever seen. It is also obviously the most disruptive and demanding yet to arise in American society. . . .

The prospective political energy in this generation is suggested by the fact that even before coming to maturity, its vanguard members helped set the pace for the two predominant controversies of the last decade: the civil rights struggle and the Vietnam war protests. These young people have also forced the most searching reappraisal of higher education in the U.S. since the borrowings from the German universities in the last quarter of the last century. And the concern of this group with the college environment has been political as much as educational in nature. . . .

The particularly virulent assault on the nation's leading universities has gone directly to the exercise and distribution of power within the educational establishment. And the university is only the first of the larger environments into which this group is moving. . . . There is even a theory that the young activists are the latest addition to the uneasy galaxy of power elites in this country. Those who ridicule this . . . fail to recognize the wells of power opening up through sheer commitment, mass numbers, the magnetism which attracts the mass media, and the informal cultural networks taking shape.

Social Activists

Another possible indicator of the potential social and political energy in this generation is provided by the hundreds of thousands of college students . . . who have regularly been volunteering part of their free time to tutor underprivileged children and do social service work. Gallup reported near the end of the sixties that a majority of all college students had done some social work. . . . The group which is intensively involved in social work constitutes a small part of the total generation, but the proportion is still at an all-time high among this country's young people. And the socially involved in the older populace constitute a much lesser fraction of that larger society.

What is perhaps most remarkable about the huge, pace-setting college group is not its proportionally few but determined protesters . . . but the fact that significant numbers of the rest at the more influential universities have rallied at critical junctures on major issues. . . . In 1970 a clear majority had joined in one or more protests. A Harris poll that year also found a third of the college students saw some effectiveness in violent tactics—but three-fourths thought other protests and demonstrations are effective. . . .

We Have to Have An Effect Now

A fundamental trait of not only the leadership group but of most of the new generation, and one likely to contribute to its influence, is a deeply instilled imperative to experience and to have effect *now*. . . . But it is a key impediment to their working within a gradualist system either willingly or well. . . . This is partly the result of the usual impatience of youth, but the forced nature of this group is also a consequence of the hurried pace of much of contemporary life. A recurring criticism by those who have worked closely with these young people is that they have no sense of history. In the words of one bitter academician, "They think Jesus Christ died in 1939." . . .

Many in this age group have sought more kinds of experience "sooner, younger" than their predecessors, and that vanguard has an unmistakable sense of nearing power, fed by a growing consciousness of the generation's size and by all the attention the mass media have given to protests and marches for many years. Far more important, the tribal self-awareness among these young people (their talk is full of *we* and *us*) has been heightened by mass advertising appeals over the course of many years to the $25-billion-a-year teen-age market—to "the Pepsi Generation," for instance, during their adolescence. Aware of all the attention and their numbers, many are entering the electorate not meekly but brashly.

In a very elementary sense, a large proportion of these young people come seeking more power and freedom. Or, as one of them has said, they demand both "to be taken into account" and "to be let alone." . . .

Increasingly they have not asked but taken liberties and authority. It is this striking feature which gives their numbers such life and thrust. It introduces into the electorate not only fresh views and energies but also the most basic kind of struggle with established patterns, without regard to whether those are economic, social, political, religious, or moral—or liberal or conservative. There is distrust of the present and disregard of the past, a challenging and testing and desire to experiment beyond what this country has ever before had to cope with and assimilate. What is most fundamentally being put in question is hierarchical authority—which just happens to be the working principle of the schools, the church, the trade unions, the family, business, and most other institutions.

Study after study has shown that the rebellious and critical element contains a very large proportion of the most perceptive, creative, and intelligent of this generation. . . . A *Fortune* poll at the end of the sixties found that less than a fourth of even the conservatives among recent college groups are ready to "easily accept outward conformity for career advancement." The percentage was substantially less among the other college students. . . .

Activism Is Not Isolated

The widespread hope that the challenges being mounted by the more active young people will ease up after this age group grows a little older, misunderstands the deeper sources of the forces which are stirring. The activism, a study at the University of California concluded, "appears to represent a relatively enduring personality disposition rather than an isolated, impetuous, ephemeral behavioral act." The power-seeking in the new generation, it seems, is as real and determined as that of earlier social groups who pushed their way into the country's political structure, from the unpropertied freemen early in the nation's history to the offspring of the 1900-to-1914 immigration wave that provided the generation base on which Roosevelt built. The new group is proportionally larger compared to the rest of the populace than were either of those earlier historical waves, and it already has a stronger beachhead within this society than those earlier groups initially had. . . .

A look at the high school students of the last few years suggests that the recent college militants and "hippies" have been having an even greater influence, in personal styles and social outlook, on much of that malleable younger set than on anyone else. Most of the recent high school students have heard the endlessly throbbing tribal drums of the new culture; and some of the more vivid of the recent college activists and hip ones have set the baseline in tastes, attitudes, and modes of behavior, from which the next wave of young people are moving on, including a great many who will never go to college. The recent young pace-setters have been exceptionally bizarre for American society, and they are being imitated even beyond the usual excesses of adolescent mimicry in search for personal definition. Through that process, their most prominent qualities are changing norms, even becoming clichés fairly rapidly. Fads come and go, of course; but in individual dress, sexual activity, social concern, use of pot, and political awareness, the current high school group has been found to be well ahead of even the recent college activists at the same age. . . .

Like every generation, the new one moving into the electorate in the seventies contains many different social and political groupings. Its far fringes include neo-Nazis, Maoists, Marxists, and Guevarists, though these are mostly labels for poses rather than commitments. There is also a plethora of fairly new organizations—a constantly reviving American phenomenon noted as far back as de Tocqueville. . . . Also, a much smaller proportion of young people is being turned on by the established hierarchies of the two major political parties, organized labor, and the churches than has been the case for many decades.

The Existentialists and the Philistines

An advance political breakdown of the main part of this generation might take as its principal categories none of those organizations, and certainly not the young Democrats and young Republicans or liberals and conservatives, but what might imprecisely be called "the existentialists" and "the philistines." . . . The suggested groupings represent attitudes and influences more than individuals in the new generation. But they also point to trends and likely tensions and counter-tensions of power in American society.

The existentialists are the vital, vocal elitists and activists of the new generation, very much the smaller of these two principal groups but the forward edge, "the prophetic minority," as they like to think of themselves. . . . These futurists are not just the still-growing New Left of the Hippies, the more concentrated political and cultural distillates of what's been happening, but a much broader phenomenon in U.S. society and the part that is increasing most rapidly in both numbers and influence.

POINT

The crying accolade by student activists that the future belongs to today's youth is much the same as arguing that night is necessarily dark. One does not disagree but merely speculates on the intelligence of he who makes the statement.

In the same manner I cannot become overly excited by the enfranchisement of these new youthful voters. Certainly a large number will fall within the 18-to-24-year-old group. But the 21-to-24-year-old age group has the lowest voting turn out of any segment of society. Will the 18- to 20-year-olds be different? Young adults may have their day, but it is usually when they have reached a more conservative middle age. Evidence indicates that the tremendous impact of the youth vote never will materialize. Like the enfranchisement of women before them, young adults will tend to participate to the same degree as any other member of the electorate. Being young does not automatically create alternatives to today's problems. Nor does the youth vote possess some secret to success at the polls.

On college campuses, students pass resolutions, attend meetings, send telegrams; but like their older brethren they soon tire of the activity and return to their own interests. Indeed, even when given specific "release time" to participate in political activity, they found other ways to spend their "vacation." Forecasts during the election of 1970 of massive participation by some one-half million youths actually resulted in participation by less than 70,000 volunteers, most of whom

COUNTERPOINT

The unknown in politics, as in other aspects of society, often tends to either create unfounded fears or cynical overreactions. Such a pattern is appearing on the issue of the youth vote.

It appears that my colleague has opted to identify with the Scammon/Wattenberg syndrome—that the "average" American voter is a midwestern housewife—as he suggests that the enfranchisement of women in the 1920s will serve as a harbinger of the youth vote in the 1970s.

As a liberal who has shed the "bleeding-heart" prefix in favor of pragmatic ethics, I cannot acclaim the 26th Amendment as the "millennium" for liberals. Yet it is politically capricious to casually discount 25 million potential voters, even if "only" 42 percent—10.5 million—vote. Though 70 percent of these new voters are in the nonstudent category, it will be the 3.9 million college students who will be disproportionately represented at the polls. Thus their high level of education will distinguish the youth voters from their older brethren. And education has been, among other things, a consistently significant variable in determining the direction of the vote; a significance that has already been evinced in the refusal of large numbers of new voters to identify with either of the major parties.

Yet of much greater consequence is the erroneous criteria of those who debunk the voting power of today's young adult. When youth get the message that a well-organized worked but once or twice. Even where active participation was encouraged and rewarded, such as at Princeton University, less than 24 percent of those released ever claimed to have engaged in political activity—less than 4 percent worked longer than a week—and the average "involvement" was 12 hours. Although it is true that some young adults showed a marked leadership potential in several campaigns, ultimately even these will be the exceptions to the rule, the same exceptions as found among the older adult population interested in politics. In 1972 McGovern's youth again demonstrated the same commitment—10 to 12 percent.

As with their older peers, if students are aroused by "short-term forces," they tend to become politically active. But usually they have too many other interests. Any "bleeding-heart liberal" who thinks that the youth vote means the "millennium" is at hand had better check the record in 1972 and 1974 before getting too excited.

RVW

minority can multiply the vote in geometric proportions, no one will question the intelligence of the major political parties in expending efforts to acquire youth support. An effective group of activists, even of limited numbers, can swing elections. Few candidates win by landslides. Congressman Robert Tiernan of Rhode Island won his seat in a 1969 special election by 303 votes out of 112,000 cast. In 1968 U.S. Senator Wayne Morse of Oregon lost by one-fourth of 1 percent. In the nation's closest U.S. Senate contest, the resolution of whether Louis Wyman or John Durkin was the junior senator from New Hampshire was only resolved by a special election in 1975. Thus I submit that the potential of politically effective groups of young adults are a more valid omen of vote power than the apathy of women in the 1920s.

VFA

The existentialists are committed to racial progress and bringing the poor into the economic and social mainstream, and they have a growing identification—*a sense of the species*—with the rest of mankind. . . .

The existentialists seek not just a "liberal more" or "conservative less" of what the nation has been doing for many years, but quite different directions. They define the good life not in terms of material thresholds or "index economics," as the New Deal, Great Society, and most economic conservatives have done, but as "the fulfilled life" in a more intangible and personal sense. They reject what they consider the compromises of the "sellouts" and "occupational idiots who pursue what William James long ago called "the bitch goddess Success" . . .

. . . [This] massive generation . . . will be living with rapidly increasing automation and could find the search for meaningful leisure as trying as the search for meaningful work has been in past times. . . . Just as the New Deal sought to solve the frustrations and failures of a Depression-wracked society, they seek to get at what they believe are the distinctive frustrations and failures of an affluent society. They see those not as wants which private prosperity or new laws or public spending can really resolve for the majority of Americans, but as problems of fairness and morality and life style which challenge the generally unquestioned assumptions of this society.

The existentialists . . . find the past and its lessons generally remote from the storm of sensations bombarding them; so they turn to present perceptions more than to history, to empirical action instead of the conventional wisdom, and to a multilevel search for an expanded being in place of the earlier emphasis on rationalism, which they perceive was never really attained or lived very much, anyway. There is, of course, a heavy dose of untested idealism in their outlook. . . . But at a minimum,

"BE CAREFUL OF THESE KIDS — ALL THEY DO IS ASK WHY"

Pierotti (Rothco).

large numbers of these young people are committed, as one observer summed it up, to a "deliberate, aggressive attempt to create a different world from that of their parents." . . . [A]s Robert Kennedy commented, "If the young scorn conventional politics and mock our ideals, surely this mirrors our own sense that these ideals have too often and too easily been abandoned for the sake of comfort and convenience. We have fought great wars, made great sacrifices at home and abroad, made prodigious efforts to achieve personal and national wealth, yet we are uncertain of what we have achieved and of whether we like it." . . .

Some observers have expressed concern that these new adults are "opting out of the political picture; they seem to be limiting their actions to the range of their perceptive selves," as Democratic Senator Walter Mondale of Minnesota put it. . . .

Senator Mondale's concern fails to take into account the range of commitment and experience which many among this generation seek. To dismiss that group as essentially apolitical or antipolitical is to misunderstand the fundamental questions they pose, the disgust large numbers of them have come to feel for the current construction of American society, and the provocative role many of them are bent on.

Instead of turning off, many of the activists will far more likely be tough, articulate leaders and social, cultural, and political agents in the coming years. . . . Their interest will generally be less in winning immediate elections than in relentlessly pressing for a fundamental recasting of values and direction, for they see elective politics as only a very limited part of the politics of social change—one of the crucial shifts taking place in American society.

The Real Revolt Is
Against Government and Politics

It is fundamental to the public prospect that the values of these young people cannot be fulfilled primarily through governmental action or a power hierarchy. The real revolt is against government, mass politics, pragmatism, gradualism, and long-prevailing liberal methods as much as against the private organization world and its establishment. . . .

Some critics have claimed to see a parallel between the ideal of participatory democracy and the concept of the people's democracy in Communist countries. . . . The more sophisticated of the new activists, however, have few illusions about being able to undo the organic arrangements very soon, if ever. The overwhelming majority are simply groping for some less-structured alternative to the institutionalized America in which they believe they and their fellow citizens are being subjugated. . . .

Whether or not quixotic, their instinctive, not just intellectual, want is to rescue the individual from a mass society of superorganizations and recover the human condition from technological domination. These young people generally accept and take easily to the spreading technologies, but a considerable number are resisting the "technologicalization" of man. The group wants to refurbish and reinvigorate individuality, and to do it through the vagaries of commitment and the imprint of each person who will speak out in either protest or affirmation—and put his body, not just his mouth, on the line. . . .

All the individuals involved would vociferously object, but there is in the young existentialists a certain amalgam of the New Deal liberal (without his economic determinism), Barry Goldwater (without his Air Force proclivities), and Henry Thoreau (without his recluse side). The mixture includes some incidental overlap. But it is primarily a reworking of historic materials in the American make-up. . . . In traditional terms, there is in this younger sector a passionate commitment to the individual—but to the full and sensitive individual; in essence, to a less competitive individualism, not the acquisitive, domineering, elephant-skinned "rugged individualism" of economic history. The accent is on personal "identity" and "authenticity," not the social adaptability extolled in the New Deal ethic. The psychological and verbal imperative is "principle," but as each individual sees it, not as society does. In such ferment, pressures for change in the basic tissues of U.S. politics and policy are at work. . . .

The philistines—the other loose major group in the ranks of the coming young people—are by far the more numberous but less active of the two. A considerable part of this group will not even vote unless very strongly stirred. Most of the philistines, however, will conscientiously comply with what they consider their minimum public duty; and the majority will uncritically follow the immediate partisan ties of their parents. Most of the present horde of young people, as sociologist Seymour Martin Lipset has summed them up, are politically passive, socially conservative, morally conventional, and largely preoccupied with private pursuits. . . .

Opinion studies of those turning twenty-one in the early 1970s have shown that a clear majority thought the U.S. could not prevent wars but should keep trying; would not participate in civil rights demonstrations and considered those either ineffective or damaging, but supported human rights in the abstract; believed in private enterprise "but thought some people could not make it no matter how hard they tried"; wanted a life of adventure but listed as their main goals "a good-paying job, money, success"; and judged themselves honest and upright but admitted they had cheated in school. . . .

This philistine majority is made up of those who pursue the traditional "American dream"; in so doing they are carriers of continuity, not agents of change. They divide on a wide range of values and viewpoints but usually reflect only the already respectable alternatives. . . . A large proportion has unquestionably been repelled by the more extreme activism of a small minority of their contemporaries in recent years, and that has had a very slight conservative effect on some of them. But . . . critics . . . concede the unwillingness of most of this age group to take on those they disagree with in their own generation. . . .

Perspectives must also be kept on the fact that the philistine group is substantially more educated, aware of the outside world, fad-influenced, self-assertive, self-indulgent, and change-propelled than the main part of any previous generation. It is inextricably caught up in the new influences at work even while trying to give the "correct answers" wanted by parents, teachers, and prospective employers. Even without the very considerable influence being exerted by the wave-making existentialists, the philistine majority forewarns of a fairly swiftly moving society and a whole new politics of change. . . .

Noncollege and College Age
Youth Agree

[A] *Fortune* survey of this age group . . . reported: "Surprisingly, noncollege youth takes nearly as critical a view of society as college youth. . . . When asked if they thought the American way of life was superior to that of any other country, only 18% of the students and 33% of the nonstudents agreed."

There are some observers, of course, who look on the coming influence of the new generation as simply "the youth myth," . . . [contending] that in politics, as in life, youth is merely a condition to be left behind, not a possession. . . . The last redoubt for those wary of this horde of young people would seem to be the more realistic expectation that if the coming power of the new generation is not mythical, may it at least not become monolithic.

What, in net effect, may be the actual impact of this flood of young people on the politics of the seventies? . . . This enormous group will influence as well as be influenced—it will batter as well as be battered.

A Diverse Approach Needed
by Politicians

The years ahead will almost certainly show politicians that diverse approaches are open with this mass of new voters. But the essence of politics is to try to perceive and affect the mold before, not after, it has hardened into history. . . . Tentative premises would at least wrap the enigma whole for working purposes. . . .

- As a starting point, it would seem that while the dominating slogans of national campaigns have long been variations on *Prosperity!* and *Peace!* new battle cries capable of reaching younger voters may evolve out of *Live!*—perhaps even *Love!* . . .
- While the prevailing personal goal of Americans in recent decades has been *security,* the objective may gradually shift not back to the older cry for *opportunity* but to *fulfillment.*
- While there have been pretensions recently of striving for the Great Society and a law-and-order society, the growing want among young people is simply a *humane society.*
- While there has long been a preoccupation with *national* purpose, the rising concern is again with *individual* purpose. . . .
- While most practical attention has long been on *special-interest politics,* the scope must be expanded in not just rhetoric but substance to include the elusive and difficult *politics of values.* . . .
- While the public frame of reference has long been *city, state, and nation,* the loyalty evoking increasing response is *mankind.*
- While the public pace which has long been extolled is *gradual progress,* there will be increasing insistence on *now.*
- And while the principal attention has been on the *Democratic* and *Republican electorates,* the vital new focus will be increasingly on the *independent electorate,* and whether to try to encourage or blunt it.

As the new generation flexes its muscles and, with other emerging power groups—women, minorities, the aged—moves toward political involvement, the traditional *majority* stands in fear and despair before the onslaught. All that the *WASP* has fought for and held dear since the establishment of the Republic seems on the verge of destruction at the hands of these *usurpers* who intend to make him a stranger in his own house. Frustration, disillusionment, and often just plain hostility are widely expressed sentiments.

The WASP

How did things get the way they are so that I am where I am? The Social Register is a laugh, the D.A.R. a disgrace. Protestantism is a blah religion, Americans can do no right, white is ugly, and just look what's happened to penis envy. I am not only a Wasp, I am a male chauvinist Wasp, and there is nothing to be done about it. When I say, "I am a Wasp," I know how

Father Damien sounded to himself that morning on Molokai when for the first time he began his sermon, "We lepers. . . ." I am a Wasp, just the way other people who now outnumber me used to be niggers and kikes and wops and dagos.[20]

[The WASPS watch as federal agents scamper] about the land with . . . little lists, searching out evidence of "discrimination" in every academic nook and union cranny, finding—what? Offenders? Who never would be missed? Or situations where Uncle Sam can intrude himself; where the government can tamper with the lives of the citizenry to "redress unbalances," "help right the wrongs of the past," "undo centuries of prejudice."

Is It Possible to Advantage One Group Without Disadvantaging Others?

The currently fashionable lists of offenders and favorite minorities touch the lives of all Americans. Benefitting who? Offending who? Nose-counting by skin color—the term is Geoffrey Wagner's, writing in *National Review* (September 1, 1972)—is supposed to help the disadvantaged minorities gain their fair share of positions in academe and other sectors of American life; nose-counting by skin color aims at the rectification of old slights, of countless incidents of negative discrimination. Surely the motivation is benign, whatever the consequences.

Of course, the consequences are more important than the motivation. Were it possible to advantage some groups without disadvantaging others, none but a churl could complain. And if all men are indeed created equal then obviously all should be equal in circumstances. *If*, that is, "created equal" means more than created thus by God—perceived as equally sharing in His blessings—and if "treated equally" means more than treated equally *under the law*. But the founding Fathers meant no more than created equal in the eyes of God, and deserving of equal treatment under law. Not that we today must take *all* our cues from the late eighteenth-century framers of America's fundamental founding documents and institutions. But to assert that the current enthusiasm for "reverse discrimination" is implied by the Declaration of Independence rhetoric (or by the Constitution!) is unhistorical and manifestly erroneous.

At bottom, there is a yawning gap in interpretation separating those who favor and those who oppose the present thrust for quotas, busing, and various other items of "reform," which are issues tied closely to the problem of eliminating impertinent, "irrelevant" discrimination in America in the seventies. Those championing quotaization, for instance, prem-

[20]John Canaday, "A Wasp's Progress," *New York Times Magazine*, 19 March 1972.

ise their opinion on the notion that if there have been grievous wrongs in the past (as there have been), then just about anything goes; those who disparage the quotaization trend assume that old wrongs are not righted by new wrongs, that quotas if once improper (as they were) are improper now. This apparently simplistic differentiation is actually complex, signifying two enormously divergent perspectives and, depending on which side triumphs, leading to two vastly different Americas in the near—and perhaps distant—future.

What passes by the name of "egalitarianism" in contemporary America, what is signalled by such rallying cries as "the new politics," "participatory democracy," and "proportional representation," was identified throughout election year 1972 with the hopes of Senator George McGovern and his *new* Democratic Party. This movement, as Ayn Rand toughly described it, was a "declaration of war on the American people by America's intellectuals." . . .

It didn't work. Senator McGovern was crushed on November 7; Middle America stayed away in droves from the McGovern polling booth levers. . . . The easiest interpretation for this phenomenon, the easiest, that is, for those distressed by it, is that a majority of American voters are simply too "selfish" at present, just too "mean-spirited," to want to redress legitimate grievances, too attached to their favored status to care about those not so favored. . . .

And that, for the moment, is where the devastated avatars of the New Politics and the Equal Society will leave it. . . . But those who never swallowed the Left prescription see the situation in another light. The conservative interpretation must be not only that the time was not yet ripe, but also that since the premise is inherently faulty, given the circumstances of American life, the time will *never* be ripe for that which Mr. McGovern and his minions wanted to do to the United States of America.

This side assumes that the "system" is basically just; that mixed-capitalism is better than statism if not, perhaps, as good as a purer unfettered capitalism; that equality of opportunity (and a healthy measure of equality of results) is not only possible under capitalism but implicit because of capitalism; that merit advancement serves the interests of vastly more people more justly, than would advancement via the "quotaization" route; that the currently fashionable minorities (by that I mean those groups who at the moment are the objects of reformist zeal) will in due course rise in America, as did other, once ill-treated minorities (those I call the unfashionable minorities: white ethnics, Gentile and Jew alike); that the rigidity of what masqueraded as "egalitarianism" in the early 1970s can never be anything other than an unacceptable brand of discrimination. . . .

**The New Politics Believe
Their Goals Are Correct**

The error in thinking demonstrated by the New Politics prophets is two-pronged: (a) they think their program is good; and (b) they thought it would work now. As to the latter, November 7 demolished that assumption. But the belief in the goal's inherent correctness. . . . I take as given the idea that America was founded on a philosophy of theoretical equality, however limited in conception, but that the practice of America was as often inequality as not. . . .

The vast majority of Negroes in America before the 1860s were slaves. The vast majority of American Indians lost their lands during the eighteenth and nineteenth centuries and were confined to the status of second-class citizens—more "denizens" than citizens, actually—throughout most of this country's history. The white Protestant hegemony often reduced non-Protestants to inferior status ("No Irish need apply") and, aside from isolated moments of equality and specific instances of high advancement, reduced Jews to an even lesser status. . . . No honest interpretation of our history could lead to the conclusion that this country has at all times and in all ways been the land of opportunity.

Yet, with all that, people abroad perceived this country as the land of the free. For economic, political, social, and religious reasons, tens of millions of Gentiles and Jews from non-English- and Germanic-speaking countries came to America to find a better life. In time they found it. All this is well-known but, strangely, often forgotten in considering the contemporary struggle over quotas, expansion of "minorities" power, and the like. The crucial point is this: for the overwhelming majority of Americans, the promise of American life became the realization of that promise. Not to understand that is to descend to the odd conclusion that Americans *should* see their lot as wretched, and that enough of them *would* so see their situation to act accordingly on election day 1972 and thereafter. But precisely because most Americans, however dissatisfied with specific aspects of their lives, perceive their lot as good, the majority opted in 1972, and will likely opt henceforth, for a basic continuation of what is—not without some changes, but without fundamental *wrenching* changes of the sort likely to cost them that which they have.

Some would say that circumstances have advantaged the majority, as if to imply: these people did not lift themselves up: "society" did it for them. But those who enjoy the blessings of American life do not believe they are fortunate because some outside force has aided them; they believe, and are correct in believing, that they themselves, and their own individual parents and grandparents, struggled against inequalities and succeeded. The Jew in America is not now the most affluent ethnic group, the most disproportionately represented in academe, the sciences, medicine, the arts, because Gentile America set high quotas and bent over backwards to help Jews. The Jew in America is where he is precisely because he advanced himself. The Irish here did not rise because the WASP said: rise, we bid you rise. The Irish rose by their own effort. The election of John Kennedy to the presidency in 1960 did not reflect a Protestant determination to advance some Irish Catholic, whoever he might have been, in that year; it reflected Kennedy's appeal to a majority, albeit a slim majority, of his fellow citizens. . . .

Warmed-Over Horatio Alger

Baldly stated, this sounds like warmed-over Horatio Alger; it is easily dismissed by cynics as Pollyannaism. Yet the phenomenon of rising from poverty, or at least from economic deprivation, to affluence, or at least to comfortable circumstances, is a reality for the vast majority of American families, from immigrant origin to the present. The white ethnics, Jewish and Gentile (largely Catholic), got little explicit help from Protestants consciously determined to help. When American Irish, Jews, Italians,

Poles and other Eastern Europeans look at their situation today, they know that they are where they are because they did it themselves. Thus, to tell them now that "quotaization" for other minorities is necessary, is to ask them to sanction for others what they never received themselves and do not think was necessary for their own groups hitherto or for others henceforth.

Who Are the Victims of Liberal Reform?

A serious error in Left-liberal thought at present is a misunderstanding of the reasons for the white ethnic rejection of the quota approach to improving American life. The Left-liberal believes that rank selfishness and base grasping are primarily to blame for the middle-Americans' rejection of what they, the Left-liberals, believe to be good. Often upper-middle class and suburban, usually well-placed occupationally and, by comparison to others, extremely well educated, the champions of "quotaization" (or busing, for that matter) do not intend to be the victims—the "offenders . . . who never would be missed." If they give it serious reflection, they realize that *their* children won't suffer. But they rarely go the next step and ponder this reality: *it is the white ethnics who will be the victims*. Those who have made it to financial solvency, to an acceptable house somewhere in a not particularly charming but nonetheless "safe" community, to a level where their children can go to college if they're bright enough and their parents save enough money, recognize that it is precisely *within* the system, and because of their own quite middle-class virtues of thrift and effort, that they have arrived at the place they now occupy. They believe that because *they* have done it, others can too.

Either those Negroes, for example, who have risen to middle-class status and to prominence in various fields of endeavor, have done so by their own efforts, or they have been pawns moved about by white benefaction. No one should seriously expect a person who knows how hard he has worked to get where he is, to turn around and accept the notion that he is merely an object buffeted about by winds—in this case, by the winds of white guilt, or white fancy. If the economic system called capitalism, and the American system of opportunity and merit advancement, has worked for John, why should John then assume that it cannot work for someone else? Not the faults in the American system (of which they are many), but the benefits of it, are those aspects upon which the large majority of Americans concentrate when considering whether or not they should approve radical changes in their way of life, radical tamperings with their traditional personal ideals and modes of behavior.

"Possessive conservatism" typifies most people who possess, except occasionally those "radic-libs," in Mr. Agnew's now abandoned phrase, who possess so much that they think they can afford to talk cavalierly about "redistributing" the wealth to those who at present do not possess it. Needless to say, the wealth to be redistributed is that of those who do *not* think they have enough to give it up, that is, of the white ethnics who are the specific objects of scorn by the white Left-liberals, and the specific objects of envy by the fashionable minorities who are manipulated by the Left-liberals to (among other actions) vote for candidates who direct their appeal to economic jealousy and race and class divisiveness.

Of course a more egalitarian America is possible, and it will come about in time. Merit advancement provides the surest, fairest route to a better America, one based on the assumptions that groups (and races) are most likely equal, or essentially equal, in ability; that individuals, not groups, are the proper focus of attention when considering opportunity and advancement; and that equality of opportunity will in due course bring roughly the same proportion of individuals from all groups to prominence in this field and that, to economic parity, to social equality. What has already occurred, and continues to occur economically among whites, whatever their ethnicity and religion, will occur eventually among all Americans, provided only that no irrelevant discriminations are permitted to suppress the legitimate aspirations of all. As for ethnic aspirations, the words of *Commentary* magazine's editor, Norman Podhoretz, apply: "Just as the black assertion set the climate for the sixties, I think you'll find a comparable Catholic, white ethnic assertion in the seventies."

Should Brain Surgeons Be Chosen by Race?

Some will excel in one field or another; at the moment, for instance, American Negroes excel all out of proportion to their numbers in the population in such sports as basketball and track, and Jews, the "people of the Book," excell at the moment in academic pursuits. Yes, Jews are over-represented on the faculties of major universities, and Negroes are over-represented on many athletic teams. If quotas are now to push Jews down to their "proper" 2.8 per cent on faculties, shall quotas likewise push Negroes down to *their* "proper" 11 per cent on the Boston Celtics? As the syndicated columnist Jenkin Lloyd Jones asked in *Human Events* magazine (May 6, 1972): "Should a man be given the right to practice brain surgery because his race is underrepresented among brain surgeons? Should bar exams be racially tilted? Should Negroes be fired from teams and replaced by second-rate white performers so that a proper racial quota

could be established?'' And Philosopher Sidney Hook asked in . . .
Freedom at Issue: "If we are going to permit colleges to advertise: 'Women
and blacks preferred,' why not 'No Jews need apply—we have too many
of them already'?''

Mr. Pottinger's Little Lists

Both questions are far from fanciful. Mr. Pottinger's little lists, and the
government's dogged determination to see those lists complied with, are
already causing college faculties to reject qualified applicants for positions
if the applicants are from the "wrong" ethnicity, race, or sex. The colleges
then hire people who may be considered by their professional peers, in the
not too distant future, to have been hired primarily because of characteristics utterly irrelevant in determining competence. The remarks of Brown
University professor Jacob Neusner, in an article in a special election
supplement to conservative Jewish quarterly, *Ideas,* speaks specifically
on Jews but relates to others as well:

> When a very able Jewish professor cannot achieve tenure, despite
> qualifications, because he is not of a racial minority, then his blighted career
> becomes the sacrifice on the altar of someone else's "idealism." When
> people are appointed to impressive professorships at the great universities on
> the strength of mediocre achievements but the "right" (for the moment)
> race, then those Jews who have worked hard and developed their abilities
> and accomplished much are made the victims of racism. And there should be
> no doubt that racism in admissions and in university appointments has
> already cost the Jews a very considerable penalty, for the Jews are poor in
> numbers but rich in talent.

"Quotaization" is not merely a temporary expediency; it is a cancer-
ous growth. To justify quotas in order to reverse discrimination is inevitably to enshrine the very concept of quotas as inherently good. The fiasco at
the 1972 Democratic Party convention, wherein a perfectly legally elected
slate of delegates from Chicago—elected by the People, by an impressive
majority of the voters of that city—was ousted by the hot-to-trot participatory democrats, is a good illustration of what happens when the notion of
quotas (in this case largely for women and colored minorities) is made into
a fetish. Those who sat on the floor at Miami representing Chicago, voting
enthusiastically for Dr. McGovern, may have thought themselves representative of the People; came election day 1972 and the results showed
otherwise. Old party loyalties weakened significantly; Jews in numbers
unknown since before the late 1920s, and white ethnic Gentiles in even
more impressive numbers, voted Republican—as did, in fact, all groups in
the United States except elite college youths (largely for ideological rea-

sons) and Negroes, for the same reasons, tinged in their case by perceived racial advantages to be gained from a McGovern presidency.

How Should White Ethnics Vote?

Should white ethnics vote conservative? Not necessarily, were the sole consideration to be the choice either of a more or less conservative Republican party championing traditional WASPish values and a more or less liberal Democratic party championing traditional heterogenous values. But such was not the perceived alternative in 1972. Instead, the Republican Party had become . . . the rallying point for the broad center—it had,

Drawings by Whitney Darrow, Jr., © 1968 *The New Yorker Magazine,* Inc.

*"This year I'm not getting involved in any complicated issues.
I'm just voting my straight ethnic prejudices."*

in kiddiespeak terminology, *co-opted* centrist moderate liberalism—and the Democratic Party at the national level under George McGovern had become the repository of drastic alterations in values and the proponent of a series of changes seen as deleterious to the center's best interests. Never mind that . . . Mr. Pottinger pushes on with his little lists, or that Mr. McGovern explicitly disavowed quotas; the perception was—and I think it was accurate—that the merit system stood a better chance of survival under Richard Nixon than under George McGovern.

Certainly there are some aspects of racialism at work here: not every white ethnic is ready to welcome Negro children into his child's school, just so long as his child is not bused to an inferior school populated at the moment largely by inner-city Negro children. Furthermore, there are certainly aspects in this phenomenon (white ethnic adherences in substantial numbers to the Republican presidential candidate in 1972) of economic elitism, even though on a lower level than that usually associated with the concept of elitism. But to infer from the facts of *some* racialism and *some* economic meanness, a general evaluation that now the People (always identified by ideologues as the folks who can be induced to vote the *right way)* have become identified as the enemy of a broad center of heartless white monsters, is to fabricate myths and distort realities.

In essence, the present shifting of voting alignments on the presidential level, and the present movement of significant numbers of previously "liberal" voters into the "conservative" ranks, are attributable to one underlying consideration: the System is seen as working well, essentially in the pattern in which it has worked hitherto; that is, the status quo is preferable to unsure "reforms." As more people come under the benevolent umbrella of a system that allows for merit advancement, "conservatism" (really liberal status quoism, for most) is on the upsurge. . . .

In any future "nation of equals," none but a fool or a martyr will mark himself down for voluntary victimization. No man, advancing his self-interest, rightly understood, wants to be on anybody's little list of offenders who never would be missed.[21]

To the *minority* who has managed to work his way up in the system, quotas, *affirmative action* programs, and legal equality mean *reverse discrimination*. Yet one might note that blacks were part of America's first seventeenth-century settlements, and native Americans were here before Columbus. If the WASP asks for time to assimilate these visual minorities, perhaps time is running out. Three-hundred and seventy-five years is a long time to work oneself into the system.

[21]From David Brudnoy, in *The Majority Minority,* ed. Drew McCord Stroud (Minneapolis: Winston, 1973), pp. 242–248.

Yet the ramifications, whether justified or not, cannot be overlooked. McGovern's disastrous defeat in 1972 well points to the general refusal on the part of an overwhelming number of Americans to support radical reform.[22] Perhaps too many Americans are happy with the way the system works to endanger their own prosperity. Whatever the solution, this socio-political question will surely revolutionize our electoral system in the future.

What then can be said for Mrs. Middle American Voter? Is she representative of "the real majority" or merely a freak accident on the political scene? As we have noted throughout this chapter, the socioeconomic issues that determine American voting behavior are indeed varied and ill-defined. They overlap in countless areas and to different degrees, creating an even more difficult climate for those who wish to predict electoral results.

Of even greater significance is the shifting impact of these issues. During the 1960s the Vietnam war and youth rebellion had a profound impact on the political climate, even, it is speculated, forcing a president of the United States to leave office. Yet the coalitions that were formed by peace groups and civil rights organizations in the 1960s are not the same coalitions at work in society today. Social movements come and go, and so do their advocates. Of greater importance is an ability to recognize these forces when they are at work, regardless of their degree of impact.

Questions of *ethnic power* (both minority and majority), women's rights, youth, the aged, and governmental integrity are all phenomena that influence politics in the 1970s. As students of the political process, we must learn to recognize these influences, while at the same time keeping enough distance to maintain proper perspective.

[22]Seymour Martin Lipset and Earl Raab, "The Election and the National Mood," *Commentary*, January 1973, pp. 43–50.

3
The Whys of Voting

The months leading up to an American presidential election are always a testy time. If times seem more threatening than usual, it is undoubtedly because the government itself is divided. Candidates abound, while inner-party struggles are rampant.

Republicans were called back into power by a public impatient with the apparent inability of the Democrats to extricate America from the pitfalls of foreign intervention. Campaigning on platforms of peace and prosperity and of law and order, they by and large accomplished their goals. But whereas war news is off the front page, inflation, a depressed agricultural market and scandal have marred Republican hopes for victory.

Not since the Grant administration has there been so much corruption in high places. Legally collected funds have been misappropriated; bribery has been discovered in the highest offices in the land. Indeed even the attorney general, a former presidential campaign manager, has been convicted of fraudulent practices.

The president claimed to know nothing of these charges, but he accepted the *responsibility* for the excesses of his subordinates. Yet, even as evidence of corruption grew, and scandal closed in from every side, he staunchly maintained his aloofness. Finally, after a surprise exit from public office, the full scope of his indiscretions has been revealed through the trials of his former associates.

But the new vice-president, an honest, if somewhat inarticulate, spokesman for middle America, has tried to restore Republican fortunes, through his "good marriage" with the other branches of government. Speaking as a supporter of progress and the American ideal, he has warned that, in order to accomplish the goal of a sound economy and progressive growth, all Americans will have to follow a "long and arduous process of self-discipline."

Your initial observations are probably in error, for the year is 1923.

That's right—1923. This is history, not current events. Every fact just referred to is out of date, even if it seems to apply. The president is Warren G. Harding, not Richard M. Nixon. The *foreign intervention* is the struggle over membership in the League of Nations, not Vietnam. The political scandal in the administration is Teapot Dome, not Watergate. The struggle among Republicans is between Progressives led by LaFollete and the conservative business interests of Coolidge, not the liberalism of Percy and Rockefeller versus the conservatism of Reagan and Goldwater. Among Democrats Alfred E. Smith and William McAdoo battle over prohibition and the influence of the KKK, rather than the struggle between the McGovern and Jackson forces.

The bribery charges stem from the illegal sale of alien land holdings, not the Milk Fund investigations. The attorney General and former campaign manager is Henry Daugherty, not John Mitchell.

Harding's sudden death, not Richard Nixon's resignation, brought into the open the breadth of scandal. The aides brought to trial are Harding's cronies, Charles Forbes, Veterans' Bureau; Thomas Milles, Alien Property Custodian; Henry Daugherty; and Albert Fall, Secretary of Interior, not Erlichman, Haldeman, Mitchell, and Dean.

The spokesman for middle-class America and the trusted vice-president who was elevated to the highest office in the land was Vermont's Calvin Collidge, not Michigan's Jerry Ford. It was Coolidge who sought to repair the damage of his forerunner by noting that, "Progress is the result of a long and arduous process of self-discipline."[1]

**To Measure
and Predict Elections**

We might jump to the conclusion that history obviously repeats itself, but historians argue that it does not, agreeing, however, that within the course of human development similar historical trends may be expected to create similar results. To predict these results has long been the desired goal of the social scientist. Through the years, as his analytical tools have improved,

[1]The idea for this introduction came from David Broder, "The Party's Over," *The Atlantic*, March 1972, pp. 33–34. (All footnotes in this chapter have been consecutively renumbered for the convenience of the reader.)

so has his ability to measure those variables affecting sociopolitical structures.

Political scientists, intent on measuring and predicting the behavior of the American electorate, have undertaken countless research projects to measure those variables that influence the voter. Some of their evidence seems to demonstrate that under normal circumstances party affiliation is likely to be an important indicator of voting behavior. Particularly in off-year elections, studies show that the party in power loses support, generally as the result of a more concerted effort of the organized opposition to bring about changes in the power structure. Because they are elections of low interest, usually with issues of low visibility, off-year elections tend, therefore, to be dominated by party influences.[2]

Personality also plays an important role in American politics. For instance, the Eisenhower election years did not represent a party realignment by the American voter, but rather widespread support for a particularly attractive candidate. Similarly, the landslide victory of Richard Nixon in 1972 represented a rejection of George McGovern, not the Democratic party. In contrast, realigning elections tend to be the results of catastrophic events, that is, depressions, wars, and the like. As a result, until the 1970s, party membership remained somewhat stable, although the number of those who claimed Republican affiliation declined slightly following World War II.

Obviously, the post-Watergate era has already had an impact on American political behavior. Though the Republican party is presently absorbing most of the electoral brunt of this political turmoil, evidence indicates that political party affiliation in general probably will be adversely affected, rather than the Republican party specifically.[3] The general upheaval of the Senate Watergate Hearings, followed by Agnew's resignation, the impeachment proceedings, and the resignation of Richard Nixon, all on national media, forebodes ill for political activity. Short-term forces undoubtedly have made any concept of a *new Republican majority* into an historical illusion. But ultimately the impact has implications for the entire system.[4]

[2]The efforts of the Nixon administration in the 1970 congressional elections demonstrates this principle. Even though the administration made a concerted effort to gain seats in both houses, the results of efforts by both parties resulted in an almost status quo situation in the Senate. This was offset by Republican loss of 12 seats in the House, an embarrassingly slight return to Republicans who had directed this full-scale effort.

[3]Address by Congressman Thomas Foley at the Manresa Conference, Port Townsend, Washington, 11–12 May 1973. Also see "Goldwater Speaks His Mind," *U.S. News & World Report,* 11 February 1974, pp. 38–42.

[4]Eight Gallup Polls compiled between September 1973 and February 1974 indicated that Republican support among the electorate has hit an all-time low of 24 percent. However, Democratic party strength has remained virtually unchanged. The significant

This is not to say that continued party affiliation will be an unimportant factor in voting behavior. In a study prepared for Edmund S. Muskie's Intergovernmental Relations Subcommittee on public attitudes, the Louis Harris survey noted that the public continues to hold a view of government that is essentially positive. Harris's findings indicated that, although Americans oppose secret political activity, feel their voice is not being heard in decision-making circles, and demand openness in government, they do not oppose political activity per se.[5]

Citizens Are Willing to Cross Party Lines

The difference in voter behavior today, compared with that of the past, seems to be the wariness of today's citizenry. In the 1970s, individuals are more willing to change political affiliation and to cross party lines in ever-increasing numbers. Yet factors related to such things as scandal do not seem to be the primary reasons for this shift. At least of equal importance is the growing affluence of the American voter, with his decreasing commitment to economic goals and his increasing concern with the quality of life.[6] The voter is therefore willing to support whichever party advocates a position similar to his own on a given issue. As party positions shift, so does the support of this group.[7]

Yet in many respects some generalizations concerning voter behavior

---

growth has been among Independent votes, now consisting of an all-time high of 34 percent. *Seattle Times,* 10 February 1974.

[5]Indeed, 66 percent indicated that, "If they wanted to see a change take place in government, they would join a political party and work to make changes." See Committee on Government Operations, *Hearing Before the Subcommittee on Intergovernmental Relations,* Bulletin no. 20402, (Washington, D.C.: U.S. Government Printing Office, 1974) pp. 6–35, especially p. 7.

[6]Address by Louis Harris to the National Conference of State Legislative Leaders, Seattle, 21 September 1973.

[7]The biggest election upset of 1974, the election of James B. Longley, stands as convincing evidence of this new force in American politics. Longley captured Maine's governorship without the support of traditional party organizations. The growth of Common Cause is another measurement of a new issue orientation among the independent-minded voter. Data collected by the Survey Research Center of the University of Michigan and the American Institute of Public Opinion, which notes that the concentration of Independent vote growth has occurred in higher socioeconomic categories in recent years, serve to provide at least a partial explanation for the increased political competence of the *new* Independent. Evaluation of these and other factors were directly related to the declaration of former Senator Eugene McCarthy's bid for the 1976 presidential sweepstakes as an Independent. Walter Dean Burnham discusses some of these implications in *Critical Elections and the Mainstream of American Politics* (New York: Norton, 1970), especially pp. 91–134.

hold true. A large percentage of voters still seem to be more consistently influenced by party than by personality or issues. The growing number of Independents do not negate this theme but rather demonstrate the fluctuation of voter support. The consistency of this behavior seems to be most disrupted when major disasters occur or when an extremely attractive candidate emerges. But even this pattern of disruption holds true only in national or statewide—congressional or senatorial elections. The charisma of the candidate in local or state legislative districts generally has less impact on the ultimate outcome than at the national level. Although the public cry for ethical politics permeates all campaign contests, local bread-and-butter issues continue to be of central concern to the electorate. In some degree this helps to explain the swing vote between major and off-year elections.

What Causes the Voter to Act?

Yet, if you ask an individual voter why he preferred one candidate to another you may hear, "Because he is good Democrat." Another will comment, "Because she is a woman and not part of that mess in Washington." Still another, "Because that's the kind of man who will do something about this inflation problem." All of these answers represent valid reactions of the American voter. Or do they? What causes a voter to decide in favor of or against a particular candidate or issue? A number of researchers have attempted to investigate just such questions. And, as Professor Angus Campbell noted, "we have [now] . . . come to an understanding of the individual voting decision and, as we extend the number of elections studies, to [ascertaining] an understanding of American elections as collective acts. . . ."[8]

Transposing [the] . . . characteristics of voters of the collective vote, we come to the following propositions regarding the elections themselves:

1. The size of the turnout in national elections depends on a combination of intrinsic political interest and the impact of short-term political forces.[9] People with a high level of intrinsic interest vote in most

[8]Angus Campbell, Phillip E. Converse, Warren E. Miller, and Donald E. Stokes, *The American Voter* (New York: Wiley, 1960), p. 573.

[9]Short-term forces refer to factors that add stimulation to the underlying political interest in a particular election. Sources of these forces include: particularly charismatic persons heading the ticket; domestic and foreign policy issues; recent political party performances; and other circumstances of the moment. See Angus Campbell, "Surge and Decline: A Study of Electoral Change," *Public Opinion Quarterly* 24 (Fall 1960): 398.

"What campaign? What election?"

Editorial cartoon by Frank Interlandi © 1972 The Los Angeles Times, reprinted with permission.

    or all national elections; people with little intrinsic interest vote only when additionally stimulated by impelling short-term forces. . . .

2. The smaller the turnout in a national election, the greater the proportion of the vote which is contributed by people of established party loyalties and the more closely the partisan division of the vote will approach the basic underlying division of standing commitments to the two parties. . . .

3. The larger the turnout, the greater the proportion of the vote which is made up of marginal voters, people who have relatively weak party identification. . . .

4. If the sum of the short-term forces is approximately balanced . . . the total vote will not vary from the . . . "normal party strength." If the sum of the short-term forces favors one candidate-party alternative over the other, it will swing the vote division toward that alternative. . . . The greater the total impact of the short-term forces, the greater will be the potential deflection from the "normal party strength."

**Cyclical Patterns
of American Politics**

If these assumptions regarding the nature of our national elections have validity they should obviously fit the facts of American electoral history. . . . Let us now consider a selection of these recurring relationships or cycles in terms of the general understanding of the nature of the vote which we have briefly outlined.

1. When we look at the two-party division of the national vote over the past seventy years, we find that the fluctuations in the two-party division of the vote in the presidential years are much greater than those in the off years. . . . The greater stability of the off-year votes over this seventy-year period must reflect some underlying differences in these two kinds of elections.

The most immediately apparent difference in the presidential and off-year elections is the greater turnout in the presidential years. In terms of our earlier language this is brought about by the presence of short-term forces in the presidential elections [and] a large number of marginal voters who do not bother to vote in the less impressive off-year elections. people are less party-identified and therefore more mobile than the regular core voters who have enough intrinsic interest in political matters to participate in all national elections. As the fortunes of politics vary from year to year, these marginal people shift their votes from one party to the other and contribute a substantial part of the large variability in the vote in the presidential years which we have noted. In the off-year elections these people do not turn out; the decision is left largely to the core regulars whose greater degree of party loyalty makes them less mobile. . . .

2. It is well-known to every politician that since the Civil War the party which wins the White House almost invariably loses seats in the House of Representatives in the following off-year election. . . .[10]

We would suggest that the familiar off-year loss . . . depends . . . on a pattern of circulation of votes which is characteristic of presidential and off-year elections. In the relatively stimulating circumstances of a presidential election the turnout is high. As we have just noted, the regular voters whose intrinsic political interest is high enough to take them to the polls even under less stimulating conditions are joined by marginal voters who are less concerned with politics but may be activated if the stakes seem high. Ordinarily one of the two candidates standing for the presidency will be benefited by the political circumstances of the moment more clearly than the others, either because of embarrassments of the party in power, the personal qualities of the candidate, domestic or international

[10]The Ford administration's efforts in 1974 to prevent a veto-proof Congress did not appreciably change this trend. The unique circumstances of Nixon's resignation and related factors merely contributed further to the severity of Republican losses.

conditions, or for other reasons. The advantaged candidate will draw to him the votes of a majority of the marginal voters, who have relatively little party attachment and are responsive to such short-term influences. He will also profit from some deflections by regular voters from the opposition party who are sufficiently tempted to break away from their usual party vote at least temporarily. In moving toward the advantaged candidate both the regular and the marginal voters, especially the latter, tend to support both the candidate and his party ticket. In the off-year election which follows, two movements occur. The regular voters who moved across party lines to support a presidential candidate they preferred are likely to move back to their usual party vote when [the presidential] . . . candidate is no longer on the ticket. The marginal voters who had given the winning candidate a majority of their votes in the presidential election do not vote in the election which follows. Both of these movements hurt the party of the candidate who benefited from the votes of the two groups in the presidential election. The loss of congressional seats is the result. . . .

Swing Elections

3. Professor V. O. Key has pointed out . . . that since the election of 1892, . . . "an unusually rapid rate of growth in the total number of voters from one election to the next is accompanied by an exceptionally high rate of increase in the number of supporters of one of the parties but not the other. . . ."[11]

What are the characteristics of these high turnout swing elections? . . . The most striking fact about the flow of the vote in the 1952 election was the universality with which the various segments of the electorate moved toward the Republican candidate. It was not a situation in which some groups became more Democratic than they had been in 1948 but were offset by other groups moving in the other direction. There was virtually no occupational, religious or other subdivision of the electorate which did not vote more strongly Republican in 1952 than it had in 1948.

A second impressive fact about the 1952 election was the relative insignificance of policy issues in the minds of the voters. There were no great questions of policy which the public saw as dividing the two parties. Instead the voters were thinking about "the mess in Washington," the stalemate in Korea, and General Eisenhower's heroic image. It would

[11]V. O. Key, Jr., *Politics, Parties and Pressure Groups,* 5th ed. (New York: T. Y. Crowell, 1958), p. 638.

appear that the flow of the vote from the Democratic majorities of the previous twenty years to the Republican victory in 1952 was a response to short-term forces which were largely unilateral.[12] They favored the Republican alternative and they were not offset by balancing forces favoring the Democrats. Having little policy content they did not set interest group against interest group, class against class, region against region.

The third important characteristic of the 1952 election was the fact that, despite the decisiveness of the Eisenhower victory, the underlying Democratic advantage in the basic party attachments of the electorate was not disturbed. We know from our national surveys that the proportions of the electorate identifying themselves as Democrats or Republicans did not change throughout the eight years of the Eisenhower administration. In 1960, when the candidacy of Mr. Eisenhower was no longer a consideration, the vote swung strongly back toward the "normal" Democratic majority, despite the severe handicap to the Democrats of a Catholic candidate at the head of their ticket. . . .

Swing Votes
Seem to Be a Reaction

[T]hese swings in the vote appear to be more a reaction to circumstances and personalities than to issues in the usual sense. Public interest in these immediate events and persons is translated into political action, with a high turnout of voters and a general movement toward the party which happens to be in a position to profit from the situation. The movement is undirectional because the circumstances which produce it are not seen as favorably by one section of the electorate and unfavorably by another. They tend rather to create a generally positive or negative attitude throughout the electorate, resulting in the almost universal type of shift which we observed in 1952. . . .

Consider 1952 as an example. This was a year which many people interpreted as a swing to the right, a conservative reaction to two decades of liberal government. In fact it was a rare person indeed among the people we interviewed in 1952 who had a program of legislation he wanted the new government to undertake. They wanted to get the crooks out of the Internal Revenue Service and the troops out of Korea and they certainly admired General Eisenhower. But far from voting for a conservative program, only a small percentage had any apparent comprehension of

---

[12]A similar example can be seen in 1964 when a massive swing to the Democratic candidate Lyndon Johnson occurred and again in 1972 when Richard Nixon carried a large number of normally Democratic voting groups.

what a conservative-liberal, or left-right dimension in politics implies. . . .[13]

If the flow of the vote in 1952 did not express a conservative mood in the electorate, how is it to be explained? It would be much more parsimonious and much more in keeping with the evidence at hand to say that it simply expressed a desire for a change in stewardship of the federal establishment. Accumulating grievances and dissatisfactions over the last years of Democratic government finally led to a vote for a new administration. The voters were not asking for any specific platform of legislation; they just wanted a new bunch of fellows to run things. . . .

We do not have [this] kind of information about earlier swings in the national vote. . . . We know there have been occasions when national crises have polarized the electorate around a major issue and brought about far-reaching realignments in party strength. Such occasions have been infrequent, however. . . . The electorate seems quite capable of expressing its intolerance of circumstances it finds exasperating and it sometimes responds strongly to the personal qualities of an attractive candidate but it . . . [usually isn't well] informed to follow a deliberate program of choice between conservative and liberal alternatives in governmental policies."[14]

Professor Campbell's observations concerning particularly realigning elections are of special interest to today's student of political behavior. By applying his principles we note that the Goldwater candidacy of 1964 did not represent a major shift from the Republican party, but rather a shift from the candidate *considered dangerous* by a large block of American voters. Likewise, the flight of Democratic party voters from the McGovern candidacy in 1972 was not a pro-Nixon or pro-Republican vote but was rather a reaction to McGovern's *seeming radicalism*.[15]

Based on Campbell's thesis, the Watergate affair and the resignation of Richard Nixon will undoubtedly bring about further shifts of at least a temporary nature but will most likely not constitute sufficient impetus for a permanent realignment in electoral patterns. Indeed, evidence indicates that the old coalition of New Deal Democrats is slowly dissolving because of socioeconomic forces and increased mobility of the electorate. Factors such as educational levels seem to be of greater impact in bringing about

[13]Campbell et al., *The American Voter,* Chapter 9.

[14]From Angus Campbell, "Voters and Elections: Past and Present," *The Journal of Politics* 26 (November 1964): 745–757. This article is particularly valuable because it represents the classic study of its kind. (All footnotes in this chapter have been consecutively renumbered for the convenience of the reader.)

[15]A discussion of the character of the Goldwater and McGovern candidacies follows; see Chapter 4.

this realignment than the activities of either the parties, their candidates, or scandals.[16]

As Fred I. Greenstein has noted, each party seeks support from different and ever-changing social and economic interest groups, that is, blue collar, businessmen, minorities, and so on. This support varies both in

[16]Address by Louis Harris, op. cit.

degree and amount depending on issues, candidates, and elections, as well as the relative voter strength and traditional turnout of each group. Parties are cognizant of the relatively lower participation of, say, youth and minorities as compared with the suburban middle class. But issues of concern even to this more participatory segment of society may not be of a broad enough nature to warrant an exclusive appeal to that particular issue. As Greenstein indicates, voters overwhelmingly support the party which they believe, at that moment, best reflects their own interest. They may change their mind between the presidential and congressional elections, but usually they will tend to support whom they feel supports them.

The growing number of Independent voters seem to represent an inability of either party to attract a certain segment of the population to their column. Although party hierarchies apparently realize the growing gap between their organization and the Independents,[17] the alienation of an increasing percentage of the population from party alignments seems to be a common phenomenon in our time. Nevertheless, while the tremendous emotional commitment to party of the New Deal days is waning, voting patterns still reflect the commitment of the electorate to the issues of individual parties, regardless of a decline in long-term commitment to the party itself. In this area alone, voter behavior demonstrates an important correlation between party and the individual voter.[18]

Each Party Seeks Support from Various Interests

As is well known, each of the major parties tends to have somewhat different clientele of supporters among the groups in society. When we look at group party-support patterns, it becomes clear that in spite of the paucity of political information and carefully considered opinions in the population, the citizen's vote *does* seem to relate his needs and interests to the actions of elected officials in a rational way.

For instance . . . we can distinguish the group bases of each party—

[17]An example of this recognition is the "affirmative action" program adopted by the Democratic party in 1974, designed to open the party ranks to ever-increasing numbers of citizens. Similar efforts among the Republicans have been debated for adoption at the next Republican convention; the appointment of Iowa's Mary Lou Smith as Republican national chairperson points to the success of this goal.

[18]To exemplify, in 1968, "86 percent of Republicans voted for Nixon and 88 percent of Democrats voted for Humphrey or Wallace." See Howard L. Reiter, "An Emerging Independent Majority," *Ripon Forum*, March 1972, p. 20. Note also that the Gallup Poll of February 1974 showed that, whereas Independent strength was at an all-time high, 66 percent of the voters were still committed to one or the other of the major parties. *Seattle Times*, 10 February 1974.

the hard-core groups that tend to support a party even in its lean years and the groups that the parties add to their coalitions in winning years.

For . . . the Republican core . . . these categories are the professional and managerial occupations, the college-educated, and the residents of those areas that are so often thought to be the quintessence of Republicanism, America's towns and smaller cities. Also "carried" by the Republicans in . . . their winning year[s] and the year[s] when they were defeated by only a small margin are a pair of population groups that are too large and amorphous to be treated as clienteles to which parties can appeal directly—Protestants and non-union members [Figure 3.1].

On the Democratic side we find three groups consistently providing a plurality of support for that party . . . unskilled workers, Negroes, and union members. . . . Further evidence of this traditional Democratic coalition—which formed during the years of Franklin D. Roosevelt's New Deal—can be found by noting the additional groups picked up by the Democrats in 1948 and carried with special one-sidedness in 1964—Catholic (in many cases representatives of the ethnic groups which emigrated from Europe between the middle of the nineteenth century and World War I), residents of metropolitan areas, and the grade-school and high-school educated.

Analysis of Group Voting

Although many Americans object to group analyses of political behavior—especially if they touch on social-class . . . [a]nalysis of group voting is one of the standard tools of the working politician. . . . [O]ne of the most difficult tasks faced by an elected official is somehow to reach down to the grassroots and gain insight into his actual or potential sources of support. To do this effectively, it is necessary to find some means of categorizing the electorate, of pinpointing groups which may be responsive—or antagonistic—to different appeals. By necessity, therefore, working politicians become students of the sociology of the electorate. . . . [however,] popular objection to class interpretations of American politics has some merit. Neither party has exclusive "control" of any of the populations groups. Each party is sufficiently heterogeneous to receive some support from all groups. And, from election to election, the winning party is capable of advancing within the groups which ordinarily provide the other party's supporters. . . .

There is a single important exception. . . . In 1964, the Survey Research Center interviewers did not encounter a single Negro Goldwater supporter. This is not to say that in the general population there were

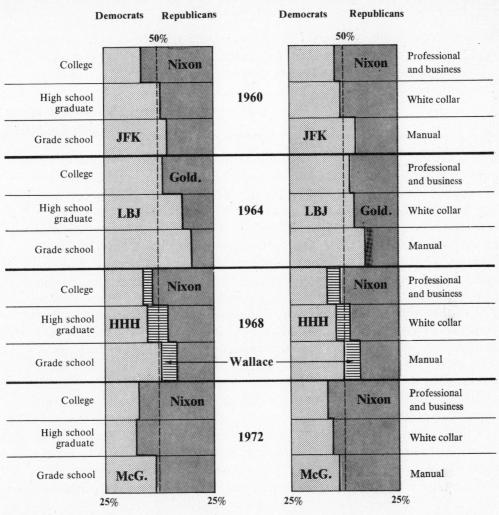

Figure 3.1. Group party-support patterns. (Reprinted by permission of the publisher, from *American Politics: Policies Power & Change,* 2d ed. (Lexington, Mass.: D. C. Heath & Co., 1974.)

absolutely no black votes for the Republicans (although a few black precincts did in fact go 100 per cent for Johnson); it simply indicates that black voters were overwhelmingly pro-Democratic in that year.

The circumstances of the one-sided Negro vote for Johnson in 1964 are instructive. Johnson had just actively presided over the passage of a major civil rights bill. Goldwater's vote against that bill had been widely publicized. In 1968 the Republican candidate also did very poorly among Negroes. . . . One of Mr. Nixon's first political ''signals'' after assuming the Presidency (on the occasion of a ceremonial visit to the Washington black ghetto) was to let it be known that he hoped to establish his, and his party's, stock among Negroes. . . . [T]he advantages of bidding for further support in this population group—strategically placed as it is in populous, closely competitive states—were obvious.[19]

Implications of Voter Sociology for Democratic Societies

Let us attempt to state the implications of voter sociology for democratic politics in a reasonably general fashion: *Under conditions of reasonably close balance between the parties, politicians who want to gain office have a substantial incentive to adopt what might be described as a "flexibly responsive" stance to the principal groups in the electorate.* They need to be sufficiently responsive to the central groups in their own clientele to hold the support of these groups and encourage them to turn out at the polls. At the same time, they have reason to be sufficiently flexible to win at least some votes from members of groups that supply the core constituents of the other party. Conditions of close party balance do not in fact obtain everywhere in the United States. . . . But in some political jurisdictions there *is* close party competition; in many others the minority party at least poses an occasional threat; and in the nation's most important jurisdiction, the presidential electorate arena, the party balance is sufficiently close to produce occasional outcomes like . . . Nixon's 1968 vote plurality of 0.68 of 1 per cent.

Such evenness of electoral balance encourage more than simple response to group demands; it encourages entrepreneurial efforts by politicians to anticipate (and shape) group desires even before they are fully crystallized. . . . [Thus] the American electorate appears to exercise con-

---

[19]That black voters had not suddenly become wholly wed to the Democrats was vividly illustrated in 1969 when Mayor John Lindsay of New York City, a Republican who had been defeated in his own party's primary (the Liberal party), was reelected with overwhelming support from black areas of the city. Lindsay was running against Democratic and Republican candidates who emphasized the kinds of "law and order" issues that in the late 1960s came to be seen by many voters as a surrogate for direct expression of racial antagonisms. The variability of voting among blacks, a group low in the resources that normally make for effective political participation, provides a striking illustration of how group voting can serve to express citizen's needs and desires. For an essay arguing that, in general, voting studies tend to underestimate voter rationality, see V. O. Key, Jr., *The Responsible Electorate* (Cambridge: Harvard University Press, 1966). Also see the comments on Key's thesis, as well as the more general findings referred to in the text above, in the SRC report on the 1968 election: Philip E. Converse et al., "Continuity and Change in American Politics: Parties and Issues in the 1968 Election," *American Political Science Review* 63 (December 1969): 1083–1105.

siderable (although scarcely perfect) control over the political actions of its leaders—even though most members of the electorate appear to be strikingly low in political activity and attentiveness. . . .

The study of group voting takes us only part of the way to an understanding of electoral behavior. For a more thorough knowledge of the voter we must move to a level of analysis closer to his actual processes of choice—from voter sociology to voter psychology. What are the voter's motivations? What criteria guide his electoral choices? . . .

Once we establish the actual mental processes influencing voters' decisions, we can begin to explain the regularities. . . .

Voter Psychology

Although only a small fraction of the increasingly elaborate findings of voter psychologists can be touched on here, we may note some of the highlights. In general, the criteria which voters use to make their choices can be summarized under three headings, *issue orientation, candidate orientation,* and *party identification.* . . .

The voter who is highly issue-orientated gathers information and weighs the policy alternatives posed in a campaign, making his choice on the basis of his agreement or disagreement with the candidate's expressed views on the crucial problems of the day. This citizen doubtless fits best into the standard civics-book conception of how voters *should* make their choices. By and large, he will be an *"ideologue."* That is, he will have a reasonably self-conscious and overarching view of the good life, usually expressed in the form of a liberal or conservative philosophy. . . .

. . . Johnson received 80 to 90 percent of the support of people who felt that the pace of civil rights advances was "about right" or "too slow," but his backing went down to 60 per cent among those who held that civil rights proponents were "pushing too fast."[20]

Findings of this sort serve to indicate that issue orientation does have an impact on voting. But at the same time, they underscore the imperfect nature of that impact: of the voters who were drawn to the kinds of views Senator Goldwater had been expressing on civil rights, more than half voted for President Johnson. There was a similar, if less substantial, vote for Johnson by people who took Goldwater's position on the other issues, as well as some Goldwater backing among those whose views matched the positions of President Johnson. . . .

[20]I am indebted to the University of Michigan Survey Research Center for providing these tabulations from its 1964 election study.

Personal Attractiveness
Is an Important Factor

Few readers will be surprised to learn that the personal attractiveness (or unattractiveness) of a candidate may have a considerable effect on the behavior of voters—an effect which is independent of the policies espoused by the candidate. In recent decades the personal appeals of Presidents Roosevelt and Eisenhower were especially potent. . . . [D]uring the two Eisenhower campaigns, "Liking Ike" seems to have resulted, to a remarkable degree, from perception of the General's personal attributes. The appeal of these qualities was especially great in a number of the population categories (e.g., high-school graduates) which ordinarily give strong support to the Democrats.[21]

In the Survey Research Center election studies, candidate orientation usually has been studied by tabulating the frequency of positive and negative references to the candidates . . . the higher a voter "scores" a candidate . . . the more likely the voter is to cast his ballot for that candidate.

It is easier to distinguish candidate orientation from issue orientation *analytically* than it is to disentangle these two classes of criteria in the "real world." To begin with, they influence each other; the voter who likes Ike will be predisposed to like what Ike likes. . . . Second, some of the very statements that are made ostensibly about the merits and faults of candidates are in fact policy statements. For example, in 1960, one rather common reason given for liking Vice-President Nixon was that "he will stop communism abroad," although those sympathetic to him were more likely to make vaguer and more personal observations about Nixon's political experience and his capacity to "handle world problems." An especially common reason given for *not* supporting Nixon's 1960 opponent, John F. Kennedy, was Kennedy's religion—a criterion which certainly illustrates the difficulty of distinguishing a candidate orientation from an issue orientation. . . .

It is part of our political mythology that Americans generally "vote for the man." . . . In 1896, for instance, the Democratic party virtually repudiated the conservative policies of its President, Grover Cleveland, and nominated William Jennings Bryan, a man who represented almost the antithesis of Cleveland. Nevertheless, a large proportion of Bryan's support came from precisely the same Democratic areas which had backed

[21]Herbert Hyman and Paul Sheatsley, "The Political Appeal of President Eisenhower," *Public Opinion Quarterly* 17 (Winter 1953–1954): 443–460.

Cleveland four years earlier.[22] Evidently, virtually any candidate named by the Democrats would have been supported by these areas.

The candidate- and issue-oriented voter to a considerable extent bases his vote on short-run factors tied to a specific election campaign. . . . Yet a remarkable proportion of voters regularly report that they make up their minds *before* the presidential nominating conventions, and many additional voters decide immediately after the conventions—that is, before the campaigns "officially" begin.[23]

On What Basis Does the Citizen Make Electoral Decisions?

On what basis are such election decisions made? For many citizens a vote is—in V. O. Key's words—a "standing decision" to support a particular political party. Party identification—the third criterion for electoral choice—is by far the strongest of the lot. If we were able to learn where a voter stood on just one of the three criteria—issues, candidates, and party—knowledge of the last would enable us to make the most accurate prediction of his vote. In any election some party identifiers—especially those whose loyalties are not strong—will vote for the opposing party, normally on the basis of issue or candidate preferences. But it is considerable more likely that a voter's choice on election day be inconsistent with either of these preferences than it is that he will bolt his party.[24]

The term "party identification" refers to what might appear to be one of the simpler and more fragile phenomena—namely, the individual's subjective attachment to the Republicans or Democrats (or, in the case of . . .

[22]Lee Benson, "Research Problems in American Historiography," in Mirra Komarovsky, ed., *Common Frontiers of the Social Sciences* (Glencoe, Ill.: Free Press, 1957), pp. 162–163.

[23]For example, in 1952, 35 percent of a sample of voters report having decided before the conventions and another 39 percent report having made up their minds at the time of the conventions. In 1960, 30 percent report deciding before the conventions and another 30 percent at the time of the conventions. In 1968, 33 percent decided before the conventions and another 22 percent at the time of the conventions. In years when the renomination of the incumbent president is in the offing, even more voters may have made their choice before the conventions—57 percent report having done so in 1956, 40 percent in 1964, and 43 percent in 1972. These findings and much further useful presentation of Survey Research Center data are to be found in William H. Flanigan and Nancy H. Zingale, *Political Behavior of the American Electorate*, 3d ed., (Boston: Allyn & Bacon, 1972), pp. 158 passim.

[24]Angus Campbell and Donald E. Stokes, "Partisan Attitudes and the Presidential Vote," in *American Voting Behavior*, ed. Eugene Burdick and Arthur J. Brodbeck (Glencoe, Ill., Free Press, 1959), pp. 356–357.

(Peters in *Dayton Daily News*. By permission.)

"That does it . . . I'm voting for Wallace."

[a small number] of the electorate, to some other political party). . . . The possession of a party identification should not be confused with a generalized belief that parties are a "good thing." While most Americans claim to prefer the present party system to various possible alternatives, by and large Americans do not think of the parties as performing the various positive functions many political scientists attribute to them. . . .[25]

[T]he 1964 Johnson–Goldwater election, bear[s] careful attention, in that [it] . . . elegantly illustrate[s] what is meant when we say party identification is the strongest determinant of voting. . . . The particular

[25]The only systematic study in this area is Jack Dennis, "Support for the Party System by the Mass Public," *American Political Science Review* 60 (September 1966): 600–615. The Dennis study is of a sample of Wisconsin citizens, and that state (because of its historical connections with Progressivism) may be somewhat more antiparty than the rest of the nation. Among Dennis's findings are that 54 percent of Winsconsinites believe that, "The parties do more to confuse the issues than to provide a clear choice on them," whereas only 20 percent reject that assertion; 53 percent agree with the statement, "Our system of government would work a lot more efficiently if we could get rid of conflicts between parties altogether," and only 34 percent disagree; 82 percent choose voting for "the man regardless of his party label"; and so forth. That the Wisconsin findings are not wholly atypical of the rest of the nation is indicated by a 1968 Gallup National Survey, which obtained virtually the identical distribution of attitudes on "voting for the man rather than his party." The national findings did, however, indicate that antipartisanship does not extend itself to positive preferences for some other kind of party system: 67 percent of the national population was "generally satisfied with the choice of parties we have now," and only 27 percent favored a new party; and the 27 percent was of such diverse backgrounds that it could not have readily been aggregated into a single third party. *Gallup Opinion Index*, October 1968.

94

aspect of issue orientation dealt with is one that was far more sharply joined in 1964 than in most election years—that of welfare statism. . . . 36 per cent of the northern Democrats agreed with Johnson's "welfare state" positions; of these, 35 per cent voted for Johnson and only 1 per cent for Goldwater. . . . [Of] the 37 percent of northern Democrats who took the Goldwater position that the government should let a person "get ahead on his own," we find that this group of Democrats also went very strongly for Johnson: 32 to 5. . . . [O]nly . . . the "anti-welfare state" southern Demo-crats—[demonstrated] any appreciable defection from a Democratic vote. Even this small group favored Johnson more than 2 to 1. . . .[26]

[Among] Republican party identifiers, we find much the same story. In every instance—whether pro, con, or neutral concerning the "welfare state," whether in the North or the South—more Republican identifiers favored Goldwater than Johnson, even in the very heavily Democratic year of 1964. Sympathy with Johnson's views does lead to a high rate of defection. Among the handful of "pro-welfare state" northern Republi-cans . . . there is an almost even (8-to-7) split, and this is in striking contrast to the other Republican extreme—the "anti-welfare state" Southerners, who were overwhelmingly for Goldwater. But what [is demon-strated] with special sharpness is the very strong tendency of voters to follow their party preferences. Given the number of party identifiers in the population, and the tendency of most of them to vote regularly for their party's nominee, it is not surprising that almost half of the voting public reports always having voted for the same party's candidates in presidential elections.[27]

In the United States an individual's identification is usually an evolu-tionary outcome of the largely inadvertent and unintended political learn-

[26]But this does clearly indicate what sociologists sometimes call a "structured effect." It has greater consequences for one's behavior to be a conservative Democrat in the South then elsewhere in the nation.

[27]In a 1966 Survey Research Center poll, voters were asked, "Have you always voted for the same party or have you voted for different parties for president?" Of those respondents who had ever voted in a presidential election, 46 percent reported that they had always voted for the same party; 5 percent said they had "mostly" voted for the same party; and 49 percent had voted for different parties. (Data supplied by the Survey Research Center.) Because Americans do not consider party voting a positive virtue (see Footnote 25), these statements probably underestimate the amount of straight-party voting. A number of years earlier, preceding the exceptionally large number of Republican defections in the 1964 election, 50 percent of a national sample reported always having voted for the same party's candidates. The contribution of party identifiers to this statistic was suggested by the fact that only 5 percent of the self-styled Independents reported such consistency. Angus Campbell et al., *The Voter Decides* (New York: Harper & Row, 1954), p. 18.

ing that is absorbed from family, peer group, neighborhood, schools, and mass media, remarkably early in childhood. By the age of ten (fifth grade), more than one-half of all American children consider themselves little Republicans or Democrats. . . .

Children as Party Identifiers

Children do not invariably acquire the party preference held by their parents: a major national survey of high-school seniors and their parents reveals much more inter-generational political difference than would be suspected from the widespread reports by adults that they identify with the same party their parents supported. Nevertheless, among parents who are party identifiers there is a better than fifty–fifty chance that the child will hold the same party identification by the age of 17, at which time the incidence of party identification is still about 10 per cent lower than it is in the adult population. Of those children who do not share their parents' party loyalty, the greatest number have not formed party identifications. The relatively few children who actually "oppose" their parents in partisanship tend to balance each other out (4 per cent of the adolescent

population appear to be Republican defectors from Democratic parents and 4 per cent to be Democrats from Republican backgrounds): by and large these are not principled departures or the consequences of adolescent rebellion, but rather the result of drift and what the report on this inquiry calls "lack of cue-giving and object saliency on the part of parents.". . .[28]

For the young child, party identification is so barren of supporting information that he may be able to say "I am a Republican" or "I am a Democrat" without even knowing the party of the incumbent President. One study found that it is not until seventh grade that even a few children differentiate between the parties in terms of what they stand for.[29] Some adults–but only a very few—manage to stay in this state of blissful ignorance. . . . [T]he Democratic and Republican voting groups tend to see the appropriate party as "best" for their group.

When asked directly what they like about each party, most voters show an awareness—with varying degrees of sophistication—of the kinds of party differences . . . associating the Democrats with high levels of government spending and support of welfare policies, the Republicans with budget-cutting and lack of governmental regulation. . . .

Group Associations

[Others] differentiate the parties on a group basis—linking the Democrats to "poor people" or "common folk" and the Republicans to business. Still . . . [others] are more fragmentary in their descriptions . . . that is, they assert that the party tends to bring "good times" or "bad times" when it is in office. (The Democrats are seen as the party of prosperity by many voters—but also as the party of war. One of the greatest Republican assets, on the other hand, is the widespread belief that the GOP is the peace party.) Finally, even among the . . . electorate that does not advance explanations of how the parties differ from each other, party preferences sometimes are consistent with the typical preference of members of the voter's socio-economic group, simply because that group (via the family, peer-group, and neighborhood) provides the setting in which the preference is acquired.[30]

[28]That is, the parties are not important to the parents, and therefore the children are not exposed to enough partisan communication to learn what the parents' preferences are. M. Kent Jennings and Richard G. Niemi, "The Transmission of Political Values from Parent to Child," *American Political Science Review* 62 (March 1968): 169–184.

[29]Fred I. Greenstein, *Children and Politics* (New Haven: Yale University Press, 1965), p. 68.

[30]Campbell et al., *The American Voter*, pp. 216–265; and various issues of *Gallup Opinion Index*.

Party identifications seem to have such an impact on voting because they are, as it were, first on the scene. They typically form early in childhood and therefore can influence later learning about issues and candidates. Moreover, even among adults party identifications are temporarily prior to issue and candidate orientations in that as new issues and candidates arise over the years they are perceived and judged by voters who already are possessed of party identifications.

Voters may describe their election choices in terms of their views of the issues and candidates and in doing so they may accurately portray their impressions of what has motivated them; they are likely to fail to appreciate what often lies *behind* their issue and candidate preferences—party identifications and the group experiences which foster and reinforce partisanship. . . .

Party Seems to Be
the Most Important Criterion

Just as voting on the basis of issue orientation seems to many Americans to be closest to the ideal of citizen participation, so party voting seems to be furthest from that ideal. . . .

[P]ublic evaluations of government and politics . . . tend to be confined to "broad considerations." . . . [O]ne of the most important of these considerations is party. . . .

For the voter, party labels simplify the task of political choice to a remarkable degree. They enable him to respond to the infinitely complex events of the contemporary political world in terms of a few simple criteria. Without such criteria, detailed research on the issues of the day would be necessary to make any sort of meaningful electoral choice. Perhaps even more important than the usefulness of party labels as devices to simplify issue questions is their usefulness for sorting out candidates and public officials. Given the complexity of American government, with its divisions between executive and legislature and between the federal, state, and local levels, there is immense value to an instrument which enables the voter, in one burst of exertion, to evaluate all the public officials he must select. Without party labels choice becomes almost impossible, especially at the state and local levels, where dozens of public officials—down to the tax collector and the county sheriff—may be on the ballot.

Although party labels, and voting on the basis of party identifications, are great political simplifiers, they are not complete blinders. Where powerful issues and striking candidates have not emerged to become the focus of public attention, most of the electorate votes on a party basis. Under such circumstances, elections will be decided by the underlying distribution of party identifications in the population. By taking account of the . . . Democratic plurality among party identifiers—but also of the lower turnout rate of Democrats (due to the lower educational and occupational levels of their core supporters)— . . . there is a "natural" Democratic majority . . . in any election which involves a ratification of party preferences.

Party identifications do not wholly dominate voting, however. The actual vote fluctuates greatly around the "normal" expectation of 53 per cent Democratic. . . . [T]he nation's electoral decision is also dependent on the voters' evaluations of current issues and candidates. Furthermore, the various elements in the equation of voting behavior—party identification, differential group turnout, response to current issues and candidates—are such as to make any single national election a matter of considerable uncertainty. This prevents the politicians from becoming complacent and stimulates the more politically interested and active members of the electorate to pay attention to the spectacle and drama of the campaign. . . .

Politicians in both parties are led to advance policies consistent with group interests by the need to maintain the backing of their core groups. This contributes to differentiation in the policies supported by leaders of both parties. At the same time, since each of the parties also needs—and seeks—support from the more or less uncommitted groups (such as white-collar workers and farmers) *and* from groups in the other party's coalition, party differences are not likely to be so sharp that changes in party control of government lead to radical reversals of governmental policy. . . . The cross-cutting nature of party appeals also tends to keep political cleavage from reaching the point at which some elements of the public or leadership consider revolutions and *coups* preferable to elections because they do not care to risk the possibility that intolerable policies will be put into effect by their opponents.[31]

Angus Campbell, drawing on the survey research of an earlier study[*] and an extension of V. O. Key's theory of critical elections,[**] classifies all presidential elections into three types: maintaining, deviating and realigning.[†]

[31]From: Fred I. Greenstein, *The American Party System and the American People* (Englewood Cliffs, N.J.: Prentice-Hall, 1970), pp. 33–42.

[*]Angus Campbell et al., *The American Voter* (New York: Wiley, 1960).

[**]V. O. Key, Jr., "A Theory of Critical Elections," *Journal of Politics* 17 (February, 1955): 3–18.

[†]Angus Campbell, "A Classification of Presidential Elections," in Angus Campbell et al., *Elections and the Political Order* (New York: Wiley, 1966).

1. A maintaining election occurs when the normal vote reaffirms the long-term attachment of the electorate to the majority party.

2. A deviating election takes place when short-term forces become significant enough to shift the voter temporarily from his normal voting pattern. Usually these elections are associated with temporary circumstances: the presence of a popular "hero" candidate and the absence of great ideological issues. However, the flow of votes is toward the personality of the candidate, not toward the minority party, for example, the Eisenhower elections of the 1950s, which resulted in widespread ticket splitting by Democratic identifiers and Independents.‡

3. A realigning election is more than a temporary departure from the partisan voting pattern of past elections. Rather, in this type of election the feelings of the voters are sufficiently intense to create a series of new coalitions resulting in the realignment of the normal vote. This infrequent shift of party loyalties has historically been associated with great national crises, whose result has created contrasting party programs. It is also interesting to note that the presidential candidates elected in realigning elections were not swept into office because of great personal popularity, as in deviating elections.

In general then, "the criteria which voters use to make their choices can be summarized under three headings: issue orientation, candidate orientation, and party identification." Although Greenstein indicates that all three are of great importance, he generally concludes, as does Campbell, that party is the "most important of these considerations." Unlike Campbell, however, he carries his point somewhat further. Party denotes voter preference, but only as long as the party represents the "primary" interest of the individual voter. The voter uses party, as James Bryce denoted, to simplify the difficult choices between a variety of candidates and issues. Evidence seems to indicate that this is probably correct. Walter DeVries and Lance Torrance, Jr., in their study, *The Ticket Splitter: A New Force in American Politics,* indicated that a considerable block of voters split their vote in a large number of elections.[32] On the national level the issues are more discernable and more easily understood, at least in a broad context. But when the voter turns to the maze of candidates and issues, his need for a simplification of choice leads him to vote a party preference.

‡In 1956, 75 percent of the Democrats and Independents who voted for Eisenhower did not support other Republican candidates.

[32]Walter DeVries and Lance Tarrance, Jr., *The Ticket Splitter: A New Force in American Politics* (Grand Rapids, Mich.: Erdman, 1972), pp. 22, 51.

Even though bread-and-butter issues may influence his vote, and the voter in the more rural community may be more familiar with candidate personalities and issues, the average voter still uses party identification as a criteria to simplify the electoral process.

Handle on Issues

Greenstein has demonstrated that this handle on the issues and candidates has often been measured at the polls by requesting self-identified Independents to indicate the party toward which they are leaning. This leaning represents, in Greenstein's view, the general willingness of all voters to support whichever party or candidate reflects their interest at a particular moment. As the needs of the voter change and as his image of the party is modified, he may split his vote, or change affiliation, although a change in party affiliation is rare (Figure 3.2).

To Greenstein, as to Campbell, most voters therefore tend to rely heavily on party labels either as "simplifiers" or because of a commitment, on either a long- or short-term basis, to one or other of the party philosophies. These "philosophies" may be the image as interpreted by the voter and/or espoused by the party candidates.

Rise of the Independent

However, the significance of the increasing number of Independent voters seems to be somewhat negated by both of these authors. Indeed the Independent, who in the finest tradition of political folklore casts his ballot for the "best qualified candidate, not the party," was apparently laid to rest a decade ago by Angus Campbell himself in the magnum opus of electoral behavior, *The American Voter*. This classic study portrayed the self-styled Independent as:

Far from being more attentive, interested, and informed, Independents tend as a group to be somewhat less involved in politics. They have somewhat poorer knowledge of the issues, their image of candidates is fainter, their interest in the campaign is less, their concern over the outcome is relatively slight, and their choice between competing candidates, although it is indeed made later in the campaign, seems much less to spring from discoverable evaluations of the elements of national politics.[33]

[33]Angus Campbell et al., *The American Voter: An Abridgement* (New York: Wiley, 1964), p. 83.

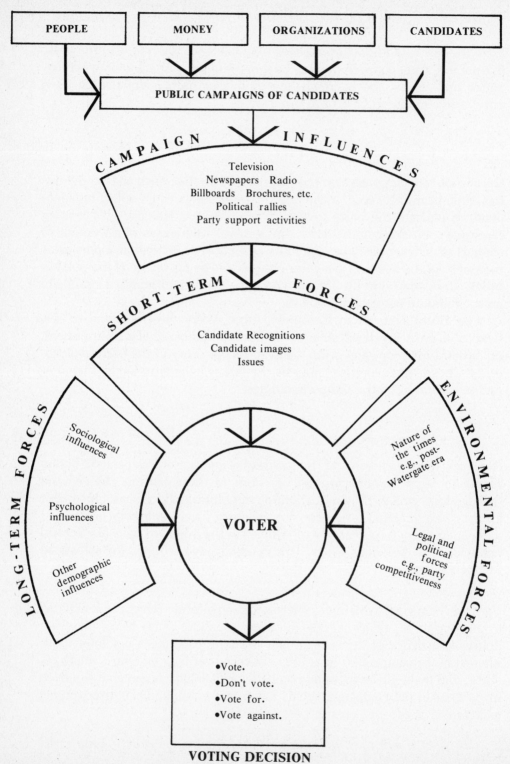

Figure 3.2. Influences on voting.

Although Campbell's conclusion has been accepted in a somewhat unquestioning manner by many sophisticated political analysts, it has not gone unchallenged. Prior to what some observers interpret as the new image of the electorate established by DeVries and Tarrance in 1972,[34] several respected scholars disputed this less than complimentary picture of the Independent.[35] V. O. Key, Jr., offered his analytical objections in what he called a "little book" that gave the "perverse and unorthodox argument . . . that voters are not fools."[36]

Whatever the arguments of political scholars, polls measuring the opinions of *self-admitted* Independents are increasing at an unprecedented rate. This trend, which began building momentum in the mid 1960s, has projected the Independent vote from 22 percent in 1964 to a high of nearly 34 percent of the national electorate. Thus Independents outdistance self-identified Republicans by nearly 10 percent and fall short of matching self-identified Democrats by only 8 percent.[37]

Who are these Independents? How do they differ from those members of the electorate who identify with the Democratic or the Republican party? Are they really some manner of political eunuch who is easily duped by the emotional pitch of a thirty-second political advertisement placed between reruns of "Star Trek" and the late movie?

Who Are the Independents?

If by the term Independent we rely not on actual voting behavior but upon the electorates' self-perception[38] of nonalignment with either of the two major political parties, there is mounting evidence that:

. . . there are at least *two* sets of independents: "old independents" who correspond to the rather bleak classical survey-research picture, and "new independents" who may have declined to identify with either major party . . . because the structure of electoral politics at the present time turns upon

[34]DeVries and Tarrance, op. cit.

[35]H. Dandt, *Floating Voters and the Floating Vote: A Critical Analyses of American and English Election Studies* (Leiden, Holland: Stenfert, Knoese NV, 1961); Allan S. Meyer, "The Independent Voter," in William N. McPhee and William A. Glaser, *Public Opinion and Congressional Elections* (New York: Free Press of Glencoe, 1962), pp. 65–77; V. O. Key, with the assistance of Milton C. Cummings, Jr., *The Responsible Electorate: Rationality in Presidential Voting, 1936–1960* (Cambridge, Mass.: Belknap, 1966); David E. RePass, "Issue Salience and Party Choice," *American Political Science Review* 65 (June 1971): 389–400.

[36]Key, *The Responsible Electorate*, p. 7.

[37]The Gallup Poll, *Seattle Times,* 10 February 1974.

[38]Self-perception, as used here, is in reference to an individual response to the survey question, "Do you consider yourself to be a Republican, Democrat, or Independent?"

parties, issues, and symbolisms which do not have much meaning in terms of their political values or cognitions.[39]

It is true that the Old Independents postponed their electoral decisions until very late in the campaign and may have voted a split ticket with greater frequency than the party identifiers, but this does not mean that they used this time for a careful evaluation of issues and candidates. Rather, the Old Independents tend to be less concerned about specific elections, less informed and less active than the remainder of the electorate,[40] including the New Independents. Despite the lack of clarity in available data, there is reasonable evidence that the Old Independents are drawn more heavily from lower socioeconomic groups and have achieved a lesser level of formal education than either Republican identifiers or the New Independents. On the other hand, demographically the New Independents are concentrated in population categories of "better-than-average education . . . [who make] a better-than-average income in a better-than-average occupation. . . ."[41] Although in percentage terms the young adult typically predominated this new breed of Independent, recent opinion polls indicate that the trend is also occurring in the over-30 age category.

The present and future significance of the Independent vote is open to various interpretations. The most radical view is that the major political parties are in the process of losing their traditional hold on the American voter. This school of thought suggests that today's young adult possesses more affluency, more education, and more exposure to political information than previous generations. As a result, the tendency is to be more politically conscious. The long-run implications of this scenario is that the New Independent population will progressively enlarge. The argument is made that as persons who presently occupy this category mature, they will remain unaffiliated with major parties, while the younger voters will constantly swell their ranks. Were this sequence of partisan erosion to take place, there would be a "mass basis for Independent political movements [with] . . . long-staying power."[42]

Other observers, however, tend to discount any profound impact by this group. Because the mainstay of the New Independent is the voter who traditionally votes in lesser numbers than party identifiers of either party, it is believed that the impact has been greatly exaggerated. The argument is

[39]Walter D. Burnham, *Critical Elections and the Mainsprings of American Politics* (New York: Norton, 1970), p. 127.

[40]Frank J. Sorauf, *Party Politics in America,* 2d ed. (Boston: Little, Brown, 1972), pp. 173–174.

[41]Burnham, op. cit., p. 130.

[42]Ibid., p. 131.

(Justus in *Minneapolis Star.* By permission.)

also made that with maturity large numbers of Independents are traditionally assimilated into the major parties. Thus the greatest long-term impact of the New Independents may be that, in years hence, they will provide new vitality to the Democratic and Republican parties. This suggestion recognizes recent data that demonstrate that Independents rank between Republican and Democratic partisans on matters of issue awareness: "with Democrats—weak and strong identifiers alike—looking like indifferent citizens by comparison."[43]

The Ticket Splitter

The other major objection to the current description and interpretation of the Independent voter was succinctly expressed by Professors DeVries and

---

[43]RePass, op. cit., p. 398.

Tarrance when they noted that the current definition of Independents "is not anchored to actual voting behavior."[44] These and other analysts argue in favor of redefining the Independent voter in terms of actual voting behavior, rather than limiting this classification to those who by their own perceptions are nonaligned to either of the major parties. Thus any voter who did not vote a straight party ticket would be considered an Independent.

Pointing to the increase in split-ticket voting in both national and statewide elections, as well as the contradiction between self-identified

[44]DeVries and Tarrance, op. cit., p. 49.

106

Independents and their actual voting behavior,[45] these analysts argued that such a redefinition would be a more realistic measure for explaining voter behavior. Not only are there more *real* Independents (that is, ticket-splitters) than self-identified Independents, but the profile of the real Independent is considerably different. As demonstrated in Table 3.1, the demographic differences are significant.

Thus, whereas Campbell saw the party as an all-important determinant in voting behavior, generally discounting the Independent as a somewhat uninformed, uneducated, uninterested individual; and Greenstein saw the Independent more in the light of an individual voting his own self-interest but generally associated with one or the other of the major parties, a view of the *real* Independent is somewhat different,

Table 3.1   Demographic Profile of Independent Voters

Self-Identified Independent	*Ticket Splitter*
50–59 years of age	30–49 years of age
Female	Male
Protestant	Catholic
Union/skilled workers	Manager/owners
Low income ($3,000–$5,000)	Middle Income ($7,500–$15,000)

Walter De Vries and Lance Tarrance, Jr, *The Ticket-Splitter: A New Force in American Politics*. Grand Rapids, Mich: William B. Erdman Publishing Co., 1972, p. 67.

Apparently Independents are not much interested in politics and government and certainly not much concerned with partisan politics—they are not emotionally involved in party clashes. On the other hand, Independents appear to have the information and the perspective on political affairs necessary for an evaluation of issues and candidates, [at least] as competent as could be expected of partisans. Independents are no wiser or more virtuous than partisans; nor are they less so. It is not clear whether their lack of involvement means that Independents are not easily aroused by political problems demanding their attention or whether their lack of involvement simply means that Independents are less biased by partisan predispositions. This uncertainty is troublesome because Independents may not be sufficiently motivated to play the role of intelligently mediating disputes

[45]The inaccuracy of self-perception of partisanship is illustrated in a 1968 post-election study conducted by the Gallup Poll. Forty-five percent of the self-identified Republicans voted a split ticket. Forty-seven percent of the self-identified Democrats voted a split ticket. DeVries and Tarrance, op. cit., p. 51.

between Democrats and Republicans. On the other hand, the self-perception of playing this mediating role may motivate Independents effectively.[46]

In summation, we have noted that party membership, regardless of the
campaign, is one of the more consistent tools in measuring the potential
success of any candidate. Yet the party label itself may not mean much to
the individual office seeker. Indeed the Liberal–Conservative and regional
splits in party membership are often broader than the differences between
the parties themselves. The increasing Independent vote may serve in the
1970s as a mediating force between the two major parties, but there is no
evidence to indicate a move away from the political mainstream by this
group. Indeed Independents as with partisans, tend to use party labels as a
handle in making their political decisions.[47]

Charisma—An Important Ingredient

Research also demonstrates that at least on the national level the *charisma* of the candidate may be an all-important ingredient to success, even
among the strongest partisan voters. John F. Kennedy's television presence
was a critical factor in his victory over Richard Nixon in 1960; at the same
time Eisenhower's father-of-his-country image certainly played a role in his
lopsided victories in 1952 and 1956. George McGovern's image as a
confused liberal was played upon by the Nixon team in 1972, emphasizing
Nixon's statesman image.

This is not to say that issues, real or imagined, are not important. A
widely publicized belief that Goldwater was an irresponsible advocate of
nuclear war caused a major shift in the normal voting patterns of Americans in the 1964 election. Johnson's use of commercials, depicting a quiet
field with a child playing, followed by a nuclear explosion, did not fail to
increase this fear among the electorate.[48] And, as we are all aware, the
Watergate affair, Nixon's resignation and the issue of political ethics were
matters of central concern in the 1974 congressional election.

However, there is a trend, particularly since the late 1960s, to split the

[46]Flanigan, op. cit., pp. 47–48.

[47]Campbell et al., *The American Voter*, op. cit., pp. 121–126; John P. Robinson et al.,
Measures of Political Attitudes (Ann Arbor, Mich.: Survey Research Center, 1968), p. 496.
Also see Gallup Poll for 10 February 1974, which demonstrated that 66 percent of the
American electorate supported one or the other of the major parties.

[48]For a complete discussion of the technique in 1964, see Philip E. Converse et al.,
''Electoral Myth and Reality: The 1964 Election,'' *America Political Science Review* 59
(June 1965): 321–336. For a discussion of the use of the Johnson commercials see Pete
Hamill, ''When the Client Is a Candidate,'' *New York Times Magazine*, 25 October 1964.

once-solid party vote. This ticket splitting is an increasing phenomenon in American politics, and as DeVries and Tarrance indicated, perhaps a more accurate description of nonparty voting than the more vague term Independent. Evidence indicates that the New Independent is a force with which to be reckoned.[49]

It is interesting to speculate on whether since 1968 this newly affluent Independent is being drawn more from Democratic than from Republican parties. For although the trend has seen an increase in New Independents, their demographic description is quite similar to that of the traditional Republican partisan. One might speculate that the generally younger nature of the New Independent is what primarily separates him from his Republican counterpart. If this is the case, we might see a continuing trend toward a new Republican philosophical majority, even though the Republican party may not benefit because of the Watergate fiasco and its aftermath. But the continuing trend of the populus to become more affluent and more educated may lead in time to a major realignment, particularly when one notes the continuing decline of the Democratic New Deal Coalition.[50] If this occurs, we may see not only a reshuffling of the population groups that support the major political parties but also a new version of the Democratic and Republican parties. That is to say, the major parties may be revamped to advocate stances that are considerably different from their recent history.

Apparently, then, a combination of influences have an impact on today's voting behavior. The American electorate, while exercising the "psychological identification"[51] with party, has become more willing to accept personality, short-range objectives, and issues as the basis of their electoral decisions.[52] With the addition of new campaign techniques and an ever-increasing dependence on media, this trend is slowly revolutionizing politics in America.[53]

[49]The presence of the Independent vote in 1972 was certainly of importance in the primaries. See "McGovern and McCloskey Competing for Independent Vote in New Hampshire," *New York Times*, 6 February 1972. See also Gallup Poll of February 1974 that demonstrated the growing strength of the Independent voter, *Seattle Times*, 10 February 1974.

[50]Address by Louis Harris, "What's Happening in America and Why," National Conference of State Legislative Leaders, Seattle, 21 September 1973.

[51]Campbell et al., *The American Voter*, op. cit., p. 121.

[52]Particularly, as the energy crisis and inflation–recession condition continue to dominate the news, groups concerned with environmental and economic issues, pro and con, will exercise increasing influence on candidates and elections. Electoral reform is already an issue and will continue to attract much interest as a result of the Watergate hearings, trials, and pardons.

[53]For an interesting discussion of issues and organizations versus the charisma of the candidate, see Jonathan Cottin, "McGovern Shapes Campaign Structure, Starts Rebuilding Party Coalition," *National Journal*, 7 October 1972, pp. 1567–1576.

"4
Party Politics: Who Runs The Show?

The Convention . . . in San Francisco was a pivot in history; like San Francisco itself, it meshed the oldest and the newest—the most complete electronic and technological political controls with the oldest of American ideas. The sound of its dominant voice bore the wisdom of the grandfathers, rising from the history of an older America; the method of its masters was entirely new and tomorrow. . . . But it is certain that few, if any, of the 1,308 delegates and 5,400 reporters from all over the world who gathered in San Francisco from July 13th to July 16th ever correctly sensed what we were living through as we lived through it. . . .

Here was the press and communications headquarters where thousands of newspapermen and electronic journalists churned constantly for two weeks, waiting for the news conferences at which the champions of various candidates would volley back and forth at one another; where the central press room stacked its mounds of releases, statements, resolutions, calendars; where the mill of gossip, rumor, whisper and occasionally fact ground twenty-four hours a day.

The press and electronic media had come prepared to report Armageddon. Trained in the analysis of political struggle, cocked for a battle of giants, prepared to report the great forces here locking once again as they had locked so many times before in mortal combat, we could not do otherwise than report what was happening as combat, and anticipate the supreme moment. "There is something about a national convention," wrote H. L. Mencken, "that makes it as fascinating as a revival or a hanging. . . . One sits through long sessions wishing heartily that all the delegates and alternates were dead and in hell—and then suddenly there comes a show so gaudy and hilarious, so melodramatic and obscene, so unimaginably exhilarating and preposterous that one lives a gorgeous year in an hour."

In stalking the gorgeous hour, one first climbed three blocks from the Hilton Hotel to the gracious old St. Francis facing out on Union Square. . . .

Outside the St. Francis all of the mammoth apparatus of television had been assembled to show, visually, the opening of war. Giant white cranes had been wheeled in from Los Angeles; technicians by the score manned the roof-high mobile cameras on the crane platforms and guarded the ropes, entanglements and cables that fed the eyes of the networks which waited to show the nation the struggle over its future. . . . Outside, on one of the days when I counted, the score read: 130-odd TV technicians waiting for dramatic personae to appear and perform; 24 pickets for the Congress of Racial Equality; 8 chubby teenagers . . . urging: RINGO FOR PRESIDENT; 3 dour pickets parading with white-lettered red placards bearing messages that praised God and damned . . . [the] Chief Justice of the Supreme Court. . . .

The Cow Palace of San Francisco, built by the early New Deal . . . sits on sixty-seven acres, a spacious but not overpowering arena, good in acoustics, an auditorium with complete visibility, generous of access and entry, perfect for conventions in all respects except for the clogged roads and highways that lead from downtown San Francisco to its site six miles away.

And here, in the plaza before the great Cow Palace, all the neat, well-barbered men and prosperous women [delegates] . . . could see the face of the enemy—as if stage-managed to rouse their anger.

First the demonstrating civil-rightsers—girls with dank blond hair, parading in dirty blue jeans; college boys in sweat shirts . . . ; shaggy and unkept intellectuals; bearded Negro men and chanting Negro women. They paraded in an endless circle, shouting, singing, sometimes clapping their hands to the rhythm "Aunt Jemima—*clap clap*—must go!" . . . "Jim Crow—*clap clap*—must go!" "Uncle Tom—*clap clap*—must go!" . . .

Simultaneously, on another patch of the fore plaza paraded the peaceniks. WOMEN FOR PEACE read their placards, and NO MORE WAR; PEOPLE WHO LIVE IN GLASS HOUSES SHOULD OPPOSE MLF; NATO MEANS NUCLEAR REARMAMENT; GERMANY HAS FORTY PERCENT CONTROL OF NATO; KEEP EIGHT NATO FINGERS OFF THE NUCLEAR BUTTON. . . .

**The Well-Dressed
Delegates Advanced**

Through all these demonstrations the well-dressed and well-mannered. . .
delegates made their way. . . .

But on Tuesday they began to roar. It was . . . [the General] who
stirred them first. The General's speechwriters had written a conciliatory,
statesmanlike address. . . . But with a personal desire to express more
human yearnings, the General had inserted a few touches of his own: "Let
us," he said as he wore to the end of his remarks, "particularly scorn the
divisive efforts of those outside our family, including sensation-seeking
columnists and commentators, because, my friends, I assure you that
these are people who couldn't care less about the good of our party"—at
which point the Convention exploded in applause, shouts, boos, catcalls,
horns, klaxons and glory. Here at last was someone cutting a bit of raw
flesh from the hitherto unnamed enemies, and the delegates could vent
emotion. . . . But . . . [the General] was not through. He had another
penciled addition to his discourse: " . . . let us not be guilty of maudlin
sympathy for the criminal who, roaming the streets with switchblade knife
and illegal firearms seeking a helpless prey, suddenly becomes upon
apprehension a poor, underprivileged person who counts upon the com-
passion of our society and the laxness of weaknesses of too many courts to
forgive his offense." A second time a nerve was twinged: an ex-President
of the United States was lifting to national discourse a matter of intimate
concern to the delegates, creating there before them an issue which
touched all fears, North and South. The Convention howled. . . .

Politics needs demonstrations. Demonstrations vent emotions. They
satisfy the citizens' desire to participate, to have a share in their own fate,
to feel themselves part of something larger and greater than themselves. . . . Senator Everett Dirksen of Illinois nominated Barry Morris
Goldwater, "the peddler's grandson," for President of the United States.
Down from the rafters cascaded flakes of inch-square gold foil; up from the
pit boomed the bass drum that beat in rhythm to "We Want Barry"; from
behind the rostrum a band blared "When the Saints Come Marching In."
Onto the floor poured the demonstrators: the Californians in golden bibs,
the Nevadans in red silk shirts, Texans carrying longhorn insignia. Gold
balloons rose from the floor. Delegates in white hats with black ribbons,
blue ribbons, gold ribbons—to distinguish themselves by states—
squeezed into parade. The cowbells and police whistles and squeeze-horns
joined the bass drum. Signs were brandished: BETTER BRINKSMAN-
SHIP THAN CHICKENSHIP; PEGGY INDIANA'S FAVORITE
DAUGHTER; OSCEOLA, ARKANSAS, TIRED OF PUMP-WATER

WANTS GOLDWATER; LAND OF LINCOLN GOES GOLDWATER. And the old favorites: WE WANT BARRY; A CHOICE NOT AN ECHO; $AU + H_2O = 1964$. And the favorite blue-and-gold portrait of Goldwater himself, jut-jawed in profile, bravery and integrity facing the world; and the state banners, state flags and spoils of victory wrenched from the Easterners. (One burly Californian, in his golden bib, had broken off the staff which bore the legend MASSACHUSETTS, having wrested it from the devoutly anti-Goldwater Bay-Staters. He had lashed it to a new stave with his own belt, and as he jiggled in the serpentine on the floor his pants kept slipping down, so that he half danced and half wiggled, holding his combat trophy up with one hand and his falling pants with the other.) . . .

"Ba-a-a-a-arry, Ba-a-a-a-a-arry." The noise grew, the sound roared, the balloons popped now as they bubbled and bounced off the rostrum to delegates who cigarette-touched them to clear them away. The gavel banged and banged and banged, and slowly the crowds subsided to listen to the hoarse-voiced man. . . .

He cleared his throat . . . then swung into his text, and it was he and the Good Lord alone, co-pilots in a rescue mission to save America at the edge of Gehenna: "The Good Lord raised this mighty Republic . . . not to stagnate in the swamplands of collectivism, not to cringe before the bully of Communism."

Gradually the dry voice picked up the force of an incantation:

"Our people have followed false prophets. . . ."

And the speaker was leading his audience way out there into a new world, a crusader's world unexpressed in American politics for generations—the visionary Prophet and the martial Patriot alternating, first the Prophet, then the Patriot, over and over again:

"This Party, with its every action, every word, every breath and every heartbeat, has but a single resolve and that is:

"Freedom!

"Freedom—made orderly for this nation by our Constitutional government.

"Freedom—under a government limited by the laws of nature and of nature's God.

"Freedom—*balanced* so that order, lacking liberty, will not become the slavery of the prison cell; *balanced* so that liberty, lacking order, will not become the license of the mob and of the jungle."

Then the Patriot reviewed the failures of the incumbent administration:

" . . . failure cements the wall of shame in Berlin; failures blot the sands of shame at the Bay of Pigs; failures marked the slow death of freedom in Laos; failures infest the jungles of Vietnam; and failures haunt the houses of our once great alliances and undermine the greatest bulwark ever erected by free nations the NATO community."

Then the Prophet again, turning homeward:

"Rather than useful jobs . . . people have been offered bureaucratic make-work; rather than moral leadership, they have been given bread and circuses; they have been given spectacles and, yes, they've even been given scandals.

"Tonight, there is violence in our streets, corruption in our highest offices, aimlessness among our youth, anxiety among our elderly, and there's a virtual despair among the many who look beyond material successes toward the inner meaning of their lives. . . .

"We Republicans see all this as more—*much* more—than the results of mere . . . political mistakes. We see this as the result of a fundamentally and absolutely wrong view of man, his nature and his destiny. . . .

"It is the cause of Republicanism to insure that power remains in the hands of the people—and, so help us God, that is exactly what a Republican President will do with the help of a Republican Congress."

Then the Patriot again, talking as Cromwell:

"It is . . . the cause of Republicanism to remind ourselves, and the world, that only the strong *can* remain free—that only the strong *can* keep the peace!"

Then the call:

"The Republican cause demands that we brand Communism as the principal disturber of peace in the world today. Indeed, we should brand it as the only significant disturber of the peace. And we must make clear that until its goals of conquest are absolutely renounced, and its relations with all nations tempered, Communism and the governments it now controls are enemies of every man on earth who is or wants to be free."

Then the message to the Party itself:

"Anyone who joins us in all sincerity we welcome. Those who do not care for our cause, we don't expect to enter our ranks in any case.

"And let our Republicanism, so focused and so dedicated, not be made fuzzy and futile by unthinking and stupid labels. . . ."

And then the final, unforgettable thrust at the Party moderates:

"Extremism in the defense of liberty is no vice! . . . Moderation in the pursuit of justice is no virtue!"[1]

The reverberation of extremism created by this convention continued through one of the worst debacles in twentieth-century politics. A small, well-disciplined group of dedicated activists, through zeal and political maneuverings, had seized control of a major American political party. The

[1]From Theodore H. White, *The Making of the President, 1964* (New York: Atheneum, 1965), pp. 221–233, 240–242, 244–245, 260–261. (All footnotes in this chapter have been consecutively renumbered for the convenience of the reader.)

significance of this victory lies in the rejection by the Goldwaterites of the normal practices of democratic politics—compromise and bargaining. Goldwater's supporters equated the long tradition of political compromise to moral degeneracy.[2] This symptom of the political *death wish* was to appear again but this time to the Democrats during the 1972 McGovern fiasco.

What Is a National Convention?

But what of national conventions themselves—the seats of party power in American politics? These assemblages of delegates, who are selected in their states by conventions, state party organizations and/or primaries, are in a very real sense the national political parties—the keepers of the White House keys. Only at this time are the divergent views and geopolitical subdivisions of the looser party confederations brought together to make joint decisions.[3] Consequently the functions and scope of these party gatherings are more complex than those of a mere nominating convention.

In all, the convention's functions of debating and approving the party platform, establishing the party government, garnering the presidential nomination, selecting the vice-presidential nominee, mending political fences, building a viable coalition, and staging, on a national basis, a campaign rally *ala spectacular,* are the ever-present activity of the assembled delegates. The interests of disparate party factions and a multitude of constituency groups—ethnic, social, sectional, economic, and religious—must be reconciled, then mobilized behind the presidential nominee. With the intent of unifying the party faithful and sympathizers with a sense of belonging to *our* national party, of adjourning the convention with the emotion of *we* among the delegates, the party platform is drafted with a sensitivity to the diverse constituencies of the party. The party platform not only praises the party's past accomplishments and slams the opposition, but, more importantly, this political document indicates future policy directions in a manner that is directly related to the constituency strengths of the party.[4] Despite a contrary belief, analysis of major party platforms between 1948 and 1968 by Gerald Pomper reveals that about 75 percent of the party platforms cannot be categorized as rhetorical generalizations.[5]

[2]Aaron Wildavsky, "The Goldwater Phenomena: Purists, Politicians, and the Party System," *The Review of Politics* 27 (July 1965): 143.

[3]Judson, L. James, *American Political Parties in Transition* (New York: Harper & Row, 1974), p. 111.

[4]Ibid., pp. 112–113.

[5]Gerald M. Pomper, "Controls and Influence in American Elections (Even, 1968)," *American Behavioral Scientist* 13 (November–December 1969): 223–227.

Perhaps the most recent exception to this rule can be found in 1972 at the Democratic National Convention. While George McGovern garnered the nomination, thus influencing the philosophical direction of the party platform, it was the position of Henry Jackson that most closely appealed to the constituency strengths of the party. The overwhelming electoral defeat of McGovern is substantially explained by his lack of appeal to regular party supporters.

It is true that American parties are not sufficiently centralized or disciplined to make this campaign document binding on the successful presidential aspirant. However, the platform does indicate the relative priorities of the party. The "bloodletting" fights over platform planks lend credibility to this assumption. To be included in the platform is no guarantee, but to be excluded is almost an assurance that the priorities of your faction or interest group will not be among future policy alternatives. As viewed by one delegate, platforms "are like college catalogue course

descriptions: never the same as the course, but designed for appeal."[6] The physical and emotional involvement of the delegates in both the long-standing "tribal rituals" and in building political bridges between conflicting elements serve to kindle a sense of common purpose and identity among the participants. Through the mass media the diverse factions of the rank-and-file members can vicariously engage in the excitement of the convention floor. When this occurs, there is also created a symbolic dimension with which party strategists hope to build a bandwagon affect—a mobilization of party faithfuls behind the *next President of the United States*.

The Basic Tool for a Peaceful Transition of Power

Yet in a broader sense, the national convention is demonstrative of the basic process which the party system plays in the peaceful transition of political power in America. Unlike the multiparty systems that are common to parliamentary governments of Europe, coalitions are formed before the election of the U.S. president. In the multiparty systems the election of the prime minister takes place with the establishment of a postelection coalition of several parties.

Thus we see that coalition building is a necessary prerequisite for the peaceful transfer of political power in any nation with an orientation toward representative democracy. Whether pre- or postelection, coalition building is that delicate process of representing the interests of at least a majority of diverse and conflicting constituencies within a political community. If the national party convention is to act as a broker for integrating these diverse policy demands, it follows that compromise is a necessary ingredient of mediating a viable coalition. To expect otherwise would be absurd, for there is considerable truth found in the definition of politics as the *art of compromise*. As expressed by one delegate, "If I can get a whole loaf, I'll take it. If not, I'll take half rather than lose it all."[7] In the post-Watergate era this statement may seem to represent an individual politically unprincipled, an individual motivated by nothing less than crass political gain. But in a representative political system, it is the task of leadership not only to represent their personal principles but also to reflect and fight for the goals and interests they were elected to represent—securing the maximum possible in every given circumstance.

[6]Denise G. Sullivan et al., *The Politics of Representation: The Democratic Convention of 1972* (New York: St. Martin's, 1974), p. 74.

[7]Nelson W. Polsby and Aaron B. Wildavsky, *Presidential Elections: Strategies of American Electoral Politics*, 2d ed. (New York: Scribner, 1968), p. 176.

Placed against the backdrop of the Goldwater debacle of 1964 and the Democratic convention of 1972, this inquiry is of vital concern to the thrust of national party politics. As noted above, the Republican convention of 1964 was controlled by a cadre of Goldwater activists who had seized power by active participation in state nominating conventions and party organizations. Not only were these delegates primarily freshmen to national convention politics; they were predominantly ideological purists who had attained control of many delegations without the "need to broaden their base or programs, or to compromise with other interests or concerns. . . . Therefore, few concessions had been made to sectional or interest group variations in the party's constituencies."[8] Nor was coalition building part of the Republican convention process in 1964. Even the long tradition of selecting the vice-presidential nomineee to balance the ticket

8James, op. cit., p. 118.

was violated. William Miller was selected because he met the criteria of ideological purity that would be consistent in offering the Republican ticket as "a choice, not an echo." Goldwater was nominated to articulate the conservative philosophy of government despite evidence that his views were not consistent with the mainstream of the electorate. In fact, opinion polls in the spring and early summer of 1964 indicated that Goldwater did not have broad support within his own party.[9] Evidence suggests that similar forces were instrumental in the Democratic convention of 1972. The *dawning of the age of McGovern* was the end product of the recommendations of the McGovern-Fraser reform commission, which shifted the power in delegate selection from state party organizations to the grass-roots level. As commented by McGovern early in 1970: "Under the old system, where national convention delegates were mainly chosen by party leaders, I would have had no chance."[10]

The Dawning of the Age of McGovern

The result was that the new rules, including a quota system for delegate selection, brought the FDR New Deal Coalition under attack by reformist elements in the party, and the old guard was ousted. Seventy-nine percent of the Democratic delegates attended a national convention for the first time in 1972.[11] The winners were vestiges of Kennedy-McCarthy fans, suburban liberals, student peaceniks, feminists, blacks, and Mexican-American activists. As noted by *Newsweek,* the delegations were "conspicuously light on moderate-to-conservative Southerners and working-class ethnic Northerners."[12] It was a convention of jumbled dress and votes cast in Sioux and Spanish. Women wore pants and demanded an abortion plank, and the debate over gay rights lasted until near sunset. But "Where," grumbled one veteran democrat, "are the working people in this convention? When the workingman sees this on TV, does he see his people on the floor? No, sir—he sees a guy in a dashiki raising a clenched fist and says to himself, 'Is that my party?'"[13]

In 1972, as in 1964, the grass-roots movements had sent delegations to the Democratic and Republican national conventions that did not repre-

[9]Ibid., p. 217.

[10]"Campaign '72: Democratization of the Democrats," *Congressional Quarterly: Weekly Report,* 17 June 1972, p. 1455.

[11]Milton C. Cummings and David Wise, *Democracy Under Pressure,* 2d ed. (New York: Harcourt Brace Jovanovich, 1974), p. 228.

[12]"Is It An Era—Or Only An Hour?" *Newsweek,* 24 July 1972, p. 17.

[13]Ibid., pp. 15, 16.

"I SURE LIKE HIM BETTER NOW THAT HE'S ORGANIZED."

sent the attitudes of the mainstream of America. The attempt of the McGovern-Fraser Commission to provide broad-based participation in the Democratic party and the resultant quota system for delegate selection overlooked the obvious. The quota system provided a representation for demographic population groupings in the states, not the rank-and-file members of the Democratic Party. The nomination of McGovern as the presidential nominee was the nomination of a minority candidate. Only 30 percent of the Democratic voters favored McGovern as their first choice for the nomination. In the primaries McGovern garnered only 25 percent of the Democratic votes.[14]

[14] "Memo from Richard Scammon," *Newsweek,* 24 July 1972, p. 40.

What we see then in the 1964 and 1972 conventions are delegates who appear to see the criteria for political decision making as a relationship between political leadership and their consciences. Although McGovern's acceptance speech and campaign were more conciliatory than Goldwater's, the delegates in both situations had defined the party without consideration of the rank-and-file, a characteristic that is common for purists.[15] Perhaps the McGovern delegates should have included a line from Barry Goldwater's acceptance speech in their platform: "Anyone who joins us in all sincerity we welcome. Those who do not care for our cause, we don't expect to enter our ranks in any case. . . ."[16]

Under differing partisan banners and articulating diametrically opposed ideological stances, the national conventions of 1964 and 1972 expose an apparent flaw in the American party system—the ability of a well-organized, highly disciplined, and unrepresentative elite to charter the course of the presidential sweepstakes. Yet what is a political party in America? Is what happened to the Republicans in 1964 and to the Democrats in 1972 a normal process, an institutional weakness embedded in the very system that those who opposed Goldwater and McGovern helped establish?

What Is a Political Party in America?

A political party in the American partisan arena is a broad coalition of diverse and often conflicting interests and values that organize for the purpose of assuming the responsibility of government; that is, controlling the decision-making centers of government and consequently public policy. With this objective in mind, the party nominates candidates and mobilizes electoral support for their nominees. It is therefore understandable why the political party must deal with the full range of public issues. If it were to confine itself to a narrow scope of issues (for example, labor, education, or civil liberties) the party could not construct the broad coalition necessary to fulfill rudimentary roles of an electoral organization. It is also of significance to note the relative stability of the major party coalitions despite the recent and unprecedented trend of ticket-splitting. That is to say, the organizational ties of major party coalitions run deep. Though the faith of any group in the coalition may be temporarily shaken (for example, the desertion of AFL-CIO from the McGovern camp in 1972), the loyalties usually return when the party returns to normality.

[15]Polsby and Wildavsky, op. cit., p. 181.
[16]White, op. cit., p. 261.

This definition of a political party exhibits what some may claim is a traditional view of the American political scene. Specifically, it is not expansive enough to cover minor parties, which are an integral part of the political landscape. Nonetheless, protest parties such as the Peace and Freedom Party of 1968, ideological parties such as the Socialist Workers' Party, or even the American Independent Party do not meet the mathematical reality of electoral politics in America.

The electoral base of these groups, if not their issue breadth, is too narrow to be considered a political party in any true sense of the word. In the past they have not been able to meet the universally accepted purpose of a political party—to control, or at least share in the control, of the governmental apparatus. Minor parties often place candidates on the ballot, but in a way these overtures are somewhat quixotic, for they campaign without hope of winning the prize of office. In a system where single-member districts predominate and a plurality of the voters is necessary for victory, Eldridge Cleaver, the presidential nominee of the Peace and Freedom Party, did not stand a chance of victory. Thus what goes under the title of a minor party has a function similar to that of an interest group; that is, it is organized to influence major parties rather than to control government. Often the issues that are espoused by minor parties inadvertently serve as trial balloons for major parties. If the issue begins to attract sufficient support from the electorate, it will eventually be incorporated into one of the two major parties.

Can the surge of support for George Wallace fit into such a categorization? In 1968, under the banner of the American Independent Party, Wallace did garner almost 10 million popular votes and the electoral votes of 5 southern states. However, his main threat to the Democratic and Republican contenders for the presidency was that he would gather enough electoral votes to deprive Nixon or Humphrey of a majority, thus forcing the presidential decision into the U.S. House of Representatives. Had that occurred, the bargaining power of Wallace in influencing the policy directions of the would-be winner would have been considerably enhanced. As it happened, the influence of the Wallace vote was more indirect. The *sunbelt* strategy of Richard Nixon, more commonly called the southern strategy,[17] was predicated on the Wallace vote. That is to say, George Wallace influenced the direction of the Nixon administration by *red flagging* a

---

[17]The essence of the rationale for the southern strategy is found in Kevin Philips, *The Emerging Republican Majority* (New York: Doubleday, 1970). For a critique of the southern strategy from the perspective of two southern newspaper editors, see Reg Murphy and Hal Gulliver, *The Southern Strategy* (New York: Scribner, 1971).

segment of the population that the president wooed after capturing the presidency. Nor has the *courting Wallace syndrome* been confined to Republicans. Early in the 1976 presidential sweepstakes pilgrimages of Democratic hopefuls to Montgomery, Alabama, have become routine. As wryly commented by William F. Buckley, Jr., "I am surprised that the Democrats in the Senate have not yet proposed rapid-transit subsidies from Washington to Montgomery."[18] This bipartisan courting of Wallace is best explained by the fact that his populist support is derived from demographic groups that have been traditionally Democrat, yet showed support for the Nixon administration with uneasy frequency. Of course the withdrawal of Ted Kennedy as a presidential contender may very well change the name of the game, so to speak, for the who's who list among presidential aspirants in the Democratic Party. Of considerably greater influence in 1976 will be the public financing of presidential elections. The rules governing the public financing of presidential candidates all but exclude 11th-hour challengers. Interestingly enough, it was Governor Wallace who first qualified for these funds.

Several theories have been advanced to explain the historical dominance of two-party politics we have been discussing: dualism, social consensus, and institutionalization are the most accepted.

Dualist Theory

Dualist theorists rely on the historical division of American interests into two camps to explain the dominance of two parties. First, constitutional issues divided public opinion groupings into two factions—Federalists and Anti-Federalists. Next, as V. O. Key notes, the initial significance of sectionalism (that is, the financial and commercial interests of the East versus the agricultural frontier) accelerated this trend.[19] The issue of states rights, which later split the nation by bloody civil war, provided a further division, eventually leading to the founding of the Democratic and Republican parties. With the groundwork so laid, the two-party system perpetuated itself. As persons entered the political system, they became socialized to one of the two major parties. At the same time, the major parties gravitated to the left or right to accommodate their supporters and respond to the changing conditions of the country. In the struggle to preserve their status as viable electoral entities, new alignments were formed, and the present two-party system evolved.

[18]William Buckley, Jr., "A Letter from Wallace (a Democrat?)," *Seattle Times,* 15 July 1974.

[19]V. O. Key, Jr., *Politics, Parties and Pressure Groups,* 5th ed. (New York: T. Y. Crowell, 1964), pp. 229–230.

Social Consensus Theory

Social consensus theorists suggest that the dominance of two-partyism results from the absence of irreconcilable differences in the population. This is in conjunction with a pattern of attitudes that is favorable to party dualism. Despite the diversity of a country as large as the United States, this nation has never faced the deep ideological riffs that have been the breeding ground for all the multiparty systems in countries such as France and Italy. The development of a partisan system in an environment that had no monarchy, feudal system, rigid class lines, or church–state entanglements allowed political debate to develop along a liberal–conservative spectrum. The choices were between self-perceived *better or worse* approaches, not legitimate or illegitimate. Americans have never had to make the choice between God and politics, as was the case in Italy when membership in the Communist party meant excommunication for Catholics. Furthermore, as Hugh Bone commented, there has been a broad degree of consensus in American attitudes on prevailing economic, social, and political institutions.[20] This agreement on democratic fundamentals, though somewhat elusive, means that there has been a centralist clustering of opinion on democratic ideals—the constitutional separation of powers, the separation of church and state, and the election of public officials are a few examples. This condition, so the social consensus advocates argue, fosters dualism because the issues of public debate are a matter of degree for most of the electorate. In current terms it is a matter of the relative size of the defense budget, defensive or offensive armaments, not a choice between whether or not Congress shall appropriate monies for defense.

Institutional Theory

Institutional theorists attribute much of the responsibility for two-party dominance to the tradition and laws that define the manner in which officials are elected to public office. Proponents of this view argue that single-member electoral districts and the plurality electoral system have caused and perpetuate a two-party system. That is to say, in a single-member district only the candidates of the two strongest parties can realistically compete in a winner-take-all type of election. There is no electoral reward for those who come in second or third as in a proportional (parliamentary) representation system. In the proportional system the minority party that gains, say, 15 percent of the vote will receive an

[20]Hugh A. Bone, *American Politics and the Party System,* 4th ed. (New York: McGraw-Hill, 1971), p. 72.

approximate representation in the legislature. In the United States, given the futile prospects of a minor party's ability to attract significant numbers, they are usually destined to defeat. The result is that the supporters of a minor party find it necessary to join the ranks of a major U.S. party or effectively disenfranchise themselves. A party that perpetually loses cannot legislate public policy. Thus the single-member district in a plurality election reinforces partisan dualism.

The same dualistic principle applies to the executive branch—the U.S. presidency—as well as to state governors. With the electoral college system the effect is to elect the president from 50 single-member districts. Similarly the state is a single-member district for gubernatorial aspirants.

And finally, the mathematical inability of minor parties to compete realistically for the executive offices of government acts as an additional handicap. The fact that minor parties are denied the most visible public offices works against their future prospects, even when the local branch of the party may occasionally elect a candidate. That is to say, public attention is seldom focused on the spokesmen of minor parties because they are unable to demonstrate a voter appeal sufficient to offer a realistic alternative to one of the major party candidates.[21]

When one argues the viability of two-party dominance in America, as opposed to multiple-party participation, the argument overlooks one important fact. Rather than speculating on multiple- versus two-party systems, we should more accurately look at the reality of one-party dominance throughout much of the nation.

One-Party Dominance

To argue the existence of only two competitive parties is not to argue that their competitiveness is spread evenly over the country. There are substantial statewide and local pockets of one-partyism in the United States. The states of the Deep South until recently spent very close to their own "four score and seven" years as the country's most celebrated area of one-party domination. Much the same could be said of the rock-like Republicanism of Maine, New Hampshire, and Vermont. And scattered throughout the country are thousands of one-party cities, towns, and counties, in which city hall or the county courthouse comes perilously close to being the property of one party or the other. Just as important,

[21]Frank J. Sorauf, *Party Politics in America,* 2d ed. (Boston: Little, Brown, 1972), p. 72. Conservative Senator James Buckley of New York is a good example. His power is diluted because he must align with Republicans, despite the fact that he represents a third party. The situation of Maine's Governor Longley is equally problematic. Though elected as an Independent, he must work with a legislature of Republicans and Democrats.

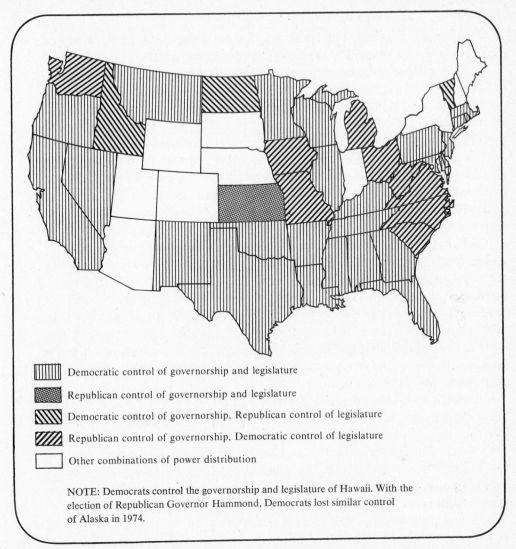

Figure 4.1. Distribution of partisan power in the states. (From "State Legislatures: Democrats Control 9 More," *Congressional Quarterly: Weekly Report,* Nov. 16, 1974, p. 3124; and "Democratic Sweep: A Story That Keeps Growing," *U.S. News & World Report,* Nov. 25, 1974, pp. 35, 36.)

therefore, as the question of the causes of the two-party system is the question of the causes of one-partyism within it [Figure 4.1].

One-partyism set within the context of broad, two-party competitiveness normally reflects a "fault" in the distribution of the loyalties that characterize the electorates of the two national competitive parties. Since the 1930's the major American parties, especially in national elections, have divided the American electorate roughly along lines of socioeconomic status. . . .

One-partyism, first of all, may result from some potent local basis of party loyalty that overrides the SES [socioeconomic status] dualism. In the classic one-partyism of the American South, traditional regional loyalties long overrode the factors that were dividing Americans into two parties in most of the rest of the country. Reaction to the Republican Party as the party of abolition, Lincoln, the Civil War, and the hated Reconstruction was so pervasive, even three generations after the fact, that the impact of the SES division was precluded. Even today, the South may be in at the process of trading in a one-partyism based on the events of the nineteenth century for a new one-partyism based on more recent racial antagonism. In either event, it is a one-partyism based on isolation from the factors that normally produce two-party competitiveness.

Second, one-partyism may result from a maldistribution of the characteristics that normally divide the parties. The local constituency may be too small to afford a perfect sample of SES characteristics and thus of nationally competitive politics. Hence the noncompetitiveness of the "safe" Democratic congressional districts of the older, lower-middle-class neighborhoods of the cities and the "safe" Republican districts of the more fashionable and spacious suburbs. In other words, the more heterogeneous are its people in socioeconomic status, the more likely the district is to foster competitiveness.

Empirical studies of one-partyism suggest, however, that its causes are far more complex than these comments indicate. Competitiveness has been associated with general socioeconomic diversity in the constituency—especially with urbanism and its industrialism, higher income levels, and ethnic diversity. Yet the relationships are not always strong or dramatic, and one recent study finds no such relationships at all.[22] We are thus left more or less to conjecture. Perhaps a homogeneous district cut from the middle range of SES factors tends to be more competitive than an equally homogeneous district at either the top or the bottom of the SES spectrum. Also, in some localities, the patterns of competitiveness may have little to do with patterns of national SES politics or with any other characteristics of the electorate. They may instead reflect the influences of local personages, of powerful officeholders, of local traditions, or of political conflict such as that between a dominant local industry and its disgruntled employees.

One may also look at these pockets of one-partyism another way. The American party system is made up of two electorally competitive parties,

[22]Charles M. Bonjean and Robert L. Lineberry, "The Urbanization-Party Competition Hypothesis: A Comparison of All United States Counties," *Journal of Politics* 32 (May 1970): 305–321.

which is really to say that it is formed by two parties competing to enlist a majority of the American electorate. The active, initiating sectors of the party—the party organization and the party in government—recruit and enlist the support of the electorate with assorted appeals. If these two parties were fully competitive in every constituency in the country, they would approach a fifty–fifty division of the electorate. They must, however, compete at various disadvantages, and frequently in some area or locality one party works at a disadvantage that it never manages to overcome. The result is the ability of the other party to maintain a one-party domination. The understanding of one-partyism, then, requires an understanding of the various kinds of competitive disadvantages a party may face.

The competitive disadvantages may begin with immobile electorates. Voters are not easily moved from their attachments to a party, even though the reasons for the original attachment have long passed. Also, a party trying to pull itself into competitiveness may find itself caught organizationally in a vicious circle of impotence. Its inability to win elections limits its ability to recruit resources, including manpower, because as a chronic loser it offers so little chance of achieving political goals. It may even find itself without an effective appeal to the electorate. The Republican party in the South, for example, found for many years that the Democrats had preempted the salient political issues in that region.

Local Versus National Appeal

Today the would-be competitive party finds the disadvantage taking another form: the formation of party loyalties along lines determined by national or statewide political debate. If the Democratic party is identified nationally with the aspirations of the poor and minority groups, its appeal in a homogeneous, affluent suburb may be limited. Increasingly, national politics may thus rob the local party organization of the chance to develop strength based on its own issues, personalities, and traditions. To the extent that party loyalties and identifications grow out of national politics, patterns of competitiveness (and the lack of them) may be largely determined for the local party organizations.

There are, to be sure, other sources of competitive disadvantage. The dominant party may shore up its supremacy by carefully calculated legislative districting. In the past the southern Democrats stifled potential competitiveness by artificially restricting the electorates to middle-class whites. In other instances majority parties have supported nonpartisanship in local elections as a way of drawing on their one-party consensus. In addition to these institutional buttresses to one-partyism, of course, it is also possible that powerful party organization and sedulous canvasing can maintain superiority. The normal processes of education and social conformity also work to the disadvantage of a party trying to become competitive. That force of conformity, a number of observers have argued, works especially against competitiveness in the closely knit, socially sensitive world of American suburbia. . . .[23]

Even when considering occasional pockets of one-party dominance, the two-party system in the United States probably lends some credence to the image of a national goliath whose organizational tentacles gird the continent. Indeed, when the politically inexperienced are first exposed to the multilevel organization chart of a major party (Figure 4.2), all too often there emerges an image of a tightly controlled, well-oiled political machine. One can imagine a disciplined hierarchy of partisan chieftains and lieutenants who delegate power, authority, and political spoils from the national chairman to legions of political foot soldiers in the wards and precincts around the country. The very jargon of campaign politics—strategy, tactics, political battle plan—conjure images of a quasi-military organization.

Image and Fact
Are at Variance

To the frustration of party chieftains everywhere, from the office of the national chairman to the living room of the precinct committeeman, public images stand in stark contrast to the organizational reality of partisan politics in America. The kaleidoscope of state statutes that define the party organizations and the by-laws of party conventions and committees may sound authoritative, but they simply are not so imposing as many outsiders perceive. In other words, the organizational condition of the major parties in many states and localities "is weak, undermanned, even torpid."[24] The American party system is characterized by organizational fragmentation rather than cohesion. Decades before urban machines were experiencing their last hurrah, Professor Schattscheider pointed to decentralization as the most important characteristic of political parties in the United States.[25] More recently James MacGregor Burns suggested that powerful state and city machines were becoming so rare that "the Democratic organization in Albany, New York, . . . should be put into the Smithsonian before we forget

[23]From Sorauf, op. cit., pp. 40–43.
[24]Ibid., p. 73.
[25]E. E. Schattscheider, *Party Government* (New York: Holt, Rinehart, and Winston, 1942), p. 129.

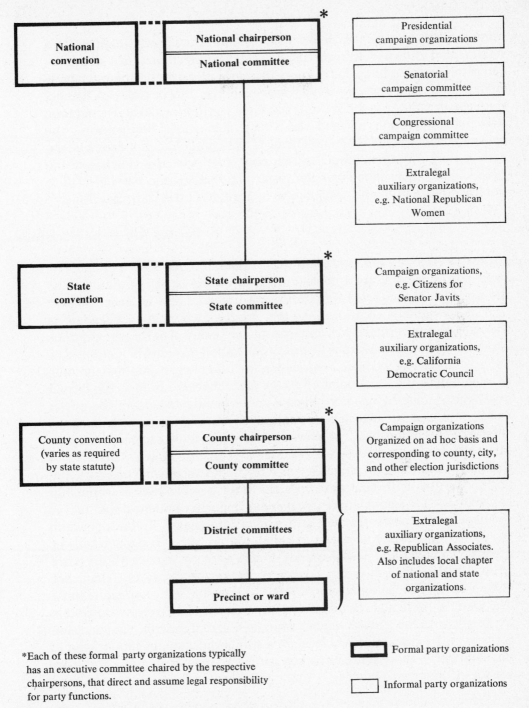

National convention	National chairperson *	Presidential campaign organizations
	National committee	Senatorial campaign committee
		Congressional campaign committee
		Extralegal auxiliary organizations, e.g. National Republican Women
State convention	State chairperson *	Campaign organizations, e.g. Citizens for Senator Javits
	State committee	Extralegal auxiliary organizations, e.g. California Democratic Council
County convention (varies as required by state statute)	County chairperson *	Campaign organizations Organized on ad hoc basis and corresponding to county, city, and other election jurisdictions
	County committee	Extralegal auxiliary organizations, e.g. Republican Associates. Also includes local chapter of national and state organizations.
	District committees	
	Precinct or ward	

☐ Formal party organizations

☐ Informal party organizations

*Each of these formal party organizations typically has an executive committee chaired by the respective chairpersons, that direct and assume legal responsibility for party functions.

Figure 4.2. Organizational hierarchy of major party.

what a political machine looks like."[26] One should not interpret this statement of Professor Burns to mean that urban machines are a phenomenon of the past. Rather, where urban machines do exist, they have fallen on difficult days. One of the most notorious examples, Mayor Daley's Chicago, is a case in point.[27] In 1972 the credentials committee of the Democratic National Convention rejected the Daley delegation. Furthermore, the power and influence of urban machines is often parochial. For example, the author of *The Walker Report,* which concluded that the violence of the 1968 Chicago convention was the result of a "police riot," was elected to statewide office in Illinois, despite the opposition of the Daley machine.

Parties Are Confederations

Parties in America are confederations of autonomous state parties. The state parties, in turn, are a confederation of county or city parties. Just as the activities of the state organization are executed in a manner independent of the national committee, so too, are the local units independent of the state central committee. Consequently the reality of party organizations is rarely synonomous with the formal organization prescribed by statutes or party by-laws. The individual who holds the title of party chairperson may or may not be the focal point of power and influence. In fact, the formal organization may be no more than a paper facade. Wherever the power exists, it is not an exercise in command—the resultant of a superior subordinate relationship. The power exists because of alliances, compromise, persuasion, or a sense of common purpose. The power of an office in the party organization often depends on the person who occupies the position. If this individual possesses the right combination of leadership capabilities—for example, resourcefulness, tenacity, patience, and tact— the likelihood of power residing in that office is increased. To have power in the party organization necessitates collaboration with those individuals or groups over which the power extends. Power does not come with the party office, for the office does not possess sufficient sanctions or "clout" for enforcement. The national committee chairperson, for example, cannot designate a particular candidate in a given state to receive favorable treatment from the state or county organization of the party. That decision is made at the state or county level. In a similar position, as titular head of the state party, the state chairperson cannot remove the county chairperson for incompetence in office—or any other reason for that matter. In the

[26]James MacGregor Burns, *The Deadlock of Democracy: Four-Party Politics* (Englewood Cliffs, N.J.: Prentice-Hall, 1967), p. 236.

[27]An excellent journalistic portrayal of Chicago politics is provided in Mike Royko, *Boss: Richard J. Daley of Chicago* (New York: New American Library, 1971).

area of finances, the dependence of the higher levels of party organization on the lower organizations is well illustrated by the county committee quota system initiated in the Republican party of California during the 1960s. Under the chairmanship of Gaylord Parkinson, the Republican State Central Committee assigned a dollar quota that each county central committee was to raise on behalf of the state party organization.[28] However, as delineated by Samuel Eldersveld's theory of party "stratarchy," "The authority to speak for the party and to request compliance is at the top of the hierarchy, but is weak and mostly formal. There is a great deal of autonomy in the lower strata."[29] And as in California, these "strata" may or may not choose to abide by the party's directives.

County Committee

What this means for political parties in most states is that the location of organizational vitality and the source of organizational authority reside in the county committee. The composition and selection of the county committees vary in different states. For example, in some southern states and Hawaii the county committee is elected by the county convention.[30] In California the county organization is a combination of persons elected from each supervisor or assembly district in the primary, party nominees and incumbents for state legislative offices that have their electoral base in the county, and ex-officio members appointed by the executive committee of the county central committee; the Republicans also extend ex-officio membership to nominees and incumbents for statewide and congressional offices. The variations are so numerous that they defy classification except to say that the members are selected from a combination of party primaries, county conventions, and appointments of other official bodies of the local party organization.

Characteristics of City–County Structures

To get an idea of what this level of party organizations means in terms of organizational vitality and effectiveness, the prototype of the *average* city or county organization constructed by Frank Sorauf is of value.

[28]Vernon F. Anderson, "An Exploratory Study of Candidate Campaigns for Legislative Office" (unpublished master's thesis, California State University, San Diego, 1970), pp. 54, 65.

[29]Samuel J. Eldersveld, *Political Parties: A Behavioral Analysis* (Chicago: Rand McNally, 1964), pp. 99–100.

[30]Bone, op. cit., p. 136.

One may mentally construct . . . the following characteristics . . .

1. An active chairman and executive committee, plus a few associated activists, who in effect make most of the decisions in the name of the party, who raise funds, who seek out and screen candidates (or approve the candidates who select themselves), and who speak locally for the party.
2. A ward and precinct organization in which only a few local committeemen are active and in which there is little door-to-door canvasing or other direct voter contact.
3. The active participation in organizational matters of some of the party's elected public officials, who may share effective control of the organization with the official leadership of the party organization.
4. A distinctly periodic calendar of activities marked by a watchful waiting or general inactivity at other than election times.

Nowhere here does one find the serried ranks of party foot soldiers. The leadership operates not with threats and iron discipline but with pleading and cajoling. There are few incentives and rewards left in the hands of these parties with which to recruit all the effort and manpower the statutory structures seem to assume.

Such a sketch of the "average" local party organization cannot, of course, begin to suggest the many forms that local parties take in the United States. It takes no account, for instance, of the oligarchic rural or small-town machines, in which a few local notables (who may or may not hold party or public office) domininate a political organization with a variable combination of patronage, local prestige and status, friendship, kinship, and private economic power. (It is one of the most durable—and least supportable—myths of American politics that political muscle, and even corruption, must of necessity be urban.)

What of Urban Machines?

A sketch of the "average" takes no account either of urban party organizations operating at a level of considerable effectiveness, albeit a level or two below that of the prototypic machine.[31] A recent study of parties in the Detroit area defined the precinct committeeman's three "critical" tasks to be the registration of new voters, the canvasing of the already registered (by phone or personal visits), and the roundup of voters on election day. Only 17 per cent of the Democratic precinct leaders and 25 per cent of the Republican leaders performed all three tasks, but another 38

[31]Sorauf, op. cit., pp. 77–78.

per cent of the Democrats and 22 per cent of the Republicans carried out two of the three.[32]

In these cases, most of the committee positions in the party's county unit are unfilled or held by completely inactive incumbents (who may have been elected without their consent by four or five write-in votes). A chairman and a handful of loyal party officials may meet occasionally to carry out only the most essential affairs of the party, or the affairs that state statutes require of them. Their main activity occurs shortly before the primary elections as they plead with members of the party to become candidates or offer themselves as candidates in order to "fill the party ticket." They are largely without influence or following, for often their party is a chronic minority party. They meet infrequently, raise little money for election campaigns, and create little or no public attention. The extent of such organizational weakness is difficult to estimate, although it is the rule rather than the exception in much of rural America. . . .[33]

This *average* prototype lies between the reality of the urban political machine and the other extreme—a paper organization that verges on the edge of nonexistence. But if this is the case, why do parties continue their decentralized approach to organization?

Why Are Parties Decentralized?

There are many reasons for lack of centralization; but among the most important are the multiplicity of constituencies, the character of the electoral system, and the statutory regulation of parties.

Political parties try to win as many elections as possible by focusing their efforts on the individual constituencies that elect public officials. *Elective offices are so numerous that the party inevitably shatters into many separate party units, each of which feels that it can most effectively compete for votes by maintaining its autonomy.* The numberless semipermanent constituency organizations are matched by a host of affiliated groups. Some of these are adjuncts to the party organization, reflect many of its conflicts, and compete with it for influence. Such groups include the Young Republicans. Young Democrats, New Democratic Coalition . . . and volunteer organizations . . . that are created temporarily to handle specific problems in a campaign, raise funds, broaden the base of voting support, or even prepare policy statements.

[32]Eldersveld, op. cit., pp. 349–350. From: Sorauf, Ibid., p. 78. David Olson has made one of the few systematic attempts at categorizing county party organizations in his article, "Toward A Typology of County Party Organizations," *Southwestern Social Science Quarterly* 97 (March 1968): 558–572.

[33]From Sorauf, op. cit., p. 76.

Constituency organizations for each electoral unit respond to the basic political fact of federalism: it "creates separate, self-sustaining centers of power, privilege, and profit which may be sought and defended as desirable in themselves, as means of leverage upon elements in the political structure above and below, and as bases from which individuals may move to places of greater influence and prestige in and out of government."[34] By following the federal pattern, however, partisans deprive the national party leadership of the means for enforcing party discipline. The local autonomy of state, county, and district party organizations assigns the fate of policy decisions to locally responsible governors, mayors, county commissioners, or congressmen, who are pretty much free of central control.

Role of Pressure Groups

Pressure-group leaders understand this party fragmentation; and when they want to influence Congress, they go to the congressman's local constituency and party politicians within it, not to the national party organizations. Parochial interests often have a voice in the party's affairs that is out of proportion to their size, particularly if the local organization depends upon pressure groups for financial aid and electoral support.

The splitting of political authority shapes social conflict representation by channeling disputes and demands through local party organizations. As a result, democratic responsibility is often so diffuse that parties cannot respond to broad social changes. Though civil rights was a problem in the 1930s and 1940s, southerners were able to keep civil rights statements out of Democratic platforms because they controlled local party organizations and threatened to bolt the national party. Ever since President Harry Truman was elected in 1948 despite a southern defection, this tactic has been less effective, but it is not yet dead.

Decentralization is further reinforced by staggered elections and single-member districts. The many offices created by the separation of powers and federalism are made even more independent of one another by provisions for nonconcurrent terms of office: the President serves four years; Senators serve six years and Representatives two years; governors and state legislators serve either two or four years depending upon the state; terms of mayors, city councilmen, county commissioners, and other officials vary similarly. Because of the nonconcurrent terms officials are elected at staggered intervals and voters respond to forces peculiar to each

[34]David B. Truman, "Federalism and the Party System," in *Politics and Social Life,* ed. Nelson W. Polsby et al., (Boston: Houghton, Mifflin, 1963), pp. 518–519.

election. Local party organizations, bent upon winning their own contest, seldom have to unify their efforts to win a single national office. . . .

Single-Member Districts

[Since] American elections are won by the candidate with a plurality of votes in single-member districts. . . . [p]arties concentrate their efforts where they know they have enough identifiers to win a simple plurality. They restrict their efforts to constituencies in which they are dominant or at least competitive, preferring not to waste resources where they at best can come in only second, winning nothing. Where it is sure to win lopsided victories because it has the most party identifiers, the party does not need strong organization. Here neither party is likely to have a strong organization, the minority party because it has no chance and the majority party because it does not need to be organized.

States are more active in regulating political parties than the federal government so they tailor their organizations to fit state regulations. *Statutory regulations decentralizes party organization.* The *intent* behind state regulation has been to promote broad participation in party affairs by the rank-and-file in place of tight control by party leaders. . . . Many also require that parties nominate candidates through primary elections, removing nominations from the control of party politicians.[35] But primary elections do not necessarily give control of nominations to party identifiers, because party lines are crossed easily in primaries. . . . The primaries are but one more force weakening central organizational control within our major parties.[36]

Thus, as demonstrated, the picture that emerges of party politics in America is not wholly consistent with popular images. Though Republican and Democratic parties do dominate, the organizational condition of these parties are fragmented, and the locus of power is diffuse. The relationships between the formal party organization and the reality of intraparty relationships vary considerably. Accordingly the actual influence and power of party officials do not necessarily come with the position. A party chieftain cannot depend on cooperation from fellow partisans, let alone obedience from subordinate levels of the hierarchy. Evidence indicates that even

[35]The blanket primary in the state of Washington, for example, allows an individual to vote for whatever combination of Republicans and Democrats he prefers. In the 1972 gubernatorial primary of Washington, the weakest Democrat was nominated to challenge the Republican incumbent.

[36]From Dan Nimmo and Thomas D. Ungs, *American Political Patterns: Conflict and Consensus* (Boston: Little, Brown, 1973), pp. 288–291.

urban political machines are becoming scarce. Where these vestiges of Americana do exist, they are experiencing their *last hurrah*.

Don't Write the Obituaries Yet

Notwithstanding the growing ranks of self-identified Independents, it would be most impetuous to start writing the obituary of either major party. Not only are the forces that created and fostered the continuance of two-party dominance still active; one cannot ignore the self-interest of lawmakers in preserving present arrangements. As for organizational conditions within the parties, they are not a new phenomenon. When Franklin D. Roosevelt organized his campaign in 1932, he "was well aware of the disjointed nature of American political parties. The lines of authority from the top down were so loose that . . . [l]iterature sent to the state might never be redistributed. Roosevelt and Farley [Democratic national chairman] agreed that a direct distribution from national headquarters to the precinct worker would be better; thus the persons in actual touch with the voters [some 100,000 precinct captains] would be supplied with party ammunition." At the same time, "A special effort was made to convince the state organizations that they had a vital part in the national campaign. All state chairmen were called to headquarters in groups of ten or twelve for three-day sessions to discuss with Farley and associates their local conditions. The plan did wonders for the morale of the state chairmen."[37]

There Are Party Differences

But perhaps even more important than these historical trends is a general recognition by most Americans that the two parties do represent fundamentally different viewpoints on many significant issues.

A veteran political reporter, reflecting on the American political system noted that, "The choice offered in an American election is never a choice of programs and specifics; it is simply a setting of direction, an attempt by two men to point the different ways they hope to go; in America, people vote . . . on what they sense the inclination and direction of the candidates to be. Traditionally, therefore, this translates into "ins" against "outs," into the wonderful baroque language of the stump: 'We point with pride to. . . .' or 'I say the time has come when we must stop . . .'"[38]

[37]Harold F. Gosnell, *Champion Campaigner: Franklin D. Roosevelt* (New York: Macmillan, 1952), p. 125.

[38]Theodore H. White, *The Making of the President, 1968* (New York: Atheneum, 1969), p. 470.

Yet the common assertion that the differences between the parties are those of Tweedledee versus Tweedledum (thus the need for more responsible parties)[39] should not smokescreen the fact that there are significant policy differences between Republicans and Democrats. Generally speaking, congressional Democrats are more liberal than their Republican counterparts. Democrats have been more aggressive in their support of income

[39]The best known advocacy of more disciplined and responsible parties is found in Austin Ranney's "Toward A More Responsible Two-Party System: A Commentary," *American Political Science Review* 45 (June 1951): 488–499. For an analysis of the

redistribution and social welfare policies, whereas Republicans have traditionally supported concepts of a free enterprise economy.[40] In the balance-the-budget versus foreign-aid debates, Republicans have more consistently been concerned with the budgetary impact. Of course, this picture of partisan policy directions is painted with broad brush strokes. It does, however, indicate that the partisan banners of the national leadership are more than campaign trappings.

The impact of partisanships on voting, explains Judson L. James, "reflects a Congressman's previous career, group memberships, friendship patterns, the nature of his constituency, House organizational outlooks, and probable policy outlooks."[41] However, this is not to suggest that any rigid partisan cohesion exists in Congress. Not only does the party organization lack the "clout" to enforce such discipline; such an arrangement is not consistent with the diversity in American society. The impact of the pluralistic nature of electoral populations is well illustrated by congressional parties, which are more conservative and less international than either of the presidential parties.[42] Similarly, the U.S. Senate is more liberal than the U.S. House of Representatives. Nor does support of party interfere with coalitions of Republicans and Southern Democrats against northern Democrats. And finally it gives no consideration to mavericks, like Representative McCloskey and Senator Javits, who stray from the partisan fold for other reasons. An in-depth analysis of the many factors that come to bear on whether a congressman votes with his or her party is beyond the scope of this book. Obviously many factors serve to weaken generalizations concerning either party, but in three areas party partisanship is demanded: (1) consideration of issues that directly affect the party as a political organization (internal organization of the legislature); (2) issues involving the support or opposition of the program of the executive branch (revenue-sharing proposals); and (3) issues that particularly affect the socioeconomic interests of the constituencies (labor versus business).[43] Forces working against partisan voting are individual orientations, judgments of the legislator, and, most importantly, constituency demands. Particularly

---

development of the responsible party concept and its major aspects see Austin Ranney, *The Doctrine of Responsible Party Government* (Urbana: University of Illinois Press, 1954). A more recent evaluation of the concept was presented in a paper by Gerald M. Pomper, "After Twenty Years: The Report of the American Political Science Association Committee on Political Parties," delivered at the Annual Meeting of the American Political Science Association, Los Angeles, 8–12 September 1970.

[40]The Nixon wage–price controls stand in contrast to this pattern.

[41]James, op. cit., p. 224.

[42]William J. Keefe and Morris S. Ogul, *The American Legislative Process: Congress and the States* (Englewood Cliffs, N.J.: Prentice-Hall, 1972), p. 314.

[43]Sorauf, op. cit., pp. 349–352.

the supremacy of the constituency is a matter of political survival respected by all in the legislative arena.

Party Pressures Are Illusive

Generally speaking, the pressures that can be brought to bear by the official party organization are somewhat illusive. What appears as the most potent weapon of the party is peer group pressure from fellow partisans. The clearest example of this leverage is in the legislature, where members can be threatened with poor committee assignments or possibly ostracism. However, even this *strength* can be asserted effectively only when partisan party demands do not conflict with those of the constituency. Not long ago a defeated senior House member was heard bemoaning the fact that, had he only been reelected, he would have been chairman of the powerful Ways and Means Committee. Support by his party colleagues had done him little good, however, in the eyes of a constituency determined to elect someone more concerned with district water problems than the financial state of the nation.

Yet how about the power of the purse—the threat of the party hierarchy to sever the *mother's milk of politics* during the next election? The question that every candidate must decide is, Who really supplies the best combination of resources to execute a successful political campaign? In an era when spiraling campaign costs are changing needs from service support (doorbelling, voter registration, and the like) to fund acquisition, parties are finding themselves in increasingly pinched circumstances. While dollars raised, such as in the Democratic Telethon, are increasing, demands by candidates are far outdistancing resources. Whatever strength parties possess is best exercised in an environment of services (for example, getting out the vote). Too many other organizations are competing to render the *power of the purse* the weapon it once was.

Political Diversity Costs Money

Within this political context, characterized by organizational fragmentation, multiple elections running simultaneously, and open nomination procedures, America fields a multitude of candidates. Since each candidate has his own need to attract attention as well as dollars, both political costs and political fund raising are directly affected. At the same time, candidates, party and non-party committees, and a miscellany of groupings, all campaign side by side, sometimes cooperating, sometimes not, but always competing to raise and spend scarce political dollars.

"Be fair, boys! . . . publish the names of my big political contributors but also expose the cheapskates who only give 5 bucks!"

Grin and Bear It by George Lichty. Courtesy of Field Newspaper Syndicate.

Thus, American politics centers more around candidates than around parties. More than 500,000 public offices are filled by election, and campaigns are also conducted for nomination both by primary and by convention. To attract dollars, a candidate must attract attention, but it costs money to attract attention in the political arena. One competes not only against one's opponent(s) for a given nomination or office, but also against others within the same party running for other offices, others who are also seeking attention and dollars. So one must spend money in order to raise money as well as to attract voters.

The emphasis upon the candidate and the value some put upon independent voting cause increased reliance upon mass communications and personal campaigning to reach the voters, and less reliance upon the party organization (if an effective one exists at all). If the media route is chosen, then a professional public relations firm or advertising agency may well be used to supplant, compliment or supplement the party's campaign. . . .[44]

The focus on the candidate is reinforced by the almost limitless array of non-party committees—committees of labor, of doctors, of bankers, or

[44]For a further discussion of the impact of media on campaigning see Chapter 8.

reformers—seeking to help him. Additionally, there are permanent independent groups with special causes: for example, the National Committee for an Effective Congress, and the Americans for Constitutional Action. One reason these committees are organized is to raise money. Some do nothing else. Some committees are only too happy to raise funds directly for candidates and thereby seek political leverage or at least influence the complexion of public officialdom.

Labor and Management Influences

For these and other reasons, labor unions and management groups enter campaigns, both directly and indirectly. Sometimes they campaign independently on behalf of candidates; sometimes they raise funds which they contribute to the candidate; sometimes corporations operate non-partisan drives among employees for funds. Corporations, business, trade, or professional associations, and labor organizations, have an advantage in politics—their members tend to identify with their political goals, and they constitute natural financial constituencies commanding ready-made channels of communication capable of reaching large aggregates of voters. Many such organizations operate at the national and state levels, while major ones, particularly labor groups, often have local affiliates as well.

It is an oversimplification to suggest that the political arena is an organizational jungle. . . . Competition for funds abounds in a system characterized by a decentralized party system, open nominations, dependence on non-party groups and financial self-reliance of candidates. . . . [The picture is even further muddied since all are dependent upon a limited number of techniques to attract] dollars from financial constituencies presently too small to serve the diverse needs of the system. There are too many candidates, too many committees, too few volunteers, and too few inexpensive ways of soliciting those who might give to permit consideration of widespread independent solicitation for most candidates. . . . No rational model exists in which party members at the local level pay dues that are then shared with state and national levels. No rational model distinguishes year-round financial support of the party organization from support of campaigns emphasizing not the party but candidates. Because no system operates, fund raising to ease deficits after a campaign runs into fund raising to sustain the party organization between campaigns; and both run into financial drives for pre-nomination campaigns or for stocking up war chests in advance. The overlap creates enormous competition for a scarce resource—dollars—and creates appalling inefficiencies.

The American party system will not readily accommodate some of the changes necessary to the achievement of the goal of widespread financial support. Solicitation of small contributions is most effectively accomplished through personal confrontation on a systematic basis. Since there are no party members as such to call upon for this task, volunteers or party activists are needed. Some local committee leaders are reluctant to seek out volunteers who might challenge their control. In any case, volunteers are relatively scarce, and many millions would be needed to solicit all possible contributors.[45] There are competing demands for the services of the few who do volunteer, to help with registration, and voting drives, to do headquarters work and other chores.[46] If these jobs are not done by volunteers, money is needed to buy such services. Yet to raise funds from a broad base requires manpower not otherwise readily available.

If money is raised locally in small sums, a rational system of finance would have the local committees take their share, then filter shares up to the state and national party committees through a quota system. But many local organizations are little more than clubs for local officeholders, with few financial or policy ties to the national party. The American party system is weighted heavily toward such autonomous local party units. Each local organization has justifiable concern for immediate needs to finance campaigns for mayor, state legislator, and other officials. Many local organizations have little incentive to achieve financial margins large enough to share money with higher-level committees. Local leaders are selected through local party processes, not appointed from above, so they normally feel no urgent need to be enticed by either money or Federal patronage; they can raise the money they need locally, and Federal patronage is not always as appealing as is local patronage, which really counts to them. Especially troublesome are dissident party organizations that reject higher authority while claiming the rights and privileges that go with the party label. Until national politicians find effective answers or incentives to offer, or can apply sanctions, or until local leaderships become more enlightened and cognizant of the financial needs of higher-level committees, widespread effort to broaden the base will not be forthcoming. Without sufficient development of big money in small sums at the local level, the filtering of money upward through the party system

[45]The United States has over 176,000 election districts; if each party had an average of 10 solicitors per district, there would be need for 3,500,000 solicitors.

[46]Numbers of political volunteers vary from four to six million an election year.

will not be readily accomplished; and the parties will continue stressing direct national fund-raising programs that emphasize large contributors, such as the President's Club and the Republican Congressional Boosters Club.

Yet there are conditions under which local organizations—even those with the best-intentioned leadership—find it extremely difficult to solicit broadly or to share funds. First, there are the one-party areas where the main election contests are between party members in primaries and party organizations do not play an active role. Despite party dominance, organization is particularly weak because campaigns are built around candidates, each with his own following. . . . If they face tough primary fights or general election competition, they need every dollar for their own campaigns; if they do not, there is little incentive to campaign at all—or to raise funds. Second, there are rural areas where distance counts heavily against broadly-based solicitation. Third, there are urban areas which contain low-income residents and where political dollars are scarce.

Too Few Resources

The party leader is working with two scarce resources, money and manpower, and his allocations must be made according to greatest needs. He must consider the demand for workers to participate in registration drives or get-out-the-vote drives, to put up posters, lick envelopes, and all the rest. In his scheme of things, the organization of door-to-door fund raising may have low priority, particularly if he has some reliable traditional source of funds. Moreover, he knows or soon learns that some volunteers do not like to ask others for money. . . .[47]

What Does It All Mean?

What does this mean to the average American voter? Are his perceptions of party still viable? The composite record of Congress so far in the 1970s is that the average Democrat votes with the party on 61 percent of the recorded votes. The Republicans have voted with their party in 51 percent of the roll-call votes.[48] In the same period the success rate of the conservative coalition of southern Democrats and Republicans dropped to the

---

[47]From Herbert E. Alexander, "Links and Contrasts Among American Parties and Party Subsystems," in *Comparative Political Finance: The Financing of Party Organizations and Election Campaigns,* ed. Arnold J. Heidenheimer (Lexington, Mass.: Heath, 1970), pp. 74–75, 98–100.

[48]"Nixon Support in Congress Hits Low in 1973," *Congressional Quarterly: Weekly Report,* 19 January 1974, p. 99.

Wright—Miami Daily News

(Wright in *Miami Daily News*, 1974. By permission.

lowest level since 1966.[49] In 1973, for example, support for President Nixon showed Senate Democrats supporting him 37 percent of the time and opposing him 51 percent. The spread of support–opposition for the president was similar for House Democrats. However, the average Republican in the Senate and the House supported their party's elected executive nearly two-thirds of the time. Obviously, as the scandal of Watergate continued to grow, this support waned. Constituency pressure for removal of the president, combined with the increasing likelihood that he would be impeached by the House and convicted by the Senate, forced numbers of Republicans to reassess their support. In the last days of the Nixon administration, even the most vocal defenders of the president encouraged his resignation for *the good of the country*, to say nothing of Republican electoral prospects. Yet to be seen is the long-range impact of the large freshman class of liberal mavericks elected to Congress in 1974.

As both titular head of his party and chief of state, the president holds a peculiar position in the American party system. Conflicts between the two roles are usually suppressed for the mutual benefit of both, but Watergate and the ensuing investigations and cover-up trials demonstrated that this dual role can often come into conflict. When it does, it becomes *every man for himself*.

[49]"Influence of Conservative Coalition Declined in 1973," *Congressional Quarterly: Weekly Report*, 2 February 1974, p. 198.

146

In this instance Republicans have become overwhelmed with the fallout from the Agnew resignation and the illegal indiscretions of the Committee to Re-Elect the President. Party representatives had to place themselves in opposition to Mr. Nixon in order to extricate themselves from his mistakes. This is not to say that blatant political considerations were the sole basis for the growing clamor among Republicans for Nixon's resignation. The evidence of malfeasance in office convinced even the most die-hard Nixon sympathizers that there were sufficient reasons for his removal. Because the Republican party hierarchy had nothing to do with the Watergate scandals,[50] it was only natural that they should wish to dissociate the party as quickly as possible. And, with an apparently attractive and experienced alternative in the form of Vice-President Ford waiting in the wings, the desire for a rapid change was even greater.

It is difficult to determine whether President Ford's vetoes will lead to a period of confrontation with Congress or one of mutual respect and cooperation. Indeed, Democratic victories in the 1974 Congressional elections seemed to create as many problems as blessings for the Democratic majority. Subsequently, a "conservative" reaction in the home districts has led to a careful reevaluation by many of the entering freshmen that may serve to reestablish some of the previous voting patterns among both Congressional Democrats and Republicans.

What Are the Roles of the Party at the State Level?

But what about party voting patterns at the state level? Until now we have been primarily interested in the role of parties as national entities. Patterns of party influence vary in form and intensity throughout the United States and are not easily contrasted.

The reasons for this are several and varied. To begin with, there are wide differences in party competition among the states. There are southern states where Republican politicians come in contact with the legislature only by visiting the state capital and northern states where Democratic legislators have a status only a notch above that of interloper—so dominant are the major parties in their localities. Under conditions of one-party rule, factions lay plans and struggle for ascendancy somewhat in the fashion of political

[50]The final report of the Senate Watergate Committee specifically noted that the regular Republican party had not only been excluded from CREEP; but had played almost no role in the presidential contest. They had had no relationship with either the president's reelection efforts or the cover-up that followed the Watergate breakin.

parties, and perform some of their functions as well, but all this bears only a dim resemblance to the idea of responsible party government.

In two states, Nebraska and Minnesota, state legislators are elected on ballots shorn of party designations. Although this leads to a nominal "nonpartisanship," other group commitments tend to take the place of the parties. In Minnesota, the House and Senate each have Liberal and Conservative caucuses which function in a party capacity, nominating candidates for the principal offices, controlling committee chairmanships, and otherwise directing the affairs of the legislature. The presence of party is felt in the open attachment of most Liberals to the Democratic-Farmer-Labor party and of many Conservatives to the Republican party. Proving further that party spirit cannot be legislated away, Liberal and Conservative caucus ("party") lines can be distinguished on certain types of roll-call votes.

A second obstacle to generalization about state legislative parties is that they function in disparate environs and under variable conventions. . . . [Finally], just as party structures differ throughout the country, the legal–constitutional systems within which party processes are carried on differ from state to state.

Comparative analysis of state legislative parties is hindered most of all, however, by "the problem," the variable practice with respect to roll-call votes in the legislatures. . . .

What Is the General Function of State Parties?

Despite the obstacles to systematic comparison of the role of political parties in fifty state capitals, the general contour of party behavior can be [outlined]. . . .

1. The model of a responsible two-party system—disciplined and unified parties presenting genuine policy alternatives—is met more nearly in certain northern state legislatures than in Congress. New York, Connecticut, Massachusetts, Rhode Island, and Pennsylvania have all considerably more "party voting" than is found in the usual state legislature. These states are distinguished by a high degree of urbanization, impressive industrialization, and competitive two-party systems. In states where rural–urban cleavage tends to coincide with major party divisions (rural Republicans versus urban Democrats), it is predictable . . . that conflict between the parties will be fairly frequent and sometimes intense. In contrast, party voting appears to be found much less frequently in rural, less populous states.

2. As in Congress, party battles in the legislatures are episodic. A great deal of legislative business is transacted with a minimum of contro-

versy. General consensus at the roll-call state is common, and in many legislatures well over one-half of the roll-call votes are unanimous. . . . This is true even in states where substantial disagreement between the parties is found, as in Pennsylvania. A conception of party which includes the notion that Democrats spend most of their time quarreling or bargaining with Republicans (and vice versa) over legislation is a gross distortion of reality, with perhaps the exception of a state or two.

3. Party unity fluctuates from issue to issue: party lines are firm on some kinds of questions, rarely visible on others, and, despite the appeals of party leaders, usually collapse on still other kinds.

4. It seems safe to say that in most states parties stay in business by being flexible as to policies. They veer and tack as electoral winds dictate.

5. There is apparently no counterpart in the state legislatures to the conservative coalition of Republicans and southern Democrats which sometimes dominates Congress. Party lines are crossed in the states, to be sure, but the biparty combinations appear to lack the spirit and continuity of the congressional prototype.

6. In northern states distinguished by rigorous party competition in the legislatures, party lines are highly visible on liberal–conservative issues. The Democratic party ordinarily originates and lends considerable support to legislation favorable to the interests of labor, minorities, and low-income groups. . . . The Republican party generally is concerned with fostering the interests of the business community, and this objective is likely to take the form of resisting legislation backed by organized labor or of blocking new regulation of business. . . . In a word, socioeconomic-class legislation often serves as a rallying point for each party.

7. Party conflict often is generated on issues of narrow partisan interest. . . . The welfare and survival of the party is a persistent theme in both legislation and legislative maneuvers. Accordingly, conflict is common on patronage and appointments, organizational and procedural matters in the legislatures, election law (especially reapportionment), bills and resolutions designed to embarrass the state administration, and measures to increase state control over municipal governments (especially where the state legislature is controlled by the Republicans and the big-city administrations are controlled by the Democrats). In sum, organizational party interest cuts through a variety of public policy questions, and its presence is felt even though dissimulated in debate. . . .[51]

[51]From Keefe and Ogul, op. cit., pp. 316–320.

Then it appears that, at both the state and national levels, elected officeholders are more reflective of their constituents' political philosophies than of any pervasive national political ideology. Variations seem to be the rule, although both parties stand for certain broad general philosophical directions that are widely supported by a majority of their adherents. Yet, even if both parties do project a certain defined image to the electorate, they nevertheless recognize that in the wake of Watergate, great difficulties face party organization.

Great Difficulties Face Both Parties

Speaking to a group of midwestern Republicans shortly before becoming president, Vice-President Gerald Ford noted that the political lessons of 1972 were that, "never again must Americans allow an arrogant, elite guard of political adolescents like CREEP (Committee to Re-Elect the President) to bypass the regular Republican party organizations." He called for "broadening the base of Republican participation—the young people, the working people, the farmers, the academians, the businessmen."[52]

Like their Republican colleagues, Democrats also see the need to strengthen party ties. As Robert Strauss, Democratic national chairman, noted in his report to the Democratic party, public trust in political institutions is at an all-time low.[53] Indeed, both Republicans and Democrats have been adversely affected by the Watergate investigations. But in recognizing these problems—most importantly, the need to rebuild the faith of Americans in their political structure—both parties hope to once again become "examples of governmental and political responsiveness."[54]

What, then, does the future hold for American political parties? At midpoint in the 1970s, we can look in retrospect at the major threats to the viability of both the Democrats and Republicans. The year 1972 produced a fiasco in the Democratic camp that guaranteed their loss of the presidency. This historic defeat closed the "dawning of the age of McGovern" in short order. Speculations are still rampant on the long-range implications. Then came the final and official report of the "Sam Ervin Show," with the investigations of impeachment by the House and the resignation of Richard Nixon as president; and the Republican Party had their cross to bear—

[52]Text of an address by Vice-President Gerald Ford to the Midwest Republican Leadership Conference, Chicago, 30 March 1974, pp. 2, 6.

[53]Robert S. Strauss, *Responsibility and Opportunity: The Democratic Party, 1973–1974. A Report of the Chairman* (Washington, D.C., Democratic National Committee, 1974), p. 36.

[54]Ibid., p. 42.

living under the cloak of the Watergate disaster. In both situations loyalty to the party chief evaporated as individual candidates scurried for their own political survival.

But What of the Future of the Two Parties?

It is one of the comforting beliefs of the conventional wisdom that social systems contain their own self-adjusting mechanisms. . . . [T]he self-correcting system of checks and balances that generations have confidently trusted to keep the American separation of powers in a well tuned equilibrium [is such as an example]. And we have long had similar hopes for the party system. For the ills of unresponsiveness and dissatisfaction in the electorate, the cure is said to be a readjustment of party appeals (spurred by competition) and a consequent realignment of party loyalties in the electorate.

Is it possible that realignment may yet come as a response to the disaffection with the parties? Indeed, it is possible. The external symptoms that ordinarily precede a realignment are evident: a third-party surge named Wallace and the instability of the vote from one election to another, for instance. It may be that the increasing disposition of voters to identify as independents and to split tickets will be reversed by a party realignment restoring the aggregate confidence in and identification with the parties.

The realignment, however, appears to be overdue. Perhaps the most striking aspect of the 1968 elections was the fact that in the end there was no realignment, that after a year of the startlingly unexpected there was a reversion in the major parties to old old voting patterns. Furthermore, an issue or ideological axis on which realignment might take place has not appeared. Burnham suggests that perhaps we are inching toward an alignment of the disadvantaged and the educated successful (the advantaged) against the strata streets in between. If that is the case, it would appear to produce a result not greatly different from the realignment strategy—the southern strategy—that a number of advisors were urging on President Nixon, whereby the Republican party would court the loyalty of middle America and its silent majority.[55] Alternatively . . . realignment cannot take place once the voters' confidence in the party system has slipped below a certain point. A considerable number of Americans may simply . . . [be deciding] to rely on cues and political organizations outside the parties. Thus they will have no incentive to change party loyalties; new non-party symbols and loyalties will be added to the old party ties.

[55]Walter Dean Burnham, *Critical Elections and the Mainsprings of American Politics* (New York: Norton, 1970), pp. 137–140.

Perhaps, too, our politics—at least for the moment—are too complex to produce the simple dualism—any dualism—around which voters can cohere in a new alignment.

What Could Cause the Parties to Regain Control?

Even if the parties should find an issue and a catalytic event for realignment, however, it is by no means certain that realigning will restore the parties to their political preeminence. Realignment is no solution to the erosion of party organizational capacity to nominate and elect candidates. Nor is it any guarantee that large numbers of Americans will then return to an unswerving partisanship or that they will again mark the straight party ticket. The truth is that a party realignment is only a readjustment of the parties to new cleavages in the society. It may even depend on the very kinds of confidence in party and need for party symbols that the American parties appear to be losing.

For the moment, therefore, a good many signs point beyond the cure of realignment to a decline of the parties generally and of party organizations in particular. Both the parties' dominance of our electoral politics and the stability of the two-party system have rested on the acceptance of the party label as a cue for action. Large numbers of voters now have cues and sources of information outside the parties. Many of them also are less and less inclined to accept the omnibus commitments that party loyalty implies. They want to pick and choose among issues and candidates. Party loyalty demands that they buy a whole collection of commitments; in effect, it asks them to divide the political world into two simple categories, ours and theirs. The simple, dichotomized choice making that party loyalty within a two-party system demands no longer agrees with an educated, issue-oriented, politically sophisticated electorate. Knowing, confident, even assertive adults are less and less willing to surrender their selective judgment in favor of an unquestioning loyalty to party.

To look at it another way, the Republican–Democratic loyalties of the American two-party system actually require a politics of low intensity and little involvement in issues. The willingness of millions of voters to buy the diverse bag of candidates and issues assumes that they have no strong feelings about any of them. Loyalty to the party as a least common denominator can bind diverse populations into one party electorate only when the other lines that divide them are weaker. But what happens when large numbers of voters repeatedly feel more strongly about a candidate or an issue than they do about a party? What happens when large numbers of voters decide that they no longer need the ready-made, all-purpose, prepackaged judgment of a political party? Above all, what happens when that voter disenchantment takes place at the same time that candidates find ways of communicating with voters outside the usual channels of the party organization?

Those questions are rhetorical, and the answers are indeed implicit in the questions. Yet, it must be clear that all this argument does not predict the imminent decline and fall of the political parties. . . . [T]here are, indeed, ample signs that the parties have and will continue to have a creative role in American politics, even if they no longer dominate the channels and resources of our electoral politics. There are hundreds of thriving party organizations, aggregate trends to the contrary notwithstanding. There are still thousands of ardent party loyalists, and millions of voters still cast straight party tickets every four years. When we talk of decline, we do not mean death.

Parties Are Alive —If Not Well

So the parties are alive, if not well, in America. But they will increasingly become a part of a richer, more diverse pattern of American politics. We may well see the repeated emergence of third parties as expressions of deeper discontent with the parties and American society. . . . The number of independent and minor-party candidates for Congress [has] more than doubled . . . and . . . independent and third-party candidates [have been] . . . elected to the Senate . . . [and a governorship]. Other political organizations—interest groups, candidate organizations, ideological movements, ad hoc issue organizations—will assume a greater importance in the electoral politics once dominated by the parties. . . . [I]n fact, organized labor's efforts registered close to five million voters. . . . And all these non-party organizations will reflect and embrace the new ideological politics in a way the parties never could. In this respect it is worth noting that the amateur voluntary organizations within the parties are probably less vital and influential today than they were in the 1950's.[56] Issue-oriented and ideological activists increasingly turn outside the party.

What seems likely, in other words, is a politics of greater fluidity and instability, carried on by a wider range of political organizations. The parties will exert their influence over nominations, elections and policy making, but so will other political organizations. In many instances the personable candidate—aided by the media—will attract the voter loyalties

[56]James Q. Wilson, *The Amateur Democrat* (Chicago: University of Chicago Press, 1962).

and activists' labors that the party organizations once did. The erosion of the one, stable, long-run loyalty in American politics will contribute to a politics more frequently dominated by the short-term influences of the charismatic candidate or the very salient issue. In its evanescent fluidity, its lack of continuity, and its lack of predictability, the new electoral politics may increasingly resemble . . . the nonpartisan politics of school board elections in many American cities.

Diversity and Specialization Characterize the Change in Parties

Diversity and specialization thus characterize the changes in American politics. The diversity goals and needs, multiplied by the intensity of feelings about them, cannot easily be met by two traditionally pragmatic, compromising political parties. Voters, too, appear to want more specialized cues for political choice and action, and the activists among them want to discriminate among the causes and people for whom they will work. All of that leads to an increased specialization and division of labor among the organizations. Just what specialized role we may anticipate for the parties is not altogether clear. Some voters will still find the party a useful cue-giver and an effective vehicle for their political goals. Indeed, there will be locales in which the party organizations maintain control of nominations and elections and in which the party loyalty of the electorate remains firm—that is, the old party roles persist. Where the parties do lose some measure of those traditional roles, they may well turn into more ideological, issue-oriented parties. The changes will be less marked in areas in which the electorates are less educated and less politicized. Where voters are politically more sophisticated and less dependent on party symbols, ideological activists will more often control the party organization.

Political life in the United States without the guiding dominance of two assertive political parties is not unthinkable. Much of our local politics has been non-partisan in reality as well as in name for some time. But a diminished role for the parties throughout much more of electoral politics suggests impacts of a greater magnitude. The question of the consequences not only for the political processes but for the quality of American democracy itself troubles many observers.

Burnham has put the point directly and simply:

Political parties, with all their well-known human and structural short-comings, are the only devices thus far invented by the wit of Western man that can, with some effectiveness, generate countervailing collective power on behalf of the many individually powerless against the relatively few who are individually or organizationally powerful. . . .[57]

The American parties—and all others for that matter—mobilize sheer numbers against organized minorities with other political resources, and they do so in the one avenue of political action in which numbers of individuals count most heavily—elections. Thus the parties have classically been the mechanisms by which newly enfranchised and powerless electorates rose to power. The old-style urban machine in the United States, for example, was the tool by which the powerless, often recently arrived, urban masses won control of their cities from older, largely "Wasp" elites. In a more fluid politics of bargaining among a larger number of political organizations and millions of more uncommitted voters, the fear is that the advantage will be on the side of the well-organized minorities with other political resources.

The Decline of Parties May Have Elitist Consequences

The decline of the parties, therefore, could have ironic elitist consequences. The educated, sophisticated, involved political minority may help impose a new kind of political tyranny on the less involved, lower SES segments of the electorate. It increasingly imposes an ideological politics that lacks salience and may indeed be incomprehensible to the less sophisticated. At the same time it contributes to the decline of the most useful cue-giver, the major political party. The removal of the political party as an organizer and a symbol in our present nonpartisan elections helps upper SES elites, both of the right and the left, to dominate those politics. The political party, in other words, is the political organization of the masses who lack the cues and information—as well as the political resources of status, skills, and money—to make a major impact on public decisions via other means. The diminished power of the parties makes the game of politics more difficult for them to play and win.

The second set of broad consequences that we fear will result from the decline of the party is the partial loss of the "unplanned consequences" of their electoral strivings: the stability and continuity the parties and their loyal electorates have brought to American politics and also their recruitment of political and governmental leadership. But most important of all, how will the country build majorities without the parties? How are we to find majorities among the congeries of adamant, articulate, even militant

[57]Walter Dean Burnham, "The End of American Party Politics," *Trans-action* (December 1969): 20.

groups? However imperfectly and hastily, the two American parties do piece together majority coalitions. American presidents do enjoy the legitimacy of majority (or virtual majority) support at their election, and the party majority in legislatures at least permits them to organize for action. Alternatively, do we face the kind of political immobilism that results from a deeply felt, intransigent splintering of political organizations and sentiments? As the cohesion of the parties in the Congress dips lower and lower, what other mechanism or loyalty is there to organize majorities for action?

It may be that the parties will come out of their present decline in ways and to degrees we cannot foresee. Were the party organizations to acquire the resources for distributing the new campaigning skills to candidates, they would redress their recent losses to the new campaign technicians and to other political organizations. The result might be a considerable revival of the parties. Or it is possible that public sentiment might lead to new electoral machinery that would restore the party role. Perhaps, too, the parties would fare better if the current mood of national self-doubt and political cynicism were to lift. But for the short-run, at least, important trends are afoot in the parties and in American politics. Regardless of whether they last, they will have their short-run effects and the long run is often nothing more than a series of short-run trends. . . .[58]

[58]From Sorauf, op. cit. pp. 415–420.

5

Campaign Fever: What Are the Symptoms?

"Politics ... has become one of our most neglected, our most abused and our most ignored profession. It ranks low on the occupational list of a large share of the population; and its chief practioners are rarely well or favorably known. No education, except finding your way around a smoke filled room, is considered necessary for political success. 'Don't teach my boy poetry,' a mother recently wrote the Headmaster of Eton; he's going to stand for parliament.'"

So spoke John Kennedy in the Spring of 1957 to a group of Syracuse University graduates. His observations continue to hold true today. A rather famous Gallup Poll of a few years ago demonstrated that mothers wanted their sons to grow up to be President, but not politicians. This despairing look at politics seems to be ingrained in the minds of most individuals. If a candidate can convince the voter that he is independent minded, sincere, and has a high degree of integrity, he runs for office not as a party politician, but rather as an independently minded individual seeking to serve his country—a statesman.

Training Is the Important Factor

Yet few other professions take as much preparation or require such a rigorous developmental period before gaining success as does politics. It is a political truism that "few candidates spring full-bloom upon the political scene. Years of preparation, learning, and building precede most success-ful campaigns."[1]

Training, preparation, planning, fighting the odds, and often "just plain luck," are needed to gain a political victory. But not everyone should run for public office. Candidates vary and so do the circumstances and offices they seek. The voter must decide if the individual candidate meets his own criteria for that office. Because an individual was a success in one particular profession, it cannot necessarily be generalized that he will, therefore, be successful in politics. The informed voter, like the informed candidate, must be able to recognize and analyze the advantages and disadvantages of anyone seeking public office.

Thus, every two years (and sometimes more often) Americans are called upon to make these electoral decisions. They become starkly aware that "campaign fever" is in the air. Potential office holders and potential candidates multiply by the thousands. Everyone of them is convinced that his particular version of campaigning holds the secret to success. Realists know that very little in campaigning is really new; only new combinations of tactics are devised. Public contact, media manipulation, research, profes-sional candidate management, and the general "hurrah" of electioneering has become more sophisticated; but little innovation has occurred, although refinements have taken place.

Why then, the tremendous effort on the part of the candidates, and their volunteers or purchased election teams to convince everyone that their position and approach deserves special consideration. Obviously, the desire to win—to be elected, and perhaps even to serve the "public inter-est" is of paramount importance.

But what is the "hurrah" all about? How does it work—or does it? Richard Harris, a contributer to the *New Yorker* magazine, asked this same question. As a temporary resident in a small town on Long Island, Harris became curious as to how the election process actually worked from "the other end of the firm handshake." His warmly humorous, as well as critical record of these hectic weeks, gives the student of politics an excel-lent inside look at a comparatively moderate election effort. Various issues, such as Vietnam, the invasion of Cambodia, and the use of atomic energy that impacted this race have merely changed to become the inflation, Middle East, or energy problems of today. Then, as now, management firms played little or no role in the campaign. Polls, when used, were not too sophisticatedly employed, while many of the "do's and don't's," of politics were violated. Yet it has been our experience that while statewide and

---

[1]"Grooming Yourself for Public Office Is Exact, and Exacting Science," *Campaign Insights* (Wichita: Campaign Associates, Inc., November 1971), pp. 1, 5.

national campaigns, and even many big-city mayors and some Congress-men, employ the latest campaign approaches and techniques, this campaign is probably more typical of the average attempt during the last twenty years at political victory in America.

However, while this campaign is reflective of politics during the 1960's and 1970s, more and more candidates are finding themselves faced with the task of establishing their image to a larger and ever more varied electorate. As the electorate increases, the distance between the candidate and the electorate increases, forcing him to seek other alternatives to the "quick smile and firm handshake." Those seeking office find it necessary to expand their use of all available media, particularly television, and to exercise an even harder reliance on polling and modern management techniques. In turn, this change costs money, and large amounts of it.

Thus, as the size of the electorate increases, the task of knowing the candidate, and the candidate knowing his constituency becomes more difficult. Parties and candidates must seek new methods of getting their message across. For good or ill, these methods may come to dominate the American political scene. Harris sees some of these changes taking place in this campaign.

How's It Look*

Shortly after Labor Day last year, as I was walking along the main street of a small town on eastern Long Island where I had rented a house for a few months, a man approached me, smiling broadly, and grasped my hand. At first, I thought he was an old friend whom I hadn't recognized. But he wasn't; he was running for office and he wanted me to vote for him. He was so earnest that I hadn't the heart to tell him I was a legal resident of New York City and couldn't give him my vote if I wanted to. In following weeks, I had similar encounters with half a dozen men who were candidates for the New York State Assembly, for the State Senate, for judgeships in one court or another, or for posts as delegates to the state's 1967 constitutional convention. All of these meetings were similarly awkward, and I grew increasingly curious about what it was like, from day to day, to be on the other side of the firm handshake. Finally, after being stopped by a candidate for the Assembly who was standing in a shopping center amid a litter of discarded and presumably unread handbills and looking very much the underdog he claimed to be, I decided to see what I could find out about the

*From Richard Harris, "How's It Look?" *The New Yorker*, 8 April 1967, pp. 48–50, 52, 55–56, 58, 60, 63–64, 66, 68–70, 75–77, 80–82, 85–87, 90–92, 95–97, 100–102, 107–108, 110, 112–114, 117–118, 120–122, 125–126, 128, 130–132, 134–137. (All footnotes in this chapter have been consecutively renumbered for the convenience of the reader.)

business of campaigning for public office. Most of the candidates who had stopped me had conveyed the impression that they would never have much more to say than "Vote for me," but friends in the area told me that there was one really interesting race—that for the seat in the House of Representatives from the First Congressional District of New York.

I had learned from a proliferation of bumper stickers and posters that the two main congressional candidates were named Pike and Catterson, and I now discovered that Pike was Otis G. Pike, a Democrat, who had been in the House for six years, and Catterson was James M. Catterson, Jr., a Republican, who was head of the Rackets Bureau in the Suffolk County District Attorney's office. (A third candidate, Domenico Crachi, Jr., running on the Conservative Party ticket, did little campaigning and got less attention.) Catterson had never before run for public office, and the papers didn't have much to say about him except that he was thirty-six years old, a graduate of Niagara University and the St. John's University School of Law, a veteran of the Korean war, and a former Assistant United States Attorney. A couple of papers did describe him as "aggressive" and "combative," and the Islip *Press,* a staunchly Republican weekly, said that he was expected to give Pike "his toughest fight" to date. As the incumbent congressman, Pike got far more extensive press coverage. He was forty-five years old, a graduate of Princeton College *(magna cum laude)* and Columbia Law School (class president), the father of three children, and a veteran of the Second World War, in which he had flown a hundred and twenty missions as a Marine Corps fighter pilot. For seven of the past twelve years, during which he had practiced law in Riverhead, his home town, he had also served as a justice of the peace, which in New York State is the rural equivalent of an urban magistrate. Suffolk County is said to be the fastest-growing county in the nation, and the First Congressional District, which has six hundred and fifty thousand residents and makes up the greater part of the county (the Babylon-Huntington section of Suffolk is in the Second District), is the most populous in the state. It contains almost twice as many registered Republicans as it does Democrats, and I gathered from my reading that Pike was regarded in local political circles as something of a miracle man. In an article in the Long Island *Press,* one of the two daily papers in the area (the other is *Newsday*), Domenic Baranello, the Democratic County Chairman, described Pike as a man who "runs for office as a Democrat, is elected by Republicans, has liberal leanings, and [uses] a conservative approach." This possibly explained another feat of political legerdemain—Pike's achieving a comparatively high rating of forty-two per cent for his congressional voting record from both the left-wing Americans for Democratic Action and the right-wing Americans for Constitutional Action. However Pike had managed it, he had clearly built up a reputation that was out of all proportion to the length of his service in Congress. In fact, such were his popularity and his political appeal, I learned, that earlier in the year the Suffolk County Republicans had offered to support him for a State Supreme Court judgeship, with a fourteen-year term and a salary of thirty-seven thousand dollars a year, presumably so that the Republicans would have some chance of capturing his seat in the House. After announcing that he was quite able to multiply thirty-seven thousand by fourteen, Pike turned the offer down, raising his prestige to a new height among both Republicans and Democrats. The New York *Times* has called him "a brilliant public speaker," and in various other papers he has been called a politician of "fierce independence" (he has frequently spoken out publicly against the President and his programs), a "party maverick" (he led the fight against the nomination of Robert F. Kennedy for the Senate in 1964), a "highly effective legislator" (in six years he authored more legislation that was passed into law than all the other representatives from Long Island combined, his most notable accomplishment being the Fire Island National Seashore bill), and a man with "unique political wit" (every election, he sent all the newspapers in his district a Blast Pike Kit, giving them information on his most vulnerable spots, so that reporters wouldn't have to waste time studying his record).

Since Pike was the more experienced politician and obviously a highly successful campaigner, I decided to follow his side of the race, if he would let me. Around the middle of September, I was in Washington visiting friends, and I arranged to see him at his office, in the Longworth House Office Building, across Independence Avenue from the Capitol. He is a tall man with wavy gray hair, blue eyes, and a face that is handsome despite a sprinkling of rather deep scars, which, I decided, must have been caused by a youthful bout with acne. He gave me the firm handshake I had expected and waved me to a leather chair facing his desk. I told him I assumed that many members of Congress would be reluctant to let a reporter in on anything but the more superficial aspects of a campaign but that I was hoping he would let me see from the inside how he ran his. Fingering his bow tie—the only kind of tie he ever wears, I was to learn—he thought for a moment and then nodded briskly, "I'd be delighted to have you along," he said. "The more people know about politics, the better off we'll all be." He added, with a grin, "I'm clean."

There's Really No Beginning or End

Congress was still in session, and I asked when he expected his campaign to begin. "I've been campaigning ever since the last election," Pike answered. "There's really no beginning or end. My wife and children live in Riverhead, and I have a small apartment here. Throughout the year, when we're in session, I go home weekends, and it's a pretty rare Saturday or Sunday that I don't go to three or four affairs—banquets, civic-club lunches or dinners, dedication ceremonies, dances, cocktail parties, educational conferences. It's all part of campaigning, and it goes on year round." This sort of off-time schedule, on top of the crushing work load that any conscientious member of Congress carries, struck me as being a sound argument for President Johnson's proposal that terms for representatives should be extended to four years, but when I mentioned this Pike shook his head. "No," he said emphatically. "When the proposal—in the form of a Constitutional amendment—came before the House Judiciary Committee earlier this year, I testified against it. In these days of big government and sprawling bureaucracy, the people's representatives should be more available than ever—and just as answerable to them at the polls. It's vital for us to be close to the people."

The next time I saw Congressman Pike was a few days later while he got close to the people at an annual dinner and dance given by the Southampton branch of the Polish National Alliance. I met him in front of the Pulaski Hall—a large gray stucco recreation center—and we stopped to chat for a few minutes before we went inside. "An affair like this is worth ten political rallies," he told me. "I concentrate mostly on going to nonpolitical events, like this one. I don't want to talk issues, and I'm not going to give a partisan speech of any kind. I just want the people to see me and hear me. Toward the end of the campaign, I'll go to some large Democratic rallies—mainly because they're covered by the press, and provide a good forum for getting your views across through the papers—but tonight is far more typical of my campaigning. Like any minority group, the Polish people are grateful for recognition. They'll appreciate my coming, and they'll go home and tell their friends that their congressman took the trouble to be with them. I like the Polish people, too. They're tough—they work hard and play hard and drink and fight—but they're good people." He smiled and added, "Not to mention the fact that forty per cent of my home town and ten per cent of the entire district is Polish."

There were around three hundred people at the dinner (fruit cup, sirloin, mashed potatoes, stringbeans, jello, coffee, and cookies), and when the main course was served Pike turned to a bulky man with a crew cut and closely cropped mustache who was seated next to him and said, "Every time I come here, I hope I'll get *kielbasa*. Why don't you ever give me *kielbasa?*" The man beamed and patted him on the shoulder. After the coffee was served, several men got up and delivered speeches in Polish, varying in length from fifteen minutes to three-quarters of an hour. Toward the end of the last, and longest, one, I noticed that Pike was making some notes on the back of a three-by-five-inch file card. A couple of minutes later, the master of ceremonies, a Riverhead lawyer named Charles Gatz, introduced Pike, who got up to give his speech. While it could scarcely have been characterized as brilliant, it seemed to me strikingly appropriate. After saying that he had never underestimated the Polish people since Gatz thrashed him in his first race for justice of the peace, he remarked that while he had been avidly following the speeches in Polish (laughter) he had got to thinking about how widely known the Poles were for their great athletes. "But to me the Polish people stand for far more than that," he went on. "They stand for justice, for faith, and for loyalty." He expanded on that theme with some eloquence for a couple of minutes, congratulated the audience on the millennial celebration of Christianity in Poland, mentioned that his secretary in Riverhead, who had worked for him for thirteen years, was Polish, and sat down. The speech took five minutes, and got the biggest hand of the evening.

Now a small band in the adjoining room began warming up, and soon burst into a whirling polka. Several people came over to shake hands with Pike and thank him for coming. As he was talking to a group of four men about the scourge of the golden nematode—a worm that attacks potatoes, which are eastern Long Island's major crop—and explaining that he had managed to get an appropriation of a quarter of a million dollars so that the Department of Agriculture could study the problem, a portly woman came up and took his arm. She introduced him to a pretty blond girl and a handsome dark-haired young man, both in their mid-twenties, and told him that he had helped get them admitted to this country.

"I'm glad I was able to do something right, for a change," Pike said, shaking hands with them, and asked how long they had been here.

"Two years next month," the girl answered. "And we just love it."

Pike told her that she spoke better English than he did, shook hands with them again, and started to leave.

The woman grabbed his arm and said, "There's a letter in the mail to you right now about her brother."

Pike looked slightly dismayed. "You mean he wants to come over, too?" She nodded, and he said, with a shrug, "I'll do what I can. But, remember, I can't work miracles."

As they walked away, he turned to me. "One of the biggest parts of my job is helping constituents," he said. "And one of the biggest problems is that once you succeed in helping someone, he comes to expect your help every time he wants something. And he gets sore if you don't, or can't, work it out."

Just then, a man with a seamed, weather-beaten face stopped hesitantly in front of Pike. "I sorry to bother," he said. Pike assured him that it was no bother at all, and the man smiled nervously and went on, "I don't speak English so good. I no want to bother, but I got problem." His problem, he explained haltingly, was that he had a retarded son and wanted to get him admitted to a special school. Pike shook his head sympathetically and said that he didn't know whether he could help but that if the man would write a letter to him at his office in Washington he would do what he could. Grinning broadly, the Pole clasped his hand, thanked him, and left.

"I don't think I can help," Pike said to me. "But he's one of those good men. He'll be grateful just for my trying."

A tall, spindly woman in a flowered dress called out as she hurried by, "How come you weren't at Luci's wedding?"

Pike smiled. "I wasn't invited," he answered. "I'm just a lowly congressman."

She waved a hand deprecatingly and went on.

I had gathered that President Johnson's popularity in the First Congressional District was not at an all-time high, and when I mentioned this Pike nodded and said, "Catterson claims that I appeal to the rebel in everyone, and that when I tweak the big man's nose people identify with me. Catterson has been going around saying that I'm not really as independent as I seem, but he's not getting very far with that."

Another man came up, and pumped Pike's hand, grinning. "I understand you're up for election this year, Otis," he said. "I didn't realize that. Who are you running against?"

Pike smiled and answered, "It's funny, Charlie, but I can never seem to remember his name."

A moment later, Pike said to me, "That's a good sign. It's surprising how many people don't know that members of the House are elected every two years. But it can be helpful. If they don't know there's an election, they haven't heard of Catterson, and if they haven't even heard his name by this time he's in trouble.

Don't Give the
Opponent Publicity

It was getting stuffy inside, so we strolled around the side of the dance floor and out the front door. It was a warm late-summer evening, and Pike suggested that we take a walk. As we set off, I asked him about his strategy for the campaign. "Right now my approach is to lie low," he said. "I used to smoke my opponent out, create an issue, drive him onto the defensive. But I think I'm ahead, so there's no reason to give him any publicity by locking horns."

I asked if it wasn't Catterson who had reason to do that, and he agreed.

"He's trying to, but so far he hasn't got hold of anything," Pike said. "Early in July, he went down to Washington to attend a three-day seminar put on by the Republican National Committee to give new candidates an idea of the best issues. So far, he's followed the Party line exactly—the war in Vietnam, inflation, and violence in the streets. I don't think he'll get very far with any of those. I support the Administration one hundred per cent on the war, and I think most of the voters do, too. As for inflation, it's true that prices are high, but so are wages, and unemployment is way down. Anyway, what would he suggest—wage and price controls? And the violence-in-the-streets pitch is a pure racist appeal. I've supported all the civil-rights bills, and I intend to go on supporting them. Sure, I want to go back to Congress, but I'm not going to crawl back."

I asked if there was any racial turmoil in his district to speak of, and he shook his head. "Oh, white people here may identify with white people in Watts or Cicero, but we have a very small colored population," he said. "It's simply not important. He's trying to create a racial issue where none exists."

We got on the subject of Pike's own issues, and he said, "My basic approach is that you should go on the offensive and stay there, and that you should have no more than three issues. The public will stop listening if you rain issues on their heads. They can't keep them all straight. As of now, there are a couple of things I plan to use. One is that a year ago last summer, when the Suffolk District Attorney resigned, the Republican Party passed over Catterson, who tried to get the job, and put in a man who had no previous experience in handling criminal matters. If Catterson wasn't good enough to be D.A., how can he be good enough to be congressman?"

Pausing, he reached into his inside coat pocket and handed me a couple of papers. They were a letter and a résumé addressed to him in August, 1965, by Catterson, who had been applying for a job on the staff of Pike's Subcommittee on Tactical Aircraft. "How can he say that I'm good enough for him to go to work for but not good enough for others to vote for?" Pike said. "I'm saving this one for the last week of the campaign."

In most political campaigns, I had long since decided, issues are like very beautiful women—widely admired but rarely approached. With this in mind, I remarked to Pike that Catterson's issues didn't seem to be issues at all, since no single congressman, and not even all congressmen together, could be held accountable for the war, high prices, and racial unrest. At the same time, I said, Pike's own issues, though they were more germane to the central question of who would be the better representative, still seemed rather peripheral.

Pike quickly agreed. "The first time I ran for Congress, in 1958, I lost," he said. "And I believe I lost because I tried to talk about the issues, in the

"GO FIND YOUR OWN ISSUE!"

same way the man I admired most in American politics, Adlai Stevenson, talked about the issues, I realized later that it just can't be done. To get such ideas across, you have to simplify them. Once you do, they become black and white. And once they're black and white, they're no longer true issues."

Stopping, he glanced around to make sure we were alone, and then he said, "Another peripheral issue could kill Catterson," and suggested that I read the last sentence of Catterson's résumé, which said, "Recently named one of 'Outstanding Young Man in America' by the United States Junior Chamber of Commerce."

"Isn't it true?" I asked.

"Not a word of it," Pike said. "The United States Junior Chamber of Commerce does pick ten Outstanding Young Men every year. But I had this checked out and found that what he was actually referring to is the Junior Chamber of Commerce of Montgomery, Alabama. It has an annual fund-raising gimmick—a book called 'Outstanding Young Men of America,' which has around eight thousand biographies in it. There's no charge for being listed, but it costs ten dollars to buy the book." Putting the papers back in his pocket, Pike added, "I hope I don't have to use this information. But I've heard that they have plans to run a dirty campaign—personally dirty. If that happens, I'll have no other choice."

If Too Many People Find Out
We're In Trouble

A couple of days later, at Pike's suggestion, I telephoned his campaign manager, Aaron Donner, a lawyer in Bay Shore, who works year round, on a part-time basis, as Pike's representative in the southwestern section of the First District, which is the most populous. Donner turned out to have a thunderous voice and a rumbling cascade of a laugh. "Come on out to the house tonight!" he roared. "You're the first person I've talked to who's even aware that a campaign is going on. If too many people find out, we could be in trouble."

When I arrived at Donner's house—a pleasant, rambling place on a quiet side street not far from the Bay Shore business district—I was met at the door by Mrs. Donner, a slim, pretty woman, in her mid-thirties with dark, curly hair and a warmly vivacious manner. "Come in, come in," she said. "Aaron's teaching the children how to answer the phone."

I went into the living room, and Donner, a heavyset man of around forty with a pleasant face and an unruly sheaf of brown hair falling forward above heavy horn-rimmed glasses, lumbered to his feet and shook hands. On a couch across from his easy chair were two girls and a boy, ranging in age from perhaps seven to eleven. Donner waved me to another easy chair and turned to the oldest of them, a girl with long blond hair and wide-set eyes. "All right, Laurie," he said, "when he calls he always says, 'This is Otis Pike.' Right?" Laurie nodded, and he said, "O.K., so when he says that, what do you say?"

Laurie giggled and answered, "Who?"

Donner boomed with laughter, "That's right, that's right," he said. "But draw it out more. Like this—'Whooo?'"

A moment later, Mrs. Donner sent the children off to watch television, and her husband leaned back in his chair and started talking to me about the campaign. "First of all," he said, "we run our campaign on the basis of ignorance, superstition, and fear—that is, *our* ignorance, superstition, and fear. We don't know what we might do wrong, so we try not to do much of anything. If we have to do something, what we do is based largely on what worked before. Above all, we avoid anything that could conceivably be turned against us. Of course, that eliminates almost everything." After another reverberating crash of laughter, he lit a cigarette, puffed on it reflectively for a moment, and continued, "Actually, we run a unique kind of campaign. It's uniquely subtle in the way Pike projects himself—as a man of independence and integrity and wit. It's not just that he has those qualities, it's the way he's able to convey an impression of them to an audience within a few minutes. Once he has spoken to a group, I doubt if anyone there forgets him. Another unique thing about our campaign is how inexpensive they are. We shouldn't spend more than twenty-five thousand dollars in all this year.''

This seemed to me an extraordinarily low figure for a district with a population of over six hundred thousand people, and I must have looked surprised or dubious, for Donner quickly went on, ''We don't believe that money wins elections. One reason we feel that way is that we *have* to, Pike being the most frugal man on Long Island. I once told him he was the only person I'd ever known who drove into a gas station in a Volkswagen and got only the emergency tank filled.''

I asked where the money would come from, and Donner explained that most of it had already been received. Around fourteen thousand dollars had been netted from a fifty-dollar-a-plate testimonial dinner for Pike that was held the previous spring, and four thousand more from a journal full of well-wishing advertisements bought by local businessmen which had been distributed at the dinner. When I asked if I could have a list of those who had attended the dinner, Donner said, ''No,'' and added, with a laugh, ''Masks are very In this year.'' He explained that many people who donated money to a political campaign didn't want it known, and that he was obliged to respect their wishes. ''I might say, though, that the defense industry was represented,'' he said. ''Representative Edward Hérbert, of Louisiana, who is a high-ranking Democrat on the Armed Services Committee, was the guest speaker, and it made their little hearts beat faster to be so close to the man who has so much to say about what arms are bought and where. But Otis has never given any commitment of any kind for money. He's very careful not to let people think they can put him in their pocket. As for the rest of the money, the Democratic Campaign Committee, in the House, gave him two thousand dollars. Then there will be five thousand or so coming in in small contributions. We'll probably spend a third on radio spots, newspaper ads, and an Election Eve television broadcast. Another third will pay mailing costs. The rest will go for posters, shopping bags, bumper stickers, campaign literature, pins, schoolbook covers, pencils—all with slogans or pictures of our candidate—plus miscellaneous expenses.''

Most People Vote Against Something

That explained how they spent the twenty-five thousand dollars, but it didn't explain—at least to my satisfaction—how they could run a campaign on so little money. When I brought this up, Donner replied, ''We found very early that we could save a great deal of money and avoid a great many

"THAT LAST HUSTLER SHAFTED YOU SO GOOD, MR. MAYOR, THAT WE'RE GOING TO HAVE TO REMOVE IT SURGICALLY."

(From *Campaign Insight*. By permission.)

headaches by staying away from public-relations men. They cost like hell, and they are likely to ruin when they rule. P.R. men have a very tenuous regard for the truth. They always want to soup things up until all resemblance to reality is lost. And in politics a lie that's exposed can kill you. During our first campaign, some fellows from big P.R. outfits who live out here came around and volunteered their time and their talents. We talked with them and looked at the campaign material they'd put together, and we were scared witless. As far as they were concerned, facts and statistics were simply things to be changed. Their time may have been valuable—to them—but their talents were in quotes, politically speaking. Basically, the P.R. approach is different. Politics has a deeply negative quality. We're convinced that most people vote against somebody rather than for somebody. They voted against Goldwater, not for Johnson. And that's what we concentrate on—making them vote against our opponent. The P.R. crowd feel they have to sell something positively. We believe in ridicule. They don't. It frightens them to death. We believe in wit. They don't. We believe in being amateurish. Our brochures look as if they were got up in our basement. But the P.R. men want to put out four-color brochures with dazzling artwork and their idea of how the Gettsyburg Address should have read. They just don't have sound political instincts. And after working with Pike for ten years I'm convinced that his political judgment is impeccable. I've never seen him be wrong on anything that counted."

We got around to the subject of how Donner had come to know Pike, and he told me they had met in 1955 at the Young Lawyers' Club of Suffolk County. At the time, Pike, who had grown up in the area and had practiced law there for four years, had been a justice of the peace for two years and was anxious to move onto a larger stage. The first step in that direction, he felt, was to take on the Suffolk County Democratic organization, which was boosting Governor Averell Harriman for the Presidential nomination in 1956, and start a splinter movement on behalf of Stevenson. "I thought Otis was crazy, but I went along with him," Donner said. "We had no money and we had no organization. We lined up twenty crazy housewifes to make phone calls and canvass their neighborhoods. To my astonishment, we won." In 1957, he continued, Pike said he had decided to run for Congress the following year, and Donner again felt that Pike was crazy but again went along with him. "In those days, a Democrat couldn't safely walk down the street in Suffolk County," he recalled. "Otis agreed with me that he didn't have a chance, but he said that if he got forty per cent of the vote he would consider it a victory and would go all out for 1960. We put on the original shoestring campaign—by selling red-white-and-blue shoestrings for a dollar a pair. They were not the most popular apparel that season. We got a few donations from Stevenson backers who were grateful for what Otis had done for Adlai, but we didn't get enough. There wasn't any money for posters, so we put out a press release saying they had all been torn down. In all, we spent less than three thousand dollars. The incumbent was Stuyvesant Wainwright. He was rich, and he had a solid Republican organization behind him, while all we had was a few committeemen bumping into each other, and he had been in office for six years and was well known in the district. When the returns were in, Otis had got forty-two per cent of the vote. We threw a moral-victory party, and went to work for 1960. Otis put together one very funny, very good speech, and went out and spoke everyplace he could. He got to be very much in demand, and by the next election a lot more people had heard of him—and he was a lot more expert as a campaigner."

I remarked that Pike had told me of his efforts to deal with the issues in his first campaign, and asked how he had changed his tactics in the second. "He chose the thing that Wainwright was most vulnerable on—his attendance record," Donner answered. "We studied it and found that he had been absent about a third of the roll-call votes. Everyplace Otis went, he would say, 'If you were paid twenty-two thousand five hundred dollars, wouldn't you go to work?' That put Wainwright on the defensive, and Otis kept him there for the rest of the campaign. By adding up the number of independents and Democrats and subtracting the total from the number of registered voters, we saw that six or seven per cent of the Republicans would control the election. That means that Pike couldn't campaign as a Democrat, so he used the old not-the-party-but-the-man routine. If you're a minority candidate, you have to appeal to people's belief in thinking for themselves—that is, you have to make them think that they *are* thinking for themselves. When the vote was counted, Otis had squeaked through by twenty-seven hundred votes. I don't think most of the voters even knew his name. They just knew that Wainwright had fallen down on the job. But Otis made sure they learned his name damned quickly. In 1962, his margin was thirty-two thousand, and in 1964 it was fifty-eight thousand. It won't be anywhere near that this time, though, without Goldwater on the ticket. Besides, I hear that Catterson is rough—a real fighter.''

**Not the Party
but the Man**

Because of the amorphous, constantly shifting nature of political campaigns, the breaks that are clearly good or bad stand out starkly, and are usually viewed with disproportionate elation or alarm by those involved. A few days after I visited Donner, he called to tell me that the Pike forces had suffered a catastrophe of the first order. He explained that although Pike ordinarily did very little in the way of sending out campaign literature, what he did send he felt was vitally important. Besides an annual report to his constituents—a reprint of a speech he inserted in the *Congressional Record* at the end of every session, which went out under his franking privilege to all registered voters, election year or not—he relied mainly on two brochures. "One of them is tailored for Republicans, and is mailed in envelopes stamped 'Republicans for Pike,'" Donner said. "That's not a front group but a bona-fide committee of Republicans that supports him. The other is tailored for Democrats and independents and is mailed in envelopes stamped 'Pike for Congress.' Altogether we mail about a hundred and seventy thousand brochures. Otis believes that most people don't get much mail and like to see a letter in their mailbox. He also believes that they are far more likely to open it if it has a real five-cent stamp, not a Pitney-Bowes imprint, on the envelope. Stuffing and sealing and stamping the envelopes is all done by hand, by our volunteer workers. Well, in the past we addressed the envelopes using the Addressograph machine in the Longworth Building in Washington, but this year the Democratic National Committee announced that it had some sort of computerized setup that would do the job at a considerable saving. After they had run off eighty thousand envelopes correctly, something went wrong and seventy thousand more envelopes marked 'Republicans for Pike' were indiscriminately addressed to Republicans, Democrats, and independents. The people running the machine took our address cards, transferred them onto magnetic tape according to a code—which turned out to be all mixed up—and then threw out the cards. That means we will have to go through the registration lists for every election district involved and make new cards for seventy thousand people. It will take weeks. Otis is in a rage. I wanted to sue the committee, but they don't have any money, and besides that wouldn't solve our problem. I suggested that we put together a new brochure—fortunately, the brochures haven't been printed up yet—and give it a neutral tone. Otis hasn't decided what to do. He's sitting down there in Washington fuming.''

A few minutes later, I telephoned Pike, and he was indeed fuming. ''I'm trying to control myself,'' he said. ''But it isn't easy. This is the worst thing that's ever happened to me during a campaign. It could cost me the election.'' He went on to say that he had decided against accepting Donner's suggestion, on the ground that it was essential for Republicans to receive brochures containing a strong endorsement drawn up by a Republican group. ''Without the Republicans, I'm lost,'' he said.

The next morning, I called him again and learned that he had come up with a solution that he hoped would save the Republican vote. This was a brochure with two sets of endorsements on the front page—one by the Republicans on the right, and one by the Democrats on the left side. ''Some democrats may be offended by getting envelopes with 'Republicans for Pike' on the front, but I don't think very many will,'' he said. ''I'm not overjoyed with the solution, but it seems like a workable compromise.'' As an inveterate non-reader of campaign literature, I was dubious about the dimensions of the problem, and suggested that he might test his theories about the importance of political mail by sending Catterson's brochures out in the misaddressed envelopes. He suggested that I never run for office and hung up.

When I received a copy of Pike's schedule for the last five weeks of the campaign the next morning, I was glad that I had no intention of ever running for office. His engagements, most of which involved making a speech, included an award-presentation dinner given by the Long Island *Press,* in Garden City; a dedication ceremony for a new terminal building at the Long Island MacArthur Airport, in Islip; a voter-registration session in Islip; the opening of his main headquarters, in Riverhead; a testimonial dinner in his honor, also in Riverhead; a banquet for the Long Island Association of Educational Secretaries, in Commack; hearings in Port Jefferson on a proposal to dredge Mt. Sinai Harbor; a rally at the Ronkonkoma Democrat Club; a dedication ceremony at the Brookhaven National Laboratories; a meeting of the Moriches Inlet Stabilization Committee; the opening of his headquarters in Patchogue; a conference with a group of Port Jefferson businessmen; a dinner at the Southold Democratic Club; a cocktail party at the Brookhaven Democratic Club; a rally at the Smithtown Democratic Club; a banquet at the Greenport-Southold Chamber of Commerce; a conference on a proposal to build an oceanographic institute in Montauk; a tour of Brookhaven shopping centers; the opening of his headquarters in Port Jefferson; a cocktail party at the East Hampton

"No matter what neighborhood we canvass today, we're covered."

(From *Campaign Insight*. By permission.)

Democratic Committee; a dance at the Riverhead Democratic Committee; the dedication of an ambulance at the Terryville Fire Department; a rally of the Three Village Democratic Club, in East Setauket; a luncheon with the Port Jefferson Rotary Club; an interview with the publisher of *Newsday;* the presentation of a flag that had flown over the Capitol in Washington to the Captree Lodge, Knights of Pythias, in Kings Park; a banquet for teachers from the Sachem High School district, in Sayville; the presentation of another Capitol flag to the Medford Avenue Elementary School, in Patchogue; a meeting with the student body of the Mercy High School, in Riverhead; a meeting with the students and faculty of the E. L. Vandermeulen High School, in Port Jefferson; a conference with representatives of the Machinists Union, in Riverhead; a rally at the Riverhead Democratic Club; a *Koffeeklatsch* in Blue Point; a dinner dance held by the Islip Town Democratic Committee, in Sayville; a tour of Islip shopping centers; a cocktail party given by the Southampton Democratic Committee; a meeting with representatives of the A.F.L.-C.I.O.'s Committee on Political Education, in Riverhead; the dedication of a fire truck at the Bohemia Fire Department; a cocktail party given by Republicans for Pike, in Islip; a cocktail party given by a group of supporters in Great River; a conference with members of the Oyster Institute, in Riverhead; a tour of the Gyrodyne helicopter plant in St. James; a meeting with the employees of the Allstate Insurance Company, in Huntington; the opening of a new office of the Security National Bank in Southold; a luncheon at the Smithtown Rotary Club; a visit to the Cenacle Retreat House, in Ronkonkoma; a meeting of the Senior Citizens Club in Wading River; a dinner at the Sag Harbor Chamber of Commerce; a rally run for the Smithtown Democratic Committee; a "Meet Your Congressman Night" in Southold; a tour of Smithtown shopping centers, the dedication of the Norwood Avenue Elementary School, in Port Jefferson; the dedication of the John F. Kennedy Junior High School, in Port Jefferson; and a Republicans for Pike cocktail party in Riverhead.

I Wouldn't See the Forest for the Trees

Concluding that I wouldn't see the forest if I followed Pike past all these trees, I decided to pick, more or less at random, a few of the events to attend with him. The first was the dedication of the new terminal at Long Island MacArthur Airport, at noon on October 1st. When I got there, I found Pike, a hundred and fifty other people, and the Suffolk County Air Force Base Drill Team and Bugle Corps inside the main entrance of the new building. Everybody was waiting for the arrival of Governor Rockefeller, who was to make a brief speech at the ceremony.

I asked Pike how things were going. "All I've accomplished so far is to talk to some other men who are running for office," he said.

I asked if he expected Catterson to be on hand, and he nodded. "I wouldn't be surprised if Rocky came in carrying him under his arm," he said.

A few minutes later, the band struck up and the crowd pushed forward to greet Rockefeller, who moved slowly through the room grinning, winking, shaking hands, and giving little fluttery waves to anyone he couldn't reach.

Catterson wasn't in the Governor's immediate entourage, but he hurried in a moment later, trying to catch up. A man of medium height with dark hair and the kind of expressionless face that would fit in well at a convention of F.B.I. men, he paused and shook hands with Pike. "How are you?" he asked. "Keeping busy?"

"Fine, fine," Pike said.

"I met your bride last night," Catterson went on.

"So I heard," Pike replied. "She's a real worker."

"I'll say she is," Catterson said, with a slight grimace, and, waving to him, moved on.

Laughing, Pike turned to me and explained that because the House had been in session he had been unable to attend the *Press* award dinner, so his wife, Doris, had gone in his place. "She went up to Catterson as soon as he came in," he said. "She introduced herself and took him by the arm to introduce him around—only to the most solid Democrats, it turned out. Then she suggested that they have a cozy little chat, and dragged him off to the bar. He didn't get to meet or talk to anyone who could have helped him.''

As Pike was talking, he kept an eye on Rockefeller, who was still moving through the crowd. A man began setting up a microphone for the Governor at the top of a flight of stairs leading to the terminal restaurant, and when Pike saw this he excused himself, saying, "It wouldn't do to go unnoticed," and headed for the stairs. At that moment, I saw a man behind the Governor nudge a man next to him and point to Pike. The two of them left the group and followed him. A moment later, Rockefeller swung around and started slowly up the stairs, followed by Catterson. By this time, Pike had reached the top and taken a place a few feet across the landing from the microphone. The two men from the Republican group hurried up the stairway just ahead of the Governor and, at the top, turned to face the crowd, pressing back against Pike in an effort to dislodge him from his prominent spot. He grabbed the railing at his side and held on as Rockefeller and Catterson took places beside him. A cluster of photographers went to work, and when the first flash bulb went off the three candidates beamed.

Pike's main headquarters, in Riverhead, was to be officially opened that afternoon at four o'clock, and I drove over there a little beforehand. On the way, I passed several large Rockefeller-Catterson billboards but not so much as a poster for Pike or for the Democratic gubernatorial candidate, Frank O'Connor, until I pulled up on West Main Street across from the headquarters—a one-story aluminum storefront, with the usual bunting, placards, posters, and flags in the windows. Inside was a room about fifty feet square, with yellow walls covered with more bunting, placards, posters, and flags. Several women were seated at desks answering telephones, and a dozen or so men and women were clustered around a long table in the center, on which were a coffee urn, a couple of gallon jugs of cider, and some doughnuts.

Donner was there, and when he saw me he shouted, "I just learned our opponent fell all over himself! He crashed a Chamber of Commerce dinner in Smithtown the other night, and they asked him to leave and then sent him a formal letter of censure. Apparently, he doesn't understand the non-partisan niceties.''

A dark-haired, bespectacled woman of around fifty, came in, and Donner introduced her to me as Mrs. Alison Russell, of East Hampton, who had been Wainwright's secretary in Washington and had stayed on to work for Pike for five years. After explaining to me that she was currently in charge of coordinating the mailing of the brochures, he turned to her and said, "You can expect to receive the eighty thousand envelopes and brochures that weren't involved in the snafu. Half of them are for Democrats and independents, and the other half for Republicans. They're all for the towns east of Brookhaven.''

''When?'' she asked, taking off her coat.

''With luck, by Saturday,'' he said. ''Can you line up enough volunteers by then?''

''Sure,'' she said calmly.

''Now, remember, I want them all mailed from friendly post offices, where Otis appointed the postmasters,'' he said. ''If necessary, I have a couple of postmasters who will let us mail on Sunday.''

Mrs. Russell shook her head, and he asked, ''Why not? Religious reasons?'' She nodded, and after a moment's thought he agreed.

''Well, we definitely don't want them to arrive on Saturday,'' he said. ''People don't read their mail carefully on Saturday. Mondays and Tuesdays are the best. Oh, another thing. We're not rich, but we're not poor, either. I think you ought to give your volunteers plenty of coffee and pastry. Would twenty-five dollars be enough?'' She nodded again, and he added, ''For God's sake, don't tell Otis.''

At that moment, Pike came in, followed by his wife, a compact, attractive blonde with a turned-up nose and a friendly, capable manner. They went around the room greeting the people on hand. There were about fifty men and women in the room by this time, most of whom, Donner told me, were Party workers and volunteers and their relatives. He also pointed out a couple of reporters from local papers. Once the amenities were out of the way, Pike nodded to Donner, who stepped forward and asked for silence.

It Helps to Have a Candidate

''I suppose you're wondering why I gathered you together here today,'' Donner said. ''Well, it seems that every two years, for some reason that escapes me, we find ourselves engaged in a political campaign. In the past, we have found that it helps to have a candidate. So this year, as in past years, we once again have a candidate. I give you Otis Pike.''

Shaking his head over Donner's introduction, Pike stepped forward, thanked each person who was helping in the campaign, and said, ''I'm told that this is going to be a particularly vicious campaign. I don't know whether it will be or not, and I don't especially care. I can take anything that my opponent can hand out. Right now he's talking about being an underdog. I hope he is, and I hope he stays that way right through Election Day. If he is an underdog, he's an underdog with all the money in the world. You've seen all those billboards and posters and newspaper ads, and heard all those radio spots. We just don't have the money to match him—nowhere near the money. It's going to mean work—hard work—for you and for me. I know that everyone is going to pitch in, and I know we're going to win."

After his pep talk, Pike took the two local newspaper reporters aside and gave them copies of Catterson's letter and résumé. They read the documents and then, in the classic Hollywood style of the nineteen-thirties, dived for the nearest telephones. I recalled that Pike had intended to save the letter until the last week of the campaign, and now I asked him why he had released it so early. "Things are too slow," he explained. "I've never seen it like this before. It's got me worried, so I thought I'd speed it up some."

A pugnacious-looking young man, who turned out to be notably mild-mannered, came up to us, and Pike introduced him as Joseph Quinn, assistant principal of a junior high school in Centereach and Pike's permanent representative in the Smithtown area.

"How's it look?" Pike asked.

"I don't like it," Quinn answered. "I'm really concerned about the apathy. And it's not just the voters who are apathetic. Our area's Democratic organization is even worse. The other day, I went over to our headquarters, and it wasn't even open. It's like a Republican organization in Mississippi. The only time our people aren't apathetic is when they're dealing with each other. Over in Islip, it's so bad that if you put a dozen committeemen together at dinner someone is sure to throw a plate of soup at someone. But the Republicans have a great organization. They have a campaign bus just for Smithtown. It has loudspeakers on top and a little balcony in the rear so the candidate can come out and speak to the crowd. And they've got all those billboards."

"But you're not going to get them," Pike said.

"Then it would help if we had a candidate around full time," Quinn told him.

Pike smiled and replied, "You're not going to get that, either, until Congress adjourns. And the latest word is that we won't be out for another three weeks." Quinn winced, and Pike went on. "The problem is that if you go home early, as about a hundred members of the House already have, your opponent says you're not looking after your constituents' interests. And if you stay in Washington, as I have, he says you're afraid to come home and debate."

I recalled reading somewhere that many of the more seasoned members of Congress were publicly complaining about being unable to get home and campaign but were privately delighted at being tied down in Washington. As long as the House was in session, the explanation went, a candidate was able to assume the virtuous stance of hard-working congressman, but once he was back home on the campaign trail he was just another candidate. I asked Pike about this, and he smiled and turned to greet a woman who was passing by, and then wandered off. Donner was standing alone across the room, so I went over and put the same question to him. He roared with laughter. "The charming thing about politics is its purely amoral quality," he said. "There is nothing to deal with but facts." Then he, too, wandered off.

Not long before the end of the festivities, I noted a poster announcing that a testimonial dinner for Pike would be held that evening in Riverhead, with "many famous personalities." Donner happened by and told me that, apart from Pike, the famous personalities were a candidate for the State Supreme Court and one for the Assembly, neither of whom had a chance of winning. "Mostly, it gives Otis an opportunity to stir up the troops and provide them with a few arguments to use with their friends and co-workers," he said. "The rest will be the usual. You know—'the man who,' 'our fine state,' 'victory in November,' and greasy roast beef."

And Greasy Roast Beef as Usual

Donner turned out to be quite right, I found—especially about the roast beef. After dinner, several local politicians got up to speak, and were followed by the two state candidates, who had little regard for the stuff of rhetoric and less for the passage of time. Fifty-odd people had paid seven dollars and fifty cents apiece for this experience, and they were beginning to look dangerous by the time Pike's turn came, an hour and a half later. Within a couple of minutes, though, they were sitting back in their chairs laughing as he told a slightly risqué story of which he was the butt. Once he had the audience with him, he moved on to the issues that Catterson had been talking about. Disposing quickly of the war, inflation, and racial unrest, Pike then brought up a few specific local issues—chiefly, I gathered, for the benefit of the troops. The first was a charge made by Catterson that Pike had done nothing about getting federal funds to stabilize the Moriches Inlet, on the South Shore, where the currents were so treacherous that several people had drowned in recent years and boating was almost impossible. Catterson had repeatedly stated that Pike hadn't even appeared before the Public Works Committee to testify on the problem. Pike said Catterson was quite right, and added, "If my opponent knew anything about Congress, he would know that the matter was pending before the Appropriations Committee, that I testified there, and that although the Administration's appropriations bill was cut by a hundred and fifty-six million dollars, I was able to get one hundred thousand dollars added to it for a study of the inlet. And every Republican on Long Island voted against that bill.'' Another issue was a second federal appropriation—forty-six million dollars to improve the nuclear accelerator at Brookhaven—which had also been passed over the opposition of the Long Island Republicans. (Actually, the votes Pike was referring to were cast against the omnibus appropriations bill, not against these specific parts of it.) Still another issue was a contest among six sites that were being considered by the government for a two-hundred-billion-electron-volt particle accelerator, which was to cost three hundred and seventy-five million dollars and was expected to create several thousand jobs. Catterson had been claiming that Pike hadn't done enough to persuade the government to build the accelerator at Brookhaven. "He's the only one who thinks so," Pike said. "*Newsday* reported that the Atomic Energy Commission stated that we had put on the best campaign in the country. I helped set up a meeting with the Atomic Energy Commission to discuss the advantages of Brookhaven. Both of New York's senators were there. Most of New York's representatives were there. People from the telephone company and the power company were there. Representatives of the Civil Rights Commission were there. Local business groups were there. And where was my opponent? I'll tell you where he was. He was at a dinner of Republican fat cats in New York City to honor two hundred and seven people who had contributed a thousand dollars apiece to the Republican Party." That was apparently as much in the way of issues as Pike wanted to rain on the heads of his audience, for he then launched into a peroration consisting of sentimental generalities and concluded, "I like human beings more than I like pieces of property or portfolios of stock or money in the bank. If I didn't like human beings, I wouldn't be in politics."

Campaigning on an Average Day

Early the following week, I drove over to Pike's headquarters again—this time to see how the campaign was conducted there on an average day. When I arrived, a harried but cheerful woman of about thirty with a plump, amiable face and brown curly hair, who I knew was Pike's Polish secretary, Mrs. Barbara Anderson, was talking on the telephone. I sat down nearby, and when she hung up she turned to me and sighed. "Awful—just awful," she said. "One of Mr. Pike's constituents, a soldier stationed in Japan, just called the Washington office. It seems that his wife died suddenly in Tokyo a few days ago. They sent her body back to this country on a cargo plane, and he followed on a commercial airliner. Now they can't find the casket. The poor man is frantic." Excusing herself, she picked up the telephone and called Kennedy Airport to see if there was any news of the casket, which was presumed to have got that far. There wasn't, so she asked the people at Kennedy so see if they could expedite the search and let her know as soon as they had any definite news.

Once she had finished jotting down the details of that call, I asked her about her part in the campaign, and she told me she directed most of the work of the volunteers, who would probably number around two hundred when things really got going, and that she also handled all the problems brought to the local office by Pike's constituents. She received an average of a hundred telephone calls a week from constituents, and took care of about half the problems on the spot, she said; the other half had to be referred to Washington for Pike or his secretaries there to handle. "Of course, dealing with constituents is one of the biggest parts of Mr. Pike's job," she went on. "And it's a vital part of his campaign over the long run." When I asked her how the constituents' difficulties figured in a political campaign, she explained that, in addition to the fifty-odd memoranda she forwarded to the Washington office every week, about three hundred letters from Pike's constituents went there direct, so that, all told, he and his staff dealt with roughly twenty thousand requests a year. I gathered that if Pike helped, or made a reasonable effort to help, most of the people who came to him, he thereby created an enormous fund of good will and publicity for himself— even if in some cases he accomplished nothing more than fixing his name in people's minds. The telephone rang again, and after Mrs. Anderson had answered it she told me that it had to do with an Italian alien who had been a stonecutter until the company employing him went bankrupt. "The government notified him that under the law he would be deported soon if he didn't find a job with a construction outfit, and that satisifed the Immigration people. Now it turns out that his salary is only forty dollars a week, which is below the minimum wage, so the Department of Labor objects to his starving." I asked what other kinds of calls she received, and, opening her notebook, she flipped back several pages and described the calls that had come in so far that day. There was one from a woman who asked for the address of the American ambassador to Japan, so that she could write to him and complain about not being invited to an Embassy party during a visit to Tokyo; one from a man who wanted to make a campaign contribution; one from a woman who wanted to know how her nephew should go about applying for admission to the Merchant Marine Academy; one from a man who insisted that Pike get him a higher rating in his government job, even though Pike had gone to bat for him on this before and had failed;one from a man whose son had been rejected for Officer Candidate School in the Army and who now wanted to get the boy on the Navy's Officer Candidate list, apparently to keep him out of Vietnam; one from a man who had lost his Social Security check; one from a man who claimed that although his son had severe rheumatoid arthritis, he had been drafted, and asked if Pike could get him a medical discharge; one from a woman who had been denied admission to the practical-nurse training program under the Office of Economic Opportunity because her husband was employed, and said that since she had five children and her husband was an alcoholic, she should be made an exception, so she would have some means of support when her husband drank himself to death; one from a former naval officer who had rented his house to an active naval officer who had decamped leaving scores of unpaid bills and, the caller feared, a black mark against the Navy; one from a young woman who had become pregnant while her husband was away in the Army and wanted to put the child up for adoption before he came back; and several inquiries about state matters, which were referred to local legislators. "Oh, yes," Mrs. Anderson added, turning a page. "There was also a call from a woman whose little boy was bitten by a dog. I don't know what she expected Mr. Pike to do. I told her to call the police, but that wasn't good enough. She wanted Washington to act."

I Love High-Priced Patriots

Donner came in just then, waving a red-white-and-blue poster bearing a picture of Catterson, his name, and below that the word "Congressman." Donner said, "Otis ought to kill him with this." Now he noticed, on the wall, a recently arrived two-and-a-half-by-three-foot poster with Pike's picture on it. "Speaking of posters, on that one, as Rocky would say, I goofed," he said. "Where are we going to put a thousand of those? After all, this isn't redwood country." I accompanied him over to the table for some coffee, and he asked if I had seen the *Press* article on Catterson's letter to Pike asking for a job. I said I hadn't, so he pulled out a clipping, with one sentence underlined: [He] blew his top and accused Pike of "brazenly falsifying' a patriotic offer to serve his country." Donner added, with a laugh. "At a salary several thousand dollars higher than he was making. I love high-priced patriots." He took another piece of paper out of his pocket—this one a press release from Catterson's office on the same subject. Again one sentence was underlined: "This letter was written because of my concern over the tactics being used in Vietnam and the headline-hunting of the incumbent congressman, sniping away at the Air Force Air-to-Ground Support System." Laughing, Donner explained, "Otis has given the Pentagon people, including Secretary McNamara, a hard time in hearings. The only way I can interpret Catterson's statement is that he intended to go to work for Otis and then sandbag him. I also heard that Catterson got sore because *Newsday* and the *Press* weren't using his releases, so he called them and complained. An astute political tactic—for our side. Nothing makes newspapers angrier than being told what to print."

A moment later, Mrs. Pike, wearing dungarees, sneakers, and a rumpled raincoat, hurried in. "I just got a call from Otis," she told Donner. "He can't make the public-school dinner in Commack Fridy night, because the House will be in session. I'm going in his place." She gathered up some papers that Mrs. Anderson had prepared for her, waved to us, and left.

"Doris is a marvellous campaigner," Donner said to me. "She's in there fighting every minute. She was a high-school home-economics teacher before she married Otis, so this Commack thing will be just right for her."

A sandy-haired, blue-eyed man in his early forties walked in. Donner introduced him to me as Robert T. Waldbauer, the Mayor of Patchogue and Pike's year-round representative for the Town of Brookhaven, of which Patchogue is a part, and which contains a quarter of the voters in the First District.

"How's it look?" Waldbauer asked.

"Peculiar," Donner answered. "Apathy is ours."

"I need some more bumper stickers and posters," Waldbauer said.

"Don't give out more than three or four stickers at a time," Donner told him. "People just throw them away. Now, if you want to get two or three hundred at Catterson's and make whatever use of them seems most appropriate, I can't see any objection."

"I could put them indiscriminantly on empty parked cars," Waldbauer said, with a grin. "People always love to find them when they come back."

"The windshield might be best," Donner said.

I left a few minutes later, and on my way out I passed Mrs. Anderson, who had just finished talking on the telephone. She beamed at me and said, "They found the casket!"

Catterson's Campaign

During most of the next three weeks, Representative Pike was in Washington, caught in the pre adjournment rush to dispose of the Administration's top-priority bills, so I followed Catterson's campaign, mostly by reading the local papers and his press releases. "The surprisingly leisurely pace of this year's campaign in Suffolk is finally beginning to pick up," the Long Island *Press* said around that time. "After a slow start, James M. Catterson Jr. has been making a vigorous run against Representative Otis G. Pike." Although the general tone of the newspaper coverage gave the impression that Catterson had a fair chance of unseating Pike, the purported new vigor of his campaign seemed to consist chiefly in his appearing in more places to say the same things about the war, inflation, and racial violence, and to charge that Pike was "afraid to run as the Administration Democrat he is," was afraid to debate, and was afraid to end the war in Vietnam by "bombing the North into submission." One of Catterson's press releases announced that because of the President's "no-win policy," Charles Staneck, Jr., of Islip, a plumber and former Marine, was "jumping on the Catterson bandwagon," in the belief that "a Republican Congress in general and Jim Catterson in particular will help develop solutions to these pressing problems." To dramatize the inflation issue, Catterson went to markets in Brentwood and Central Islip and gave each passing housewife eight pennies—the amount that the price of a loaf of bread had risen since the Democrats took over in 1961. And to dramatize himself, he passed out a costly-looking "Catterson Congressional Cookbook," with a cover photograph of him and his family having a cookout; among the favorite recipies of "noted Republicans" around the country were Iowa Cucumber Saccharine Pickles (Representative H. R. Gross), Kansas Space-Age Homemade Bread (Representative Robert Ellsworth), and Oklahoma Peas, Pickle, and Peanut Salad (Representative Page Belcher). Catterson also sent out twenty thousand copies of a questionnaire asking the voters such things as "Do you think the United States should be involved in Vietnam?" and "Do you favor federal government subsidy of a birth-control program?" and "Should George Hamilton be deferred?"

Since the beginning of October, I had been hearing both candidates' radio spot commercials, all of them more or less standard campaign fare. However, on the sixteenth, as I was waiting my turn in a barbershop, a commercial that I hadn't heard before came over the barber's radio. "Here's the latest official Vietnam casualty count from the Pentagon," a man's voice boomed out. "Five thousand five hundred twenty-eight American boys dead. Thirty thousand eight hundred twenty-three wounded." After asserting that President Johnson's recent trip to Manila had been a political "trick," the voice concluded, "And where will it all end? With the death of your son, brother, nephew, friend? . . . It'll take united action to win this one. Elect Jim Catterson to Congress on November 8th to help get it."

A man who was being shaved pushed the barber away and sat up. "Why, the son of a bitch!" he said.

Later, I called Donner to ask if he had heard the commercial, and he said he had. "This may be the big break of the campaign," he told me. "I understand the radio stations carrying the spots have got a lot of angry calls from listeners. Right now I'm busy organizing spontaneous calls from outraged wives and mothers."

A couple of days later, Pike struck back at Catterson through an interview in the *Press*. "It's a sick and cruel ad," he said. "If he wants to blame the war on me, that's his business. . . . I hope he keeps it up until Election Day, because I have confidence that most people will recognize it as nauseous, contemptible demagoguery."

Catterson retorted that he would stand by the commercial. "Distortions, innuendoes, and smears are conceived by candidates failing to camouflage their basic inadequacies," he told the press. "All this is a cover for a man who is frightened." Catterson soon had cause to be a lot more frightened, politically speaking, than Pike, for *Newsday* then ran an editorial entitled "Reprehensible!" in which the paper attacked Catterson for attempting to "make capital out of a war in which Americans are dying." This, Donner assured me, all but guaranteed Pike *Newsday's* endorsement—the most influential factor in the entire campaign. The following day, Pike got the endorsement of the weekly Suffolk County *News,* which stated, "He is the finest Congressman this district has had in many years." And the day after that the Long Island *Press,* which is the second most influential newspaper on the Island, came out for him, too, in a lengthy editorial. "His talent for persuasion and debate have won him respect and made his an effective voice for his district," the paper asserted, and added that Catterson was "simply not in the same league."

Congress finally adjourned on Saturday, October 22nd, and the next day Pike began campaigning full time. That afternoon, I joined him and Mrs. Pike at the Terryville District Firehouse, near Port Jefferson, where an ambulance was being dedicated to the memory of a deceased volunteer fireman named Peter Seitz. Pike made his way through a crowd of perhaps fifty firemen and as many of their relatives and friends. He paused here and there to shake hands and chat for a moment, being careful not to make any partisan remarks. "I'm surprised they invited me to a non-political affair this close to election time, especially since Catterson lives near here," he told me. "This is the best kind of thing for me to attend—like the Polish dinner." At the dedication ceremony, Pike spoke briefly, and non-politically, about how men like Setiz contributed to their community instead of merely taking from it, and thanked the firemen for the kind of tribute they had chosen and for letting him join them in it. Then, after shaking some more hands, he left.

I went along with the Pikes on the ride to their next engagement—a rally of the Three Village Democratic Club, in East Setauket, a few miles away. During the ride, I mentioned the newspaper stories I had been reading, and Pike told me that when it came to endorsements, he expected to split the district's two dozen weekly newspapers with Catterson but to get the support of both *Newsday* and the New York *Times.* "I've been getting a better break with the weeklies than usual," he continued. "For instance, the Long Island *Advance,* which is an arch-Republican paper, always used to run five pictures of my opponent to every one of me. Last week, I was surprised to see that it had only one of Catterson along with one of me. In fact, I was so surprised that I wired the publisher and asked if the paper had been surrepticiously sold." He went on to tell me that Catterson's claim of having been chosen one of the "Outstanding Young Men in America" had appeared in both the New York *News* and the Riverhead *News-Review,* and in a couple of Catterson's brochures as well. "I'm not sure what I should do," Pike said. "If I attack him, I could just create sympathy for him. Does the public really care about a thing like a lie of that sort; I just don't know."

"Otis, I feel very confident about the east end of the Island," Mrs. Pike interjected. He nodded, and she said, "I think you'll do better there than last time. The only area I'm worried about is Smithtown."

At the rally—a cocktail party in the ballroom of a restaurant called the Country Corner—I saw Quinn, Pike's man in Smithtown, and went over to ask him about the prospects in his bailiwick. "I've been out knocking on doors and talking to people, and most of them have never heard of Catterson," he told me. "They know that Pike's their congressman. That's the big thing. And many of the people who *have* heard of Catterson don't care for the way he's blaming everything except cancer on Pike. They're particularly sore about that radio spot."

I asked Quinn what else he had been doing, and he said, "Well, we sealed, stamped, and mailed thirty-five thousand brochures for the Smithtown area in two days. That was one time my nine children came in handly. We had about twenty volunteers—maybe eight or nine of them other kids. Tomorrow night, we start with brochures for four thousand newly registered voters in our area."

Mrs. Pike came up to Quinn and asked, "Did that Cook girl who called headquarters get in touch with you?"

He nodded. "She's already typed up address labels for the new registrants in two election districts," he said.

"Good," she said. "How's it look?"

"I think we're there," he answered.

I Think We're There

At noon the next day, Pike attended a luncheon meeting of the Port Jefferson Rotary Club, held at the Elk Hotel, and I dropped in at the end of the meal to see what was going on. Just after I sat down, Rotarian songbooks were passed around, and the hundred or so men on hand began singing to the accompaniment of a piano in the back of the room. I had never been to a Rotary meeting before, and was surprised when they batted out "It Had to Be You" and "Five Foot Two, Eyes of Blue." But Pike was obviously used to such occasions; he sang along with the rest, without using the songbook. Afterward, he got up to speak on what the master of ceremonies described as "a non-partisan subject that is expected to have a great effect on the election this year"—the war in Vietnam. Pike started out by saying that he was aware he was in enemy territory, Port Jefferson being Catterson's home ground and generally a Republican area—facts that he said he had been reminded of when he entered the hotel through the bar and a man there had snarlingly identified himself as a Republican. "Then he bought me a drink," Pike said. "It's nice to see that things don't change." Having established his association with Republican voters, he went on to tell a joke that lumped President Johnson with Ho Chi Minh, and, having disassociated himself from the Democratic Administration, he said that he supported the President all the way in his conduct of the war. He talked for a few minutes about the purposes of the South Vietnamese, and to stop the growth of Asian Communism without excalation into a world war. Toward the end of his speech, he told about a woman from East Hampton whose son had had both legs blown off in Vietnam. She had called Pike's office for help in expediting a visa application so that she could fly to Manila, where the boy was in a hospital, and Pike had told her to get on the plane and promised that the visa would be waiting at the other end. "I've never met that woman, but I'm gonna meet her before I die," he said. "Do you know that, with all her grief, she took the time to write and thank me all the way from the Phillipines? A letter like that makes up for all the draft-card burning and street demonstrations. Yes, the war comes home to you in all sorts of ways. The worst of them is when you're asked to expedite the burial of a soldier in the Arlington National Cemetery."

Like every political challenger who wants publicity, Catterson repeatedly called for a series of debates, and, like every incumbent who wants to keep the limelight for himself, Pike repeatedly ignored him. Finally, though, he agreed to participate in four debates during the final two weeks of the campaign—primarily, I gathered, because it would have been impolite to avoid the challenge altogether, and because he was convinced that few voters changed their minds so late. The first debate was held on the afternoon of October 25th at the Connetquot High School, in Bohemia, before a student audience. I met Donner outside the school shortly before the time set for the debate, and we went into the still empty auditorium and took seats in the front row. Almost at once, the students—around a thousand of them—poured into the chamber. I was surprised that either candidate wanted to spend his time talking, let alone debating, before an audience of people who couldn't vote, and when I brought this up Donner said, "The audience has no importance at all. What counts is the press coverage." He seemed edgy. So did Pike when he came onstage and sat down at a table there; he fumbled through some papers and began licking his lips. "He always does that when he's nervous," Donner said, watching him. "Must be a wreck today. He looks like a lizard." I asked what sort of approach Pike intended to use, and Donner shrugged and said, "I advised him to use humor or schmalz, but he'll probably go his own way. He usually does." As soon as the auditorium was full, the moderator went to the lectern, even though Catterson had still not arrived, and began describing the backgrounds of the candidates, beginning with Pike. Just as he had finished introducing Pike and was saying, "The other candidate is James M. Catterson, Jr.," Catterson walked onstage. He received a big hand.

"Nice," Donner whispered. "Very nicely timed."

Although the debate turned out to be little more than a rehash of what the two men had been saying for the previous couple of months, it produced several surprises. For one thing, Pike, who spoke first, was neither humorous nor schmalzy; instead he was declamatory, drawing on a full range of arm-waving and table-thumping. Catterson, on the other

hand, leaned casually against the lectern and spoke in a relaxed, conversational manner. For another thing, Pike immediately went on the defensive in his speech, describing the charges that Catterson had made against him and denying them one by one; Catterson, for his part, pressed the attack. And, finally, Pike allowed the debate to center on Vietnam—a topic that I had expected him to avoid, since the male half of the audience would soon be eligible for military service. Actually, he brought the subject up almost as soon as he rose to speak. Waving one of Catterson's recent press releases, he said, "See if you can figure out from this release whether he's a hawk or a dove: 'I feel peace should be achieved, and our boys safely brought home, but only by acting from strength and not adopting the peace-at-any-price tradition of the Democratic Party. A peace parley, by Asians, for Asians, should be sought, but not where it creates the impression of American weakness and confusion.'" Chopping the air with both forearms, Pike shouted, "What does he stand for? This is—this is mush!" He went on to read a statement in which Catterson called for increased bombing of North Vietnam, for a blockade of all ports in the North, and for the use of "more Asian troops, particularly from Nationalist China." Waving his arms again, Pike said, "He should've stuck with the mush! I can't conceive of anything more likely to escalate this war into a great big nuclear war, with the Red Chinese coming down from the north, than for us to bring in Nationalist China from the south. The Vietnamese don't want them. The most militaristic members of the Army and the Navy don't want them. My opponent wants them. He can have them."

Catterson, when his turn came, responded, "I have called for a stepped-up war—not an escalation but an intensification—to convince Ho Chi Minh and the rest of the Communists that it's about time they came to the conference table. It was said better last week by General Eisenhower when he said, 'I would use whatever force is necessary to bring the Communists to the council tables.' And the only thing they understand is force. . . . *His* Administration"—he pointed at Pike, as he did whenever he referred to the President or the Democrats—"has done nothing. We have attempted to go forward and the configuration now in a limited-war situation. He says he stands with the Administration. We all support our nation, but I reserve the right to criticize a no-win policy. If he wants to take the credit for what's going on in Vietnam, he's got to accept the responsibility." Pike had got a respectable round of applause when he sat down. Now Catterson got an ovation.

Watch Your Tactics

"Bad tactics—very bad," Donner said to me as the students began leaving the auditorium. "Otis not only put himself on the defensive but didn't act like a congressman at all. He should have played the seasoned legislator. You know—'I've voted on a thousand bills in the interests of the people of this district. What would you have done differently? Tell us of one vote affecting Vietnam on which you would have voted differently from me. And I've voted on dozens of them. If my opponent wants to challenge my record, let him tell us what *he* would have done? Then you wind up with the there-are-no-easy-answers-to-hard-questions routine.''

Pike, looking drawn and tight-lipped, joined us, and we walked out into the main corridor, where the principal, a bespectacled young man named Charles Adams, was waiting to invite us into his office for coffee. Pike apparently wanted to keep busy, once inside the office, he said he would do the honors, and poured the coffee and served it to us. We sat around a long, narrow conference table in silence, until Donner, trying to soothe Pike, said, ''It's difficult for the incumbent in a situation like this. He can't brag. He can't say he did this or he did that for his constituents, or that he's worked for them for six years, and worked like hell.''

Everyone waited for Pike to reply. He sipped at his coffee moodily for a long time, then looked around at each of us and said, ''Do you suppose it's really a gut issue—that we should drop the bomb? Do you suppose that's what the people really want?''

''I can't believe so,'' Adams answered. ''You've got to remember that a lot of these students come from conservative homes—very conservative homes, in many cases. And, of course, the boys will be facing the draft soon.''

''Maybe that's what they really want,'' Pike said, unheeding. ''Maybe we're just fooling ourselves.''

He lapsed into silence again, and a minute or two later an assistant came in and told the principal that Catterson was outside, waiting to say goodbye. Adams went out, and returned with Catterson and an aide. Pike looked discomfited, but he got up and shook hands with both men and then poured them some coffee. He gave the first cup to the aide and the second, without a saucer, to Catterson, who said, with a smile, ''Don't I even get a saucer, Otis?''

''If there were any left, you would,'' Pike said peevishly.

Continuing to smile, Catterson slouched casually in his chair and said, ''It's refreshing how alert and interested these kids are. Much more so than their parents. Don't you think so, Otis?''

Pike nodded gloomily and began drumming on the table with his fingertips.

''But don't forget,'' Adams said, ''most of these youngsters are from Republican families.''

Catterson smiled, without replying, and after another brief silence

Adams said, "As difficult as it is to get at the truth in anything as short and confusing as a debate, the people usually decide correctly in the end."

"Yes, they do," Catterson said, with a nod.

"They have so far, anyway," Pike said.

Everyone laughed, and Pike, smiling for the first time, got up to leave, saying he had an appointment in Southampton in an hour.

"I'll see you tonight at the Smithtown League of Women's Voters, won't I, Otis?" Catterson asked.

Pike frowned and shook his head. "That's not on my schedule," he said. "We told them weeks ago that we had something else planned for tonight."

"Should I give them your apologies, Otis?" Catterson asked.

Before Pike could answer, Donner hurriedly said, "Do that—but nothing more."

"You mean I might say something like 'I debated with Mr. Pike today, and I guess he was afraid to show up tonight?" Catterson asked, grinning. "Now, that would be too childish, wouldn't it?"

I left with Pike, and on the way to his car he shrugged his shoulders and sighed. "He won that round—no question about it," he said.

Strictly on the basis of debating points, I felt that Pike had won, but when I said as much he shook his head sharply. "He got most of the applause," he said. "In a debate, it's not who wins but who appeals most to the audience." When I brought up what the principal had said about most of the students' being Republicans, Pike replied, "So is the whole district. If I can't win with the kids, I won't win with their parents." When we reached his car, he stood gazing abstractedly into the distance. Then, turning back to me, he said, "He's a tough little guy—by far the smartest opponent I've ever had. I could be in trouble."

"PIKE, CATTERSON MEET WITH DEBATABLE RESULT," said a headline in *Newsday* the following morning. This was the general press reaction, but, as I learned when I dropped in at Pike's headquarters that afternoon, it did not change Pike's opinion; he was still convinced that he had lost decisively. His chance to recoup came that evening, when he and Catterson had another encounter—before a meeting of the Bellport League of Women Voters, in the auditorium of the Bellport Junior High School.

This time, there were only adults in the audience, and the event was not in the strict sense a debate but a session in which members of the audience addressed questions to one candidate or the other and then each man had two minutes to answer. Although more or less the same topics were covered, the results were quite different. Pike was calm and aggressive, Catterson uneasy and defensive. Pike put his opponent off his footing at the outset by refusing the offer of a microphone and speaking directly to the audience, of seventy or so; Catterson did the same, but his voice was rather thin, and it tended to rise and crack when he tried to reach the people in the rear of the hall.

Who Supports Waste in Government

There was more discussion of domestic issues than there had been the day before. A curly-haired woman in the audience asked Catterson what he would do about inflation, and he replied that he would cut back on Great Society spending, and not impose wage-and-price controls, as Pike recommended. Pike, who had never recommended anything of the sort, got up and said so. Then he went on, in a way that showed that he had taken Donner's advice, "As far as domestic programs are concerned, my opponent talks about wasteful government spending. I have yet to hear any candidate anywhere take a firm stand in favor of wasteful government spending. Where are you going to draw the line? I think some parts of the poverty program are good and some parts bad. We have a vote in Congress called 'Yea' and a vote called 'Nay.' We have no vote called 'Maybe.' He spends a lot of time running against Lyndon Johnson and his Secretary of Defense, Robert McNamara, but he hasn't really talked about how he would have voted differently on all the votes I have had this year. There have been two hundred and thirty-two roll-call votes this year, and I have not heard him criticize one. I think you are entitled to specific answers about specific programs."

A lanky man with glasses rose to ask Catterson if he favored Brookhaven as the site for the new nuclear accelerator, and Catterson answered that he did. Then he used the question as a catchall and took the rest of his two minutes to discuss various other views he held. The man got up and objected, saying that his question had been answered, whereupon Catterson called him a "plant," received a scattering of derisive laughter, and sat down, red-faced. When Pike's turn came, he pointed out that the Republican representatives from Long Island had voted against the appropriation to improve the existing accelerator, and asked, "How can they say that they would support a new one when they wouldn't even vote for the old one?"

Aside from a few exchanges of this sort, most of the time was again devoted to the subject of Vietnam. The same woman who had asked about inflation rose to ask Pike how he would approach world problems in general. "The answer to the problems which confront us in the continuing struggle between ideologies is not an answer which we are going to impose by bigger bombs or by fear," Pike replied. "A man who is hungry, a man who has not food today and no hope for tomorrow, doesn't really much care what is happening to his government, or even what his government consists of. I believe that we have got to win the struggle for man's mind not by fear but with hope.''

That got a big hand, and when Pike sat down Donner whispered to me, ''That's it—the old H.I.P.D.'' I gave him a puzzled look, and he explained, ''You know—war, clashing ideologies are not the enemies. The enemies are man's oldest enemies—hunger, ignorance, poverty and disease.''

A man at the front of the room asked Pike whether he advocated dropping a nuclear bomb on North Vietnam, and Pike got up, said loudly, ''No, I do not,'' and sat down—to resounding applause.

Catterson rose slowly and looked at the audience for a long time. ''This is a ticklish subject,'' he said finally. ''The whole campaign in 1964 was won and lost by a picture of a little girl in a field of daisies and a nuclear bomb going off. Americans get nervous when we talk about nuclear weapons. I can see no reason to go into non-conventional or nuclear weapons. However, I do know that an army is made for the primary purpose of killing people, and to do that in the most efficient way possible to get to its objective. I don't think anyone could advise a nation to take such a drastic step. But if need be, if the nation's welfare was at stake, then I would support the President if he decided that it could be handled only by nuclear retaliation.'' He passed, stared out at the audience again for a time, and then continued haltingly, ''It depends on too many factors. This is a major vote as far as I am concerned, whether they have it in the House or not.'' He stopped once more, and with a shrug added, ''This may not satisfy you. You may not feel I'm answering your question. But I'm giving it to you as I feel.'' His voice trailed off, and the meeting ended.

Donner turned to me and nodded once, and his face broke into a wide smile. ''Otis certainly left him with his mouth hanging open,'' he said.

I had the impression that Pike had been ready for a number of the questions, and I asked Donner whether any of them had been planted. ''Most of them,'' he answered without hesitation. ''That tall fellow is a high official at Brookhaven and a good friend of Otis's, and the curly-haired woman is one of our volunteers from Southold. Otis reacted so badly to that unfriendly audience yesterday that I decided I had better get some friends here tonight. Catterson has his claque and we have ours.''

I asked how many people were there because they were interested, and he answered, ''Oh, maybe five to ten per cent. As I said yesterday, it's all for the newspapers.''

Out in the corridor, I saw Mrs. Pike stop Catterson as he was leaving.

"You told me that night at the *Press* award dinner that you weren't going to run a dirty campaign," she said.

"I haven't," Catterson answered, giving her an angry look.

"How about those posters you have on every telephone pole?"

"What posters?"

"You know very well what posters. The ones that say you're a congressman."

"They don't say that."

"That's exactly what they say, and you know it."

A man standing beside Catterson took his arm and led him away. Pike had come out into the corridor in time to overhear the last of the conversation, and he chided his wife for personally attacking Catterson.

The posters had struck me as being deceptive, and I asked Pike why he had not objected to them publicly. "I guess I've lost my instinct for the jugular," he replied. "Besides, I'm not sure the public would care."

The members of his claque gathered around to congratulate him on what was clearly a victory. "I must say I feel a lot better than I did yesterday," he told them. "But just remember one thing—I was down then and I'm up now, but at least when I was down I knew it."

Donner peered at him solemnly for a moment. "Worthy of Lincoln," he said, and burst into a wild laugh.

It's the Newspapers that Count

The theory that it was the newspapers and not the audience that counted was verified in the next day's *Press,* by way of a long article on the meeting that ran under the three-column headline "ADVOCATES NUCLEAR WARFARE IN VIET NAM IF NECESSARY." Catterson immediately called a press conference to deny that he had said anything of the sort, but no one paid much attention—not even the *Press.* A couple of days later, its political columnist, John Maher, wrote that among Catterson's supporters his statement had raised the spectre of a trigger-happy Goldwater, and added, "They fear that this incident may have turned a respectably close race into a rout."

The next meeting between Pike and Catterson took place the night after the Bellport meeting, in a debate held at the Port Jefferson High School and sponsored by the North Brookhaven League of Women Voters. Much the same material was covered once again, but the result was closer to a standoff. The only disturbance came at the end. Catterson's manager may have reacted to the largely pro-Pike audience at the second meeting of the candidates just as Donner had reacted to the audience at the first, for this time the audience included half a dozen noisy, tough-looking men who cheered almost every time Catterson completed a sentence.

Just as Donner remarked to me, "They look like guys he couldn't convict as head of the Rackets Bureau," one of them got up and said, "Mr. Catterson, thank God you don't play the ukulele!"

There were laughs and catcalls from the audience, and then Pike jumped up and shouted, "I learned to play the ukulele in the Pacific during World War II, when I was being shot at by experts, and if you think I'm going to stop now because of his puny political popgun, you just don't know me."

I was bewildered by the exchange, and asked Donner what it was all about. He told me that Pike occasionally played the ukulele, and that because of a recent incident this hobby had become a campaign issue— "one of those nonsense issues" Donner called it. A couple of weeks earlier, he explained bad weather had shut down all the airports, and Pike was prevented from appearing as the main speaker at a testimonial dinner for Howard Lee Koch, the conductor of the South Shore Symphony Orchestra. "Howard is an old, old friend, and Otis really wanted to do something for him," Donner said. "Finally, I arranged for the telephone company to rig up a line so that he could speak to the crowd at the dinner over an amplified telephone—at a cost of around a hundred dollars. Just before he was due to go on, the special line to the place where the dinner was held was cut. When a telephone lineman told me that, I didn't believe him. I told Doris Pike, and she didn't believe me. She told Otis, and he didn't believe her. But the lineman said there was no doubt about it—the line had been cut. He finally fixed it, and Otis came on and played the ukulele for Howard. I presume that Catterson was aware of the incident. Anyway, he started making cracks about Pike's lolling around in Washington playing the ukulele instead of debating him. Otis is angry as hell about the whole business."

**Nonsense Issues
Can Be Important**

When I stopped in at Pike's headquarters the next day, I found that he was also angry about a story in *Newsday* on the previous night's debate. He showed me the article, which said that the audience in Port Jefferson had been harder on him than the one in Bellport, and that he had been hooted and jeered for playing the ukulele. I said my impression had been that the hoots and jeers were for the man who had asked the question, but Pike said he agreed with *Newsday* that they had been meant for him.

Cheering up somewhat, he produced a copy of that morning's *Times,* which endorsed his candidacy, saying, "Although Representative Otis G. Pike . . . voted against several worthwhile programs, notably rent subsidies and foreign economic aid, we think that his energy and ability are sufficiently impressive to warrant his return for a fourth term." Pike remarked that the endorsement was less enthusiastic than he had hoped it would be and added, "It would help me with my constituents, though, since most of them are also against rent subsidies, but unfortunately, those who are against them don't read the *Times* and those who read the *Times* are likely to be for them."

Glancing at his watch, Pike said he had to leave if he was going to be on time for the *Kaffeeklatsch* over in Blue Point, on the South Shore, and invited me to join him. On the way to his car, I asked whether he had made up his mind about using Catterson's claim that he had been named by the United States Junior Chamber of Commerce. He shook his head. "Donner is afraid it may backfire, and so am I," he said. "This morning at breakfast, I told my thirteen-year-old son, Robert, about it, and he said that maybe it was a lie but it didn't stir him up any. I'm afraid that's the way most people would react."

After we had passed through Riverhead and were on the Sunrise Highway, Pike took a battery-powered razor out of the glove compartment and began shaving as he drove. "We have a crisis," he said as he ran the razor over his scarred cheeks. "It's the same one that comes up every election year around this time—money. We have only three hundred dollars in our account. The Republicans for Pike Committee has about three thousand. We'll probably get another thousand in donations by Election Day, but we have four thousand dollars in debts, and I want to run ads in all the weekly papers during the last week. That would cost around two thousand. I could get the money easily, but I don't want to be obligated. Maybe I'll forget about the ads."

I asked if he felt that he was in danger of losing, and he said, "Not really. An incumbent who does his job has a hell of a leg up. That alone should make it safe. And then, the people I have working for me—Donner and Quinn and Waldbauer and Mrs. Anderson and the four girls in my Washington office—are all pros. I don't have a single political hack on my staff. In many areas, you have to make a lot of promises to get nominated—promises that you'll hire party workers if you're elected. I know some congressmen who can afford to have only two staff people in Washington because they have to pay the salaries of some hacks back home who do nothing but sit around in the local clubhouse."

Pike finished shaving, and we drove along in silence for a few miles, until I asked how he had first got interested in politics. "It began when I was fourteen," he answered at once, as if he had often asked himself the same question. "It was on a Sunday during the Depression. My sister Betty, who is ten years older than I am, came home from her job with the Suffolk County Welfare Department and told us about a family she had just visited. They had a big farm—around a hundred and fifty acres, as I remember—and she said that all they had for Sunday dinner was boiled potatoes. I was surprised that in a great country like America such a thing could happen. All my family had always been Republicans, but that kind of thing, and what Franklin Roosevelt tried to do about it, turned me into a Democrat." He fell silent for a time, and then went on. "I guess I wasn't really aware of how I felt that early, but it was there. And when I went to Princeton, I studied at the Woodrow Wilson School of Public and International Affairs, with the intention of going into the diplomatic service. The more I learned about history and world affairs, the more I came to believe in the Democratic Party and its awareness of the problems of our time. Then, not long after I turned twenty-one I got two letters. One was from a cousin, Edward Lupton, who was a Republican state assemblyman. As a kid, I had often talked about starting a weekly newspaper out here. He'd heard about that, and he wrote me that if I hoped to get anywhere with a paper in Suffolk County I would have to be a Republican. The other letter was from a woman lawyer named Syrena Stackpole, who was a Democrat and a justice of the peace in Riverhead. She told me that now that I was twenty-one I had to choose a political party. She said that being a Republican would bring me more economic rewards but that being a Democrat would be more fun. I was already a Democrat intellectually, and her letter made me realize that I was also one emotionally. I'd always been a maverick."

I asked why he had given up both diplomacy and publishing, and he explained that after his wartime experiences in the Marine Corps diplomacy had seemed too slow, and after he had finished at Princeton starting a newspaper had required more financial resources that he could summon. His parents had died when he was young, he said—his father when Otis was two and his mother when he was six—and though they had left enough money for his education and support, there hadn't been enough for any sizable business venture. "So I went to law school and then set up practice in Riverhead," he went on. "Doris and I moved into my family's old house in Riverhead the night Harry Truman was reëlected. I stayed up all night listening to the returns."

**Small Meetings
Are Helpful**

As we pulled up at our destination, a modest green-shingled house on a pleasant side street, Pike remarked that small meetings like the one coming up could be fairly helpful. "Aside from me working directly with constituents when they want a favor, this is about the closest contact with voters that I have," he explained. "I figure that each person present can be multiplied by ten votes. They go home and to work and to parties and they talk about meeting their congressman and tell what he said."

Pike's host, a hulking, amiable man named John Foley, introduced him to the people who were waiting—fifteen men and women, ranging in age from around thirty to around seventy. Pike shook hands with each, saying, "Hi, I'm Otis Pike. I'm delighted to meet you." As soon as he had completed the circuit, a woman with reddish hair and harlequin glasses came over to him and said that her son had applied for admission to the Merchant Marine Academy, at Kings Point, and had written him asking for a recommendation. "I wondered if you could help him," she said. Telling her that he didn't recall the circumstances of the case but would find out, Pike went over to a telephone near the stairs and called his Washington office. He asked his secretary to get the boy's file, and, after waiting for a minute, inquired what the young man's standing was. He listened, said, "Fine, thanks," hung up, and came back to the woman. "I can tell you that he is one of three boys that I am seriously considering for a recommendation," he said. She beamed and thanked him several times.

With this detail out of the way, Pike pulled a chair into the center of the room and sat down. "I'm ready for questions," he said. In the course of the next hour, he casually fielded questions about how he answered his mail, what sorts of problems he spent most of his time on, how he felt about our relations with the United Nations, what his standing was, what the chances were of getting the nuclear accelerator located in Brookhaven, how he felt about a proposal to build a bridge connecting Long Island with Connecticut, whether the white backlash was an issue on the Island, how a high-school student who wanted to be a dentist in the Army should choose a college—and, naturally, what should be done about the war in Vietnam.

A blond woman of about forty who was wearing an aquamarine silk dress and large coral earrings brought up the last subject by asking, "What would happen if we dropped the atomic bomb on North Vietnam?"

Pike swivelled around in his chair to face her. "Where on North Vietnam?" he asked. "If you dropped it on Hanoi, you would kill two million civilians."

"But they're killing our boys," she said.

"That's true," Pike said. "They have killed five thousand Americans."

Another woman, sitting across the room, leaned forward and said, "The entire world would hate us."

"But it would end the war," the blonde retorted.

"I don't think so," Pike put in. "At worst, you would have a nuclear war. At best, you'd find that millions of people from all over the world would volunteer to go and fight for North Vietnam.''

"I just think we ought to get it over with," she said. "Why not bomb the harbor?"

"And hit neutral or Russian ships?" the other woman demanded, her voice rising.

The blonde dismissed the question with a wiggle of her shoulders and went on, "Nostradamus said that the yellow race is going to defeat the white race in 1977 and that the white race will come back and defeat the yellow race in 1999. Then we'll have a thousand years of peace.''

Pike looked at her levelly. "Did you come on a pogo stick?" he asked.

That ended the discussion, and after drinking a cup of coffee Pike said good-bye all around and got ready to go. Out on the front porch, Foley asked him if he had time to stop off and greet the nuns at an Ursuline convent a few blocks away. Pike replied that he would be happy to, and drove Foley and me over to the convent, a large, dun-colored building set in a grove of pines. A severe-looking nun with gold-rimmed glasses met us at the door, and Foley introduced her as Sister Joseph. She took us into a small reception room, and a moment later we were joined by the mother superior, a square-faced Irishwoman named Sister Philomena, who gave Pike a sly look and said, "I don't know you, Mr. Pike, but Sister Joseph here has given me her word that you're a good man, so I'm going to vote for you.''

"I hope I'm as good as her word," Pike said.

"I'm a registered Republican, so you can believe my word," Sister Joseph broke in, and her dour look was replaced by a broad smile.

"Goodness!" Pike said. "I thought I was in a hotbed of Irish Democrats.''

Sister Philomena replied that she wouldn't be surprised if he got the votes of all twenty-four sisters in the convent, whereupon Pike asked her if she would like to be his campaign manager on a full-time basis. "I have sin enough to deal with, surely," she said, smiling.

A moment later, Pike got up to leave, and the two nuns accompanied him to the door. "God bless you, Mr. Pike," Sister Philomena said, giving him another sly look. "We'll vote for you." With a sudden peal of laughter, she added, "And we'll pray for you.''

That evening, there was a fifty-dollar-a-plate dinner given by, and for, the Islip Town Democratic Committee, at a restaurant called Land's End, in Sayville. Pike, who was to be the main speaker, wasn't there when I arrived. Donner was, though. He explained that Islip was a part of the area that he was personally responsible for. "Besides," he said, "I have the uneasy feeling that something is up.''

Something was up, we both learned as soon as Pike and his wife came in. Once they were seated at the main table, Pike waved to Donner, who went over and chatted with him for a minute. He returned holding a couple of sheets of yellow legal paper. "God help us all," he said. "Otis has written a song about 'the outstanding young man of the year.' It's called 'Ballad for a Bad Boy.'" He sat down and bent over the paper, wincing from time to time and then glancing over at Pike, who laughed each time. Finally, he returned to Pike's table and talked again for a couple of minutes. Afterward, Donner slumped into his chair beside me and said, "I told him it was a mistake. I can't imagine a more unsuitable occasion. But he has that determined look."

After dinner, the master of ceremonies, a local politician, introduced Pike as "the man who has installed vim and vigor in each and every one of us," and Pike got up to make a couple of jokes and go through what had by now become his standard campaign repertoire concerning the "issues." Then he asked the audience of around two hundred people to write down on whatever paper might be handy the words "But they never, never ever, no they never, never ever heard of his name." A few minutes later, after some more jokes and some more talk about the campaign, he described Catterson's claim of being chosen one of the "Outstanding Young Men in America" by the United States Junior Chamber of Commerce, explained what the actual situation was, and, reaching under the table, brought out his ukulele. "What has got under my opponent's skin is my love of music," he went on. "I've written a song just for him. If you'll look at the words I asked you to write, I think you'll understand them. And I hope you will join me in singing them as the chorus." The song, which Pike played to the tone of a raucous old Army marching song, had six stanzas, plus the chorus. The first stanza went:

> Oh, he claimed that we was one
> Of the big men in the sun
> That the U.S. Junior Chamber
>   gave him his fame.

At the end of each stanza, the audience joined in, at first halfheartedly and then with more enthusiasm, to sing the chorus. When Pike finished and sat down—to laughter and applause—I went over and asked him why he had chosen that occasion and that method to refute Catterson's claim.

"First of all, it's a friendly crowd, so I don't have to worry about any backfire before I make my point," he answered. "And, second, the lie really isn't a very big one. I want to use it without seeming to make a big fuss. This seemed just right to me—light and mocking." With a smile, he added, "And, most important of all, done with the ukulele."

Shopping centers may have disfigured the American countryside and ruined downtown merchants, but they have proved a boon to anyone running for public office, since they provide ready-made gatherings of voters and easy access to them. The following morning, a Saturday, Pike was scheduled to make a tour of half a dozen shopping centers in the Islip area in a motorcade, so at nine o'clock I arrived at the assembly point—a large parking lot in front of Gimbels, on the Montauk Highway just east of Bay Shore. When I drove up, Donner, who had organized the tour, was busy taping poster pictures of Pike onto his brown Buick convertible. "And I could be home raking leaves," he said when I joined him. The motorcade was scheduled to leave at nine-thirty, but it was almost ten before all the vehicles had assembled: half a dozen cars with posters on their sides or signs on their roofs; an ancient bus carrying two dozen uniformed adolescents, who made up the East Brentwood Fire Department Raiders Band; and a gleaming aluminum Greyhound-sized bus. When the Raiders piled out and began tooting and banging away, Donner winced. "Three notes and you know it's a Democratic affair," he remarked.

I asked about the aluminum bus, and he said, "Some character out in the Midwest had it built, at a cost of a hundred thousand dollars. It sleeps four and has a kitchenette and a bathroom. The guy didn't know what to do with it, so he sold it for thirty thousand dollars to some character here. He didn't know what to do with it, either, so he lent it to Charlie Melton, our local assemblyman. He and Otis are campaigning together today. It's pretty stylish for us—maybe a little too stylish."

I asked Donner how the motorcade had been set up and how it would operate. "I spent a couple of weeks arranging it—an hour here and an hour there," he told me. "I called a few of our more zealous committeemen and asked them to get some cars and some helpers to distribute literature and shopping bags. I had to clear the route with town officials, arrange for the police escort, and hire the band. Altogether, it cost about a hundred dollars. The plan is for the Raiders to go to each shopping center fifteen minutes before we do. They stomp around and play whatever they call it. Then the sound truck—that mockup railroad engine over there—circles the center and announces, 'Your congressman, Otis Pike, is on the way, folks! Be sure to step up and say hello to your congressman!' After they have revived all the people who have fainted from anticipation, the bus pulls in. Otis makes his pitch over the loudspeaker, and then he gets out and mixes with the crowd."

A tall, sleepy-looking man in a houndstooth jacket came up to Donner and complained that they were already forty minutes late. Introducing him to me as Robert Smith, a local Democratic committeeman, Donner said to Smith, "Who do you think we are—Republicans? Anyway, Otis isn't here yet. We could go without him, of course. It's bad enough running a campaign, without having a candidate around."

Just then, a five-motorcycle police escort roared up, sirens howling, and stopped at the head of the motorcade. A moment later, Pike arrived, followed by Melton, a plump man of around fifty with yellowish gray hair.

"How's it look?" Melton asked Pike.

How's It Look?

"Pretty good for both of us, Charlie," Pike replied, and followed him into the big bus. They sat down on an upholstered seat in the rear, beside a microphone and loudspeaker system.

If repetition is not the political campaigner's best friend, it is surely his closest companion. As the bus pulled into the first shopping center, the Bay Shore Farmers Market, Pike took the microphone and delivered a brief speech, which he repeated, with a few variations, at all the other stops. "Good morning, ladies and gentlemen, this is your congressman, Otis Pike, speaking," he began, and, to make it clear that the stylishness of his transportation was none of his doing, he added, "I'm here on Assemblyman Charlie Melton's beautiful bus. Charlie will do his best to answer any questions you may have about state matters, and I'll do my best to answer those on federal matters. I'm sorry that I wasn't able to get home earlier to campaign, as my opponent has been campaigning for the past six months, but Congress was in session until just two weeks ago. You hired me to do a job for you, and I had to stay down in Washington and do that job. I've been serving you in Washington for the past six years, and I'd like to go right on serving you. I like being your congressman, and I've done the very best I could for you. I won't pretend that I've got all the answers, as my opponent pretends to have. There are no easy answers to the great problems of our time. If there were, they wouldn't be great problems. I'd like to meet as many of you as I can. I'd like to talk to you, and hear your problems, and try to help. In the past six years, I've helped thousands of people in Suffolk County. Some of the problems I deal with are big problems, like defense contracts for Grumman and Republic. Some are as small as a lost Social Security card. But all of them concern human beings, and all of us are concerned about human beings. Now, I've been trying to talk about my record in this campaign. My opponent has been talking about everything except my record. I think that's pretty flattering, too. I've had the endorsement of every independent paper in the district. We need newspapers that don't accept slogans and scaremongering, newspapers that think for themselves. But we need more than that. We need people who think for themselves. Are you going to think for yourselves on Election Day? I hope you do. This is Otis Pike, your congressman.''

As he circulated among the shoppers, Pike used many lines that also became increasingly familiar through repetition. To people carrying shopping bags with his name and picture on them he said, ''I see you're carrying my shopping bag, and I hope you'll help carry me back to Congress.'' To women with infants *and* his shopping bags he said, ''That's a precious package you've got there. Don't put *that* in my shopping bag.'' To men who had just made purchases and were putting their change in their wallets when he came up to shake hands he said, ''Always put your money away before you shake hands with a politician.'' To small children with their parents he said, ''Do you know what a congressman is? A congressman is someone who goes down to Washington and spends all your old man's money.''

During the time that I had been following Pike, I had heard him reiterate jokes, arguments, and replies many times, but never in such concentrated doses as on this morning. By the third stop, I had begun to wonder what this sort of repetition does to a man's sensibilities, and as soon as I got a chance I asked Pike if it had any effect on him. Giving me a slightly surprised look, he said, ''I'm hardly aware that I'm doing it anymore. In the first campaign, it drove me crazy. I felt as if I were hearing a record of myself. But I soon got used to it.''

That brought me to something else I had been wondering about—how much Pike actually enjoyed traveling around his district meeting different kinds of people and attending such diverse affairs as Polish dances and Rotary Club luncheons. ''At the beginning, I got a terrific kick out of it, but now I'd rather stay home with my family,'' he told me. Just then, the bus pulled into another shopping center, and Pike looked out the window and shook his head wearily. ''Almost five minutes of this kind of thing would last me a long, long time,'' he said. In the previous few days, I had noticed that Pike was beginning to show the strain of the exhausting schedule he was keeping, and when I asked him if he was tired he nodded. ''It can be murderous—literally,'' he said. ''More than once, I've fallen asleep at the wheel when I was driving home late at night after a long day of campaigning.''

Donner had told me that Pike was uneasy about approaching people on his own, so Party workers in the motorcade had been instructed to bring shoppers up to him as he stood outside a store or walked along the sidewalk in front. Donner was apparently uneasy about approaching people himself, for at each stop he stood off to one side with an armful of shopping bags and chanted, "Take a shopping bag for Congressman Pike." Smith, on the other hand, went up to passersby, called out, "Come on, folks, don't be bashful! Come and meet your congressman," and dragged one couple after another over to shake hands. But a good many people came over on their own. Most of them, it turned out, had something on their minds. There was a man who argued that his military service should be added to his employment record for Social Security benefits, a man who rebuked Pike for not helping him in an income-tax dispute with the Internal Revenue Service, a woman who told him he was going to be President someday, and a man who asked what he should do about his wife's drinking. Pike told the first to write him a letter explaining his views, apologized to the second for being unable to help, thanked the third for making his day, and advised the fourth, "Join her." There were some shoppers who refused to shake hands with him, or even to look his way, and at each refusal of this sort he flushed slightly and hurried on.

In front of one supermarket, Smith gave a brochure to a pinched-looking woman as she came out and urged her to "say hello to Congressman Pike."

Without breaking stride, she slapped the brochure into Pike's extended hand, said, "Hello Congressman Pike," and stalked off.

"A good Republican face," Pike said, watching her go.

I mentioned the incident to Donner a little later, and he nodded. "It happens," he said. "But it's not important. The important think is how many people know his name. It's never been like this before. We used to spend thousands of dollars to advertise him and then hand a shopping bag to someone and they'd say, 'Who?' That's what hurt—that 'Who?' But now they take the bag and say, 'Oh, yes, Congressman Pike.' It's taken years to get to that stage."

Campaigning Can Be Murderous

Donner had heard rumors that Catterson's supporters were going to picket Pike that day, but the hours wore on with no sign of them, and Donner concluded that they had probably failed to find the motorcade because it was so far behind schedule. "That's the advantage of being a

Democrat,'' he said. ''Your schedule is always so loused up that even you don't know where you are.'' At the next-to-last stop, four boys of about eighteen, with tight black pants, black jackets, and slicked-up pompadours, who looked as if they would like nothing better than to get into trouble, clustered around Pike in front of a market and began shaking hands with emerging shoppers, each introducing himself as Lyndon Johnson, Nelson Rockefeller, or Robert F. Kennedy. They were clearly acting on their own, but they struck me as being far more menacing than organized pickets would have been. Apparently, Pike felt the same way, for he eyed them nervously, and moved on to another doorway. Donner watched them as they started off in the same direction. ''You know,'' he said, ''I'm not so sure I'm against police brutality.''

Finally, at the last stop, the Catterson pickets showed up. There were three of them, all middle-aged women, and they were carrying signs reading, ''SWEEP OUT THE MESS IN WASHINGTON.'' ''SWEEP OUT THE BIG DEM SPENDERS,'' and ''TRADE IN YOUR PRESENT CONGRESSMAN FOR A LESS EXPENSIVE MODEL.''

Pike waved at them and shouted, ''Welcome! Where have you been? We've missed you.''

The crowd laughed, and as Pike went back to shaking hands the three women closed in and tried to cut him off from the shoppers.

One of the committeemen who were passing out Pike's brochures—a tall, heavyset man with a double chin—stopped the leader of the pickets, a small redhead. ''You shouldn't behave like that,'' he told her. ''The Democrats would never do that. If you want to follow the motorcade or picket farther away, that's fine. But you have no right to stop him from meeting the voters.''

The woman glared at him, and then suddenly cried, ''You fat rat!''

Pike heard her, and at once went over to the sound truck, which was parked nearby. Taking the microphone, he began telling the crowd about Catterson's Junior Chamber of Commerce claim. As Pike started to refute it, the redhead rushed up and swung her sign at him, missing his face by inches. ''You're not a congressman!'' she shrieked. ''You're a maniac!'' Flushing, Pike finished his account, and then he moved off toward a group of people who wanted him to autograph some posters. Just as he put the first of the posters down on the hood of a car and raised his pen, the redhead hurried over and tried to cover the poster with her sign. Smiling, Pike quickly autographed the sign. With a look of contempt, she jerked it back and moved away. Just then, a comely woman in her mid-thirties made her way up to Pike and shook hands with him. ''I want to wish you every success,'' she said. ''I went to law school with Catterson, and I'm certainly going to vote for you.''

The Final Encounter

The final encounter between the candidates took place on Tuesday evening, November 1st, a week before Election Day, at the Nassakeag School, in Setauket, under the sponsorship of the Three Village Junior Chamber of Commerce. I met Pike at the Three Village Inn, in Stony Brook, for dinner beforehand, and no sooner had we sat down than he said, "I hear Catterson is steaming about my song. I expect him to make a violent attack on me tonight." He went on to say that since the newspapers had failed to report his rendition of "Ballad for a Bad Boy," he had prepared his first, and probably his last, press release—consisting of Catterson's claim, his own refutation of it, and the text of the song—and had mailed it to the weekly papers in the district the day before. "On this, the timing is the big thing," he said. "The weeklies, which come out on Thursday, will call Catterson for a response to my charge. However, on Wednesday I'll send the dailies my documentation—Catterson's claim, the story of the Montgomery Junior Chamber's book, and a telegram from the United States Junior Chamber denying that they ever named him. That way, the dailies will print the hard evidence on the same day the weeklies come out with his explanation."

The day before, *Newsday* had endorsed Pike, stating that he was "able and industrious" and had "established a fine record of service to his district and to the nation." I assumed that he would be pleased by this, but he was more interested in the paper's assertion, in the same editorial, that Catterson, "the aggressive young chief on the Rackets Bureau . . . favors more aggressive war policy." Reading the line to me, Pike said, "That could hurt me badly, because most of the voters out here also favor a more aggressive war policy." I asked Pike about a report in the papers that Catterson had organized a group of a thousand housewives, who were planning to picket the final debate. "That won't hurt me at all," Pike said. "First of all, it will create some publicity. And, second, it will make the sponsors of the debate angry before things start. That may affect the way the program is run." He laughed and added, "I did consider planting a woman to throw a tomato at me. That would be worth ten thousand votes."

When we arrived at the school, we found not a thousand women picketing but twenty-two. They were marching in two circles side by side—one circle of fourteen women and the other of eight. At first, I assumed they were all Catterson supporters, but then I saw that the larger group carried pro-Democratic posters. The others had signs reading, "WE WANT BREAD AND BUTTER, NOT JOKES AND BALONEY," "HAD ENOUGH? VOTE FOR CATTERSON," "PIKE'S NO PIKER WITH OUR TAX DOLLARS," and

four thousand votes for him to a little under twelve hundred for Catterson—with about three per cent of the votes counted. Pike pointed to the Islip returns approvingly, and I saw that he now had a two-to-one lead there. Smithtown still hadn't come in, so he called the headquarters, but got no news.

That's Wonderful News

While he was on the phone, I went over to stand with Donner. An awesomely pretty girl with long blond hair hurried up to him and cried, "We're way ahead in Huntington!"

Donner patted her on the shoulder. "That's wonderful news, Alice," he said. "Except Huntington isn't in our district."

At eleven o'clock, there were still no returns from Smithtown, so Pike decided to drive over to the Democratic headquarters there. He and his family and I again piled into the car and sped off. On the way, Pike kept nervously switching the radio dial from station to station to get the returns from other races—particularly the one in the Third Congressional District of New York, which he expected to be close. The Smithtown headquarters for the evening turned out to be the Villa Pace, a large, glossy restaurant that was crammed with people with drinks in their hands and cigarettes and cigars in their mouths. As soon as we came in, Pike peered through the smoke, spotted Quinn, and hurried over to him. "How's it look?" he asked.

"They haven't put it on the board yet, but it's about thirty-five thousand to twenty thousand," Quinn answered.

"That's not good enough," Pike said, licking his lips.

A moment later, Domenic Baranello, the Democratic Chairman of Suffolk County, whom I had seen at various Party functions, came up to Pike and pinned to his lapel a large button that read, "Otis Pike for United States Senate."

"No, no," Pike said quickly, taking it off. "You wear it."

Baranello put the button on, and a photographer posed the two men against the election-returns board. Afterward, several other people came by wearing identical buttons, and Pike stopped one of them, a middle-aged woman. "That looks awfully good," he said.

Within an hour, it was clear that Pike had won handsomely, especially considering Rockefeller's victory in New York and other Republican victories around the country. Pike stood up on a chair and made a brief speech to console the local Democratic candidates who had lost and to thank everyone for helping him win, and then we left.

In the parking lot outside, his younger son pulled one of the Pike-for-Senate buttons out of his pocket, held it aloft, and cried, "I got one!"

Pike grinned at him. "Atta boy," he said.

Most of the Fun
Is Being an Amateur

When we got back to the house, at one-thirty, a couple of dozen people were there, waiting to congratulate Pike on his victory. Donner was sunk in a large easy chair in a corner holding a highball and gazing blearily at the milling crowd. I asked him how he felt now, with another victory behind him. "It's not much fun anymore," he answered. "Most of the fun is in being an amateur and figuring out how you're going to correct all the mistakes you've made. I've become too professional. There aren't many mistakes anymore." Recalling the sudden appearance of the Pike-for-Senate buttons, I said that I assumed any more in that direction would mean challenging Senator Jacob Javits. Donner gave me a noncommittal smile, and I asked whether he and Pike meant to take on Javits, and if they did what strategy they might use. "We could leak it that he's Jewish," Donner said, with a shattering burst of laughter.

Although by this time Pike's margin was forty thousand votes out of a total of a hundred and seventy thousand, he was told that Catterson still hadn't conceded—which, in fact, Catterson did not do until around two o'clock, when his secretary called Pike and read a brief statement wishing him luck in the Ninetieth Congress. Pike shook hands all around and then undid his bow tie and opened his collar. "I didn't think I could get so tired," he said, and slumped down on a couch in the living room. Resting his head against the cushion, he closed his eyes and folded his hands on his lap. After a few minutes, I thought he had fallen asleep, but suddenly he opened his eyes and sat up. He looked around wearily, then rose and went over to the television set and switched channels. "I wonder how it looks in the Third," he said.

Perhaps the spirit of the Pike campaign was best recognized by Donner, when he noted that "most of the fun is in being an amateur and figuring out how you are going to correct all the mistakes you've made." However, to the candidate who makes the mistakes and loses, victory is a sweetness he would certainly be willing to trade for the "fun of it." Indeed, across the country defeated candidates far outweigh victorious ones. Many are defeated in the preliminaries before the main events ever get under way.

The Losers

The losers, as documented in *The Politics of Defeat*[3] have much in common. They are generally non-incumbents, about 46 years of age, and may

[3]Robert J. Huckshorn and Robert C. Spencer, *The Politics of Defeat: Campaigning for Congress* (Amherst, Mass.: University of Massachusetts Press, 1971).

or may not be college educated or members of a profession. They have overextended themselves financially, often insist on running their own campaigns, tend to be naive as to party help waiting on the sidelines, and generally misjudge the *feel* of the campaign. Additionally they occasionally make costly mistakes that reveal an unflattering side to the voter, a view that cannot be recouped. Many of these candidates felt their chances were excellent and victory was in their grasp, yet they still lost by varying pluralities.

On the national level the *losers* react to defeat in different fashions. Many of them look forward (so they say) to the next time. They have planned and schemed for years, to get a *crack* at a particular office, and their professionalism won't let them accept defeat. Yet in the pressure of the moment, defeat is a bitter pill to swallow, and many candidates buckle under the emotionalism of the hour. Richard Nixon's 1962 statement, after his California gubernatorial defeat, that the press would "not have Nixon to kick around anymore" was such an outburst. But the professional who is defeated generally reacts in such a way as to close no doors nor burn any bridges.

On the local level, however, this is not always the case. Bitterness, a self-agonizing reevaluation of ideals, a rejection of the system, a leveling of blame, all are reactions by the *smaller* defeated candidate. Thus, *sweet victory,* has its bitter antithesis, and the student of politics, as well as the potential candidate must be prepared for both.

THE MORNING AFTER

In May of 1972, the campaign of America's *new* Abraham Lincoln, Senator Edmund Muskie of Maine, came to an abrupt end. The following morning the excitement of the campaign was gone.

Up a flight of 24 stairs, each riser bearing the banner, "Believe in Muskie," to the scene that best depicts the end of the road for a candidate:

The sad, spacious, almost-empty floor of a campaign headquarters that is closing down.

NO SONG AND DANCE HERE

While national campaigns often close down and move out of town in the tradition of the *big tent shows,* there is no song and dance act for the small office seeker. The *morning after* scenario of a defeated state legislative candidate from a large midwestern state is illustrative.

The campaign office was a small storefront squeezed in between a barbershop and a local drugstore; not on the main street but a block from a busy intersection. The bunting and streamers seemed to sense that "it was all over," for the rain had weighted some of them to where only the slogan could be seen:

Over in the corner, behind closed doors, one hears a man singing at the top of his voice, entertaining himself no doubt: "Who shall I turn to . . . now that it's over?"

The door opened and the substantial figure of the usually ebullient Mark Shields stepped forth. Mr. Shields was to Senator Muskie what Harry O'Donnell was to John V. Lindsay, what Jim Hagerty was to Eisenhower, and what Harry Hopkins was to Roosevelt—the real, political savvy guy that all the politicians and press respect.

"If it had to end," Mr. Shields said, tripping about the room a bit to indicate that he was in a song-and-dance mood, "it should end in Ohio—the mother of presidents."

. . .

The phone rang and Mr. Shields went to his desk and said to whoever was at the other end of the line, "I'm standing in Dunkirk, and the Titanic is steaming toward me." Then he paused and in mock gravity added: "Joe, it is time for people like us to be nice to each other. These are moments when we need each other old buddy."

Ted Meader, Ohio campaign coordinator for Sen. Edmund S. Muskie, joined us about there, just in time to get into the zany act of political workers who were simply slap-happy and numb from the endless hours of work that now had ended in the sudden shock of tragedy.

"What are you," I asked Mr. Shields, trying to remember whether his exact title was "national campaign

"The Man for Tomorrow." Unfortunately for Mr. Ames, the electorate had decided otherwise.

Inside, the hubbub and noise of only a day or two before seemed to echo in the now empty room. It was even darker, almost gloomy, I thought as I stood looking at the posters piled here and there in a general disarray.

In the corner, Bill Johnson, the campaign coordinator for Ames's legislative race sat in his shirtsleeves (I can never recall seeing him in a jacket), talking in interrupted staccato fashion to the party on the other end. As I closed the door he waived, motioning me to a folding chair leaning against the wall. As I sat down, he hung up.

"The damn skinflint." With a wry grin, he asked me what the hell I was doing here. I'd been doing research for a book on politics and had visited several campaigns throughout the state. This one had fascinated me since it seemed to represent all that was supposedly good in American politics, the volunteerism, the enthusiasm, the will to participate in that "game." But at the same time I also recognized all the flaws of an amateur organization.

coordinator'' or ''national campaign director.'' He was the latter: But Mr. Meader supplied this answer: ''He's unemployed, that's what he is.''

''Yes,'' said Mr. Shields, taking another fancy walking dance around the room, ''I'm now just another statistic on Nixon's desk. Do you think he has a retraining program for me?''

He paused in flight for a moment to cite Pat Moynihan's famous words: ''We Irish,'' he said, ''always know that sooner or later life will break your heart.'' He added: ''My heart has been broken about eight or nine times in the last few weeks. . . .''

Someone picked up a card that had fallen from the wall on which was typed: ''Against stupidity even the gods themselves battle in vain.'' All seemed to agree that while the Von Clausewitz comment was a little bitter, it somehow fit the decline and fall of candidate Muskie.

They all spoke well of their candidate. But they all held strong misgivings about the way he had run his campaign. . . .

I pressed to find out what they believed had really gone wrong. They were reluctant to speak ill of their leader; but they seemed to agree that Muskie suffered from a ''small-state syndrome, meaning by this that he always sought to run his national campaign the way he had run his campaigns in little Maine— and that this simply had not worked out well.

The complaints were along these lines:

I told him I had come to see if Ames was planning on dropping by, as I would like to ask him a few questions about his campaign.

He grinned, leaning back in his chair, his rather longish hair falling into his face. In a moment he said, ''I thought you were only interested in winners.''

I remarked that a view of a losing campaign that seemed to have so much going for it would be a valuable addition to my research.

He shook his head. ''I can tell you what went wrong—everything. No money, no help when we needed it, the damn party never really recognized our needs.''

At that moment the door swung open and Ames walked in. He looked tired, almost haggard, but immediately upon seeing me smiled with an outstretched hand.

''Hello, Rog. How's it going? What are you doing here?''

As Ames seated himself on the corner of the desk, pushing Johnson's feet out of the way, I explained my goal. He looked a bit strangely at Johnson, then shaking his head he said with a half-hearted grin, ''What are you doing, writing a chapter on losers?''

I explained to him that everyone was willing to write about winners but there was little available on losing campaigns. I then reiterated on losing campaigns. I then reiterated my desire to show both sides of the campaign; to point out where, in the views of the candidate and manager, the campaign effort had gone wrong. Perhaps because he was too tired at this point, or he thought it might help, Ames began to talk of political defeat. It was a difficult task to put lost dreams into words.

That Senator Muskie had attempted to sell "image" not "issues" and the people were interested in taxes, war, and other problems, not whether Muskie was going to bring the country together and could be trusted and believed in, and so on.

That when Senator Muskie finally decided to hit hard on the issues, it was too late.

That all major decisions of this kind came too late, simply because the Senator, from a small state where he always had been able to handle all the policy and planning, never came to realize that in a race for president he must rely on an expert staff for making these turns in the road.

A voice from another room called in with this comment at one point: "Muskie always wanted to be trusted—but he never really trusted those around him enough—never enough to delegate authority."

But the mood had become too sober for Mark Shields. He floated across the room again, disappeared into the next, and levitated back in again on wings of song.

"How now my love?" he asked, now wailing, plaintively, "now that it is over."[4]

[4]From Godfrey Sperling, Jr., "Scene from Muskie Closing Night," *The Christian Science Monitor*, 1 May 1972, p. 2. Reprinted by permission from The Christian Science Monitor. © 1972 The Christian Science Publishing Society. All rights reserved.

"I don't know really where we got into trouble. Perhaps we were all along." Johnson nodded in agreement.

"I guess money was the worst problem. Everybody pledged, but not nearly as many delivered. As the money ran out, and it became more desperate, I finally decided to mortgage my house."

I looked up rather startled. It was supposed to be a prime rule that the candidate didn't put any more money into his contest than he could afford. Mortgaging was definitely out of the question. He saw my reaction.

"I know. I know it was wrong. But we needed money. 'Stoney' Hills, my campaign finance man who also handled media, said we had to have more exposure." He shook his head. "You know you can only reach so many people by pressing the flesh. As the opposition opened up its final leg, they just buried us. They had billboards, yard signs, TV. My God, I never saw so much at once!"

Johnson joined in, "I warned you, Jim. I told you we had to stick to the plan. But you had to listen to that S.O.B. ad salesman. If they had to have it, we had to too. You just can't . . ." His voice trailed off and ended with a negative shake of his head.

Ames sighed. "I know . . . now."

"Even the volunteers didn't help too much," Johnson noted. "They were all as eager as hell, but not too organized. The coordinator was a college professor who really didn't know what the hell he was doing. We had those kids all over the place. They . . ." The phone rang, and Johnson picked it up.

"Yeah! Hi, Harry old pal! Glad you returned my call. Yeah! I want to get those desks and chairs back to Overlakes. Well, I thought maybe you and some of the boys could get that truck. . . ." His voice trailed off. "Yeah! O.K. Forget it." He hung up shrugging his shoulders. "Nobody wants to help."

Ames looked at me rather embarrassedly.

"What about the volunteers?" I asked.

"Oh they were all right, I guess. . . ."

"Are you going to run again?" I looked at both men.

"Well, I don't know. I thought I could do a good job. Hell! I did do a good job on the commission. But I don't know."

There was another pause.

"First I've got to pay off that $10,000. Then . . . it's really hard on the wife and kids. I don't know if it's really worth it. Sometimes I think nobody cares."

He stood up.

"Well, I've got to get to work. I'm in business you know, and it's been hurting lately. Nice to see you again. I'll look forward to that chapter on losers."

He forced a weak grin and moved toward the door. The phone rang again, echoing in the empty room.[5]

Bedfellows Make for Strange Politics

The bitter taste of defeat has always been an accepted risk for those who joust in the affairs of state. Whether this potential cost has been carefully calculated often depends on how serious the contender pursues politics as a way of life. Yet there is another group of individuals whose vulnerability is not eased with the glory of victory. In fact, the anxiety of victory may cause them silently to reject public life. These are the wives of politicians. Though

[5]From composite interviews conducted by the authors during the 1972–74 political campaigns, although most of the conversation was from recorded interviews with a California candidate.

"That's the difference between just a politician
and a real statesman."

given little fanfare and even less tribute, their attitudes can have major implications for a campaign. The morale of a candidate can be impaired by a wife whose anxieties over family and other personal matters becomes obvious. Whether in the turmoil of the campaign or the demands of office, even the small amenities that she has given the private man may now be efficiently provided by staffers. But even though removed from the power and glory of victory, these wives too are a special caste of political veterans.

. . . In a sense, both Betty Ford and Pat Nixon were veterans. No so the younger, more fragile blonde who . . . sat silently in the Heritage Room of Boston's Parker House and watched her husband bow out of the 1976 presidential contest. Joan Kennedy, demonstrating the rigid control expected of political wives in America—especially Kennedy wives—stayed calm and clear-eyed, her gaze focused on a point near her husband, her hands folded demurely in her lap. She remained all but immobile when her husband said that he would not subject his family to the rigors of a presidential campaign. Then her control began to give way at the edges, and she blinked back tears. Joan, whose life has been made miserable by a political role she neither sought nor was capable of handling, could no longer completely conceal her feelings. Said a longtime Washington friend who watched the drama on television: "You could hear her relief 500 miles away."

The ordeal of the political wife . . . is more than a matter of mere gossip, more than a personal problem. It was important enough to help knock the leading Democratic contender out of the 1976 presidential race. Under the steady glare of television, the personality and character of the political wife is more crucial than ever, but the treatment she receives has not caught up with her importance. Torn between the role she feels she ought to fill and the part that is handed her, she understandably grows distraught. The problem is most conspicuous in the U.S., where traditionally politicians' wives have played a far more public role than elsewhere. . . .

Some women, to be sure, would be unhappy no matter what their husbands' occupations and would turn in their despair to drink, to drugs, to affairs. But probably no other career makes such relentless demands on wives and families as politics. Witness Pat Nixon in virtual exile at San Clemente. "We are worried about Pat," an associate of the Nixons confides. "She has not been in touch with any of her close friends. It's not like her." Witness Eleanor McGovern, once again on the stump in South Dakota, confessing with her customary candor: "I would like to have had another year before campaigning."

The Wife
Is Public Property

Marriage to a high-level corporate executive, educator or military officer has similar strains—but not really comparable. Those pressures can be worked out in relative privacy and obscurity. Not so with the office-holder's wife. She becomes public property, an extension of the public man, subject to unending scrutiny, judgments, accolades and criticism. She is often used and then abandoned or ignored or forced to turn the other way as "power groupies" cluster around the Big Man. She must sparkle to help her husband but beware of outshining him. She must know the issues and the arguments for and against. She must often maintain two homes without really living in either. Many such women want out. And yet, for all the pressures and drawbacks, quite a few would have it no other way, particularly after their husbands reach the real heights.

Almost all resent the near-total loss of privacy. Ellen Proxmire, former wife of Wisconsin's Democratic Senator William Proxmire, characterizes the experience in a book about her life in politics, *One Foot in Washington*. "I sometimes think that goldfish in a bowl are much better off than the public figures they resemble," she writes. "Those who study their silky movements from outside the glass don't critize what they are wearing, what they do, what they say, what they mean, nor do they ask the fish lots of questions or expect them to do much more than entertain."

While many wives prefer to remain in the bowl, an increasing number are openly expressing discontent and looking for means to change the system that ensnares them in a variety of ways. Some, like Abigail McCarthy or Mieke Tunney or Phyllis Dole, have left their husbands and named politics as the corespondent. Others, like Betty Ford and Joan Kennedy, have sought psychiatric help and owned up to it—something that would have been unthinkable a few years ago. Occasionally there appears a Cornelia Wallace or a Martha Mitchell who does not hesitate to speak her own mind whatever her husband may think.

A Contradiction in Terms

A political wife, in a sense, is a contradiction in terms. She is expected to manage a household and raise a family, often with little or no help from her husband; yet, at the same time she is called upon to make speeches and win votes for her husband. She must be the model of purity and probity at home, but she must be Everywoman outside, with a ready smile and a cheerful word for all the importuning bores on the campaign trail. Writes Ellen Proxmire, "She is first and always a mother, a cook, a chauffeur, a seamstress and a homemaker, but she is also an adviser, a social secretary, a campaigner and even a TV personality."

In a book of reminiscences just published, appropriately titled *Uphill,* Eleanor McGovern tells about being late for a press conference during the 1972 Democratic National Convention in Miami. "I was in the penthouse pullman kitchen washing the dishes after cooking bacon and eggs for George and the children and the grandsons and the other relatives and staff who wandered in and out." One of her aides reprimanded her: "I can't tell the press that you're late to talk about being a potential First Lady because you're scrubbing a frying pan." Eleanor shot back: "Then go and find me a cook." That night she got one.

During a campaign, a wife is considered a surrogate for her husband and the closest approximation to him. She must perform as skillfully as he does but without his experience or all-consuming drive. Seasoned campaigner that she became, Joan Kennedy was forever wondering whether Ted would approve of what she said. Even such an articulate speechmaker as Abigail McCarthy worried constantly. In her reminiscences, *Private Faces/Public Places,* she wrote, "After each interview, I lay awake in a black nightmare of anxiety, fearful that I had said something which would do Gene irreparable harm."

Occasionally this nightmare becomes a reality for political wives. During the critical New Hampshire primary campaign in 1972, Jane Muskie was reported in the Manchester *Union Leader* to be fond of drink and salty jokes. Incensed at what he considered to be a snide attack on his wife, Muskie was reduced to tears in a public appearance one snowy evening. This display of emotion, observers agree, cost Muskie a considerable number of votes in the primary and slowed his momentum as a Presidential candidate.

The political wife is essential to the campaign, and then again she is not. For the jealous staff surrounding the candidate, she may become an adversary—a rival claimant on their hero's time, which they think should be devoted exclusively to getting elected. "The wife sees the staff as a rapacious group of self-serving people, and they see her as a jealous old bag," says Washington Psychiatrist William Davidson. "The political wife is at the whim of the staff," adds an aide to Eleanor McGovern. "When the candidate can't be there, she is expected to give the speech and know the issue. When he *is* there, she is expected to cross her legs at the ankles and listen adoringly." Eleanor, in fact, got in trouble with the staff in 1972 when her speeches began to earn better press notices than her husband's. She was instructed, in so many words, to cool it. Be good, but not too good.

Can a more dutiful, adoring, enduring wife be found on the campaign trail than Muriel Humphrey? Nor is her husband inconsiderate. Nevertheless, she was taken by surprise when Hubert announced that he would run for the presidency in 1960. She sent him a wry wire: LET ME KNOW IF I CAN BE OF HELP. . . .

Given the conflicting demands, a political wife begins to wonder who she is. She may lose her sense of worth and identity. "Politics has nullified my personality," claims Joy Dirksen Baker, who has suffered double political jeopardy, as it were. Her father was the sonorous Senate orator Everett Dirksen; her husband is Tennessee Senator Howard Baker. "The problem started with my father, who was famous," she says. "Then the Watergate hearings came along, and Howard catapulted to prominence. I've always felt I was sort of an appendage."

To avoid that danger, political wives are carving out lives or careers of their own. Says Marion Javits, who has managed to do so with considerable éclat: "The wife who accompanies the man who shakes the hands knows what 'impersonal' means best of all. She is completely left out . . . You become part of your husband's audience. Although the ego of people in public life doesn't quite equal that of Orson Welles, who is supposed to have wanted applause when he climbed out of the bathtub, it is there."

It was after being elbowed aside once too often that Angelina Alioto decided to punish her husband Joseph, the ambitious mayor of San Francisco, by disappearing for 17 days . . . without telling him where she was going. "At five feet," she says, "I'm the right size to be elbowed in the head." Her husband often failed to introduce her at functions they attended together; he even appropriated her quotes, she claims, without giving her credit. "Son of a biscuit-eater, I'm nobody's robot."

A Friend in Power Is a Friend Lost

Henry Adams wrote that "a friend in power is a friend lost"; that may apply to a husband as well. He becomes a different man, and not necessarily a better one. However humble his office or aptitude, he develops an exaggerated notion of his power. "His ego is constantly fed," observes Jane Muskie, who periodically denies such nourishment to her own husband. "A little kick in the behind sometimes helps," she adds. "Politicians are not a lovable lot," says an internist who has treated countless numbers of them and their wives during nearly 30 years of practice. "They are self-serving egomaniacs, and I take off my hat to their wives. I don't know how the husbands get away with it." He believes that no more than 3% or 4% of political wives genuinely enjoy what they are doing. . . .

Political wives find that theirs is the last cause to which their husbands devote themselves. California Representative Pete McCloskey, recently divorced from his wife, regretfully seconds a friend's assessment: "Pete's a great guy. He'll do anything for his country, his friends and his family, in that order—which is not very good for his family." Adds McCloskey: "You get so involved with the cause that you lose your sensitivity to people." Nancy Riegle, who is divorced from Michigan's Democratic Congressman Donald Riegle, acidly agrees, "The trouble is these guys think that what they're doing is so important they lose perspective. They think they're being unselfish worrying about the kids in Viet Nam and the poor in the ghettos, but that's a bunch of crap. All they want to do is see their name in print. It's all for their own aggrandizement. When it comes to being a daddy or a husband, there is no time."

Psychiatrist Davidson, who traveled with the McCarthy presidential campaign in 1968, argues that "politicians have overextended themselves physically and emotionally to the point where their judgment is impaired.'' Rather than lead the errant husband back to reality, the family tends to become over-protective for fear of letting him down. Through the best of intentions, they thus confirm him in his illusions. Barbara (''Bootsie'') Mandel, whose husband of 32 years, the Democratic Governor of Maryland, deserted her . . . in order to marry a younger woman, concurs. ''A man like Marvin Mandel, he starts to believe what his staff tells him, and they only tell what he wants to hear. Then he comes home, and his wife tells him the truth.''

A constant stress on politicians' wives is the frequent absence of their busy husbands. ''Those wives may talk about hating politics,'' says a Washington woman who has worked closely with the wives of two presidential candidates. ''But what they really mean is that they hate being abandoned. . . .''

After having her husband to herself for much of an idyllic summer, Happy Rockefeller fretted . . . about the separation that the vice presidency will bring. She greeted the appointment with distinct coolness. It is not that she is displeased, says a family spokesman, but she is ''less than enchanted with the idea, and her sons are having trouble getting used to it.'' Said a family friend: ''She's not throwing her hat in the air about getting back into public life, but she is throwing her hat in the air because her husband is so happy.''

Left very much on her own, a wife learns to cope with problems that a more conventional husband might take off her hands. Knowing that she will be seeing even less of her husband than before, Helen Jackson, wife of Democratic presidential hopeful Henry (''Scoop'') Jackson, has enrolled in a course in home maintenance so that she will be able to repair plumbing and electrical appliances. Last year two Senate wives—Barbara Eagleton and Ann Stevens—took an auto-repair course.

Long or frequent absences by a politician father can be hardest on children. Susan Ford, 17, wandering about the White House family quarters in T shirt and carpenter's pants, recalled that ''not having a daddy at home made it really hard on Mother. She had to put up with three boys— and me.'' But she added, ''Dad really just wasn't home a lot, so when he was there, it was so special we did everything we could to make him happy—and he did everything he could to make us happy.'' When John Lindsay was a Congressman he left his family at home, as do many others. His wife Mary recalls that ''when our daughter Margie was six, John walked in with a couple of friends and she said in a loud voice, 'How come everybody else gets to see Daddy and we don't?' That did it. We moved to Washington, and I think it saved the children.''

There is also the danger of an absent husband's taking permanent leave. Other women are an ever-present threat. Political office, or campaigning for it, can convert the most unlikely prospect into a Casanova. For the first time in his life, he discovers that he is irresistible to certain women with a craving for power. The temptation is hard to resist, and many scarcely try. "It's a very heady business," says Jane Muskie. "You go to a party alone, and when your husband arrives you see all those women advance on him like vultures. Well, that does something to a man that's not normal."

Barbara Howar, a shrewd observer, and participant in the Washington sex-and-politics scene, refers to all the secretaries and stewardesses available to the vulnerable politician as so much "cannon fodder." Says Howar, who has been linked more than once with familiar Washington names: "The kind of man who will stand up and say, 'Vote for me because I am better than he' has just the kind of ego that needs that physical contact, that someone saying, 'I want you.'" The protective devices against these dangerous liaisons have broken down, she feels. "Washington never has had any standards. This town has no morality at all. It was always the stern standards of their home communities that people brought with them to Washington." Now, she maintains, morals are almost as relaxed in the provinces as in the nation's capital, and wives suffer for it while their husbands make the most of it.

Beyond these already severe stresses is one that plagues every political family: the hatred that even the well-motivated, understated politician arouses. "I'm no stranger to hard-fought politics," says Jo Hall, wife of Oklahoma Governor David Hall. But she was appalled at the vehemence of the attacks on her husband, who lost a recent bid for re-election. "You can't imagine how troubling it is to look into the faces of people with absolute hatred in their eyes. I've caught myself remembering that these were the people who cheered when President Kennedy was assassinated. If you love someone, be prepared to be hurt, and hurt often, in today's political climate."

Though it is something of a minor miracle, given the problems, some wives survive and even thrive in politics. To do so, they must set some of the rules and reserve some time, space and independence for themselves. One way is to insist on the primacy of the home. Except during a crisis, Mary Lindsay took the phone off the hook at Gracie Mansion for 1½ hours every night of the week during her husband's mayoralty. While all callers—county bosses, job seekers and cranks—got busy signals, John Lindsay had an interval of enforced leisure during which he could catch up with his family.

When he is not embroiled in campaigning, Pittsburgh's Democratic mayor, Pete Flaherty, makes a habit of coming home for dinner every night so that he can chat with his five children. Once he is finished, he usually goes off to an officially scheduled dinner. "He gets there after everybody has eaten," says his wife Nancy. "But they don't seem to mind." And meanwhile, she adds, "Pete has told me and the children what is going on." Junie Butler, wife of a Virginia Congressman, states this creed for the wife determined to avoid being submerged by the political life: "If my husband doesn't like my image, he can get a new model. If his constituents don't like my image, they can get a new Congressman. I feel my part is to have a solid family."

An Independent Course of Action

Other wives are striking out on independent courses of their own. Betty Talmadge, wife of Georgia Senator Herman Talmadge manages a meat business, Talmadge Farms, which grosses $3.5 million a year. "I have shaken hands," she says, "but I have never made a campaign speech in my life." Even Muriel Humphrey, a notably docile political wife, recently declared a measure of independence from the indefatigable Hubert. She now spends most of her time at their lakeside house in Waverly, Minn. "What is the life of a Senator's wife anyway?" she muses. "I find more satisfaction in doing the things I really care about, seeing my children and grandchildren, playing the piano, the artistry of needlepoint. I love being alone."

Some wives turn out to be a political match for their husbands. Jane Hart, who holds a helicopter pilot's license, is often a provocative step ahead of her husband, Michigan Senator Philip Hart. She refused to pay her 1972 federal income tax because of the Viet Nam War and journeyed on her own to Hanoi to talk to American P.O.W.'s. Hart, who candidly admits that his wife financed his political career, quips, "Bedfellows make strange politics." Carolyn Bond, wife of Missouri's Democratic Governor Kit Bond, relishes campaigning as much as her husband. She has visited every state hospital in Missouri and is considering running for office herself some day. . . .

Political wives are agitating for something more than politics as usual. For them a career of scrambling for office and then struggling to stay there is not enough. The rebellion of the political wife—and her passive protest of divorce, alcoholism and withdrawal—is a plea not just for women, but also for a more human politics.[6]

[6]From "The Relentless Ordeal of Political Wives," *Time,* 7 October 1974, pp. 15–17, 20–22.

A candidate usually decides to seek public office with the intention of winning victory. He considers all the advantages and disadvantages possessed and then, in the consultation of friends and colleagues, reach what perhaps will be the most significant decision of their life—to go before the electorate. The spotlight of public acclaim and recognition is often a severe task master. For a congressman like Pike, the strain is obvious, but to the comparatively unknown challenger electioneering often proves to be an unmerciful ordeal.

6

The Decision: Running for Public Office

George J. Delaney lost 17 pounds last June and hasn't regained them. That's when the director of community relations for Consolidated Edison won a tough primary fight for the Republican nomination for state senator in the Riverdale section of the Bronx.

Bert N. Mitchell is down to 173 pounds from his spring weight of 200. "And it's not November yet," says Mr. Mitchell, an accountant who's seeking election as state senator from the Sixth District in Nassau County.

Neither of these six-footers intended to diet. A lean and hungry look is one of the bonuses reaped by the businessman-politician trying to scale two greasy poles of prestige at the same time. . . .

If, like Bert Mitchell, he is a partner in an unincorporated firm of certified public accountants such as Lucas Tucker & Co., he has some flexibility and can "get a little backstopping" from his four partners and the staff of 35. Being a partner, however, means "you're saddled with a heavy load of responsibility," he points out.

It's Not Sufficient to Be
Elected by Black People

Mr. Mitchell is up and running (without breakfast) Monday through Friday at 6 A.M. to assemble a crew of campaign workers. They arrive at a Long Island railroad station at 6:30 A.M. where, until 8:15 A.M. they distribute literature and introduce the candidate to Manhattan-bound commuters.

Exposure is crucial to Mr. Mitchell, a Democrat and a Negro running in a conservative Republican district that is 90 percent white. "I contend that for black people to make political progress, it's not sufficient to be elected by black people," he says. His campaign committee is 60 percent white.

At 8:15 A.M., Mr. Mitchell heads for campaign headquarters in Hempstead for coffee and conferences. At 10 A.M., he arrives at his office in Harlem where he proceeds to juggle his accounting practice with campaign necessities (telephone calls, interviews, strategy revision) and manages to miss lunch at least three days a week.

Some days he leaves the office at 4 P.M. to ring doorbells in his district from 5 P.M. to 8:30 P.M. Other days he stays until 8 P.M. In either case, the hours from 8:30 P.M. to midnight (and sometimes 3 A.M.) are a round of meetings, coffee-klatsches and innumerable ploys aimed at making himself known to voters and keeping supporters busy and enthusiastic. "If I'm lucky, I have dinner three times a week," he says.

Weekends, from 10 A.M. to 6 P.M., are for ringing doorbells and meeting voters in supermarkets and shopping centers. Many candidates pound the pavements because house and apartment dwellers are afraid to answer their doorbells. The street scene is also much cheaper than radio and television advertising in a year when campaign contributions are hard to come by.

Saturday evenings, he makes the banquet and party circuit with his wife. "I show up at any group that has more than two people," says Mr. Mitchell, who recently rapped with the local Gay Liberation Front and was promised their backing. Sunday evenings are for campaign committee meetings until 2 A.M.

Three years ago, Mr. Mitchell won a hotly contested seat on the Roosevelt (L.I.) School Board while working as comptroller for the Hamilton Life Insurance Company. Then, as George Delaney is now, he had to be vigilant about separating his 9-to-5 career from his community self. . . .

For George Delaney it isn't that easy. His state senatorial campaign obliges him to condense his open-ended community relations job at Con Ed into an 8:30 A.M. to 5:30 or 6 P.M. bind and to use lunch hours for political chores such as interviews or correspondence. Evenings and weekends follow the inexorable pace of meetings, speeches and street campaigning with office homework sandwiched in or tacked on at the end.

Like Mr. Mitchell, he is grateful for a cooperative wife and photogenic children. Maura Delaney is a Republican committeewoman. Three of their four sons (ages 5, 8, 9) are clubhouse regulars and astute street corner campaigners.

Considering himself an underdog, Mr. Delaney is concentrating on the local issues and trying to gather nonpartisan support. The most exhilarating donation he received was a $100 personal check from Charles F. Luce, Chairman of Con Ed. "It pleased me more than anything, especially because he's a Democrat," Mr. Delaney said exulting. . . .[1]

There are also serious questions of economics for a person considering elective office, particularly if the individual is the family breadwinner. Not only will the campaign significantly dilute the business and professional activities of the candidate, with a consequential reduction in income, but what happens if the candidate is elected? There are many "almost" candidates who changed their minds when they face the economic realities of a successful campaign. Take the example of a $22,000-a-year salesman. The median average state legislative salary is about $7,000 to $8,000. This results in a loss of nearly $14,000 in family income—a stiff penalty for serving the public interest. Although these dollars do not reflect per diem expenses, they nevertheless do constitute a considerable loss. Thus, a decision to run for public office must be based on a careful evaluation of all the pitfalls.

However, victory in terms of acquiring office is not necessarily the final achievement of a political candidate. Many times, in deciding to run, candidates want to make a *political point.* That is, they wish to focus attention on a particular issue, change the direction of their party by demonstrating the popularity of their cause, or perhaps gain political recognition for themselves by challenging a political incumbent. A congressman, such as Paul McCloskey,[2] who tried to redirect the Republican party, could not hope to defeat the incumbent president in the primaries; nevertheless, he could perhaps gain additional stature with a certain segment of the electorate (youth) or demonstrate that he is a dedicated statesman looking for alternatives to the quagmire of administration policies. Such individuals must be as careful as any other candidate in considering their ultimate objective. For this type of candidate has the added risk

[1]Marilyn Bender, "After-Five Politics, Ambition and Jobs May Clash," *New York Times,* 4 October, 1970, pp. 1–2.

[2]Republican, then Independent, congressman from California, who challenged Richard Nixon's conduct of the Vietnam war by opposing him in the 1972 primaries.

of not only endangering his political base, but in making powerful enemies within his own party or group.[3] As citizens interested in the political process, we must be able to judge the worthiness of the McCloskeys as well as the candidates who genuinely strive for their party's nomination.

Indeed the process that the candidate goes through in making his/her decision to run for public office is often as important to the voter as it is to the candidate. The characteristics that eventually lead an individual to seek the nomination, the liabilities, and the assets offer a clue to the candidates' abilities and sometimes forecast future chances of success, both as a politician and as a public servant.

Challenge, Excitement, and Satisfaction Are Central

What, then, drives an individual into America's "most neglected, . . . most abused and . . . most ignored profession."[4] Today's student of politics is too often willing to jump to the conclusion that it is to obtain riches at *the public trough*. This argument follows that of George Washington Plunkitt, the corrupt politician from Tammany Hall, who said that *honest graft* was the goal of all politicians.[5] Yet, if this is a prime or even important reason, it is difficult to explain why individuals like Nelson Rockefeller or California industrialist Norton Simon would spend millions of dollars on campaigning to obtain an office that would return only a fraction of their expenditures.[6] Obviously there are other attractions to an individual such as Rockefeller, or indeed any person of means, to seek public office. Perhaps in this instance, the prestige is attractive, the idea that, for one who has everything else, prestige is an added factor to consider. But does not an individual of Rockefeller's stature already command such acclaim? Public service is also a viable, and in this example perhaps the most viable, explanation. Challenge, excitement, and satisfaction are still other factors.

However, for the average candidate seeking office many more considerations besides those that are obvious will impinge on the decision. The

[3]During the 1972 congressional elections, McCloskey became a target for Republican politics in his home district, attempting to unseat him. After a bitter and hard-fought campaign, he narrowly retained his seat.

[4]John F. Kennedy, spring commencement, Syracuse University, 1957.

[5]See William J. Riordan, *Plunkitt of Tammany Hall* (New York: Knopf, 1948). George Washington Plunkitt was a member of the corrupt Tammany Hall political machine during the "guilded age." He achieved his niche in history by explaining the legality of "honest" versus "dishonest" graft.

[6]See James M. Perry, *The New Politics: The Expanding Technology of Political Manipulation* (New York: Clarkson Potter, 1968), p. 135; and Herbert Alexander, "Political Broadcasting in 1968," *Television Quarterly* 9 (Spring 1970): 42, in which costs of campaigns are discussed.

"I've always prided myself as spokesman for the grassroot voters . . .
Lately, though, I'm worried about the image of the word 'grass'."

Grin and Bear It by George Lichty. Courtesy of Field Newspaper Syndicate.

political novice, besides seeking prestige and other possible benefits, may
be aiming at higher positions of responsibility. The office for which they are
running is a stepping stone for attaining this other goal. Some find that
public office affords them the opportunity to influence, for good or ill, their
own political fate. Still others discover that the humdrum of a corporate
and/or professional career does not provide enough excitement to suit their
tastes. All of these considerations are weighed when the individual decides
to toss his hat into the ring.

Christopher T. Bayley, an attorney in a large West Coast city, considered these and other possibilities when he decided to seek the office of
county prosecutor. In discussing the experience, Bayley divided his decision
into five phases: (1) a personal desire to seek office; (2) the consideration of
friends' opinions; (3) the pre-decision phase; (4) the final private decision,
and (5) the final public decision. When we evaluate a potential candidate,
should we consider some of these same points?

What is it like to seek public office? . . . For discussion purposes, I have
divided the process into five phases, from a complete blank in your mind
about running for office until the time you are formally and publicly a
candidate.

229

It is very difficult to determine a beginning of phase I. Anyone who runs for public office usually has some background that interests him in this kind of career. Usually it means having worked for other candidates, causes or issues, or having been involved in political activities or something similar. There are an infinite variety of experiences that can set the stage for seriously considering yourself a potential candidate. I believe that most individuals who become candidates get the idea in their mind, and then proceed from there. Seldom does a group of people approach an individual guaranteeing him financial support and workers if he will seek public office. That is an unreal model. If an individual has the motivation required to win an election, he will self-start.

My experience is somewhat typical. I graduated from law school in

1966, and went into the standard law school practice. I returned to my home town, became associated with a law firm, and for the first two years was a young lawyer in a large firm doing the usual corporate and probate legal business. I was also active in a number of statewide activities usually involving political issues. One organization I helped found was CHECC (Choose an Effective City Council). This was a bipartisan group interested in electing new people to the city council. Although occurring before my phase one, this activity contributed to my decision by providing me with a political frame of reference. During 1968 I was very active in a number of statewide campaigns and was cofounder of a group devoted to getting young people involved in the political process. It postured itself as an organization that did not ask people what their party preference was, but simply wanted them to get involved. Before 1968, I had harbored the thought of seeking public office. After the election the state attorney general asked me to join his staff, heading the Consumer Protection Division. This was a period of decision making. If I look at it from the advantage of hindsight, it is easy to see that this decision was the first step toward a public career. By accepting a position with the attorney general, I decided to leave the world of private law with its various positive factors of financial security and regular schedules, for a public life and one which I knew would have considerable exposure. So from the early part of 1969 until I decided to run for prosecuting attorney, I was chief of a division which had more contact with the public than any other part of the attorney general's office. By late fall of 1969 the situation was stable. I was satisfied with my position; it was a great challenge. I had always harbored the thought that if the right opportunity presented itself, I should like to run for public office. But in my own mind the position would have to be one which I felt was as interesting as the one I now possessed and secondly, be one I had a chance of winning. In the fall of 1969 there was one position that met both these criteria. Thus in my own mind I had proceeded through phase one before I had discussed the possibility with anyone else.

The position available was that of county prosecuting attorney. Basically the prosecuting attorney's position was one with which I was quite familiar. It is a position of tremendous responsibility, with a large staff, and an ability to initiate positive action. If an individual is interested in public service, there are few other positions around that can match the possibilities of this office. One of my stipulations had been met—it was an office that offered a challenge. In my own mind the question was whether or not I could win the election.

There was a Republican incumbent who had been there for over 21 years and never been defeated. No one had even come close to doing so. In the view of the public, he was an entrenched political figure, and no one in his right mind would even think of challenging someone of that stature. However, I believed he had some vulnerabilities. He had been in office a long time, and problems had been uncovered that indicated the possibility that his political base had eroded. Perhaps people would vote for a change. During the first phase of thinking about it myself, I had reached the conclusion that he was a viable target. I suppose in thinking back in November and December of 1969 I thought a lot about this myself; then I began to talk to other people. At this point I had entered phase two.

Phase II:
Discussing Possibilities for Public Office

Phase II began with a very general discussion of the possibilities of seeking this office. The people in whom I had confided, as you might imagine, were individuals with whom I had worked in CHECC, earlier political endeavors, and individuals I had known from my college and even earlier days. This "thinking-about-it-with-others" phase lasted until the end of January. We put together a small group of five or six people to analyze the situation. The first thing I had to do was to convince this group that the position was worth seeking and there was an opportunity to win. This took some selling because the members of this group felt the incumbent could not be defeated if he chose to seek reelection. One of the unknown factors was his intention in this regard. After an extensive period of discussion, the group finally decided that the effort was worthy of further consideration. As a result, we moved into phase III.

Phase III:
The Pre-decision Phase

The third phase of consideration, which I call the predecision phase, is something I think most candidates, if they have a well-organized approach, must consider in a conscientious manner. It's not just a haphazard approach of contacting people who might become financial contributors or are political sages. You have to do it in a well-organized fashion. What you are trying to find out in this predecision phase is whether or not resources are available even to consider a campaign. Additionally you want to know whether the people really have good political judgment and are not biased by a personal commitment to you. This is actually an operation of expanding the original group of five or six persons to include a larger number. We did have a series of meetings with people who had raised money, and, although they were receptive, they considered the undertaking to be a long shot. They did, however, recognize the need for a change. During this predecision phase the committee was able to measure the general feeling of the populace, as well as to obtain some commitment of financial support. This later commitment was initially obtained through people who were not wealthy but were friends of mine from law practice and other contemporaries who agreed to pledge a certain amount of money per month. The first pledge was for three months. If the campaign actually proceeded, then pledges would be continued throughout the campaign. At this point I am unable to give you the exact numbers involved, but they were in excess of 20 people all pledging between 5 and 20 dollars a month. Later we organized a pledge breakfast, which is a standard technique for raising funds similar to a payroll deduction plan. Thus during the predecision stage the campaign began to take shape. Unknowns such as the incumbent's indecision on whether or not to run for reelection or the likelihood of other candidates and similar factors were still unresolved. In my opinion one of the key factors in a political race is to get involved early enough to discourage other likely candidates.

In the Republican party no one else seemed interested in the prosecuting attorney's position. I believe one reason to be that most of the party rank and file felt that unless the incumbent retired it was foolish to challenge him. In the Democratic ranks, the challenger who ended up being the final candidate was probably making similar considerations. He was working behind the scenes and, by announcing early, he discouraged other Democrats from seeking the position.

Phase IV:
The Private Decision Phase

The fourth and fifth phases the candidate must consider, I term the private decision phase and the public decision phase. The private decision is decided for oneself in your "heart of hearts" that you are going to run. Naturally, through the first three phases I have discussed, there is a desire to run. You would not be maneuvering and going through the time and energy getting your friends interested, if you did not really wish to seek public office. However, the basic underlying motivation is extremely important, more so than might be realized. If a candidate is reluctant or if his friends must talk him into it, it is unlikely he will win an election unless he falls into a vacancy or good fortune makes the position a political plum. This private decision is similar to an airplane flight. You eventually commit and then pass the point of no return. You decide you are going to run, and it is almost impossible to turn back. In my own particular position

I suppose I made the private decision some time in March. After having made that decision, it was a matter of further expanding the interested core group and trying to increase the financial base.

Phase V:
The Public Decision Phase

We decided that the formal announcement, phase V, would come on the first of June. We met with a media advisor, not exactly an ad agency representative, who had some experience in these matters and designed a theme for the campaign. The brochures, letterhead, buttons, and other paraphernalia were produced during the month of May before the official announcement. The idea of the campaign was to center on the theme *equal justice for all*. But before we made any announcement publicly, we were working on the basic ingredients of the campaign. It is necessary to have these ingredients ready when you make your formal announcement. Items such as tabloids, brochures, and so on are necessary to have on hand immediately after the announcement. Additionally it is extremely important to demonstrate concern from the beginning. Start doorbelling. Organize coffee hours. Pass out literature. The campaign really gets started when you have all of your materials ready to go at the moment you announce. Some candidates make the error of announcing publicly with no follow-up. The psychological dip that follows for three or four weeks makes people believe the individual is uninterested or perhaps even unannounced.

We were able to finance the intiial printing of the brochures based on the financial resources already raised. The final public decision phase, phase V, was made around the first of June at a press conference. The same day we also held a breakfast announcement gathering.

One of the most important factors in making both the private and public decision was that the federal grand jury had been sitting during the early months of 1970 and had indicted an assistant chief of police, the first to be brought to trial in a series of officials involving police corruption. The police payoff system had been rumored and written about, but little had been done. The grand jury intended to expose this corruption, and it was quite clear to us that this would reflect poorly on the incumbent prosecuting attorney. Obviously he had been in a position to act but, for whatever reasons, had failed to do so.

As the trial progressed, it soon became evident that a significant portion of the community felt the incumbent prosecuting attorney should have done something, the revelations at the trial providing a fortuitous boost in the early phases of the campaign. . . . I attended part of the public testimony and, as the trial continued, I began to ask where the prosecuting attorney had been when most of these crimes had been committed. I must admit those events were considerations which helped me reach my public decision to run for office.

In the end analysis perhaps I can summarize by noting that the potential candidate's general ability, his character, and his willingness to work hard in public office are perhaps more important considerations in terms of qualifications than is direct experience in a similar position. Perhaps that is a self-served observation, but let us hope it remains a true one.[7]

GROOMING YOURSELF FOR PUBLIC OFFICE IS EXACT, AND EXACTING, SCIENCE*

Question: What is the objective of your current activities?
Answer: . . . [My] own candidacy.
Question: What steps do you see as necessary to a political aspirant?
Answer: Accomplishment, recognition and a wide power base.
Question: What sort of accomplishment?
Answer: I would almost say 'any sort,' but that is not quite accurate. . . . The accomplishments that generally recommend themselves to voters seem to be the same kinds of accomplishments they expect from their public servants. Something that benefits the public in some way.
Question: How are you going about making such accomplishments?
Answer: In several ways. Politically, I am helping the Republican Party by working on the formation of a Chinese Republican Council in San Francisco's Chinatown, which has been a Democratic stronghold. . . .

I am also active personally and by cash contributions on campaigns for individual candidates, sometimes against hopeless odds. The political pendulum makes wide swings, and today's unsuccessful candidates become tomorrow's upset winners.
Question: Are you also aiming at accomplishments outside the political arena?
Answer: For a beginner, as I am, this is the only really open path toward

[7]Christopher Bayley sought the office in King County, Washington (population 1,200,000), the county in which Seattle is located. This article is a compilation by the authors of Mr. Bayley's comments to a group of students, reporters, and visiting administrators to the Center for the Study of Practical Politics, Seattle, Washington, September 28, 1971. By permission.

*Excerpt from an interview with George L. Scott, *Campaign Insight*, November 1971. Scott is 25; his goal is elective office.

the recognition one needs to run for anything. But I don't think you can enter outside activities without having a profound conviction of their importance regardless of whatever political benefits they might eventually provide. In other words, you have to be a man of integrity *before* you start thinking of politics—not as an expedient afterthought.

Question: Where have you found opportunities for expression of this principle?

Answer: In organization, for one thing. I served as chairman of a Junior Chamber of Commerce Committee on playgrounds for disadvantaged children. I have rung doorbells for our Young Republican Club. Right now, I am serving as Vice Commander of a post of the Veterans of Foreign Wars.

I am also vice-president of my union, and a member of the San Francisco Labor Council. . . .

Question: Do you also get into broader public-service areas?

Answer: . . . As an officer of the local chapter of Project Concern, I have directed fund-raising activities for overseas medical aid to peoples of Asia and Latin America. And here in our home town, I am active in the Godfathers, a group of businessmen dedicated to helping our local version of Boys Town.

I have spent summer vacations in Mexico, helping to conduct eye examinations for poor children who would perhaps never have seen an optician if Project Concern had not organized a group to aid them. . . . I am very suspicious of candidates who give lip service, but who never expose themselves to the conditions they bemoan. . . .

Question: "Going out," as you put it, takes time. How do you manage that? What does your wife say about it?

Answer: Getting married is one thing I *haven't* had time for. . . . You don't simply "go out" if your interests are political. You have to maintain a very careful schedule, to be sure you attend the "right" civic and social functions—and skip any potentially harmful ones.

Question: How do you insure that?

Answer: By contacts. I check by telephone with every one of my contacts, of whatever kind—political, social, organization—about once every two weeks. . . . I pick up some helpful piece of advice or information on each call.

Question: Is this cultivation of contacts costly?

Answer: Somewhat. It *does* lead to big phone bills. Dinners, entertainment, campaign contributions and tickets to fund-raising dinners add up too, although these are frequently covered by my union duties.

One more expense. . . . I occasionally invest in ghost-writers for important speeches or letters. Good politicians all seem to know the best ways to take advantage of services like ghost-writing and research work. . . .

Question: How do you bring your name to public attention?

Answer: My ghost-writers are unusually fecund with suggestions for publicity. They have had me named "Citizen of the Day" by one Bay Area radio station, and they have distributed copies of speeches and other publicity material to newspaper editors and columnists. Magazines of my various organizations, and the Chinese community press, have all treated me very well. I try not to be pushy or overt about it, but I do see that any personal stories that seem worthwhile get a chance for public exposure. Too, as a member of the San Francisco Press Club, I am fortunate in having a number of good friends working in the media.

Question: . . . [Our] publisher recently identified exhaustion as the "candidate's worst enemy." Is this a problem with you at your age?

Answer: It would be, if I neglected either my very careful diet or my exercise. Despite the temptations to drink freely, which are faced by anyone who goes out as much as a political person does, I keep my alcohol intake down to no more than about a drink a day. I follow a simple diet regimen, even to eating breakfast in the same restaurant every day. And I work out with heavy weights and handball in a public gym at least three times a week, in addition to a daily swim in the Press Club pool, usually just before dinner.

One more thing about keeping in shape: a public figure should *have* a figure he can show in public. I keep my weight steady, and my muscles toned. I also work at maintaining a slightly tanned but not weatherbeaten complexion. Too much sun could suggest to voters that I'm a beach bum!

Question: Do you take strong public positions?

Answer: Only on clear issues. Nobody can fault you for soliciting funds for the work of a Project Concern or fighting for the rights of your union or ghetto children. Besides, there's plenty of need for applying power in causes like these. I feel it would be premature, and perhaps foolhardy, to come down heavily on one side or the other of controversial issues at this stage, when my opinion would weigh so inconsequential[ly] little, although I do keep up on the issues. I *know* the various viewpoints. But by concentrating whatever strength I have on clear and vital issues, I can do more good both for the causes and for myself.

Question: What is your political career timetable?

Answer: I have learned patience. A party hierarchy does not form itself over many years simply to be displaced by any ambitious newcomer. My first step, as I see it, is to work closely with my County Central Committees of Labor and charitable groups. When I go for a political office, I want to be sure of all the support I should be entitled to. I want to know, and I want them to know, that I am really ready!

"SO THAT'S HOW THEY DECIDE TO RUN FOR OFFICE."

Mr. Bayley's decision to run ultimately won him victory in one of the state's most hotly contested elections. The knowledge that it is necessary for a candidate to seek active support, to self-start, was the basis of his political decision. After considering the five phases—the candidate's idea to run, discussing with others the possibility of seeking office, the predecision phase, the private decision phase, and the public decision phase— Bayley declared for the office of prosecutor. Although not all candidates follow the same procedures, successful ones usually take similar points into consideration.

Indeed most candidates, if they plan on achieving victory, must carefully weigh not only the decision itself but also the advantages and disadvantages they possess in reference to the opposition. Innumerable beginners enter their first political campaign after giving extensive thought to the decision and little regard to their own actual chances of victory.

It Is Important to Recognize What Your Chances Are

A psychology professor once said that it is a great day in a man's life when he recognizes what he can and cannot do—that is, when he recognizes his potential. Some of us, unfortunately, never learn this. I think it is a good idea for the candidate and his advisors to look at the nominee as a product, omitting the human element, and ask: "What is wrong with this product? Is there anything that might go wrong because it is not the way we would like to have it?"

Recognize Liabilities

In looking at my campaign, I discovered that there were [several] . . . factors that might be considered liabilities.

. . . One of the clients of my public relations agency was the American Medical Association. The A.M.A., in some minds, is an orgnization that wears the black hat of the bad guys on television Westerns. Therefore, we assumed that my opposition would advance the idea that I was not a very good guy or I would not have time to represent the A.M.A. We were right. This was one of the key issues in the campaign, and I was accused of being the tool of the American Medical Association.

. . . Because I had not been a long-time resident of the district in which I ran, it was assumed that my opposition would label me a carpetbagger. . . . My opponents did use this as one of the key issues in the election.

. . . I am a member of a small religious organization in the United States known as the Seventh Day Adventists. We knew this would be a factor whether it was publicly proclaimed or not. It was also going to be a hindrance in terms of my inability to campaign actively on Saturday, which is an extremely important day for campaigning. Who in his right mind would think of running for public office if he could not get around to all the county fairs and do all of the gladhanding on Saturdays? True, my opposition made the most of the Saturdays while I was "recharging my batteries."

. . . The last liability was the decision to retain professional management. I consider it one of the wisest things we did, and we expected my opponent to use this as an issue against me. I might remind you that I represent a district which includes some very rural areas, such as the Mojave Desert which is composed of numerous small, isolated towns. My opponent assumed these people would resent a man who had professional management, and he made a great deal of the fact that his campaign was an amateur production. He emphasized he was his own manager and did not need professional counsel.

These, in general, were the . . . principal liabilities with which I began.

Change Your Liabilities
into Assets

As you recall, the first liability was my association with the A.M.A. We discovered, by polling, that while people may have a negative image of the

A.M.A. as an institution, everyone likes his own doctor. People may change doctors now and then, but at any particular moment a person has a good relationship with his own physician. Therefore, why fight the idea of the A.M.A.? Why not identify with doctors as individuals and stress the fact that I had represented the physicians of America? At that time Medicare was an important national issue and my opponents thought this would be the way to shoot me down. They sponsored newspaper advertisements, some of which were full-page and run daily, that were designed to show how terrible the doctors and their lobbyists were. We took the opposite approach and set out to show that a doctor was a pretty nice guy. We used an advertisement depicting a little boy walking across the street saying, "Mr. Pettis, what's wrong with my doctor and minister supporting you?"

The second liability was the carpetbagger issue. It just happened that I was chairman of the board of a local university and had played a key role in moving that institution out of Los Angeles and into the district. This relocation meant about 25 million dollars to the district and brought in about 3500 new people, people who would contribute to the intellectual climate of the community. The university included both a medical and dental school. By identifying with the good causes of the local community and pointing out that in the . . . years I had been in the district I had done some things which might be considered significant in terms of public service, we hoped to counter the carpetbagging issue. This was just one of the numerous ways we tackled that problem. . . .

The [third] . . . liability was my affiliation with the Seventh Day Adventists. California State Senator Milton Marks has said that you have to take time out in the campaign to "recharge your batteries." Every candidate has to take some time for reflection, for stepping back and taking the long view. If you do not do this, you can go on in the campaign so that right before the election you get so close to the trees that you cannot see the forest.

I believe that . . . [candidates] everywhere ought to learn the value of reflecting upon the total political scene. Even though I missed a few of the county fairs and parades, I used my Saturdays for retrospection and in the end I do not think I lost anything. This abstinence from political activity on Saturdays called attention to my religion and revealed that I was devoted enough to my faith not to betray my religious convictions for political gain. I found that many members of the church to which my opponent belonged . . . were identifying with me and offering assistance because they had found one or two instances in his record in Congress where, in their minds, he had voted against his own conscience. He had made the mistake of violating his own conscience in the minds of the people with whom he identified religiously.

A person ought always keep this uppermost in his mind. If you are going into public service, you have to make up your mind to keep faith with yourself. You have to say to yourself, "I'm not going to pay the price of compromising my convictions, particularly my religious feelings and convictions, for a political goal which may or may not be right." Even though this was not difficult for me, I think it was one of the more important decisions I made.

The [fourth] . . . issue concerned the professional management. I was very fortunate in having very fine professional management, and its advantages far outweighed any disadvantages. I wish there were more people who had the competence to be managers of campaigns, even at the city council or supervisorial level. We do not have enough of these people around the country. As a result, the candidates wind up being their own advisors, lacking the ability to stand back and see themselves objectively. As a candidate, you cannot do this because you are behind that face of yours, you are behind that voice, and you are behind your total personality. Objective managers can take a good look at you, as would any organization that is packaging a product, and they can tell you what is good and what is bad in your campaign. . . . I shall never have a campaign in which I do not employ professional management.

The specific incidents I have related to you are probably applicable to very few candidates and campaigns. Each reveals, however, that what appears to be a liability can be transformed into an asset. If you can analyze your potential liabilities before the campaign actually gets underway, you will be in a better position to cope with them if and when your opponent tries to use them to put you at a disadvantage.[8]

For most of us, the decision at first seemed simple, but the difficulties to be overcome are what make an election interesting, while at the same time calling attention to the potential of both protagonists.

When discussing the *liabilities* and *assets* possessed by political candidates, a minority candidate must add to his list the consideration of race. He is forced to fight for victory as a successful politician—overcoming the problems of any campaign, plus trying to convince the 80 percent nonminority electorate that he is interested not only in the problem of the minority but in the concerns of the majority as well. The facts of life for the black candidate are that, unless he is running in an all-black constituency, his decision to run must take into account the factor of race.

Edward Brooke of Massachusetts made this difficult decision and

[8]From Jerry L. Pettis, "Recognizing Liabilities and Winning With Assets," *Ways to Win* (Washington, D.C.: Republican National Committee, 1968), pp. 23–26. (All footnotes in this chapter have been consecutively renumbered for the convenience of the reader.)

successfully campaigned his way to the United States Senate.[9] As the 1970s progress, one might interpret Brooke's astute handling of this decision as a harbinger of similar decisions by other black political aspirants. The late 1960s and mid-1970s witnessed, for example, the elections of black mayors from Newark to Los Angeles. In 1972 Andrew Young was even sent to Congress by an Alabama constituency in which 62 percent of the registered voters were white.[10]

Tough Facts of Life for Black Politicians[11]

The plight of the black candidate in the 1970's is the same one that has always snared minority politicians in America. He must ask himself: "Am I a *minority* politician, or a minority *politician,* or both?" and then try to choose a stance. In resolving this problem, the Negro candidate must face certain facts of life. In the first place, since Negroes currently account for only 11 per cent of the total population, most black office seekers who campaign largely on the basis of "black appeal" will remain in broad constituencies *minority* candidates. The lesson of the success of two well-known black officeholders, Sen. Edward Brooke of Massachusetts and California superintendent of public instruction Wilson Riles, is that they campaigned simply as candidates, pitching their appeal to voters of all races.[12]

In the second place, the black politician cannot escape the fact that America's political system—unlike the European model—is a non-proportioned one. This means there is no guarantee that parties or groups will be represented according to their degree of support in the electorate. In the U.S., the winning candidate takes all . . . [T]he point of the exercise [is] "majority building." To be successful a politician must put together a larger, broader coalition than his opponent. For the black politician in most districts, success means getting as much as he can by working within the winning coalition.

It is a task full of obvious pitfalls. By seeking to hold the favor of his own constituency, the black politician may push the larger coalition to the

[9]John F. Becker and Eugene E. Heaton, Jr., "The Election of Senator Edward W. Brooke," *Public Opinion Quarterly* 31 (Fall 1972): 346–358.

[10]Hamilton Bims, "A Southern Activist Goes to the House," *Ebony,* February 1973, p. 87.

[11]From Richard Scammon, "Tough Facts of Life for Black Politicians," *Newsweek,* 7 June 1971, p. 33. Copyright Newsweek, Inc., 1971; reprinted by permission.

[12]For a further discussion of the need to seek office as the best qualified candidate, not as a "minority" candidate, see Chapter 2, Hamilton Bims, op. cit., pp. 35–43.

breaking point. For instance, a black politician running in a district comprising both ghetto voters and white suburban voters could win Negro support by campaigning for low-income housing in the suburbs—but in present-day America such a tactic would surely alienate a large part of the white suburban vote.

This is not to suggest that black politicians today lack in substantial clout. Thanks largely to the enormous influx of Negroes into the cities and to the exodus of whites to the suburbs, black voters now wield a potential influence in certain local and Congressional races that is disproportionate to their share of the electorate at large. . . . And because of their heavy concentration in such strategic states as New York, California, Pennsylvania, Illinois, Ohio and Michigan, Negro voters may well play a vital role in deciding the outcome of . . . Presidential elections.

To use this ammunition effectively, the black politician will have to assess Negro voting habits with special care. The conventional wisdom is that blacks vote Democratic and—given the choice—vote black. Still, it would be a mistake to presume monolithic voting behavior among them. In 1956, for instance, nearly 40 per cent of the black electorate voted for President Eisenhower's re-election. And in mayoralty contests . . . in Atlanta and . . . in Philadelphia, black voters were far from unanimous in choosing between black and white candidates. . . .

A . . . viable exercise might be the proposal to run a black candidate within the Democratic nominating process—a candidate who might symbolize black aspirations and, backed by his expanding electorate, press vigorously for Negro goals within the broad (and volatile) Democratic coalition. Whether he chooses to work inside or outside the Democratic Party, however, the black politician faces the old questions: "If I am a black politician, am I a black or am I a politician?" Plainly, the answer is both—but that doesn't make his choices any easier.

As Senator Edward Brooke of Massachusetts once noted, his constituency is only 3 percent Negro, and he has always resented being typed as a *Negro senator*. But a reflection of the difficulties in playing such a role is plainly visible among the members of the congressional "black caucus." "Brooke's skin is nearly black," says one, "but his mind isn't black at all." Barbara Jordan, the first black woman elected to congress from Texas, cannot be so stereotyped. Though most independent, she is a member in good standing of the "black caucus."

In some respects any candidate who is different, or who desires to step outside his party or peer group runs into similar difficulties. If you want to win, it becomes necessary to follow the rules of the game. Congresswoman Jordan is a good example. Some individuals are successful while opposing the system.

**GUIDE TO
CANDIDATE RATING CHECKLIST***

I. Campaigning ability
   A. Public speaking
      1. Availability to speak any time, and willingness to spend time in preparation
      2. Forcefulness and clarity in presenting ideas
      3. Pleasant voice
      4. Ease and spontaneity in speaking situations
         a. Naturalness of expression in formal speeches
         b. Ability to speak extemporaneously
         c. Wit, sense of humor
      5. Ability to project his personality on television and other mass media
      6. Debating skill
   B. Personal contact with voters: Ability to mix easily with a crowd and establish rapport
   C. Ability to attract campaign funds: Affiliations with business, labor, civic, or professional groups
   D. Ability to allocate resources effectively: Personal energy, campaign funds, etc.
   E. Mental and physical stamina
   F. Ability to adapt to unforeseen circumstances and turn them to his advantage
   G. Ability to keep a campaign running smoothly: Keeping staff and workers enthusiastic by his own personal confidence, poise, and vitality

II. Appeal to voters—first impression on voters
   A. Physical appearance
      1. Attractiveness
      2. Choice of dress
      3. Age and health
   B. Personality
      1. Personal dynamism, "charisma"
      2. Manner
   C. Ethnic background
   D. Religion
   E. Regional background

III. Appeal to voters—background as perceived by voters
   A. Character

*E. John Bucci et al., "What Really Decides an Election . . . The Six Key Factors,"
E. John Bucci & Associates, 1971, pp. 29–30.

1. Philosophy and values: Sense of honesty, reliability, integrity, justice and fair play
2. Record for speaking out on issues, personal courage
3. Clear record, no skeletons in closet
4. No conflict of interest

B. Personal background
   1. Home life, marital status, wife and children; strong support from family?
   2. Social standing
   3. Personal "success story"?

C. Military record

D. Community affiliations (church, civic, social, business)

E. Education

F. Professional and/or business experience

G. Political experience
   1. Past positions, present office
   2. Past attempts at election

H. Relevance of experience to probable issues

I. Possible points of hostility among voters
   1. Prior public statements or actions
   2. Undesirable personal habits (drinking, . . . etc.) or affiliations
   3. Position on civil rights, religion, ethnic groups

IV. Value to the party

A. Record of party allegiance
   1. Willingness to donate time, money, and effort
   2. Willingness to work through chain of command
   3. Consideration of and dedication to the interests of the party as a whole

B. Effect of candidacy on the entire ticket toward balancing the ticket

C. Appeal across party lines

V. Potential performance in office

A. Leadership
   1. Ability to generate support for new ideas . . .
   2. Keeping his word to the voters, delivering on promises

B. Administrative talents
   1. Recruiting capable workers
   2. Delegating authority effectively; ability to make use of others' talents
   3. Setting up an effective organization
   4. Attention to details

C. Application and dedication to the work of the office

D. Qualifications for the office
   1. Previous experience
   2. General education

Usually, however, their success is relative to the goal they wish to achieve. That is, they may be seeking political recognition for themselves, or attempting to change the status quo. If this is the case, political advancement may be of secondary importance.

Paul McCloskey, the *maverick* Republican, then politically independent, congressman from California campaigned during the 1972 presidential race in opposition to Richard Nixon. Desiring a modification to the president's policy on Vietnam, McCloskey fought to establish a principle—a decision for him and the voter with far-reaching political implications.

McCloskey, The Unlikely Rebel*

In background no less than appearance, McCloskey would not seem to be an apostate. A fourth-generation Californian and a Marine second lieutenant in Korea, he served his rich, suburban San Francisco community quietly for three Congressional terms until he decided . . . to begin challenging Mr. Nixon's conduct of the war. He is an active, outdoorsy man, a golfer and tennis player whose favorite pastime is hiking in the Sierras with his wife and four kids—which he plans to do for a month again this summer. Meanwhile, he jets to Minneapolis, Miami, Chicago, Portland and Philadelphia to throw up the war to the President, and he has opened a $750-a-month campaign office in Washington as he points toward the six or so Presidential primaries that he plans to enter.

Back in Burlingame, some think that McCloskey sounds like one of those hippie radic-lib Democrats—so much so that one conservative Republican group has already voted, 153–129, to ask him to get out of the party. [The reaction?] . . . "Hell, if we kick Pete out and he becomes a Democrat, we won't be able to get anybody to beat him." That drew a scattered nervous laugh because no one really needed to be reminded that in last year's election McCloskey won by the highest margin of any Republican in the nation who had opposition.

"You get angry with me for challenging the party leadership," he went on patiently. "But if we don't do something to change our image, we are going to be the minority party permanently. If we keep registering kids and 57 per cent register Democrat against 17 per cent Republican—the figures for San Mateo County—we aren't going to elect anybody. Look, there are different ways of looking at how a man best serves his party."

"But how do you justify the attacks you have been making against the President?" a tight-lipped man rose to ask.

*From Karl Fleming, "McCloskey, the Unlikely Rebel," *Newsweek,* 51, May 1971, pp. 19, 20. Copyright Newsweek, Inc., 1971; reprinted by permission.

I'm Trying to Make Him Change His Policy

"I'm not ridiculing his status as President," McCloskey replied. "I'm trying to make him change his policy. My position forces him into public debate on the subject of bombing about eight months earlier than he'd have to talk about it otherwise. He has to go to the American people *now* and justify his policy. And if that makes him stop the war just 30 days earlier, it's worth it even if I lose my seat in Congress, which is possible."

The audience never did come over to McCloskey's side; even some of his friends concede that he does the wrong thing politically on occasion. "He hasn't changed any since I've known him," says investor Al Schreck, a longtime friend and finance chairman of a fifteen-man "executive board" that has advised McCloskey since he first ran against Shirley Temple Black.

The days I spent with him, McCloskey waded in on several touchy issues without any apparent regard for the consequences. "Most municipal governments," he told a League of California Cities dinner, " . . . are incompetent or corrupt or both." In Lockheed country, where the aerospace recession is a matter of urgent concern, he argued that the government "should not bail out a corporation under ordinary circumstances." Among the Republican faithful, he says flatly: "You can't get on the House Ways and Means Committee unless you are a guardian of the oil industry."

McCloskey's district office at home is a graceful, old white house in San Mateo, where he props himself up at a 40-degree angle on the front of his desk and receives visitors in his shirt sleeves. One day, eight wives of American prisoners of war in Vietnam sat in a semicircle to question his attacks on the President's war policy, especially in regard to their husbands' safety. "Ending the war seems to me to be the best way of getting your husbands back," he said. "The President is perpetrating a cruel hoax when he says we will keep fighting until the prisoners are released. If he does what I think he's going to do—get all the troops out before election but continue the bombing for two or three years—I don't think you can have an expectation of any prisoner coming home. If I were President, I would have only one condition for getting out—and that is the release of the prisoners."

McCloskey recalled his own service in Korea. "I was much more afraid of being captured than being killed," he told the wives sympathetically. "So let me ask you the crunch question"—and he put to them what he described as the choice between Mr. Nixon's policy of long-term bombing while negotiations continue on several issues, the liberal Democratic policy of pulling out unconditionally, or his own of making the release of prisoners the only condition of withdrawal. Hesitantly, six of the eight women raised their hands to support his position. . . .

One of McCloskey's themes is that the Administration has lied to Congress about bombing and its impact on civilians. Rattling toward the San Francisco airport in a banged-up Maverick one day, he told me: "I'm going to break it off into them on this issue. . . ."

Norton Simon, the millionaire industrialist who has indicated that he would back McCloskey through the end of the year, . . . had second thoughts about "how strong my feelings are about his going against Nixon. If we make Nixon lose, will we wind up with Reagan? I don't want that to happen." McCloskey admitted that it could happen, and he admitted further that he is "under no illusions about upsetting the Republican Party system, which is essentially hostile to rebels. Even if I made a hell of a showing in the primaries," he went on, "the prospects of getting the nomination aren't very great. The party could never forgive me." . . .

Victory as a Viable Candidate
Was Not the Real Issue

As Fleming notes above, McCloskey was "trying to make him [Nixon] change his policy." Victory as a viable presidential contender was not the real issue. Such a decision on the part of a candidate runs to the roots of the entire political process in America. Unlike Christopher Bayley, who in earnest sought the office of prosecuting attorney, McCloskey's decision to run was based on his desire to change the policy of the winning candidate. Fortunately for McCloskey, he was able to fight off a strong primary challenge by his Republican peers in California, winning the nomination for another congressional term. However, the battle was a bitter one. McCloskey found it necessary to solicit and receive significant financial help from opponents of Richard Nixon. He won reelection to Congress, but only after waging the single most expensive congressional campaign in history.[13]

For most candidates, personal success such as experienced by McCloskey in winning reelection is not the reward for the role of *rebel*. Indeed, to most Americans such a stance smacks of political turncoatism. Even of

---

[13]The Common Cause Campaign Monitoring Project noted that McCloskey spent $321,588, which "was the highest recorded expenditure for any House candidate in 1972." "Editorial Memorandum on Congressional Incumbents' Campaign Finances," Newsrelease of Common Cause, Washington, D.C., September 1973.

those who agree with the candidate, questions are often asked concerning his motives.

In many respects the woman who wishes to test the waters of electoral politics has to overcome an even more unique set of difficulties. Her *assets* and *liabilities* take a variety of forms, sometimes quite the opposite of what one would expect. One female candidate running for a state legislative office reported that while doorbelling in what seemed a perfectly respectable neighborhood, she was propositioned, then accused of soliciting, by an irate male. At another house the same candidate was offered considerable financial assistance by a male physician who told her more women were needed in public life.

Women often find it difficult to overcome the broad-based prejudice associated with the male-dominated political arena. "Honey, whatever women do, they do best after dark,"[14] is a sentiment that is all too widely held by male politicians. "Women do the lickin' and the stickin',"[15] seems to characterize the generally held view. While these attitudes are changing,[16] they nevertheless represent an additional hurdle for the woman candidate to overcome.

It's Difficult to Be a Woman and a Politician

On congressional or state levels, women often try to run as *nonwoman* candidates or, rather, as candidates who wish to be dissociated from their sex. One newspaper man referring to a "crusty" female congrssswoman, noted that she was the "biggest male chauvinist he had ever met." Indeed this position often seems necessary if a woman is to become effective in politics. Esther Newberg, executive director of the New York Democratic Committee, once noted that men "assume that the reason you're in politics is for sex."[17] "If there's a kind of semiattractive woman around a candidate, the assumption that she's there to sleep with him," is a widely held philosophy.[18]

[14]Mayor John Lindsay of New York, in Susan and Martin Tolchin, "Getting Clout," *Esquire*, July 1973, p. 113.

[15]Mayor Moon Landrieu of New Orleans, in ibid.

[16]See Senator George McGovern, "Mandate For Reform," *Congressional Record*, no. 138, 22 September 1971; and Robert S. Strauss, *Responsibility and Opportunity: The Democratic Party, 1973–74: A Report of the Chairman*, (Washington, D.C.: Democratic National Committee, January 1974), for a discussion of changing roles for women in politics.

[17]Tolchin and Tolchin, op. cit., p. 113.

[18]Richard Reeves, journalist, in ibid.

The decision for a woman to seek office is, however, more often dependent on family situations than on problems related to sexual stereotyping. Women, when deciding on a career in public service, often must consider the occupation of their spouse, his position in the community, and his willingness (or lack of it) to relocate or be subjected to long periods of separation. Usually male candidates seek support from their wives as part of a team. The wife in generally willing to give up her career outside the home and, if she is not so occupied, finds little difficulty in accompanying and supporting her husband's political ambitions.

Ambition Versus Family Is a Special Consideration to Women

However, the woman candidate finds it necessary to weigh more carefully her goals, as her spouse, while giving support, is less likely to relinquish his career for that of his wife. Children also play an important role in the decision process. Women with young families invariably find it impossible to devote the necessary time and efforts required to gain experience and success in electoral politics. Husbands, on the other hand, experience no such handicap. Indeed, a pleasant family is an asset to the male, whereas women seeking public office are often accused of "deserting their husbands and children."

Women candidates with families sometimes are also faced with the difficult task of choosing at least temporarily between motherhood and political office. They find it necessary to be missing from home during the after-school and evening hours as well as on weekends. When one harried housewife, who was running for a local city council position, was asked why she didn't campaign around her family obligations, she proclaimed plaintively that she would, but no one else seemed to be available during those hours. Everyone was either working or too busy to meet a candidate.[19] Sometimes in the prenoon hours, grocery stores provided a forum, but the danger here was that she would appear as a candidate appealing to only the women's vote. Because she was already being charged by the opposition as being the "kitchen kandidate," she had to be available at the more popular hours. This caused difficulties at home, including added financial burdens for child care. Even the most understanding spouse sometimes finds it difficult to become a political widower.

Problems in organizing campaigns is another burden for the female

---

[19]For a more complete discussion of the difficulties in trying to combine occupational and political ambitions, see Bender, op. cit., pp. 1–2.

candidate. Unlike Christopher Bayley, who reached his decision confident of the necessary backing of his friends and associates, women often run into opposition from social contacts who do not believe they should get involved in the "dirty game" of politics. One female candidate for a congressional seat noted that "her friends were her biggest headache." Rather than an asset, they were liabilities, questioning her *reasons* and ability. One term in Congress, however, dispersed much of this opposition.

Social Contacts Are Less Available for Women

A lack of political and the more beneficial social contacts represents another major stumbling block for the potential woman candidate. Although men create lasting political alliances through service and professional organizations—contacts that can be effectively drawn on during a political campaign—women usually lack these avenues. Certain service clubs do accept them, but the overwhelming number of these organizations do not. *Male-only* associations are primary growth areas for potential candidates. *Female-only* clubs are generally oriented to social or social-welfare goals, and women's professional organizations are few. Those professional societies open to both sexes are most often dominated by the male membership. A lack of a firm political base in service and other organizations has often been the decisive factor in an election.[20]

Thus, while the minority candidate must convince the electorate that he represents all the voters, the female candidate must try to convince voters that she represents all the males, all the females, and all the minority electorate. Public acceptance of males to represent the entire constituency, be they minority or Caucasian, is far more widespread than a willingness to elect a woman to office.[21]

Many times, therefore, a woman candidate finds it necessary to fight sexual stereotyping, as well as a reluctance on the part of her spouse to support her, her family to allow her the necessary time, or her friends to take her seriously. In addition, the opposition many times plays on her role as housewife and mother rather than seeing her as a legitimate candidate. In making a decision to seek office, a woman has to accept these limitations, working within them, and, like minority politicians, seek office as the best-qualified candidate.

Today both parties recognize this new awakening among women and are encouraging their increased participation in the electoral process. Party reform by the Democratic McGovern Committee as well as the new national role for Republican women is indicative of these changes.[22]

As with their male counterparts, then, women recognize that the decision to run is based on many factors. In the end analysis perhaps the most important of these is an ability to recognize one's *liabilities* and *assets,* whatever they may be. No one can or should convince an individual to seek public office. Potential candidates must be willing and able to make their own commitments. No other area of campaigning is so much neglected, yet of so much significance, as the initial decision. Once this decision has been made, there is seldom opportunity to turn back. Everything from real issues of vital concern to constituents in their district, to nuisance issues such as Congressman Pike's ukulele, to the motto that "a woman's place is in the home" can and will be used by the opposition.

[20]"Contacts" are extremely important to the potential candidate. The margin of victory between male–male, female–female, and male–female contests may often rest on such relationships.

[21]For an interesting discussion of what happens when a minority woman decides to seek office, see "Clear It With Shirley," *Newsweek,* 18 October 1971.

[22]See *Responsibility and Opportunity: The Democratic Party . . .,* op. cit. and minutes of the Republican Credentials Committee, Republican National Committee, 1972. Both indicate a growing awareness and acceptance of women in politics.

To the citizen who is deluged with the tools of the *image makers* it can be a very valuable asset to understand the forces that are present when a candidate decides to run for public office. If we can comprehend, in a general way, the factors that impact such a decision, we will have a better grasp of the real issues and what constitutes a nuisance factor in the campaign. Hopefully a more involved and informed electorate will result.

7

Strategy,
Technology,
and Politics

To be turned from one's course by men's opinions, by blame, and by misrepresentation, shows a man unfit to hold an office.

PLUTARCH

It is the folk wisdom of American politics that campaigns are run like well-oiled military machines. If they are, most are closer to Custer's strategy than to that of Eisenhower's, and with similar results. If there is a universal rule in campaign strategy, it is that there is no universal rule. Most campaigns, even some congressional and gubernatorial races, stumble along from one apparent disaster to another. As the campaign manager for New York Congressman Pike noted, "We run our campaigns on the basis of ignorance, superstition, and fear—that is *our* ignorance, superstition, and fear."[1]

A young college intern joined a state legislative race. Drawing on one of the many "how to win a campaign" pamphlets, he asked the manager to see the campaign's battle plan. "What was the real strategy of the campaign?" The manager, an old hand at politics, looked a little credulous, and answered, "To win. What the hell did you think it is?" Typical with most such races there was no carefully laid-out plan, but rather a general commitment to get *our candidate's* message across and ignore the opposition.

Campaign Battle Plans—
The Great "Sustainers"

The belief that a political strategy somehow connotes a carefully laid-out, well-planned, and minutely directed scheme

[1]From Aaron Donner's comments to Richard Harris in "How's It Look?" *The New Yorker,* April 8, 1967. (All footnotes in this chapter have been consecutively renumbered for the convenience of the reader.)

for victory is one of the great *sustainers* of American politics. Like similar folktales that denote the honesty of George Washington—"I did it sir. I chopped down the cherry tree"—this belief in the inviolatability and inflexibility of campaign strategy should be laid to rest.

If there is a carefully plotted plan for victory at any level in politics, it probably is found at the presidential or senatorial levels of government. Occasionally, congressional or statewide campaigns are also tied to a well-planned strategy, but these tend to observe strategy plans more in the breach than in reality. The reason is obvious. Only at the highest levels are new media techniques and the impact of technology most viable. Thus more planning is required, with less allowance for flexibility of approach.

But in the overwhelming number of the remaining campaigns, the strategy is simply to try and get through the campaign, hopefully achieving victory. These organizations tend to be "underorganized, underplanned, and undermanned."[2] As one manager noted, half "the fun is in being an amateur and figuring out how you're going to correct all the mistakes you've made."[3]

Campaigns Vary a Great Deal

In reality, then, for most campaigns the strategy depends on a great number of variables, most of which are unmeasurable.

In truth, . . . optimum campaign strategy. . . . will vary with the following:

1. *The skills of the candidate:* Does he project on television? How does he handle a press conference or an informal coffee hour?
2. *The nature of the constituency:* Is it several square miles of urban slum or 30,000 square miles of prairie?
3. *The office being sought:* Is it a city councilorship or perhaps a judgeship, which will call for a far more restrained campaign?
4. *The nature of the electoral system:* Is the ballot partisan or nonpartisan? Is the general election two or six months after the primary?
5. *The party organizations in the constituency:* To what extent can their organized resources be counted on? What can they do?
6. *The availability of political resources:* How much manpower, skills, and money will be available and when?
7. *The nature of the electorate:* What are the electorate's political norms, party loyalties, perception of issues and candidates? What political styles and tactics do they approve?[4]

[2]Frank J. Sorauf, *Political Parties In America* 2d ed. (Boston: Little, Brown, 1972), p. 239.

[3]Donner, op. cit.

[4]Sorauf, op. cit., p. 245.

Flexibility Is the Key Factor

Obviously the strategy of a campaign is based on many additional variables. Incumbents are exposed to one set of problems, for instance, and the challenger to quite another. Considerations of group support, the influence of economic issues such as inflation, and the credibility of the candidate in the post-Watergate era—all have an impact. However, it is necessary to remember that strategy must be flexible enough to adapt to the cyclical variations of elections (two, four, six years) and to the possibility that issues during a campaign may fluctuate.

An example was found in the 1974 congressional elections. With the resignation of Richard Nixon and the subsequent elevation of Vice-President Ford to the presidency, Republican candidates saw a major shift in their fortunes. They began to campaign on the issues of government spending, inflation, and the *good marriage* apparently being forged between Ford and the American people. However, President Ford's surprise pardon of the former president forced another shift in strategy with a downturn in fortunes. Thus flexibility, not the preciseness of a *battle plan,* is the key to good strategy.

For instance, many candidates must vary their approach to strategy because of geographic concerns. A Republican living in a major urban center cannot afford to appeal exclusively to those groups from whom Republicans have traditionally sought support, that is, businessmen and middle-class Protestants. In an area that tends to be heavily pro-labor and contains significant minority religious and ethnic groups, the candidate is required to seek broad support from anywhere he can get it.

What Factors Are Associated with Being a Republican or a Democrat?

Evidence indicates that Republicans more often appeal to the overall electorate than to individual groups because most identifiable groups tend to be affiliated with the Democratic party, that is, labor, Blacks, Catholics, Jews, and so on.[5] This affiliation stems from the depression New Deal Coalition of Franklin Roosevelt, which many experts feel may be in a state of decline. Nevertheless, although the coalition may be dissolving, the issues on which it was built are, in many instances, still prevalent.[6] Thus candidates work at building their own coalitions by appealing to the

[5]John Kingdon, *Candidates For Office, Beliefs and Strategies* (New York: Random House, 1968), pp. 116–121.

[6]*Louis Harris Survey for Committee on Governmental Relations,* Bulletin no. 20402 (Washington, D.C.: Government Printing Office), 1974, pp. 6–35.

"And that, I take it, goes double."

perceived needs of this past socioeconomic attachment. Democrats tend to be perceived as liberals and "for the little guy," whereas Republicans are believed to be conservative and pro-business.

This exercises at least a psychological attachment on a significant percentage of the electorate that considers themselves to be among the little guys, at least as far as politics and government are concerned. The fact that most of the little guys are affiliated with what is probably the nation's largest and most powerful lobbyist—labor—does not seriously negate this philosophy.

On the other hand, Republicans still tend to be more socioeconomically conservative and thus attract a different following. While Watergate and its ensuing scandals forced the G.O.P. to reevaluate their issue and group appeals, the negative voting patterns of 1974 were more likely a reaction to short-term economic and ethical questions than a major realignment in voting patterns. Once these short-term forces have abated, Republican strategy, tempered by the Watergate experience, may return to former patterns.

The interesting question, of course, is whether or not the apparent shift to the Democrats in 1974, considering the record low turnout, really represents support for the Democratic party or simply an expression of the voters' desire to choose the lesser of two evils.

The significant growth of self-identified independents may lead to a major strategy shift by both parties (see Chapter 3) and a subsequent realignment of issues and new group appeals under old party labels.

Whatever the outcome, strategy and tactics will be forced to vary a great deal, depending on group appeal, issue questions such as inflation and integrity in government, and the setting in which the election takes place.

A Most Important Part of Strategy

[T]he most important single datum to be considered in devising a strategy is . . . past election statistics and public-opinion polls for the election district. How the voters are distributed in terms of party affiliation is . . . most important. . . . The percentage of Republican and Democrats in the district is related to a number of social and economic factors over which candidates have little control. . . . Hence, most candidates must work within a particular election district in which the number of hard-core potential supporters is already pre-determined.

The second most important fact to know is whether the opposition candidate is an incumbent. There are many opportunities for incumbents to do favors . . . to lessen the effect that [opponents] . . . will have in the forthcoming election. Also, an incumbent has already developed a winning coalition and has probably had a good deal of exposure to the public. . . .

This disadvantage is compounded by the fact that they are also likely to have fewer party followers in the district than the incumbent has.

The third most important fact is what the opponent is going to do. Is he planning a vigorous campaign? Is it clear that if one candidate conducts a vigorous campaign, the other candidate must also.

Given these three factors affecting election campaigns (again, factors over which the candidates have little control), it is possible to plan a number of strategies, but the strategies will be severely limited in effectiveness for the minority-party candidate because of these factors.

The first point to be made is that, by and large, small turnouts favor the incumbent. . . . Hence, one may conclude, small turnouts are likely to favor the status quo (the return of the incumbent to office); large turnouts are more likely to favor the challenger.

Opposition Strategy Dictates
an Increased Effort

When faced with an incumbent, then, the strategy of the opposition party will be to increase election turnout. There are, generally, two ways in which this can be done. The first is to run a candidate who can attract a large personal following regardless of party. This is the so-called hero strategy in which the minority party attempts to make up for its minority status by running a candidate who can appeal to voters on a basis other than party affiliation. . . . [T]here are many reasons why such a candidate is not likely to be desirable to the minority party, even if he is available. The prospects of victory with such a candidate must also be weighed against the likelihood that the candidate will feel independent of the party (which in fact he is). Party leaders may not be enthusiastic about a candidate whom they know will not be as obliged to them as some other candidate might be. As the same time, however, they must be concerned with winning, and a minority party may run a "hero" as one way of overcoming its minority-status handicap.

The second way in which a party can attempt to overcome its minority-party status is to run a candidate who is close to the candidate of the majority party in his stands on issues. That is, if the incumbent or the party of the incumbent is Republican, then the Democrats might choose a conservative Democrat as their standard-bearer. If, on the other hand, the incumbent or his party is Democratic, then the choice of the Republicans might be a liberal Republican. But because issues are not salient to most voters, this strategy would appear to be a good deal less successful than that of running a hero-type candidate.

Also, although this seems to be one way of overcoming a minority-party status, there are a number of factors inhibiting its use. First, the power within a minority party very often falls into the hands of those who are most unlike the incumbent of the opposite party. Hence, as Miller and Stokes demonstrate, minority-party candidates are likely to be quite atypical of general constituency opinion on issues.[7] Second, it is usually difficult to get a party to unite on an extreme end of the continuum. That is, it is difficult for the Republican party to unite on a liberal (or, for that matter, an extreme conservative), and it is difficult for the Democrats to unite on a conservative or an extreme liberal.[8] Although the minority party may be more likely to win with such a candidate, for many party leaders it

---

[7]Warren E. Miller and Donald E. Stokes, "Constituency Influence in Congress," *American Political Science Review* 57 (March 1963): 45–56.

[8]Most recent examples are the Goldwater (1964) and McGovern (1972) defeats.

is more important to maintain the "purity" of the party than to win. For the candidate with the best chance of winning to gain the party nomination, therefore, many institutional factors must be overcome. Hence, another powerful restraint is operating on the party in choosing its best candidate: the candidate with the best chance of winning is difficult to find and, if found, is difficult to nominate. There is a built-in tendency for minority parties to run candidates who reflect the general locus of power within the party and who, as a consequence, have little chance of beating the incumbent.

Minority-Party Candidates Must Appeal to Other Party Supporters

The major hope of the minority party is to choose a candidate who either appeals for his supporters above party lines or whose appeals are similar to those of the majority-party candidate. However, [because] . . . of factors operating to inhibit the success of such a candidacy. . . . The only alternative, then, is for the minority-party candidate to get a higher turnout of his supporters on . . . and, hopefully, to cut into some of his opponent's support. This is not very feasible because, by and large, the candidates chosen by minority parties are quite atypical of the constituencies which they are to represent. The fact that the incumbent already has built a coalition of support makes it even more difficult to garner commitments . . .

As has already been suggested, low turnouts at elections usually favor the incumbent. There is only one circumstance in which this may not be the case. . . . If the minority-party candidate can quietly go around to his supporters and increase their rate of turnout while the majority-party candidate is doing little campaigning, then there is a chance that a low turnout will benefit the minority-party candidate. This also may happen if the majority-party is overconfident or too busy to campaign.* It is, however, quite difficult to pursue this strategy successfully. Campaigns, by their very nature, are public, and it is quite difficult to sneak around an election district without being spotted. As soon as the majority-party candidate finds out that a vigorous campaign is taking place, he will (or certainly should) step in to do some campaigning.

The majority-party candidate also has a number of advantages which the candidate of the minority party does not have. To the extent that campaigns create a general awareness of an impending election—for

---

*The campaign of Mike Gravel unseated his incumbent opponent, Senator Gruening, with this strategy by waiting until the final weekend of the election to unleash a media blitz on the voters of Alaska.

example, through television speeches to heterogeneous audiences—the majority-party candidate is more likely to reach more of his supporters than is a minority-party candidate. The minority-party candidate, when speaking to nonspecific, heterogeneous audiences, runs a greater risk of including in his audience those predisposed not to support him.

Also, the candidate of the majority party will find it less necessary to seek support outside his already established coalition. He will also find it easier to campaign in that he can concentrate on style issues (which have a stronger appeal for supporters than for opponents). A minority-party candidate, on the other hand, has to concentrate much more specifically on concrete issues, a difficult task at best, and one complicated by the fact that the position which the candidate takes is not likely to be shared by a majority within the district.

All in all, then, organizational factors, the influence of mass media, and simple arithmetic all lead to the conclusion that minority-party candidates are not likely to win. Basically, the factors against them (minority-party status, nonincumbency, and organizational factors producing weak candidates) are all beyond the control of the candidate. He must play the game according to rules which are not of his own making and which cannot be adapted to the needs of the campaign. The fact that the "best" strategy for the minority party is to run a "hero," or someone whose issue positions are close to those of the incumbent, does not mean that either of these alternatives will occur very often. The restraints on the minority party, in fact, insure that they will not.

Along with the strategies already mentioned, there are a number of more specific actions which are useful to candidates regardless of the general strategy pursued. Although tactics vary a good deal, depending upon available resources, the following are probably useful in any situation. With more resources, more can be done, but these tactics may be followed by candidates with any amount of resources.

Get Others Involved

1. *Get others involved.* It is important to elicit the support and participation of groups during a campaign. As Klapper and Brown (among others) have pointed out, the most effective pressure on people is group pressure.[9] It is generally not enough for the candidate himself to tell people to vote and to vote for him, he must also get others who are more familiar with the voter and who are in a position to exert some social pressure and

[9]Joseph T. Klapper, *The Effects of Mass Communication* (New York: Free Press of Glencoe, 1960); and J. A. C. Brown, *Techniques of Persuasion* (Baltimore: Pelican, 1963).

to communicate more personally with the voter to tell him to vote and
. . . the best candidate. . . . As more people are directly involved in the campaign (making telephone calls, sending out literature, going from door to
door), they are likely to get others involved also. These "others" might include perhaps, just a narrow group of close friends, family and relatives, and
perhaps business associates, . . . or others with whom the person is in intimate contact. The more people who work in the campaign, the more likely
friends and neighbors will become involved indirectly through the active
persons. It is by increasing the number of people directly involved in the campaign that one increases the number of people indirectly involved. If as many
people as possible are given a personal stake in the outcome (through ego
involvement), they are more likely to become informed about the campaign,
to talk about it, and generally to spread a certain amount of enthusiasm. This
tactic, in a sense, involves creating opinion leaders who will be in a
position to influence a small group of others around them. These opinion
leaders will be likely to discuss the campaign with others who are similarly
situated (such as family, friends, and co-workers) and who will undoubtedly also have the same preference if they voted. The purpose of getting
as many people as possible to work directly for the candidate is to
proliferate the number of people indirectly exposed to the opinion leaders
and providing impetus to go to the polls and vote.

Use Personal Contact

2. *Use as much personal contact as possible.* Social scientists are now
verifying what politicians have suspected all along: the more personal the
communication, the more effective it is likely to be. For the candidate,
then, the major effort of the campaign should be on meeting, personally, as
many people as possible. Preferably, the meetings should be in small
groups where the contact can be more intimate. Large, but live, audiences
(rallies, speeches before large groups) are the next best thing. The emphasis should then be on television, radio, newspaper, and handouts (in that
order). Although it is probably a good idea to try all kinds of communication, the emphasis in terms of expenditure of resources should definitely
be on the more personal form of communication.

Be Brief

3. *Be brief.* If radio and television are used, six spot announcements . . .
at various times during the day are likely to be a good deal more effective
than one thirty-minute program. First, it is important to avoid competition
with regular half-hour programs (by and large politicians cannot compete

with westerns, situation comedies, and "medical" programs). Second, short announcements are more likely to reach captive audiences. . . . Third, short announcements at various times during the day are likely to hit a variety of audiences who watch or listen at different times during the day.

Don't Publicize the Opponent

4. *Don't publicize the opponent.* A campaign is a method of exposure and a mechanism for persuasion. It is not an intellectual exercise in the sense that a high school debate is. Arguments with the opponent should be avoided, not only because they give him free advertising (on the candidate's time and money), but also because he might win the argument. The now famous "Great Debates" between Richard Nixon and John F. Kennedy only served to give the lesser-known Senator Kennedy a good deal of free publicity and exposure.

Have a Simple Campaign Theme

5. *Have a simple campaign theme.* It is advantageous to a candidate to have a few general points around which he can center his campaign. Under the necessities of time and money, most of the campaign will be spent with many heterogeneous audiences. Under these circumstances, it will be better to concentrate on a few general issues rather than attempt to cover all issues. It can certainly be said that . . . [Richard Nixon's theme of "Law and Order" in 1968] was a help, not only in organizing his own thoughts but

also in helping the general public to understand what he would do if elected.

These are but a few of the general tactics which all candidates can employ, regardless of whether they are majority- or minority-party candidates.

The purpose of the campaign . . . is threefold: reinforcement of party supporters, activation of latent supporters, and conversion of the supporters of the opposition party. The ease with which these purposes can be accomplished is in the same order: reinforcement, activation, and conversion. There are many reasons why this is the case, the most important being the existence of predispositions among the general population to support one party's candidate over that of the other party, and the psychological factors of selective attention, perception, and retention. Group conformity and the mediating role which groups play between candidates and voters is also of paramount importance in promoting reinforcement and activation, and inhibiting conversion. Most of what the candidates say and do, then, will be limited in its ability to change or convert people, and will serve, rather, to reinforce and activate supporters.

Facts Alone Are Not Enough

There are also, however, several technical points which should be made clear in discussing the effects of campaigns and the attempts by politicians to use the campaign for the purpose of winning office. The first of these is the fact that, in attempting to persuade people, facts alone are not enough. Facts do not "speak for themselves." They may be perceived and interpreted differently, depending upon the way in which a person looks at them, the value system which he brings to the facts. Hence, in attempting to persuade people it is quite important also to provide the value context within which the facts should be considered. One must give some direction to the audience as to how the facts are to be considered. If one wants to increase his chances for effective persuasion, it is necessary not only to provide facts, but also the framework in which they are to be used to change or reinforce people's opinions.

This, quite obviously, is another impediment to the free discussion of issues in a campaign. Given their goal of winning candidates must necessarily attempt to present a winning case, not just a case. They must mix fact with value, and at times "truth" must be handled gingerly. This does not mean that a candidate must lie, but it does mean that he may be playful with the truth. For example, when a person takes an oath before a court of law, he swears to tell the truth, the whole truth, and nothing but the truth.

It is quite possible for a candidate to tell the truth, but not the whole truth (that is, to leave out some important facts), or to tell the truth mixed in with a little imagination and speculation (guesses, hunches, and so on). If candidates were limited in their campaign oratory as court witnesses are in their testimony, the candidates' opportunities to persuade people would be severely inhibited.

Explicit Material Is More Important Than Implicit Material

A second technical point of some importance in being able to persuade people (either through reinforcement, activation, or conversion) is that explicit material is more effective than implicit material in guiding people to action. How far one can go with implicit material or subtleties of argument quite obviously depends, in part, on the level of intelligence of the audience and how informed they are about the matter being discussed; generally, however, innuendoes, irony, and other forms of subtle and sophisticated communication should be eschewed in a political campaign. It is like the famous dictum to teachers (although a good deal more appropriate for the heterogeneous audiences with which politicians are more likely to face): "Tell them what you are going to tell them, tell them, and tell them what you told them." A politician should leave none of his communications and messages to chance. And he should not let the audience draw its own conclusions about the material being presented. The communicator himself should make the conclusions clear.

Attribute Material to Prestigious Sources

A third factor increasing the chances for effective communication is the attribution of material to prestigious sources. In many cases this amounts to parading before the public party heroes of another era as well as current high-status people. This is why one will almost always find references to Lincoln at a Republican rally or references to Franklin D. Roosevelt at a Democratic function.

A fourth factor of some importance in presenting material to the general public in a campaign for the purposes of persuasion is that appeals which are based on fear are less likely to move the audience in the desired direction than are less threatening and anxiety-producing communications. That is, fear tactics (and, by extension, one may also assume that campaigns based on hate should be included here) seem to have the reverse of the desired effect. Tactics which attempt to elicit deep-seated emotions are

"Bad news, Senator. Your opponent has come up with a device so sophisticated that it makes recorded calls, goes door-to-door, kisses babies and raises money. But what's even worse, every time we put a bug on it, it eats the damned thing."

(From *Campaign Insight*. By permission.)

likely to boomerang in that people who are threatened are not likely to follow the advice but rather to follow their own line of defense. In many cases this line of defense is withdrawal rather than action. Psychological mechanisms of repression are likely to lead people away from the desired action rather than toward it. This is probably one factor which serves to keep campaigns on a relatively ethical and moral level (at least in terms of public charges against the candidates). These fear and hate tactics are not employed much because they are not successful—as well as being, in most cases, unethical. . . .

[T]he ideal that candidates in campaigns should debate alternative policies and that voters should listen, consider all sides, and then choose among the candidates rationally, is not only a hopeless ideal in that it does not square with the empirical facts as seen through the eyes of the candidates and voters, but also that it is not even a useful ideal in that it does not take into account either the limitations under which candidates and electorates operate or the necessities of the situation. . . .[10]

Computers and Polling—
Major Strategy Tactics

As demonstrated in countless campaigns, two of the major tools in strategy formation are computers and statistical analysis based on polling. Although neither of these techniques are particularly new, their usage in recent years has come to have a major impact on the electoral process.

[10]From Lewis A. Froman, Jr., in *The Electoral Process,* ed. M. Kent Jennings and L. Harmon Ziegler (Englewood Cliffs, N.J.: Prentice-Hall, 1966), pp. 11–19.

Many Americans, using the guidelines of Marshal McLuhan and Alvin Toffler, have expressed fears that technological political manipulation, as practiced by such organizations as Decision Making Information (associated with Spencer-Roberts of California) or Joseph Napolitan Associates, Inc. (Washington, D.C.) will lead to what Adlai Stevenson referred to as the "ultimate indignity to the democratic process."

The use of computers in particular has a tendency to alarm the general population. The idea that vast quantities of information on each American are being fed into some data bank for further recall smacks of 1984. But computers have been used in statistical analysis and politics for decades. The difference is the major upsurge encountered during the 1970s. This change is at least in part attributable to new campaign laws that fail to regulate computer use as they do media expenditures.[11] Unlike the more blatant abuses of the last-minute television blitz (see Chapter 9), computers offer a more subtle form of voter manipulation.

Since the 1970 census computations became available, computers have become even more valuable. Until those figures were obtained, demographic and other data were based on the 1960 census.[12] Unless a candidate were willing to spend a fortune on gathering more current data, computer predictions always suffered from an information lag.[13] Now, however, this research is available on a district-by-district basis and at a marginal cost.

Even the party pros are becoming convinced that they can add an extra 2 or 3 percentage points to their turnout through the use of computers. In close elections (which, as we've seen, many are) this small percentage is the margin of victory.

The Computer Helps in Several Ways

. . . Armed with dramatic examples from recent elections, the computer fans are out to sell it to the entire party [system] as a vital tool, perhaps even more valuable than television.

The computer helps in half-a-dozen different ways, all pretty much tied to one idea: To identify [partisans] . . . and thus lets precinct workers rifle-shoot their registration drives. It breaks the electorate down into dozens

[11]"'72 Campaign Trends: More Computers, Fewer T.V. Spots," *Congressional Quarterly: Weekly Report,* 15 April 1972, p. 56.

[12]Ibid., p. 857.

[13]Bill Boyarsky, "Computers Take the Guesswork Out of Elections," *Los Angeles Times,* 5 June 1970, p. 1.

of different interest groups, and prints and mails letters tailored to each group. It pinpoints those citizens most likely to respond to calls for volunteer help or campaign funds.

It makes incredibly easier the job of "be sure to vote" phone drives in the closing days of a campaign, and gives precinct workers super-systematic block-by-block lists . . . to use on election day for late-afternoon turn-out-the-vote efforts.

Computers, of course, don't really do much that political organizations haven't long been doing with three-by-five cards and other tools; they simply do it far more quickly and efficiently. Nor is the political use of computers precisely new; they have been so employed for . . . [more than] a decade now, with their use steadily spreading and growing more sophisticated.

Thus far, though, computers have been most heavily employed by Republicans, particularly well-heeled ones like . . . Nelson Rockefeller . . . or by GOP organizations in places like Arizona and Texas, where Democrats long were solidly entrenched. The GOP will, of course, keep using computers more and more, installing them where they haven't been used, perfecting them where they have.

A New Tool for Democrats

. . . [A more recent] ingredient is that Democrats seem finally to be recognizing the computer as a tool potentially far more valuable for them than for the Republicans. The reasons for this are simple. There are more Democrats than Republicans, but Democrats don't usually register and vote as readily. Generally poorer and less educated, they aren't as motivated, nor as self-starting. Any device that makes it easier to prod men and women to register and vote is almost bound to help Democrats more than Republicans.

Democrats also tend to be far more diverse—ethnically, racially, economically. Anything that helps target appeals to different groups more precisely is also likely to help Democrats more.

"If we install an efficient computer operation in every large state, the states where Presidential elections are decided, it could easily be the key to victory," says William Welsh, executive assistant to [the] Democratic Chairman. . . . "Those are our people who haven't been turning out." . . .

In Minnesota, for instance, Democrats scored a notable sweep. . . . Mr. Humphrey's strong coattails were generally credited; less known, both outside and even within Minnesota, was the ambitious computer effort he staged for himself and the entire Democratic ticket.

The effort was organized by Valentine, Sherman & Associates. . . .

In July the firm began putting on magnetic computer tape the name, address, phone number, county and Congressional district of every telephone subscriber in Minnesota—about 1.1 million names, more than 85% of the total electorate.

Then the computer printed this information on individual survey forms suitable for later "reading" by an optical scanner. The forms for each county were shipped to a supervisor there, and volunteers began phoning each house for additional data: the party preference of each adult, whether he or she was registered, the number of children and old people, union membership, whether the person farmed. The results were added to the personal histories on the master tape.

Then thousands of computer-produced letters started going out, with arguments and appeals aimed at specific groups—farmers, educators, parents of young children, old people, residents of a particular area. The letters plugged not just Mr. Humphrey but all his running mates, down to the candidate for the state senate and house—a fact given major credit for minimizing the usual drop-off as voters go down the ballot.

Precinct lists were produced, with Democratic-inclined households recorded block-by-block, so that local candidates and party workers could make door-to-door calls. Then, for several days before the election, volunteer-manned phone banks used computer print-outs to remind Democratic-leaning citizens to vote. The callers even asked whether the voter needed a ride or babysitter on election day, duly noting those who did. Party officials estimate 280,000 homes were reached, and each time the message specifically called for support of the entire ticket.

"It was the most significantly effective role in our campaign," says Jack Chestnut, the young Minneapolis lawyer who managed the Humphrey drive. Minnesota Republican Chairman George Thiss, whose party has been perfecting its own computer operation for the past several elections, admits; "We just had no idea how much they had come along in getting out their own vote. And they did it in a way to help the ticket all the way down."

The computer gets major credit, too, for the lopsided re-election of Nevada Sen. Howard Cannon. . . . Mr. Cannon's staff spent more than a year researching all the Federal goodies he had arranged for each Nevada county or neighborhood—park funds, airport aid, school money, defense contracts, pensions. Then Nevada's voters were put on tape, 110,000 households in all, and every household got a letter spelling out just how Mr. Cannon had helped it.

There were different paragraphs for men and women, for oldsters and families with young children, for each neighborhood. In all, more than 12,000 combinations were used; campaign manager Chester Sobsey insists the technique was refined to the point where a paragraph citing Mr.

Cannon's success in winning funds for a local airport would be deleted in letters to voters with homes in the flight patterns. . . .

Voters Appreciate
a Little Personal Contact

[V]oters seem to appreciate any little personal contact in this age of impersonalized campaigning. Willian Butcher, executive vice president of American Computer Resources in Los Angeles says most voters don't realize the letters are computer-written, but even those who do still seem to like the attention and the candidate's familiarity with local issues and their own needs. Over and over again, phone canvassers are told, "This is the first time anyone ever bothered to ask me for my vote. I'll be glad to support your man."

Enthusiasts claim a first-rate computer operation is surprisingly cheap—and growing cheaper as more states and cities have voter names already on tape and as mail-list companies offer more complete coverage. . . .

Moreover, advocates argue, cost-conscious politicians should remember that the computer permits them to pinpoint their mail and other efforts, thus eliminating a great deal of wasteful spending. The annual cost is markedly less if the party keeps the tapes up to date year by year, eliminating heavy start-up expenses each election.

Computer sketptics remain, to be sure—party pros who say this will always be far too costly for all but the wealthiest men and organizations; that it breaks down on the local level when volunteers fail to carry out their assignments properly; that people resent interrupting phone calls or visits by canvassers; that computer bugs will get letters to the wrong people and backfire.

Candidates who won with the help of the computer are talking up its virtues, however. And there's still no better ad for a product than a satisfied customer.[14]

Management Techniques Are
As Important As Computers

Even more important to the future of the political process than computers, some experts agree, is the implementation of modern scientific management priorities of staff organization and responsible resource allocation based on computer output. Politicians are slowly realizing that antiquated

[14]From Alan L. Otten, "Computing Democratic Winners in '72," *Wall Street Journal,* 11 December 1970, p. 14.

management techniques are one of their major handicaps.[15] Systematic planning based on such devices as the Critical Path Method offer revolutionary possibilities for campaign organizations.[16]

While several critics have charged that computers are a dehumanizing influence in politics,[17] pollsters have fared little better. The argument is made that polling supplies information not only on past electoral preferences but also on the current *whims* of the electorate. Thus, when politicians use polls to formulate their strategy, *they* may have no position at all. The irony of this possibility was reflected in Joe Napolitan's remark, "There go my people; I must follow them. I am their leader."

But what critics fail to realize is that, through the broad exposure that most candidates receive either personally or through media news coverage and advertising, the public is generally able to determine whether or not the candidate actually understands the issue or really supports or opposes a particular program.[18]

The difficulty arises when candidates discover that the really crucial issues in a campaign may be of only slight interest to their constituencies. The voters are more concerned with sweeping events and major problems than with those the candidate may actually be able to impact.[19]

During the Vietnam war, candidates for state or local office often found themselves in the uncomfortable position of having to issue "policy statements" on the conduct of hostilities. If they insisted, quite accurately, that such questions were beyond the scope of the election, they were accused of lacking candor. But if they were drawn into the *trap*, they found themselves in political hot water.

In such cases polling is designed to discover not only which way the *political wind* is blowing but more importantly what issues are of significance to the electorate. Candidates cannot hope to attract a sufficient coalition of voters unless they are addressing the issues with which the electorate is concerned. Thus the poll is designed to establish not necessarily a candidate's position on the issues, but rather what the issues are.[20]

---

[15] "'72 Campaign Trends," op. cit., p. 859.

[16] For a complete discussion of the Critical Path Method of winning campaigns, see William Wilcox and James J. O'Brien, "How To Win Campaigns . . . ," *National Civic Review*, May 1967, pp. 265–269.

[17] Senator Edmund Muskie, for example, complained that some computer techniques (telephone and message solicitation) were the ultimate in insensitivity. "'72 Campaign Trends," op. cit., p. 859.

[18] For a further discussion of media and polling effectiveness, see Chapters 8 and 9, Shelby Coffey III, "Out of Control."

[19] For an interesting discussion of this phenomenon, see "Campaign American Style," CBS News Special, 1971.

[20] Stephen D. Shadegg, *How to Win an Election: The Art of Political Victory* (New York: Taplinger, 1964), p. 141.

**An Issue Survey
Is an Important Adjunct**

One consultant recalled the difficulty he had in trying to convince the candidate that an issues survey was an important adjunct to any campaign.

. . . The candidate was an ardent golfer and I knew it. After 30 minutes discussing other subjects, I switched the conversation to golf. I happened to have my putter with me. Clubs can be rented at almost any good golf course but a putter is a purely personal weapon. I engaged the candiate in a discussion of the problems of putting. I had him show me his stance, then I deliberately picked it to pieces—he was too erect, his grip was wrong, his stance was awkward—and with each critical suggestion I cited some great golfing authority. Then I dropped a couple of golf balls on the hotel room carpet, suggested the candidate try putting my way. He spent five minutes absolutely absorbed with the problems attendant on trying to knock that golf ball into a glass at the other edge of the carpet. After this exercise we returned to politics and sometime later I deliberately switched the conversation to a discussion of the fine points of quarter horses. The candidate had spent most of his life in a city and while he could recognize a horse as being different from a Mercedes-Benz, this was about the extent of his knowledge. He very promptly lost interest in the conversation and turned to something else. Then I made my point.

"When we were talking about golf," I said, "you were eager to listen. You didn't agree with anything I said but you listened because you were interested. When I started talking about horses, you refused even to carry on the conversation. When you are touring this state, you'd better talk about something in which the voters are interested or they'll give up on you the way you gave up on the horses."[21]

**A Good Poll Measures
a Variety of Problems**

Thus a good poll does more than tally voter opinion. It should give the candidate enough information to plan accurately a strategy by measuring:

1. His electoral strength as compared to that of his opponent.
2. The probable quota of votes he can expect in each political subdivision, such as district or county, showing his areas of strength and weakeness.

[21]Ibid., pp. 149–150.

3. Voter motivation—why citizens intend to vote for him or for his opponent.
4. His personal political profile—the image he projects to voters.
5. The issues on the minds of voters as they pertain to this particular contest, and which they regard as most important.
6. Any unusual circumstances of attitudes which may affect the course of the campaign.[22]

It is important to remember that polling is only as good as the information received and evaluated. Polls deal with people and are interpreted by people—and people are not infallible. Secondly, one should note

[22]E. John Bucci et al., *What Really Decides an Election . . . The Six Key Factors,* E. John Bucci and Associates, 1971, p. 25.

" I'M REPUBLICAN, MY HUSBAND'S DEMOCRAT, AND FIDO'S RADICAL. "

Reprinted courtesy of the Chicago Tribune.

him, but he still has to connect with the voters and make his own campaign. No poll . . . has made the candidate a different man, has changed his position on an issue, has made him into what he is not. Especially with television, it is impossible to perform such transformations, even if it were proper. However, such polls can singularly alter the strategy of a candidate. They can tell him where to spend his time and money; which national issues he has working for him, and which are boring the electorate to death; and how he can campaign most effectively. In all . . . polls [probably cannot] change an election more than 3 to 4 percentage points, but since most elections hover around the 50–50 mark, . . . they can affect the outcome. More accurately stated, a candidate using polls effectively can alter the outcome.

Poll Taking Is a Rapidly Expanding Industry

Despite opposition to the use of private political polling . . . its growth has continued unabated. And for good reason. Much as with market research before it, such polls pay off. They are helpful and by now have a proven track record—not that they are always right, and not that they cannot be misleading. They are subject to the same frailties as is any science-art, such as medicine, for example. . . . But if a man stands a 50–50 chance of making the right decision by flipping a coin, and if he can be right 70 per cent of the time if he has some good native judgment going for him, then with polling instruments as now developed, polls should be right better than 90 per cent of the time. This is a better record than that of reporters, editors, political science professors, even sociologists, and perhaps soothsayers, without the use of survey research.

Ethical Considerations

As we develop polltakers who better understand the mechanics, language, and Gestalt of politics, and as we develop candidates who are better informed about polls and social science research, inevitably the mating of the two professions will become more frequent and relations will become closer. The polltaker who is knowledgeable about politics will inevitably be invited to sit in on strategy meetings, mostly as a resource but also as a man of balanced judgment. The polltaker will more and more be in the position of recommending when and how many polls should be conducted for his client, rather than simply waiting for the political powers-that-be to call him and set the time schedule. This, too, is for the good, for if this tool is to be used to optimum advantage, the fullest and best thinking of the polltaker should be obtained. . . .

[T]he day will not arrive when an army of polltakers will take over the political machinery of this country. Politicians with power have a singular way of not passing that power over to strangers, especially those who have been retained as professionals. Neither will the people allow this. . . .

It has been stated that a polltaker who sits in on strategy sessions will acquire a biased and warped point of view that will color his ultimate findings. But if there is any sense to the discipline of . . . method and [an] . . . adherence to that discipline, then it is simply nonsense to believe that the social scientist who employs proper methodology will be swayed by emotion. What is more, the polltaker is hired specifically to be objective and to turn up the bad news wherever it is.

It has been stated that favorable polls are always leaked to give a candidate advantage in getting a bandwagon effect rolling or to line up a nomination. Long before polls were used, candidates tried to use whatever means they could to create such an effect. Yet leaks of polls are the exception rather than the rule. . . . Should the polltaker take cognizance of every mention in the gossip columns and newspapers? . . . [Probably] not. . . . Some . . . practitioners, it is true, have done polls paid for by partisan sources and put them out as impartial public polls; or have done private polls that have squirted out in partisan leaks; or, worse yet, have consented to the publication as campaign literature of parts of polls that hide the essential weaknesses of the candidate and, to the contrary, make him out to be the strongest candidate. But . . . such charges have been grossly exaggerated and are the handiwork of those who believe the whole field should be indicted because of a few cases. To blow these cases out of proportion ill befits a discipline wedded to the proposition of cross-section sampling and balanced reporting.

Polls Are Having a Profound Effect on Politics

Polls are having a profound effect on politics, and politics is having a profound effect on polls. But our free and democratic system will not be less free or less democratic as a result. At long last, the province of political research has come to include functional operations, and the worth of such polls is now appreciated most by the practitioners of politics. If the purpose of knowledge is to put it to use, then surely this is a desirable development. . . .

If, in some small way, such polling can reduce the number of irresponsibles who achieve high office, if it can make a candidate face the issues of concern to his electorate, if it can make the voice of the people a little clearer and more articulate, if it can make democracy function somewhat better in an hour when it is on trial, then, indeed, there will be a higher purpose in polling. . . .[25]

As one critic noted, the ethical questions of using polls is endemic to any consideration of the ultimate *good* or *evil* of the technique. But the "if"-y benefits to the public of such devices are difficult to substantiate. If a pollster wants to make money in the political arena and is hired to do a particular survey, do not the findings belong to the organization paying for the effort? If this is the case, is it not the right of that organization to use the poll in any manner that will assist their candidate to victory?

Leading pollsters generally agree that polls influence the morale of campaign workers as well as help or hinder the candidate's fund-raising activities.[26] But the influence is not generally felt thoughout the public sector until such polls reach the media. The ability to raise money and volunteers is of paramount importance to any campaign. In this regard, negative or positive indications in the press have an impact.[27]

The Underdog Effect

Polls also have a tendency to impact elections through what is described as the *underdog effect*. This occurs when polls indicate that one candidate is so far in front that the other receives a sympathy vote. Obviously the numbers are small and the impact is generally negligible.

Another possible influence on elections can be the *hedging* that some pollsters commit in order to excuse errors disclosed by election returns. This process assigns undecided voters on a weighted basis between the two candidates. Predictions of victory on such projections can, in a close election, cause certain individuals to change their vote in order to back the winner. Whereas the overwhelming number of major pollsters do not engage in this strategy (Gallup between 1950 and 1972 was accurate within 1.40 percent of the actual vote),[28] some private pollsters may try to create a bandwagon effect through such tactics.

[25] From Louis Harris, "Polls and Politics in the United States," *Public Opinion Quarterly* 27 (Spring 1963): 3–8.

[26] "The Facts About Political Polls," *U.S. News & World Report,* 7 October 1974, p. 34.

[27] Bogart, op. cit., p. 27.

[28] "The Facts About Political Polls," op. cit., p. 34.

These individuals may, as an example, *leak* information to the press, showing that candidate B is supported by 70 percent of the labor force. However, the additional information—that an insufficient number to constitute a legitimate sample was used—is withheld. Similar techniques have long been employed by merchandisers when they claim "9 out of 10 New York doctors choose brand Z for relief of headaches."

The Bandwagon Effect

Pollsters point to academic studies of voting behavior that refute the idea of a "bandwagon" effect following published polls in the days before an election. They refer to 1948, when polls forecast an easy presidential victory for Republican Thomas E. Dewey, who lost to Harry S. Truman. If there had been a bandwagon effect, the pollsters claim, the polls would have increased Dewey's lead.

Such studies do not, however, refute the charge that polls in three-way races might lead voters to switch from the bottom candidate (Goodell [D—New York]) to the middle one (Ottinger [D—New York]) in order to prevent a victory by the frontrunner (Buckley [Conservative—New York]). In the race among the liberal Ottinger, the liberal Goodell and the conservative Buckley, Ottinger gained nearly five points between the last poll and the election.

Pollsters counter by saying that switching choices in a three-way contest is a legitimate strategy for voters and that information about the relative strengths of the three candidates is fair information for a poll to provide.

Publication of polls poses a greater question of ethics when the polls are leaked in partial form or without adequate disclosure of their methods. Early in 1968, the Democratic National Committee leaked the results of a poll taken in one heavily Democratic county in New Hampshire and used the results to argue that President Johnson would run well against Republican opposition that fall. Pollster Archibald Crossley, who had taken the survey, repudiated the Democrats' interpretation, charging that his information had been unfairly manipulated. . . .

There are other ways that public polls and leakage of private ones can influence the outcome of elections. Pollsters cite the example of Richard Hughes' uphill campaign for Governor of New Jersey. . . . Hughes, a Democrat, was thought to have little chance of defeating Republican James P. Mitchell, a former Secretary of Labor. But a publicized private poll showed Mitchell to be vulnerable, induced [the] President . . . to campaign in the state for Hughes and helped bring about Hughes' narrow victory.

Some Problems in Polling

The *Detroit News,* which formerly commissioned public polls in primary contests, ceased the practice after an experience [some years ago]. . . . John B. Swainson and James M. Hare opposed each other in the Democratic primary, and a *News* poll showed Hare comfortably in the lead. The poll alarmed United Auto Workers officials, so the union waged a campaign to save Swainson, and Hare was defeated. Editors of the News felt they had unwittingly influenced the outcome. They gave up primary polling on the grounds that primaries were too volatile and subject to easy manipulation based on poll results.

Some newspapermen are vehement in their opposition to published candidate polls. Executive Editor Douglas Turner of the *Buffalo Courier-Express,* once an advocate of polls, now uses only "unscientific surveys" in his newspaper. "It's a great circulation builder," Turner said of the formal poll, "but it's against the principles of the secret ballot. We gave it up as unreliable. It's like going to mediums or playing with a ouija board. It's against the principles of a republic. It's a corruption, and we'll never run one again."

Proposed Congressional Action

In Congress, the major proponent of efforts to regulate the flow of poll results has been Rep. Lucien N. Nedzi (D-Michigan). . . . Nedzi has introduced legislation placing requirements on those who conduct polls for publication. According to the bill . . . pollsters would be required to disclose the name of the person who commissioned the poll, the method of sampling, the size of the sample, the time of the interviewing, the questions asked, the method of interviewing, the number of responses and the results. . . .

Hearings would turn up at least one fact annoying to professional pollsters: the most scientific surveys are sometimes not the most accurate. Congressional Quarterly's survey of 1970 polls revealed that two of the most accurate polls in statewide races were postcard surveys, a method long discounted by professionals. KAKE-TV in Wichita, Kansas, mailing postcards to about 1,000 voters and receiving less than a 45 percent response, came within 0.3 percent of the correct result in the state's race for Governor. The highly scientific and much-admired Iowa Poll, using methods perfected by national pollsters, was 5 percent off in that state's gubernatorial election. . . .

A Variety of Techniques

Polling techniques, and the reliability and accuracy of each, vary widely for published political polls. Major types include:

Personal In-Home Interview. An in-depth technique but time-consuming and costly. Teams of interviewers canvass designated residential areas and administer questionnaires to selected respondents.

Telephone Interview. A generally short interview with respondents whose names are selected in a predetermined order from telephone directories or voter registration lists or whose telephone numbers are randomly generated to computers (thereby including individuals with unlisted numbers).

Mail Poll. Returnable postcards or letters mailed to individuals selected in a predetermined order from voter registration rolls or telephone directories. Response rates are usually lower than 30 percent.

Man-in-the-Street Quota Interview. Infrequently used in modern scientific polling. Interviewers question individuals at any location so long as the sample is of a certain size or meets certain criteria such as a specified quota of women, young people, Catholics, blacks or other groups.

One major factor separating the different types of published polls [is that] . . . those done by private pollsters generally tended to be more scientific.

Public and private polls differ in their use of strict statistical methods.

Probability Sampling. . . . is the basis of all modern "scientific" polling and requires that every person in the population being sampled has an equal and predictable chance of being included in the sample. Such a sample should have the approximate characteristics of the population, and the sample's chances of representing the population can be stated mathematically.

Because of the difficulty of enumerating a complete list of citizens or voters, let alone the cost of tracking down the ones selected in any wholly random sampling, scientific polling organizations rely on variations of what is called an "area modified probability sample." All voting precincts or counties in the country (or state or region) are listed, and a sample of those is selected randomly. Then blocks or other residence areas within the larger jurisdictions are selected the same way. Finally, in the more scientific surveys, particular residences and exact persons to be interviewed are predetermined by a set procedure (such as every third address) and are not left to the discretion of the interviewer.

Most personal in-home interview polls are the probability type. . . .

Telephone, mail and quota polls are based normally on less exacting methodology. A sample may be drawn from some established list of individuals (telephone directories, commercial mailing lists, voter rolls, etc.) or by seeking respondents with certain specific characteristics. The pollster cannot be sure, no matter how large his sample, that the sample does not have the same bias that the source may have had. For example, the source may over-represent high-income individuals or under-represent young people.

Sampling Is Important for Accuracy

Although such samples do not have mathematically predictable margins of error, many have improved their techniques, particularly in the use of voter registration rolls and randomly generated telephone numbers. . . .

Most statewide area modified probability samples of published polls range from 600 persons (Utah Poll) to 5,000 persons (*New York Daily News* Poll). Nonprobability samples vary from reporters talking to a few dozen people on the street to thousands of phone, mail or man-in-the-street interviews.

The size of samples is one of the most misunderstood aspects of polling. The size of a sample is not nearly so significant as the care with which it is drawn. National pollsters such as Gallup and Harris use about 1,500 or 1,600 interviews. Both claim that 95 percent of the time, their samples allow for statistical confidence that the results will not vary more than 3 percentage points from the results if the entire population were polled. In order to lower the statistical tolerance by one point, the sample size would have to be doubled—a costly step. . . .

The Gallup organization has maintained that "the addition of many thousands, or even millions of persons has very little effect on the result after the first few hundred have been included in a survey." . . .

What Are Pollsters Attempting to Discover?

Almost all polls make some attempt to determine which individuals in a sample are most likely to vote. A series of questions might include whether the respondent is registered, how he voted in the last election, how he intends to vote in the next election or whether he knows where his polling station is. Large survey organizations frequently use scales of questions to assign a probability factor that a certain person will vote. Accuracy of these polling procedures often can be checked by later examining registration rolls. Several polls take their samples directly from voter registration lists in order to improve their accuracy.

All pollsters emphasize that the dates of field work for any poll must be taken into account when interpreting results. National or local events— even the weather—sometimes can cause measurable differences in the results of two similar polls conducted only a few days apart.

Ever since the disastrous experience in 1948 of pollster Elmo Roper and others, who stopped polling in September and did not detect a late shift of support from front-runner Thomas E. Dewey to Harry S. Truman, polls that offer vote projections have conducted their final surveys as close as possible to election days.

What Influence Does Interviewing Have on Polling?

Interviewing creates another potential source of error for polls. The order and wording of questions can affect the answers, especially if they make it appear to the respondent that the pollster hopes for a particular response. In polls taken to determine the popularity of a single candidate in a field of several candidates, respondents are not supposed to know which man is the subject of the poll.

A further problem is created by respondents who are not available the first time they are visited or called. Many pollsters report reaching only about half the sample on first visits. In a strict probability sample, absentees are contacted again and again and are finally dropped from the sample only if they are permanently unavailable. But this is too costly and time-consuming for most surveys. Many polls substitute another member of the household for the one originally sought for the interview, or simply move to the next house. The problem with this technique is that the substitute may change the result. The Gallup Poll neither calls back absentees or substitutes for them. Instead, Gallup interviewers ask respondents if they are normally home at the hour of the interview. If they say no, their answers are weighted more heavily, on the assumption that they speak for those who are unavailable.

Pollsters also have to be careful not to mix interviews done at different times, especially in situations where opinions are likely to change. A cumulative pre-election poll based on information gathered regularly between Sept. 1 and Nov. 1 is not likely to measure the extent of voter shifts that take place during the campaign.[29]

[29]"Public Polls: Variance In Accuracy, Reliability," *Congressional Quarterly: Weekly Report,* 18 September 1971, pp. 1927–1930.

To the novice all of this interest in sampling techniques, timing, question validity, computers, and so on may seem like political double talk. However, to the candidate it may very well represent the margin between success or failure in one of life's most competitive sports. The average voter reads a statistical analysis to either support his own view, or reinforce his philosophy that others "don't know what the hell they are doing." But the candidate uses this information to tell him where he should concentrate his time during the campaign and on what issues. Such an approach would seem to be of benefit to both the voter and office seeker. The majority of voters will be where the candidate concentrates his time, and the issues they consider important will become the basis for his discussions.

Is Polling Inimical to the Continued Existence of Democracy?

Perhaps, then, the underlying question of importance when discussing computer technology and polling in the electoral process is whether or not it is "inimical to the continued existence of democracy. . . . It seems . . . the answer must be no, for several reasons.

In the first place, [technology does not] . . . create attitudes, . . . [it] merely measures them. A good survey does not try to sway opinions. Rather it tries to find out what really is on people's minds. Too often in the American past political campaigns have been based on what politicians think is important. With the development of a scientific [approach], . . . campaigns can now be based on what voters think is important. . . . [This technique becomes] . . . the essence of democratic leadership.

Second, much of the attack on polls assumes that voters are semi-competent boobs. There is increasing evidence, however, which indicates that voters can and do distinguish between candidates and that elections are meaningful in terms of electoral choice—despite the fact that few voters are Ph.D.'s in political science. . . . Though some may be foolish, voters are not fools.

Finally, it is important for leaders in a democratic society to know what people think. If politicians are to be elected or re-elected they must relate what they do and believe to what voters do and believe. It is the height of political irresponsibility to argue that the information about voters that politicians have should be incorrect, that it should not be gathered in the most sophisticated manner possible. Decisions, in politics as in business and education, are best when based on good information.

Certainly this is not to suggest that . . . [technology] will not be used by venal men for corrupt purposes. But this is true of universal suffrage, free speech, and a host of other desirable political practices. It is the men . . . who are at fault.[30]

[30]Timothy D. Mead, "The Use of Private Opinion Polls in Political Campaigns," *Memo*, February 1971, pp. 13–14.

8

Control:
The Art of
Campaign
Management

"Out of control. He's simply *out of control!*" shouts anguished Bob Bonitati, who has been around political skirmishes long enough to know that you might as well giggle a little when a skittish congressional candidate just *won't do as instructed.* Hefty, jocular Bob Bonitati's dilemma is standard for the political consultant: cooling off the candidate, outclassing the arguments of the passle of yes-men surrounding the candidate.

As president of Robert-Lynn Associates, a public relations and political management group . . . Bob Bonitati is part of the . . . mushrooming of political consultants that sprang up over the 1960s—accelerating the past two years as more young hustlers and older "pols" took stock of just how much of those millions and millions of dollars spent by candidates might help pay off their own mortgages. It's a hell-and-ambrosia field: jittery, lucrative, very cyclical, and possibly more fun than anything else in the world when it's not more frustrating than anything else.

If the Candidate Has Money, He Is Harder to Handle

For instance, Bonitati's Dilemma: "The Candidate has a lot of money . . ."—ever a prime consideration in a field where bad debts are strewn about like '57 Fords in an automobile graveyard. But this very wealth makes the candidate harder to handle. "He's been though *three* advertising firms already." (It was late September.) And it seems that an old FTC charge against one of the Candidate's lucrative mail-order companies (a charge launched before he took over, according to Bonitati) had been brought up by the Opponent and created a one-day splash in the local newspapers.

"Like most candidates, he's very insecure," says Bonitati, his great chocolate eyes slying, "he wanted to mail *massive* explanations, deny everything, throw lawsuits at them. I tried to calm him down . . . 99 per cent of the people in the street won't remember the charge in 10 days." But hell hath no explainer like a candidate's conscience pricked: at the next rubber-roast-chicken meeting of Republican biggies, what does the Candidate do but ramrod right up to the mike and start blasting away: "I want to explain about a terrible article!" "Most of those guys," says Bonitati, shaking his stylishly shaggy dark head at the wonder of it all, "most didn't even know what he was talking about. We have no control."

Control is a major part of the political consulting game—almost as major as winning. Political consultants are witchdoctors of the computer campaign, slick political inheritors of the McNamara myth of systems analysis. At 500 bucks a day, they'd better be good (some of the younger firms, like Robert-Lynn, get considerably less, but well-publicized media people like Joe Napolitan get the top buck).

**You Have
to Have Control**

And to be good they have to have . . . control.

As one remarked, "You're always fighting the guy who's the candidate's best friend or next-door-neighbor, the guy who always has his ear." Amid the generally bitter factional strife of campaigns, consultants adore control; the more established demand it before accepting a campaign.

They are both the hired guns (as Brad Hays was called when he tried to get the Virginia Republican nomination for Harry Byrd, Jr.) and the staff generals (as Spencer-Roberts' . . . Reagan campaign) of million dollar statewide shootouts for the ballot box.

They're the experts from out of town—who, often enough, are experts only because they're from out of town. "We're the objective" factor, as cool, gray-haired Doug Bailey of Bailey, Deardourff, and Bowen puts it: the factor that soothes harassed candidates pumped to bursting with adrenalin and desire.

And if they don't pull that off—well, you have Bonitati's Dilemma.

This minor but growing glamour industry has its origins in the population explosion; the rocketing of America's post-War affluence; the monster-baby growth and power of teevee; the erosion of traditional party structure and machines; the advent of the jet; reduced long-distance telephone rates; our peasant-faith in technology and "experts," and God-blessusall, Greed.

One study shows that some 200 firms are now doing political work—media consulting, polling, management fund-raising, data processing, research, advertising, etc.

It's All Electronic Now

It's gone way beyond Ernest Dichter and motivational research—it's all caught up in the electric fury of data speed, all the oohing and aahing over the fellows with the slicked-down hair who come into your territory and tell you, yessir, that you have to limit your billboard messages to just a few key words, mind you, and to keep your teevee-interview answers short and crisp. And they will even tell you (if you have an advisor like young John Lorenz with "diachronic analysis" of speech) "scientifically" what words to slip into your sentences when you are in one territory and what words to avoid when you are in another territory.

This is the sort of effort that sets the new campaign professionals off from the old seat-of-the-pants touts: the use of technology. They attempt to use more scientific methods in determining voter attitudes; they bring a technocrat's view to the methods of mass persuasion. And, having monitored the public's attitudes, they fit it into a Grand Strategy, more elaborate than the often frantic, day-to-day old-style campaigns. (Which is not to say that they don't need local expertise or that they aren't often wrong.)

The firms that have jumped into this lucrative whirlpool include

It's okay for the computer to schedule my speeches, but damned if I'm going to stand for it picking out my ties.

(From *Campaign Insight*. By permission.)

smallish, essentially one-man operations (like that of Clifton White in New York—he has what is generally considered to be one of the finest political minds in the United States) and the mammoth full-service factories like Spencer-Roberts, which has scores of employees and even went so far as to conduct a school for fledgling Republican campaign artistes out in Chicago (a school from which, it might be added, a number of the young free-lance consultants of today have sprung).

The consultant has become so obvious in political Americana that now, across this fine November land, you hear contests described in terms of epic consultant-battles. Chivalric champions of passive, scarf-fluttering candidates. As young Mike Rowan of Napolitan's vaunted firm notes, "This is the first year people have been mentioning races as *between* consultants. . . ."

All of this is costing great sums: [in the late 60's] political expenditures . . . were estimated at $300 million [a year]; near $60 million alone went for air-time for television and radio spots, and production costs are estimated by the Citizen Research Foundation . . . to have accounted for another $30 million. Specialists and orchestrating generalists are demanding even higher prices . . . [as the seventies progress].

The only possible relief in sight might have been the . . . vetoed bill to limit campaign spending on t.v. and radio ("it's an incumbent's bill," complains Mike Rowan). A lot of media people might be hurt. Organizers like Matt Reese might prosper. But Doug Bailey (media-oriented) thinks that big business men ("the major contributors, anyway" . . . who can empathize with high television costs) might not see the need to contribute so much for organization.

Many contemporary political consultants would have been the Jim Farleys (and his imitators) of yesterday. Practically all of them are lined up with one party or another (Baus and Ross of California being one exception; they worked for Pat Brown but also in Barry Goldwater's presidential primary. Dave Garth of New York also works both sides). "It leads to less potential conflict," as Charles Guggenheim, a top Democratic filmmaker, puts it. . . .[1]

But here the similarity ends.

Competition Has Intensified with Dollars

The competition for political power in America has intensified as the Gross National Product has swollen. If campaign spending has risen well over a

[1]*Potomac,* 9 February 1969.

hundred million dollars since 1945, then there are more new post-War fortunes available to meet those bills. The number of seats of power stayed nearly static (with the exception of two new states), but the competition has grown more fierce. It's not just the Jaycees deciding that old Al ought to have a shot.

As the power of patronage declined ("Who needs those Post Office jobs?" wonders Bob Bonitati), so has the power of the party—though it is by no means as defunct as some consultants might have you believe.

In turn, that decline has led some pols to split off and make considerably more money on their own than they would have braving the flows and eddies of life in the national organization. The cool medium's unmatched power has spawned not only a host of firms like Guggenheim's and Harry Treleaven's, but also has forced Bob Squier's Communications Company and Robert Goodman's Baltimore ad agency to turn major time to political work. It has also spawned the Instant Candidate—the obscure man with great cash, like Milton Shapp in 1966 and Howard Metzenbaum in 1970 (both Napolitan-Guggenheim productions), who could emerge from obscurity to victory mainly by virtue of a media campaign.

With the growth of consulting has come the consultant with diversified interests. Firms the size of Spencer-Roberts, the West Coast octopus with a full range of services, are able to handle many clients at once. . . . But other campaign professionals, both consultants and specialists, are able to handle several campaigns at once just by jetting in and out. A man like Roy Pfautch, a former Methodist preacher turned poltical operator, can be in Wyoming one night, then flip up to Utah to check on his associate Brad Hays and the next morning be back in Washington to look at co-worker Ed Grefe's work . . . all the while keeping tabs on local developments and national trends via long-distance telephone.

Consultants generate a certain amount of power—by reputation as well as by knowledge.

"Goddamit, . . . are you going to work for me or not?" a badgere[d] Ronald Reagan is quoted as telling a group from Spencer-Roberts. . . . The boys from Spencer-Roberts just sat back and waiiiiited a couple of days before deigning to assist Reagan to the landslide that caused him to be considered a presidential possibility. . . .

Pollster-interpreter John Lorenz, youthful head of Cyr, Pickard and Associates in Washington, giggles and swears that one wealthy senatorial hopeful was scared out of a race by a badly done poll. . . .

The knowledge of even the mere presence of consultants can affect a campaign.

Some candidates, fearing the cries of outsider, hide their consultants. . . .
This fear is especially pronounced in the less urbanized states.

For instance, down in Tennessee, senatorial candidate Bill Brock's
press man claimed, to this reporter, that Brock's campaign director, Ken
Rietz, was no longer associated with media massager Harry Treleaven.
Rietz is. . . .

As counterpoint, the presence of high-powered consultants can help
keep others out of a race.

When Sargent Shriver was Hamleting about, trying to decide whether
to run for governor of Maryland, Gov. Marvin Mandel scampered off to
Joe Napolitan. Soon enough, stories started appearing in great metropolitan newspapers that shall here go nameless. The stories, near-breathless
with inside info, noted that Joe Napolitan (management), Bob Squier
(teevee) and Tony Schwartz (radio) . . . were on Mandel's side. Other
pressures were applied . . . polls did not show much . . . and Sarge didn't
run—another illustration of the power of consultants to affect the race
before it reaches the teevee-glazed malleable unwashed. . . .

A biting smoke clouds the large central office down at Bailey, Deardourff and Bowen. Fred, the Xerox machine, had become ill in the
afternoon and belched smoke for quite some time. It has made hardly any
difference to Doug Bailey. . . .

At the moment, . . . [he] is practically purring with delight, having
helped befuddle John Gilligan in the Ohio governor's race. Sitting across
from him is his television expert, John Bowen, who used to be assistant
media director for the Chevrolet account ("largest ad account in the
world"). Bailey recalls, "Gilligan said some words he probably wishes he
could take back—allegedly encouraging 'revolution.'

"We put a spot on the air citing the quote. . . . He apparently was prepared; he had some guy swear out an affidavit saying he was misquoted."

But the backers of Bailey's tiger, Roger Cloud, also were secreting
evidence that Gilligan had indeed said it. They were oozing with desire to
blast Gilligan with their confidential info. But Bailey, out-of-town Bailey,
cool hand consultant, said wait. Grumbling, they did. Gilligan presented
his evidence and stations took off the ad. The press leaped after the story
like dogs panting after a bitch in heat. . . . Then, cool hand Bailey sends
the Ohio pols off with their confidential memo, and again the papers bound
after the story and the teevee people reconsider the evidence and, hallelu-
jah, the ad is replaced.

"He (Gilligan) would have been much better off if he had just let it pass," says Doug Bailey. "That's right," says Bowen. "It wasn't even a very good spot. It was thrown together too fast." (After further Gilligan evidence several stations banned the ad again.)

Consultants Inject Timing

"If there's one thing that consultants can inject," says Bailey, "it's timing, timing. We may start building these little jabs up in August . . . some of the things may not seem to make much sense but by October, they come together."

This sense of orchestration courses throughout Doug Bailey's talk of consulting. Actually, his firm is more of an advertising company now. In fact, it's sort of a clearing house that lets out bids to production companies like Jerry Schnitzer in Los Angeles, Summerhill, also in L.A., Ernie Lukas in Chicago and Gordon Hyatt in New York. His firm keeps 15 per cent of the production costs and is paid 15 per cent of the advertising costs by TV stations on which it places the ads. "We combine political expertise with advertising know-how, so that you don't use methods to try to sell soap when you're selling a candidate," says Bailey, who adds the claim that the firm also does consulting for roughly $250 a day. . . .

[P]olitical consulting is fun [he notes]. A campaign has great emotional dynamics. Although it sounds frivolous, it has all the combative elements of any game. . . . you're totally exhilarated or totally destroyed on election night.

"I'm a great fan of pro football," continues Bailey. It has two elements that appeal to him: violence and science and he sees these two elements carrying over into politics in slightly transmuted forms. "A campaign should be viewed as a million dollar operation . . ." with many diverse pieces. . . .

"There's only one day that counts and as you approach it, you have to draw all these pieces (all the hundreds of thousands of dollars, the thousands of people, the masses of figures) together into . . . the . . . right . . . place." . . .

Now a don of the consulting world, cool Joe Napolitan no longer bounces around Springfield, Mass., politics, boostering one man into the mayorship one year, then boostering his opponent into glory a few years later. Cool Joe Napolitan has gone international. He no longer grows so effervescent with reporters, describing how he told rich little Milton Shapp, 1966 Democratic candidate for governor of Pennsylvania, to forget it when Milton first came in—and then told Milton to sit down when the industrialist mentioned having a million or so to spend in the campaign.

Cool Joe Napolitan

Cool Joe Napolitan has been burned by that kind of talk and the publicity it generates. Now when you meet him at his little Connecticut Avenue offices, he is restrained and quiet. . . . Modestly, he'll mention that he doesn't think having the Humphrey account in 1968 hurt his reputation at all. Very seriously he'll talk about the American and International Associations of political consultants, which he and Clif White have organized.

That low-key impression tickles Mike Rowan, Cool Joe's 28-year-old assistant: "People think" Joe's not so smart, since he's so low-key. It seemed to me like a quiet cunning. Grinning, Mike agrees.

A native of New York, mod-suited Mike Rowan was school-teaching in Alaska, enraptured with politics and helping manage Mike Gravel's successful Senate campaign when he met Joe Napolitan, who had come up for media consultations. After several months' work with Gravel's office, the slender, ebullient Rowan hooked up with Napolitan. His voice lifts a full octave when he talks about Joe's expertise and diversity. One of the more fascinating parts of that diversity is Public Affairs Analysts. . . . That firm was started up by Napolitan, Larry O'Brien, Clif White, international government student Martin Ryan Haley, Nicholas Constantine, an international lawyer and several others. . . . [T]he PAA ("nonpartisan") board meets "once a month" and provides a full range of governmental issues in relation to clients: "intelligence services," "political feasibility studies for a client's proposed activities," "counseling on the most effective political use of client personnel and other resources," and so on. All of which adds up to a nice little package of services, especially if and when a Napolitan- or White-advised President clambers into 1600 Pennsylvania.

**Politics Is Too Important
to Be Given to Advertising Agencies**

At the moment, Rowan says, things are going well for the political arm, which advises mainly Democrats and claims 10 victories out of 11 primaries this year. "As Joe says: Politics is too important to be given to advertising agencies," says Rowan. "That's why we can win 10 out of 11."

Napolitan's specialty is polling, interpretation and hauling in media specialists like Tony Schwartz and Bob Squier. Many in the field consider him one of those few true and good minds who can determine when and how the swing vote will go and how to get it—the truly crucial test of a campaign consultant. But others, most notably Milton Shapp . . . think

Napolitan doesn't leave candidates the kind of support they need for a general election—where a "media blitz" is not as effective as in a primary.

Rowan delights in talking about the media and its implications. He claims to have read articles denouncing the use of trains in campaigns when they were new to the "whistlestopping" game. He thinks television has been a great liberating factor. . . .

People Are Afraid of Television

"People are afraid of television but maybe years from now we'll look back on this period with great humor . . . and besides look at what we're *doing* with television—electing an Andy Young in *Atlanta*."

Rowan, who says he is receiving only around $5,000 for "20 days of work" . . . delights in the power of his position. Like a lot of consultants, he has no intention of running for office at the moment.

"I can do more from right here than I ever could if I were elected to Congress," he bubbles, gesturing about his cramped offices. . . .

Handsome Davy Hackett ("looks and talks like a Kennedy," gushed a 1961 Associated Press biographical blurb) was schoolbody tennis chum of the late Sen. Robert F. Kennedy and helped invent the "boiler room" in the 1960 presidential campaign; and when John Kennedy was elected President he became a special assistant to Attorney General Kennedy, specializing in juvenile delinquency; and when John Kennedy was laid to rest in Arlington, Dave Hackett bided his time; and when Sen. Robert Kennedy ran for President in 1968, Davy Hackett worked hard in the Washington headquarters; and when Robert Kennedy was laid to rest in Arlington, Davy Hackett . . . went into the consulting business.

His firm specialized in "statistical analysis based on extensive use of polls; media recommendations and financial counseling." Their candidates . . . first (and possibly final) year of political counseling were: Robert P. Casey, who ran for the Democratic gubernatorial nomination in Pennsylvania; Mr. Violent World, former pro footballer Robert Lee "Sam" Huff, who ran for Congress in West Virginia; and the blondest astronaut of them all, John Glenn, who shot for the Ohio senatorial nomination.

Harvard law grad Fraser Barron bravely says he did much of the political work for David Hackett Associates. Fraser Barron is now working for the Alaskan Indians. . . . None of the Hackett stable survived the primary. Huff turned out to be, well, not really a viable candidate, and lost by around 2 to 1; Casey "listened to the touts" and blew it to Milton Shapp; and, upset of upsets, John Glenn lost to a rich unknown named Howard Metzenbaum.

All this political carnage seems to have left a serious scar on Fraser Barron. When, to put him at ease, I mentioned that "several sources" had said he was very efficient, Barron slouched deeper in his swivel chair, stared at his shoes and murmured: "Maybe you better get some new sources."

Strewn about his office, Barron has great black notebooks, thick as two shoulder-to-shoulder Polish sausages, packed with information on Ohio. Another smaller green notebook contains frantic polls charting the eroding popularity of John Glenn (who was leading roughly 62 per cent to 9 per cent in January). A *Time* magazine-style Sam Huff brochure smiles mockingly up from another shelf. (The picture on the cover is hopelessly saccharine, unconvincing; "He insisted on using *that* picture," mourns Barron.) And the Casey campaign? God, it was like something out of a parody of *The Last Hurrah*.

"I remember one meeting in the Casey campaign," says Barron, who is baldish, 33, and screws his face into a mask of bloated arrogance when imitating the old style pols, "those 'touts' kept saying (face contorts), 'We don't need a poll' . . . At one meeting they turned to a media consultant—a media consultant, ha—and asked him 'what's the situation in Philly' and he says (face, voice bloat again), 'Well, you gotta watch out for those colored people . . . People are pretty uptight these days.' Fraser Barron just shakes his head. "You asked where they got their information and they say 'Well, I been in the right bars in Philly.'"

But, of course, the Glenn campaign was even more painful. John put up a big staff in a big suite in Cleveland, but "never could develop a field staff."

One haunting factor that shadowed the Glenn campaign, Barron thinks, was the Glenn financial state after the '64 Bathtub Campaign, from which Glenn was forced to withdraw after suffering a bad fall in the shower. "He came out of it $64,000 in debt," says Barron, "It was very humiliating and embarrassing for him. Personal friends were sending his kids to college . . . (More recently) He got an awful lot of stock out of Royal Crown . . . but it's my understanding that it's all mortgaged. He had a paranoia about a repeat of '64. Not being able to pay off his debts . . . If he would just have put 25 or 30 grand (into television ads) in the northeast part of the state . . ."

As it is, though, Glenn still hasn't paid off his debts to David Hackett Associates, alleges Barron. And "as close as he and Dave were, we could never get him to believe (in our approach) . . . All this raises the main reason why we don't want to go on with this: you do all this work, but it's an exercise in futility."

(For his part, former candidate Glenn says that he did believe in many of Hackett Associates' plans but simply didn't have the money to carry them out. While he does "own a block of RC stock," he also "owes money" and says he didn't have extra personal cash to put in the campaign.)

Adds Barron:

"You have to contend with a bunch of touts—sons of the *Last Hurrah* days, treating campaigns like they were in 1900 . . . thinking up corny press stunts, getting a 'big crowd' at rallies, getting a head table at the Knights of Columbus dinner . . ."

Barron waves his hand, falls silent. Perhaps he is thinking of the Alaskan Indians again. He goes to a storage closet and fumbles about with the thick black notebooks jammed with Ohio printouts and voter analyses.

"We've got a helluva lot of crap about that state," he says, and finally changes the subject.

Where Are the Democrats and Republicans?

Where are the Democrats? Where are the *Democrats?* Where *are* the Democrats? The DEMOCRATS ARE STILL IN THE DARK AGES.

And the Republicans? The REPUBLICANS ARE STILL IN THE NINETEENTH CENTURY.

But, thank Mammon and Bill Buckley, Dick Viguerie and Associates (40 in all, including 18 executives, according to Viguerie) are in the bloody TODAY world of fund-raising for politicians. "As the kids say 'our bag' is direct mail," says Viguerie, relaxing in his plush Connecticut Avenue office. Only certain politicians need apply; those with impeccable conservative credentials. Viguerie's acknowledged clients include men like 'the Blue Max' Rafferty, who knocked off Sen. Tom Kuchel in California and then lost a squeaker to now-Sen. Alan Cranston ("We put $700,000 in his campaign," claims Viguerie); Judge Harrold Carswell, who was trounced by Rep. William Cramer, down in Florida ("an inept campaign," complains Viguerie); Rep. Phil Crane of Illinois, one of the brightest young conservatives to come out of that state since Ev Dirksen; Sen. John Tower of Texas, and a host of others. Some 30 in all, according to Viguerie, who bemoans that a lot of them turned out to be ingrates.

Candidates are not the only sort of clients Dick Viguerie handles. "I have a list of close to a million names of contributors to conservative causes around the country," claims the soft-spoken, personable executive, who grew up on the hard side of Houston.

With that cast of hundreds of concerned thousands developed over the past decade of fund-raising . . . Viguerie has also been able to raise enormous amounts of cash for various conservative political organiza-

"THE ALL-AMERICAN GAME"

tions. He refused to name any of the 40 groups, considers it unethical to do so. (One already mentioned in the press was the United Republicans of America.)

But back in the recesses of his sprawling offices, under lock and key, glitter well over 700 plastic-jacketed computer tapes. Each is marked with certain names and addresses: On one roll of mud-brown plastic are etched the names of all people who contributed to Judge Carswell during one month; one has all the names of contributors to sad-faced John Marchi's losing campaign for Mayor of Fun City; others are marked with the organizations' names. Rows of "conservative books" like *The Suicide of the West* line one office, remainders of an abortive direct-mail book-selling operation. Charts of mailing schedules stuck with red tape clutter the walls of another office in the busy operation.

You Can't Get Away with Baloney

"You can't give a client a lot of baloney in this business," says Viguerie. . . . "In advertising, who can tell if [the ads] do any good? Our letters go out on Monday and we have to live with the returns the next Monday. We can't say 'you have a lot of friends.' (Except maybe when they do voter mailings.)

Processing each letter costs roughly in the range of 15 to 16 cents but it can cost less or more depending on the speed and number. (They say they can handle up to 400,000 in six days.) It's a wide shrewd bicuspid-flashing grin he manages when asked the secret of his success: "I've studied direct mail six days a week, 12 hours a day, for years." One letter, which never reached Mrs. Ola Critcher of Cromwell, Ala., does show part of the Viguerie magic. Dated Aug. 17, 1970, the appeal for Judge Carswell comes under the letterhead of United States Senate, Edward J. Gurney, Florida. It begins, "First let me say that I know it's only been a short time since you generously contributed $2.00 to Judge Carswell.

"And because you have been so generous this is a difficult letter to write . . ."

Part of the secret is this super-personalization. Instead of just using an MTST machine to put the person's name into the body of the letter, the amount of the previous contribution is also mentioned. (How did they know, Ola? All those whirring IBM 2401s helped a bit.) A sharp blast at

Senators Kennedy, Fulbright, et al., for their "crushing" blow to us "conservatives" is mentioned, as is a request that Ola write in NO on an enclosed form if she can't send any more money, so I'll have an idea as to how much we can expect to raise! That NO might be a little harder to write since the return envelope is marked for "PERSONAL ATTENTION: SENATOR EDWARD J. GURNEY." (Ola's letter came back marked unknown.) This is super-personalization and part of the key to what Viguerie, proud as a Medieval scientist mentioning his philosophers' stone, calls "the secrets."

Not that those secrets aren't widely imitated; Viguerie says various opponents sometimes copy letters almost verbatim. "But the coffee doesn't taste as good in another cup." That's part of the secret, too.

"We also keep a lot of dummy names" in the data bank, just in case some scoundrel should break through and steal. "We should know immediately" if someone had swiped the million and their addresses. (Many, according to a source outside of Viguerie headquarters, gathered at the Clerk of the House's office and in state capitols where campaign reports are filed. Viguerie will neither confirm or deny.)

For all their expertise (and high prices; Viguerie says he keeps 50 per cent of the income while detractors say he keeps more), the generally low-key Viguerie leaps just adjacent to outrage when he talks about some politicians.

"Steve's life was miserable for a year," says Viguerie, gesturing to assistant Steve Winchell, who worked furiously as the account executive for the Rafferty campaign. And did the Blue Max send so much as a postcard? No.

"I never even talked to John Marchi in my life," and he too sent no word of thanks. "Just a postcard or a pat on the back . . ." And one candidate who ran an awful campaign let his staff grouse bitterly because Viguerie only raised 75 per cent of his self-estimated target.

So now, Dick Viguerie is thinking of doing more commercial mailings. There will be more money, though "We'll be small potatoes in that field."

But at least there won't be so much incompetence, so much panic, and back-stabbing and penny-pinching. Despite attacks for soliciting out-of-state, Viguerie thinks he has helped make politics a better place by giving candidates "with lots of small donors" as much cash as ones "who have to take checks for ten thousand" from one big money man. "When big contributors come in and tell him to do something," he can tell them off.

All the Last-Minute Hassles

But there remain all the hassles and the last-minute calls stirring account executives out of their beds to go down and start up the battery of computers and line up speedy printers to land another 25 grand in some ingrate's coffers. "Sometimes," says Viguerie, "you go in and you're almost throwing up with tension . . . they're nightmares," those days of pressure.

And then this utter lack of appreciation and complaining from campaign workers. "I'm getting tired," says Viguerie, his firm, tan face set grimly, "of dealing with all the stupid people you have to in politics."[2]

Although the professional campaign consultants and managers may complain about the "old school" politicians and political hacks with which they must contend, the ranks of these professional politicians are growing. The composite message of consultants is that these inconveniences are overshadowed by the excitement and challenge of the campaign arena, not to mention the field's lucrative financial aspects.

Services Have Numerous Commonalities

The scope of services available to a candidate in the 1970s may vary from the design of a brochure to the full services of a campaign management firm.[3] A promotional brochure of the Los Angeles-based Spencer-Roberts and Associates exemplifies the degree to which an organization can be "rented" by a candidate.

Once into a campaign, the Spencer-Roberts management team emphasizes timing. It schedules the opening of the campaign headquarters, the distribution of printed brochures, the purchase of advertising and all media and the coordination of volunteer get-out-the-vote-effort. Spencer-Roberts has settled on touch stones that they consider essential to any campaign plan. They will usually devise three or four key projects tailored to the particular problems of the individual campaigns. And they like to play to their clients'

    [2] From Shelby Coffey III, "The Tentacles of Management Firms Grow," *The Washington Post/Potomac,* 1 November 1970, pp. 8–14, 21–24, 26–27. (All footnotes in this chapter have been consecutively renumbered for the convenience of the reader.)

    [3] For a further discussion of the scope of campaign consultants and their role in political races, see Dwight E. Jensen and John F. Burby, eds., "Professional Managers, Consultants Play Major Role in 1970 Political Races," *National Journal,* 26 September 1970; "Campaign Costs: More Specialization, More Dollars," *Congressional Quarterly: Weekly Report,* 11 September 1971, p. 1912; Vernon F. Anderson, *Professional Consultants in the Campaign Arena,* Washington Association of Educational Media, 1973; "Campaign Management Grows into National Industry," *Congressional Quarterly: Weekly Report,* 5 April 1968, pp. 706–710; "Campaign Consultants: Risking Sincerity in 1974," *Congressional Quarterly: Weekly Report,* 4 May 1974, pp. 1105–1108.

"I was packaged by Candidates Limited. Who packaged you?"

strength, looking for undecided voters among demographic groups which are generally favorable to the candidate.[4]

Despite the variations of the candidate service firms, a recent nation-wide study by *National Journal* revealed that their

. . . services are characterized by numerous commonalities:[5]

1. Scheduling of a candidate, not so much to draw big crowds, as to draw television cameras.
2. Heavy reliance on polling, not to determine a candidate's standing in

[4]Jensen and Burby, op. cit., p. 2078.
[5]Ibid., p. 2077.

a race, but to select issues on which he should campaign and areas and voter groups he should concentrate on.

3. Independence of party structure so that the candidate moves closer to his party if polls shows that will help him and cuts his party ties if polls show the party label hurts.[6]

4. Total control of every step of a campaign from selecting precinct appearances on the basis of computer printouts to organizing the get-out-the-vote-activities.

What these new campaign techniques mean when they materialize on the campaign trail was well exemplified in the successful effort of W. E. Brock to unseat the tenure of Albert Gore in the U.S. Senate.

Brock's campaign manager . . . [was] Kenneth Rietz, 29, a partner in a New York campaign management and consulting firm of Treleaven and Associates. The firm accounts among its successful clients Gov. A. Linwood Holton, Jr., R-Va., and Sen. Edward J. Gurney, R-Fla. It is engaged in several major contests . . . for Republican candidates.

Rietz, a fair-haired stylishly dressed political scientist and adviser to the Republican National Committee, said that early [the year] . . . Brock asked the Treleaven firm to assess his chances of defeating Gore. The firm conducted a two-week survey of the state and prepared a confidential report, dated May 5, . . . which still serves as the basic strategy blueprint.

Organization— A Well-Oiled Effort

Brock organization: Rietz moved to Nashville in November to put the operation together, a task made easier since a chart had already been drawn up by the Treleaven firm. . . .

The Brock organization has hired several professional campaign specialists:

- Harry Treleaven, head of the firm bearing his name, is advertising director in charge of designing all media and other advertising materials.

[6] A good example of this approach was demonstrated during the last days of the Nixon presidency when Republican congressional candidates, fearing a debacle at the polls, sought to increase their distance, politically, from the president and the party he represented.

- Glen Advertising Inc. of Dallas produces the ads.
- Tully Plesser of Cambridge Opinion Studies, Inc., New York, is the candidate's pollster.

The campaign chairman is Dr. Nat Winston, a prominent Republican, former state mental health commissioner and country music enthusiast.

Chairman of the policy committee, an 11-member group similar to a corporate board of directors, is the candidate's brother, Patrick Brock.

A paid, full-time staff of about 25 works under Rietz on the nuts-and-bolts functions. Major elements of the organization include:

- The publicity section, which produces press releases, photos and radio tapes (changed twice a day for use on noon and evening news shows).
- The research section, responsible for producing speech materials on major issues (as indicated by the polls) and information on the opposition candidate.
- The advertising committee, a high-level, five-member board including Republican National Committeeman George Ed Wilson, that screens all major advertising materials prior to release.
- The nine district coordinators, full-time staff men who oversee developments in each congressional district. Under them are eight part-time field staffers and the district, county, city and precinct chairmen. (These campaigners are responsible for such tasks as distributing literature, organizing meetings and appearances by the candidate, distributing news releases, working on voter registration and transporting people to the polls.)
- A speaker's bureau, which ensures that someone from Brock headquarters is available to address meetings when the candidate is unable to attend.
- A canvassing section, which reviewed primary election results in each congressional district and assigned priority numbers to each precinct within a district where a Republican bias was indicated. As part of the canvassing operation, 600,000 voters' names were fed into leased computers at Brock headquarters. Printouts showing name, age, address, telephone number and voting preference in the Aug. 6 primary were then made available to Brock workers throughout the state.
- A women's division, which coordinates coffees, teas and other fund-raising and campaign affairs involving women's groups around the state—and seeks endorsements of the candidate from other women's organizations.
- An advancing section, which, in conjunction with the scheduling sys-

tem, sends at least one staff member ahead of the candidate to contact party chiefs, alert news media, arrange rooms, meals, telephones, and keep the visit on schedule.

- Brockettes and Young Volunteers for Brock, mostly college and high school age volunteers, are asked to appear at rallies, knock on doors and collect "Bucks for Brock" in supermarket parking lots.

Other assignments on the Brock organizational chart include ballot security (election day poll-watching), coordination with state party head-quarters and state legislators.

Numerous citizens groups for Brock, often headed by a nominal Democrat or independent, have been formed. They usually reflect varying interest groups. Lawyers, hunters and "Walking Horse People," the latter being fans of Tennessee's show horses, each have an organization supporting Brock. While usually inactive, these groups serve two main purposes: they help spread the candidate's name within specific groups and provide material for news releases. . . .[7]

This contest was also of interest because the campaign style of Senator Albert Gore made the race a study in contrast. The Senator "hired no professional managers, pollsters or outside advertising firms. . . . 'I'm a volunteer,' said Gore's campaign manager, James F. Schaeffer, 41, a Memphis lawyer and former legislator. 'We don't even have a public relations consultant.'" Schaeffer said Gore's organization was approached by one campaign management firm looking for business. The total fee for organizing the operation and shaping campaign themes would have been $175,000. Schaeffer also said of polling, "Senator Gore has never believed in polls, and so far as I know has never caused any to be taken." He said that Gore's convictions on issues would not change regardless of what the poll showed and that "we don't have the money to spend for polls anyway."[8]

Not in the Stump-Thumping Tradition

Nonetheless, Senator Gore's campaign was not necessarily in the "stump-thumping" tradition of old Tennessee politics. As in many major political contests that adhere to some traditional campaigning techniques, traces of the new politics were evident. At a cost of $85,000 Guggenheim Productions created and produced a series of television spots for the senator in both the primary and general election. It is also of interest that a "Demo-

[7]From Jensen and Burby, op. cit., pp. 2081, 2083.
[8]Ibid., p. 2083.

cratic National Committee official said on a not-for-quotation basis that Gore . . . [was] the only democratic Senator facing a tough campaign . . . who [had] not commissioned polls, but that the committee on political education of the A.F.L.-C.I.O. . . . [had] taken polls in Tennessee on the Brock—Gore race and made the results available to Tennessee Democrats."[9]

We see, then, that there is an ongoing but subtle revolution taking place in national electoral politics. Perhaps the most blatant expression of this occurrence is found in an advertisement that has intermittently appeared in a Los Angeles newspaper: "Leading Public Relations Firm with Top-Flight Experience in State-Wide Campaigns Wants Senate Candidate."[10]

Costs Are Being Driven Upward

Aside from the much discussed topics of voter manipulation and the less recognized issue of the substitution of the traditional party organization for a cadre of professional consultants, the growth of technological politicking in major political races is a significant factor in driving the costs of campaigning ever upward.

For a candidate who engages the available professional campaign services in a competitive race for the U.S. House of Representatives, costs could easily amount to more than $125,000 plus the additional expenses of purchasing television time.[11]

During the 1972 election candidates for the Senate and the House of Representatives spent over 77 million dollars between April and December.[12] The most costly race in the House was that of Paul McCloskey with a total expenditure of $321,558, while John Towers's campaign expenditures of $2,301,870 topped all contenders for the Senate.[13]

However, in considering campaign costs one must look beyond aggregate data and even the dollar outlay of particular campaigns. The costs of electioneering services vary from consultant to consultant. But also the needs of any given campaign differ. Consequently, to obtain a reasonable

[9]Ibid., p. 2083.

[10]Robert Wernick, "The Perfect Candidate," Life, 3 June 1966; partial reprint by Public Relations Center.

[11]As an example, in 1968 over $89,000,000 were spent on radio and television; in 1972 the figure had risen to $110,000,000. An average 60-second spot in New York television in prime time can run to $50,000.

[12]"Editorial Memorandum on Congressional Incumbents' Campaign Finances," News release of Common Cause, Washington, D.C., September 1973.

[13]Ibid.

understanding of campaign costs, including the expenditures for consultants and technological services, it is of value to focus on the specific cost components of a major political race.

Consultants

The political consultant may visit his candidate's state or district only occasionally, preferring instead to closet himself with poll results, computer breakdowns of voting patterns and demographic profiles. He prefers to plan a campaign as early before the primary as possible. He generally prefers newcomers for whom he can build an image. He is expensive. Some consultants command $500 a day for their full-time personal services. One firm requires about $80,000 for an average House campaign; the firm claims it must clear $1,200 a day to meet salary and travel expenses.

A well-versed campaign consultant must be qualified to work in public opinion surveys, electronic data processing, fund-raising, budgeting, media, research, public relations and press services, advertising and volunteer recruitment. Some participate in policy decisions as well.

No organization has the talent or resources to take on all these jobs at once, but some offer prospective clients a "package" of related services. This practice assures that one firm will be responsible for victory or defeat. Some experienced politicians, however, still prefer to draw on a variety of experienced individuals and firms for their campaigns.

Other firms, such as Matt Reece and Associates, of Washington, act only as consultants for work contracted out to other individuals or agencies. Reece has charged as much as $25,000 for a plan detailing a timed approach to campaign management and control, staff, county organizations, finance, communications, party contact, scheduling and advance management, advisory committees, other special committees and the specific "Citizens for John Doe" committee. Reece will also prepare campaign budgets.

Contention exists whether advertising agencies, because of the charge of "selling the candidate," should be in campaigns at all. . . .

Yet political consultants regularly refer clients to advertising agencies. This expansion of campaign services brings good profits to the consultant, one observer explained, either by collecting automatic referral fees from outside agencies or by charging the candidate directly for advertising campaigns run by the campaign management firm itself.

Polls

William R. Hamilton and Staff is a division of a Washington public opinion and marketing research firm, Independent Research Associates, Inc., one of dozens of such firms that play an increasingly important part in campaigns. . . .

Hamilton claims that polls' total costs vary only plus or minus 15 percent. What do vary are costs per interview and the amount of information and analysis provided. The cost of Hamilton's statewide personal interview poll of 300 to 800 probable voters ranges from $5,000 to $10,000. Telephone polls are usually about 50 to 60 percent of the costs of a personal interview polls, he said, or $2,500 to $5,000. Telephone follow-ups can range from $750 to $2,500.

The sample size for congressional or metropolitan area constituencies is usually 200 to 400, depending on the size and complexity of the area, says Hamilton. A personal interview poll, Hamilton says, should cost between $3,000 and $5,000. The basic telephone poll costs between $2,000 and $3,500, and the telephone follow-ups are slightly less than for statewide studies.

Scout studies vary, depending on the type of voter desired in the sample. Hamilton says the costs should range from $250 to $1,000. . . .

[Herbert] Alexander estimates that the total for polling for all candidates at all levels in 1968 was about $6-million. . . . [which] broke down to 1,200 polls at an average cost of $5,000, he said. . . .[14]

During the presidential primaries and general election of 1972 alone, the two major parties expended 2 million dollars on polls.

Broadcasting

The total amount spent by candidates on television and radio in 1972 was 59.6 million dollars according to Federal Communication Commission reports, a slight increase from the previous presidential election year of 1 percent. A breakdown of this figure reveals that the most significant stabilizing force was a decline of almost 50 percent in the presidential contest, down from 28.5 million in 1968 to 14.3 million in 1972. Other factors included a 4.0 million decrease from 1968 for senatorial candidates and a federal law requiring stations to give candidates their lowest rates.[15] These figures include the commissions of consultants who are time buyers—the individuals who purchase television and radio spots that will provide candidates with the best combination of media exposure. Their fee is generally 15 percent of the cost of the media purchased. Time buyers

[14]From "Campaign Costs," op. cit., pp. 1913–1914.
[15]"Broadcast Spending: Presidential, Senate Costs Drop," *Congressional Quarterly: Weekly Report*, 12 May 1973, pp. 1134–1135.

calculate their decisions on a combination of the media exposure needs of their clients and complex charts that categorize the types of individuals who watch and listen to which stations at what times.[16] These totals do not, however, cover the costs of production and production related costs, which can easily run an additional 30 percent.

Though the 1972 campaign year indicated that overall media costs remained relatively constant, the relief was probably temporary. Because television is primarily an exposure medium, the year of Nixon versus McGovern was somewhat unique. Nixon trimmed his 1968 media budget by over 70 percent (15.6 to 4.4 million) because he had no need of name identification exposure. In the Democratic camp, where McGovern needed name identification advertising, the 1972 media budget was comparable to the 1968 budget. Furthermore, the post-Watergate pressures to limit campaign expenditures are countered by an inflationary spiral in the cost of television and radio. Between 1972 and 1974 alone, candidates noted a 20 to 25 percent cost increase for television and radio.[17]

Print Advertising

"Television has done to print what the jet did to railroads," Michael Rowan said. "You could run a political campaign without print, but there are certain things you want to use it for—information too complex for electronic media, information that needs a fuller explanation. The big thing with print, after all, is identification. The last thing you're going to see in the campaign is a name on a ballot. . . ."

A slight identification can be the turning point in local and state races, according to Reece. "One advantage in a lesser campaign is that nobody much cares who wins, unless he has some personal reason," Reece said. "A slight identification or superficial contact is enough to get someone to vote for the candidate. That's easy for the consultant, because he can see that you do have that letter in your mailbox." . . .

Agencies determine the execution of posters, billboards, brochures, newspaper and magazine ads and handouts. While some politicians discredit the effectiveness of newspaper ads (Rep. Charles E. Bennet (D. Fla.) told the House Committee on Standards of Official Conduct that he bought newspaper advertising only "so they won't get mad at me"), the medium consumed 10 to 15 percent of the total budget of a modern statewide campaign in 1970.[18]

Billboards are bought by market, rather than by state, and by what are

[16]"Campaign Costs," op. cit., p. 1914.
[17]"Needy Candidates: Why Campaign Chests Are Low," *U.S. News & World Report,* 30 September 1974, p. 57.
[18]*Guide to the Congress of the United States,* p. 484.

called "showings," according to Jack Bowen of a Washington advertising agency, Bailey, Deardourff and Bowen. A showing is a projection of the percentage of people in an area who will see a billboard message at least once during a week. Billboards are bought in advance, by the month.

In the New York metropolitan area, Bowen said, a billboard for one month at a 100 showing would total 232 different boards costing $34,160. At a 75 showing, or 174 boards, the cost would be $25,620.

In the Billings [Montana] area, a 100 showing, or 14 boards, would cost $1,050; a 75 showing, or 11 boards, $825. In Atlanta [Georgia] a 100 showing, or 80 boards, would cost $8,630; a 75 showing, or 60 boards, would cost $6,480, he said.

Persons buying billboards for a presidential campaign, Bowen said, usually buy within a selected list of 50 to 100 top markets. Besides the agency fee, campaigns must pay for the advertising itself. . . . [Costs vary. A one-page ad in a national magazine, for example, can run between $50,000 to $110,000.]

Ad agencies also oversee campaign paraphernalia. Feely and Wheeler, a New York advertising agency, handled the following list for . . . [a Nixon] campaign: 20.5 million buttons, 9 million bumper strips, 560,000 balloons, 400,000 posters and placards, 28,000 straw skimmers, 30,000 brochures, 3.5 million speeches and position papers and 12,000 paper dresses and jewelry. The total cost was $1,124,626 but did not include two books, *Nixon Speaks Out* and *Nixon on the Issues,* published by campaign committees, Alexander wrote. . . .[19]

Fund Raising

"To raise money, you have to spend money," emphasized Bob Odell at a recent political fund raising conference of the American Association of Political Consultants.[20]

To the chagrin of candidates and other types of political committees alike, this has become a fact of life. The costs of fund raising may actually absorb as much as two-thirds of the dollars raised.[21]

One of the most lucrative fund-raising enterprises is the warm steak and cold peas at the $1000-a-plate dinner. The overhead can be held at 5 to 9 percent. In contrast, the overhead on a $10-a-plate dinner can easily skim the profits by as much as 50 percent.

[19]From "Campaign Costs," op. cit., pp. 1914–1915.

[20]Remarks of Bob O'Dell, Staff Director, Republican National Finance Committee, to the American Association of Political Consultants Political Fund Raising Conference, New York, 11, 12 February 1972.

[21]"Political Fund Raising: Methods and High Costs," *Congressional Quarterly: Weekly Report,* 14 August 1971, p. 1711.

ONE MAN'S ACCOUNT OF CAMPAIGN COSTS*

Reacting to the Watergate scandals, four New York Democratic gubernatorial candidates have begun what is likely to become a trend in politics—full disclosure of their campaign finances periodically during the campaign.

In doing so, they have gone considerably beyond the seldom enforced State Election Law, which requires financial reports just before an election and afterward, when it is often too late to make an issue of questionable practices. They will probably force other politicians to reveal their finances. Perhaps more significantly, the reports give voters a glimpse into the vast organization behind a political campaign. It is, in effect, an instant corporation. Probably the best organized, yet still fairly representative is the campaign organization of Howard J. Samuels, millionaire industrialist and former president of the city's Off-Track Betting Corporation. He is conceded, even by his opponents, to be the leading Democratic gubernatorial contender.

'Gearing Up' Expenses

A total of $403,843.97 was spent in the "gearing up" period, the 10 months between May 7 last year and March 7. Recently, spending has increased sharply. In the three-month period ending early next month, at least that much will be spent again. In April, the budget was $113,000. The May budget is said to be more than that. And the primary is still four months away, the election, six.

A year ago, the paid campaign staff for Mr. Samuels was four part-time researchers; some other part-time workers were tucked away on the OTB staff. Now, there are 50 full-time paid workers in the Samuels campaign, 30 full-time volunteers and hundreds of part-timers. The last reported weekly payroll was $6,250.

Five volunteer accountants ride herd on the vast operation. Campaign credit cards are taboo, in order to control the "big spenders."

Media Expenses

The campaign bought its own $11,000 printing press to help cut costs. The press was installed at a printing plant under an agreement in which the printer would provide campaign literature at cost and in return, after the campaign, will inherit the press. Even so, the printing bill was high: $33,013 for the first 10 months.

Telephone bills came to nearly $10,000. To be sure the bills are paid, the New York Telephone Company demanded a $17,100 deposit when the phones were installed.

Consultants, the hired guns of politics, were supposedly kept to a

*Frank Lynn, "One Man's Account of Campaign Costs," *New York Times*, 5 May 1974.

minimum. "The instant experts who come in from out of town and give you the same advice they gave a guy in Illinois, four years ago," was how they were described by Mr. Samuel's campaign manager, Auletta. Nonetheless, at least $50,000 was spent on consultants in 10 months.

Even Christmas cards can be an expensive proposition for a candidate trying to win friends and influence politicians. The Samuels stamp bill for Christmas cards was $720, enough for 5,760 holiday greetings.

The huge entertainment bill, $5,381.57, reflects luncheons and breakfasts involving the candidate, top staff, political leaders and potential contributors. One whopping bill for $301 paid for a dinner at Sardi's at which Mr. Samuels and two aides were hosts to eight upstate county leaders who are supporting him. Often the only way a candidate can draw a crowd of politicians he needs to impress is to host a cocktail party or lunch.

Of necessity he is also fair game for politicians, political clubs and other organizations selling tickets and ads in dinner journals. While according to Mr. Auletta, restrictions were put on ticket purchases, the tab came to $5,376. The biggest bill was $1,000 for the annual dinner of the Inner Circle, an organization of present and former political reporters. Mr. Samuels even bought $300 worth of tickets to help pay off the Congressional campaign debt of Representative Hugh L. Carey, of Brooklyn. Mr. Carey apparently was unimpressed, as he is now running for Governor against Mr. Samuels.

Outrageous Expenses

Because of the fair-game syndrome, Mr. Auletta said the campaign had been confronted by some outrageous demands. One congressional candidate, for instance, was more than willing to endorse Mr. Samuels but thought that in return the Samuels campaign should pick up his telephone credit-card bill. The answer was a blunt no.

Who are the financial supporters of this instant corporation? The Samuels staff reported about 1,000 individual contributors as of Feb. 28, and total contributions of $189,775.

However, $109,760, or 60 per cent of that, came from 23 "fat cats" who contributed at least $2,000 each. Five of the 23 also lent the campaign a total of $70,045, while the candidate himself provided "loans" of $95,185.

The income and outgo make it apparent that despite Watergate and all the talk of campaign-finance reform and contributions from [the] little man, political campaigns are still mostly the games of rich men.

Small contributions from large numbers of people is a popular concept these days. Yet, as was discussed in Chapter 4, there are not enough volunteers to raise sufficient money in this manner on the basis of face-to-face solicitation. The alternative, ferreting out a broad base of financial support through direct mail, can prove a very expensive undertaking, particularly for organizations that sporadically use direct mail as a fund-raising technique. Even for committees that do have an ongoing direct mail program with their own in-house or past contributor lists, costs can range from 20 to 40 percent of the contributions.[22]

Nonetheless, direct mail solicitation has become the mainstay for increasing numbers of major campaigns. For example, much of the $14 to $15 million received by the McGovern campaign in small contributions can be attributed to the 600,000-plus names developed by his committee for its fund-raising solicitations.[23] As much as 80 percent of the Republican National Finance Committee's receipts have come from direct mail, programs that include solicitation for sustaining membership categories as high as $1000 or more a year.[24]

Staff and Office Expenses

Although headquarters and staff generally account for less than 20 to 30 per cent of most campaign budgets, a long-time aide to a western Senator refused to estimate a probable cost for his boss' next campaign. "It depends on who you find," he said, "a retiree who will work for just about expenses or someone you hire away from a full-time job. Staff costs are among the imponderables."

At campaign headquarters, costs continue through election day for items such as rent, supplies, utilities and salaries of some employees. There are expenses for transporting voters to the polls if not enough persons volunteer for such duty. And poll-watchers may have to be paid.

Volunteer workers' services, though nominally free, are costly to administer. Indirect expenses include recruitment drives, maintenance of headquarters, transportation of canvassers, "socials" to sustain enthusiasm and other items.

Speechwriting and Research

Speechwriters and researchers are usually included on the campaign staff, but occasionally freelance writers are hired. Commercial research firms and clipping services are often contracted, besides, to provide extensive background information and continuous updating on candidate publicity.

Professional gag men have been retained by parties or candidates at least as far back as the Herbert Hoover–Al Smith campaign, but these

[22] O'Dell, op. cit.
[23] "Democratic Party: Start of a Big Repair Job," *Congressional Quarterly: Weekly Report,* 2 December 1972, p. 3095.
[24] O'Dell, op. cit.

have been partisan volunteers whose activities were kept as secret as possible. Today the candidate's joke writers have been openly credited with making or breaking several campaigns.

Jim Atkins, a Washington public relations man who has supplied 20 campaigns, including three presidential races, with humorous lines, charges $100 a campaign, no matter what the campaign, for "whatever I happen to turn out." . . .

Travel

Stated campaign travel costs may be considerably inflated, according to Alexander, since as much as half the total is reimbursed by the organizations of reporters traveling with candidates. Most of this reimbursed transportation is for flying on a plane provided by the campaign or in the candidate's plane, but some ground transportation, such as press buses, may also be paid for. . . .

[Though accommodations vary considerably, the travel expenses of the George Wallace for President race were not atypical. That campaign] . . . reported at least $1,235,000. had been spent on planes, rental cars, hotels and so on. . . .

Freebies

Some candidates receive goods and services without charge from their supporters. For instance, a friend may lend his private plane to a candidate or may lend a building rent-free for an office. Incumbents have certain financial advantages, too, such as computerized mail files of correspondence during their tenures.

Furthermore, when campaign totals are given, they represent committed costs, not actual expenditures. Some of the debts from the Kennedy, McCarthy and Humphrey campaigns . . . were settled for less than their full amount. . . .

Campaign loans are often canceled in part or in total. Bills from telephone and telegraph companies and airlines are sometimes simply not paid or are "written off as uncollectible," as the companies put it. According to a General Accounting Office study requested by Sen. Hugh Scott (R Pa.), $2.1-million in political debts has been incurred in airline bills and about $400,000 in telephone bills.[25]

As alluded to, the growth of the political consulting industry also raises questions concerning the future role of parties in campaigns. In the 1972

[25]From "Campaign Costs," op. cit., pp. 1915–1916.

presidential election, Richard Nixon, in effect, organized an in-house consulting firm to direct his reelection effort. The Committee to Re-Elect the President (CREEP) carried out activities completely independent of the Republican party structure. The party saw its nominee turn his back on those who had supported him in his quest for the presidency, in favor of a group of individuals whose "nuts and bolts" expertise in campaigning was undeniable, but who, in the words of President Ford, "violated the historic concept of the two-party system in America and . . . ran literally roughshod over the seasoned political judgment and . . . political experience of the regular Republican Party. . . ."[26] The results, Watergate, are all too familiar to Americans.

Throughout much of the nation, the increasing ranks of free-lance consultants are continuing to usurp the power of both political parties. These consultants, whether individual entrepreneurs or sophisticated companies such as Robert-Lynn Associates, may gradually replace the parties as the backbone of the electoral system. Obviously the candidate for lesser office is not generally involved in this movement; but as this trend continues, the ability of parties to assist even the lesser candidates will be considerably weakened.

What Future for Political Parties?

Unless the political parties modernize themselves in the coming decade, consultants could assume many of the functions now exercised by the parties. The consultants have already introduced new expectations and demands for party performance and their role will continue to expand into new functional areas in the 1970's. Consultants, for example, will play a critical role in determining how open or closed the presidential selection process will be. A successful preconvention strategy now requires professional advance work and planning in both primary and party convention states as well as a sizable convention-city operation and convention strategy. In the 1970's, polls and simulation will be even more important in weighing alternative candidates and strategies. Consultants, trained in the party process and familiar with party politicians in a wide number of states, will be among the relatively small number of people capable of mounting presidential campaigns for either major- or minor-party candidates.

Major Consulting Firms May Fill Party Roles

If the national parties do not develop effective, integrated national headquarters, operations centers and communication nets, the major consulting conglomerates themselves could begin to fill *national* party roles.

---

[26]Text of an address by then Vice-President Ford to the Midwest Republican Leadership Conference. Chicago, 30 March 1974, p. 2.

Suggested party reforms could in many instances be just as easily adapted for use by a large consulting complex with clients over a sufficiently broad geographical region. The multifunctional conglomerate consulting firm is thus a serious competitive rival to unreformed national committees.

If party politics remains fluid and temporary coalitions replace the still dominant New Deal Democratic party coalition, consultants will play an increasingly crucial role in negotiating with various elements of prospective party coalitions. New York City and New York State politics provide a ready example with a four-party framework, numerous extra party lines added to the ballot and enormous shifts of voting blocs between parties, depending on the candidate choices offered. If party activists become more ideological and issue-oriented in their approach to electoral politics, more neutral actors will have to assume the brokerage role traditionally performed by a broad-based two-party system. The alternative to coalitions within the parties is some form of multiparty system, an option that would afford consultants a new range of opportunities.

Brokers of Cable Television

Consultants will also be the political brokers of cable television, perhaps the most important political media innovation of the coming decade.

The continued growth of the political consulting industry raises major new issues for party responsibility. To the old problems of making officeholders and party officials accountable for their actions in a decentralized party and governmental system that diffuses lines of responsibility, there has been added the new factor of an echelon of political professionals with no formal public or party accountability either in statutory or party rules. The professionalization of the parties will have the added effect of concentrating new political resources in national and state party committees with wide discretionary authority in hiring trained professionals who often have little or no public visibility.

As consultants have become a quasi-staff arm of the parties and as complicated new relationships have evolved, new forms of political unaccountability have emerged in the clear absence of any clear party guidelines on the use of political consultants. Several examples indicate the potential conflicts of interest.

A consulting firm retained in several major 1970 election campaigns by candidates at the state level received directions from national party headquarters recommending that it shift key personnel from one race to another. Since the party served as reference for the consultant in the first place and controlled national funds going to these and future races, the consultant had little choice but to comply with the recommendation.

A state party precluded by the law from making preprimary endorsements used consultants as a front to back candidates in primaries that it favored. In another instance, a candidate discovered that a polling firm he had retained to do surveys was also doing polling work for the opposition party and sitting in on strategy sessions with his opponent.

Consultant Firms Are Shaping Parties

Besides participating in campaign decision making and operations, consultants are shaping the parties and the decision-making structures of the future, but no representative agency is overseeing and/or participating in this process of political modernization.

Another problem is the broader responsibility of the consultant for the functioning of the governmental process. These are not entirely new problems for representative government, but the growth of the consulting industry and the new techniques it is introducing to party politics have made them urgent topics for public and party discussions. From where is political leadership to come, with the ever more sophisticated means to find out what people are thinking and then communicate campaign appeals back to them to maximize votes? Moreover, as one party official notes with concern, "If more and more legislators, if governors and even Presidents, gain public office as men running against the machine—the established party—the governmental process is bound to become more and more fragmented and disjointed. These public officials are likely to assume an increasingly self-centered view of their public responsibilities, in a period when our democratic system can least afford the luxury of such fragmentation." . . .[27]

Nonetheless, although it is important to recognize the significance and potential of consultants and other free-lance specialists, one should be careful not to attribute mystical powers to these forces. Several primaries in the 1970s serve as cases in point. There were spectacular campaign casualties suffered by some of the best-known leading consultants. Several met with not only one but many defeats.[28]

[27]From John S. Saloma III and Frederick H. Santog, "The Expanding Role of Political Consultants; New Issues for Party Responsibility," *Parties: The Real Opportunity for Effective Citizen Politics* (New York: Vintage, 1973), pp. 306–308.

[28]See particularly "Political Consultants: Mixed Results in 1970 Elections," *Congressional Quarterly, 1970 Almanac,* 1970, p. 1098. Among 9 firms, there were 20 victories and 24 defeats. See also Roger Ailes, "Candidate + Money + Media = Votes," *Politeia* 1 (Winter 1972): 29–31.

Maximum Organization Is Still the Exception

Furthermore, in considering the overall picture of electoral politics, it is important to remember that the maximum organization, with maximum technological involvement, is still the exception and not the rule in American politics.[29] For every major congressional, gubernatorial, or big-city mayoralty contest there are many more individuals seeking lesser office. These candidates cannot afford the services of a political personages such as Joe Napolitan or Roger Ailes. Not only from a financial standpoint would it be ridiculous for most of them to consider such an alternative, but the contribution of, say, a major advertising firm diminishes in contest for lesser office.[30] Local campaign requirements for a school board position or even that of a state legislative race are considerably different from that of a congressional or senatorial campaign.

Some Campaigns Are Run from Under the Candidate's Hat

Some American political campaigns are run literally from under the hat of the candidate. He may raise his own funds (often on his own local credit rating), write his own speeches and press releases (which his wife may type), drive his own car from speech to speech. These one-man campaigns are found chiefly in campaigns in small constituencies, in rural areas, and for less noted offices—for example, the campaign of a rural candidate for state legislator or unimportant county office. More common and perhaps the modal campaign organization in American politics includes the candidate, his campaign manager, perhaps an office manager, and a small number of faithful political friends, who devote part of their time to major campaign tasks. Together they constitute something of a general council for the campaign. Candidates adopt these modest campaign organizations for one or both of the following reasons. First, an organization costs dearly, and many candidates cannot afford it. Second, for many offices and many political cultures, campaigning does not require a large organization; minimal campaigning demands only minimal organization. . . . But regardless of the form the campaign organization takes, in most campaigns the key man remains the campaign manager. Most candidates find it necessary to shift the burdens of directing the campaign so that their time,

---

[29]Frank J. Sorauf, *Political Parties in America,* 2nd edition (Boston: Little, Brown, 1968), p. 256.

[30]Address on campaign advertising by Lee Bartlett, vice-president of Cole-Weber and Associates, Advertising, Center for the Study of Practical Politics, Seattle, 10 October 1972.

physical energy, and concentration can all be spent on the campaign itself. Yet, few candidates abandon complete control of their campaign, even to a talented veteran or a professional manager. Thus the possible points of conflict between candidate and manager are ever present, especially over the strategic decisions of the campaign. . . .[31]

Candidate – Manager Relationship Most Important

Many times when the candidate – manager relationship breaks down, it leaves in its wake potentially disastrous situations. After several weeks of arguing over direction and strategy, the campaign manager of a midwest-

[31]Sorauf, op. cit., pp. 255–256.

ern congressional candidate resigned. When he left, he took his own records with him. The new manager became frantic, for contained in those records was the *only* list of volunteers. The resigned manager then took an extended vacation. After several days of absolute bedlam it was discovered that the candidate had a copy of the list. Indeed, the argument that had eventually split the campaign manager from the organization had been the candidate's insistence on being consulted on all details, including the use of volunteers.

In a California congressional campaign, the manager's resignation led to similar difficulties. A cocktail party fund raiser had been scheduled at one of the "posh" private clubs in the area. Given the demands of other responsibilities and the candidate's assurances that everything had been arranged, the campaign coordinator, a young college student, did not bother to reconfirm the location of the event.

On the night of the cocktail party guests began arriving, much to the surprise and chagrin of the club. Because no one had contacted them with a firm commitment, they had given the space to another organization. Contributors arriving for the unscheduled party were shunted onto a small terrace where within a short period nearly 100 people were squeezed together. Arriving late, the coordinator hastily produced a *punch* to accompany hors d'oeuvres of tuna fish on crackers. Thus individuals who had paid $50 a couple were subjected to the result of poor planning and a lack of campaign leadership.

He Runs the Campaign

As we have seen, the role of the campaign manager is of paramount importance in organizing any campaign. His responsibilities can be summed up in a brief phrase—"he runs the campaign." If the candidate is a skilled politician, the manager may have an easier task, but the reverse can also be true. All too often the incumbent feels that, because he has several times won elected office, he should be able to make all the decisions. In the 1974 off-year elections, one such candidate came hurriedly into campaign headquarters frantically waving a copy of *Newsweek* magazine. He paced back and forth, repeating that the campaign wasn't facing the issues. A national pollster had indicated that inflation and the energy crisis were foremost in the minds of the nation's voters. However, his manager reminded him that a city councilman's campaign could not really be built on national issues and that reform of city government was still a more viable goal.

If a candidate is allowed to run his own campaign, he is courting disaster. As F. Clifton White, chairman of the board of Public Affairs

Analysts, noted: "If he wins, it is luck. He was at the right place at the right time."[32] This is not to say that the experience of the candidate is without value, but the candidate is too close to the campaign really to make unbiased decisions.

Same Man Can't Be Both Pitcher and Catcher

[A]s in baseball the same man cannot be both pitcher and catcher. In politics the candidate cannot successfully manage his own campaign. . . .

The candidate is on public display twenty-four hours a day. He must keep a schedule of appointments and appearances. He must shake hands with the voters and never appear to be hurried. He must be competent and compelling on television. His speeches must be addressed to subjects which concern the audience and to be effective they must be meaningful.

It is the job of the campaign manager to make the candidate look good, to map the strategy, to command the supporting troops. To do these things successfully, he must enjoy the full confidence and trust of the candidate, and he must be given authority to make all decisions.

Candidates rate the headlines. Campaign managers are shielded from public attention by the shadow of the candidate. This is as it should be. The manager must retain a perspective and objectivity which is denied to the central figures on the political stage.

A proper campaign organization will enlist the special skills and the talents of many people. The manager must direct and inspire. His job is to build an efficient, effective group of specialists who can produce under the terrific pressure and tension of political battle. Unless there is a clear line of authority, the result is likely to be only so much organized wheel spinning. . . .

The manager must know the constituency—its geography, its people, its commercial interests and those special sectional rivalries that frequently complicate a . . . political contest.

The manager should have some acquaintance with the media that will be employed in the campaign . . . television, radio, newspaper, direct mail. Since no single individual is likely to possess great competence in all of these fields, the problem becomes one of finding a manager who can enlist the right talents for these specialized activities. . . .

The manager must be able to get along well with people, to control the

[32] Disscussion among F. Clifton White, Michael Rowan, and Joseph Napolitan (of Public Affairs Analysts) at the National Education Association School for Politics, Seattle, March 1971.

overly ambitious and to be able to resist the pressures which build up when human egos clash.

The manager must be able to say "no" without giving offense; to say "yes" and stick to it. Frequently he must say "no" to the candidate. And when he makes a commitment it must be kept.

In this regard candidates have much more latitude. They can, by innuendo or suggestion, imply a promise for future delivery. When the manager says something will be done, it must be done—and before the day of election which ends that campaign.

The campaign manager must be cold-blooded and hard-nosed about spending campaign funds. In every political contest there are literally hundreds of people who come forward with a sure-fire scheme to bring victory. If only—if only the candidate advertises in their particular program, sponsors their barbecue, gives financial support to a project being urged by a minority group.

Party Pressure on Manager

Party leaders will put pressure on the manager to favor their choice for a campaign itinerary. Important supporters will insist the candidate spend what may be an unnecessary amount of time in their bailiwick. And to all these pressures and requests the manager must find a diplomatic refusal.

In addition to all these things, the manager must understand how the voter is motivated to reach a decision and be able to devise an over-all strategy which will increase the popularity of his candidate. . . .

[B]ut out of all the prescriptions for victory offered here there is one I regard as paramount—the manager must command the campaign effort. Any division of authority between the manager and the candidate or between the manager and his assistants will, at some point in the campaign, produce disaster.

I argue this not because I think the campaign manager is in every case or in any case more competent than the candidate. The campaign must have unity. The campaign must move steadily forward from its starting position to its objective of victory. Any delay or deviation from the basic strategic plan will waste precious time and money.

The manager can be objective; the candidate cannot completely divorce himself from the emotional stress of being the candidate.

The manager who has selected the strategy, after consultation with the candidate and his crew of experts, must be in a position of authority to implement that strategy. . . .

I suffered through my first political experience more than thirty years ago. An immensely popular political figure, who was then the elected Secretary of State in Arizona, decided to enter the primary and seek the gubernatorial nomination. His supporters wanted to publish a campaign newspaper. This was in the depths of the depression and when they offered me $50 a week to edit their propaganda, I accepted promptly.

Our candidate's two opponents were relatively unknown politically. Our man was backed strongly by the mining and railroad interests in Arizona. We had a handsome campaign budget. At the outset victory seemed inevitable.

As the campaign progressed, confusion increased. There was no unity, there was no theme. Our man, like Don Quixote, went around the state tilting at windmills. But for all of this he was still in the lead the night before primary election day.

The Democrat Party in those days held a final climactic public meeting in the largest outdoor arena in the state. More than 10,000 people gathered to hear the candidates make their final appeals. In addition to the three men running for governor, there were ten or fifteen candidates for lesser offices included on the program.

Our man spoke first. He had refused to prepare a written text; he was the old, experienced campaigner, proud of an ability to deliver stirring oratory extemporaneously. He did. He talked for one hour and eighteen minutes. He alienated the affection of every Democrat in that stadium. Supporters of other candidates resented his usurping all the time. His own supporters were bored. His two opponents spoke for less than ten minutes each.

I watched the agony on the campaign manager's face. He knew and I knew we had lost the election. Our man ran third. If there had been five candidates, he would have been fifth. And he lost through an unbridled display of that ego which is standard equipment with most candidates.

A poor campaign manager is almost certain to lose the campaign regardless of the candidate's qualifications, but even a poor manager who has the authority to act is better than no manager at all. . . .

In this key relationship of any political campaign, when the candidate agrees to accept the ruling of the manager, it is equally important for the manager to recognize that he is not the candidate. The manager who takes to the hustings with the candidate, who makes all the appearances, who is as much on the go as the candidate himself, really isn't a manager at all. He's nothing more than a functioning political valet. The effective manager, like the man in charge of a good baseball team, must call the plays and let someone else run the bases.

Relationship Must Be One of Mutual Trust, Responsibility

The manager–candidate relationship should be one of mutual trust and divided responsibility. It is not the manager's job to think for the candidate or to manipulate him like a puppet on a string. What the manager must do is help the candidate to express his ideas, to display his true personality and to avoid mistakes. The manager should have time to think; the candidate has precious little time for anything. The manager . . . will coordinate all of the activities of the entire campaign staff into an effective team effort with the special skills of each member adding strength to the candidate's image.

This is a delicate and precious relationship—one that is not often achieved, but one well worth striving for. . . .[33]

The Henry Kissinger of Domestic Politics

Though not all managers are the "Henry Kissinger" of the domestic campaign scene, "the campaign manager is a unique person. He mends fences, puts out fires, holds hands, soothes ruffled feathers, stays on top of a dozen projects. He does all things in addition to keeping the organization on target and the activities on schedule. No matter how well the campaign is going, he anticipates 'Panic Week' . . . and is ready for it. He makes sure that there is some time blocked out in the candidate's schedule during each of the last three weeks before election. . . . When the troops start reacting to what the opponent is saying, when they decide that the direction of their campaign is all wrong, ONLY the candidate can reassure them. A few words from him, backed up by the manager, and the panic will be short-lived. The campaign will be back on target and the chores will be done."[34] The manager must be personable but is more effective if he is not the candidate's best friend. Few individuals can run their brother's campaign as did the late Robert Kennedy. The manager cannot be so close to the candidate that he loses perspective.

Executive Ability Is a Key Factor

Perhaps one of the greatest tools of the manager is not his political knowledge but his executive ability. He must be an organizer but not try to

[33]From Stephen D. Shadegg, *How to Win an Election: The Art of Political Victory* (New York: Taplinger, 1964), pp. 25–34.

[34]*The Campaign Manager,* prepared for an Action for Washington Campaign School, Bellevue, Washington, 1971.

accomplish all tasks himself. During a 1972 western gubernatorial primary, the manager notified the candidate's wife that he was to be at a luncheon on a certain day to address a gathering of Rotarians. On the appointed day the manager arrived late but found no candidate. Two other individuals spoke and the manager rose to express his apologies, having earlier tried to reach the candidate at home. After a rather lengthy explanation of why the candidate was unable to attend, the program chairman, looking somewhat startled, said that he had already been contacted by the candidate who had expressed his apologies to the club, using another set of circumstances for being absent. Obviously everyone was embarrassed, particularly the manager. The candidate's image was tarnished before an important constituency because the manager had been too involved in details to carry out his responsibility properly; that is, to see that each area of the campaign was accomplishing its task but not try to direct each individual effort. If he had been in contact with campaign headquarters as he should have been, he would have been notified that the candidate's wife had been taken ill.

The Trick Is to Multiply the Effort

Discussing the role of the campaign manager, Congressman Joel Pritchard noted that the "trick in politics is to multiply the effort. If there are 50,000 voters in the district, the candidate cannot hope to meet them all. However, if he has 500 supporters, all who talk to ten people, who talk to ten more, etc., the whole district is contacted."[35] It is the manager's responsibility to organize this multiplication of effort. He must direct the activities and take into account the varying needs and priorities of the campaign. Timing should be his decision so that all efforts are building to the climax of election day.

Everyone wants to be a strategist. Each of the candidate's friends has his own sure-fire plan for victory. An example occurred in a recent New York congressional race when, two weeks before the primary, a group of business associates decided to have a $10-a-person-dinner for the candidate. The idea was to have hundreds turn out and thus gain considerable media coverage. The candidate agreed and the manager reluctantly acquiesced to the scheme. On the day appointed, fewer than 40 people showed up, including 10 representatives of the media. The cost of the dinner was estimated to be over $1600; thus the campaign went in the hole $510 and received poor news coverage as a bonus. From a strategic standpoint it was

[35]Address by Congressman Joel Pritchard, "The Role of the Campaign Manager," Center for the Study of Practical Politics, Seattle, 18 November 1972.

a disaster. The opposition picked up on the sparse attendance and used it as an example of the waning support for the candidate. The manager had allowed the strategy of the campaign to be sidetracked in favor of something that showed little chance of success.

In today's campaigns, on all levels but particularly for lesser office, volunteers play a dominant role. Indeed, in many instances they are the margin between victory and defeat. But many volunteers believe that they have been recruited to assist on all levels of the campaign rather than to perform a specific function. As a result, volunteers often become spectators *cheering on* their candidate and planning instead of working. The *last hurrah* experts discussed earlier must be kept in check without hurting egos or alienating support. The campaign manager must weld this corps of volunteers into a smoothly functioning machine. Excursions into "blind alleys" and meaningless "side shows" must be prevented if victory is to be achieved. The candidate's charisma attracts and holds the loyalty of the team, but it is the manager who must make it into an effective tool.

The Manager Is Not the Candidate

However, as important as is the campaign manager, it must be reemphasized that he is not the candidate. A good manager stays in the background and runs the show. The candidate answers questions and meets the people. Too many campaign managers have political aspirations of their own, which tend to conflict with those of the candidate. If they are to be successful and effective in their duties, they must realize where their role and that of the candidate differ. Often unnecessary strains have been placed on a candidate–manager relationship because of an *overactive* manager.[36]

If the area of campaign management is the most important of the organization, then fund raising is certainly of near equal value.

Fund Raising— An All-Important Ingredient

Obviously, without money a campaign will never succeed. . . . However, many campaign organizations fail to appreciate the significance of a well-planned, highly-organized fund-raising operation, even for communities of small size. . . . It is important to give minute attention to the establishment of a fund-raising organization because it can serve as the source of manpower for the over-all campaign organization. With a workable and realistic plan of operation you can create interest and activity for your

[36]Ibid.

candidate. A contributor has an investment. He will take more interest. By means of fund-raising efforts you can find new workers and can generate favorable "talk" about the candidate.[37]

To direct this important venture, the manager and the candidate must assume direct responsibility for recruiting a finance chairman. Too many campaigns try to combine several areas of responsibility in one individual. The campaign manager, although obviously concerned with funds, should not do the job himself. His tasks are too broad to deal with this area. In choosing someone to direct this activity,

[37] "Fund Raising and Financing," *Campaign Techniques Manual* (Washington, D.C.: National Association of Manufacturers), ND p. 47.

. . . an energetic man of major substance who is known and respected by a great number of potential major contributors [should be chosen]. He should have previous fund raising experience and should be reasonably acceptable to the [p]arty's district fund-raisers. The campaign manager should work hand-in-hand with the finance chairman to help assure a successful fund-raising operation.

Hopefully, the finance chairman will have been appointed by the time the campaign manager goes to work preparing the budget. If not, the manager should prepare a preliminary operational budget including minimum requirements to cover the initial period of campaign activity.

What Are the Needs of the Campaign?

In developing the budget the manager and the finance chairman should consider the needs of the campaign in this light:

1. a "bare-bones" budget covering just those things necessary to run the campaign with hope of victory;
2. an "operational budget"—adding muscle to the "bare-bones" budget where it is most needed and most likely to gain the maximum number of votes per dollar spent;
3. an "ideal budget" which includes all logical expenditures necessary to assure victory.

The manager and finance chairman should also agree upon a cash-flow, or spending, schedule for the various budget items. This schedule should be based on the campaign strategy and campaign timetable prepared by the manager.

The finance chairman should organize a broad-based committee to provide direct approaches to the district's principal financial bases. Before the committee begins solicitation, the finance chairman and the legal advisor should review the legal aspects involved and agree upon the ground rules for committee members. Also, a respected member of the community should be selected to serve as campaign treasurer—often a certified public accountant or banker will accept this assignment. The finance chairman may need, as well, a staff, or volunteer, assistant to help with day-to-day detail work and telephoning.

The manager should help the finance chairman find people with the time, devotion, and fortitude to see the job through. Otherwise, some of the fund-raising effort may revolve back in the direction of the campaign manager's office.

Among the time-proven ways to raise money, the most productive is direct solicitation by the chairman and key members of his committee. Their efforts may occasionally require brief meetings between potential contributors and the candidate. The manager should reserve some time in the master schedule for this purpose. Usually, a breakfast meeting or small reception will give the potential contributor adequate time to meet the candidate and help the finance committee member conclude the "sale." Certainly, the finance effort should not ignore a number of other effective fund-raising techniques, including the use of direct mail, testimonial or other fund-raising dinners and special events.

What Are the Sources of Funds?

The most common sources of campaign money are: the [p]arty central committee and [p]arty organizations; previous contributors to campaign or [p]arty solicitations; business, professional and other special interest groups; volunteer workers; fund-raising events.

The basic mechanics of a successful fund-raising campaign are simple but important:

1. ledger cards or lists showing the name, address and record of contributions given to the party and previous campaigns;
2. names and addresses of potential contributors who have reason to give even though they have not done so previously;
3. pledge cards, prepared in advance, for all potential contributors— for use by the finance committee members;
4. a clear statement of the need for the funds solicited;
5. special budget-items that allow a contributor to ear-mark his contribution (billboards, etc.);
6. good office procedure to assist fund-raisers and to avoid duplication of effort. . . .[38]

The Flow of Money Is Equally Important

It is, of course, necessary to remember that in any campaign the flow of money is as of great an import as the actual raising of dollars. When television time is desired in a campaign, it usually comes at the end of the effort, not at the beginning. Thus less *startup* money is needed to get the campaign going than to meet later expenses.[39] The problem arises when

[38] From *Manual for Campaign Managers*, Spencer-Roberts and Associates, pp. 18– 20. This is particularly important because most states have adopted new and stringent finance regulations as is the federal government. New laws formulated in the wake of Watergate make it imperative to carefully review legal ramifications of campaign finance.

[39] F. Clifton White et al., op. cit.

the candidate is unknown and to get money must become known. He approaches his close friends and associates for sufficient dollars to start an organization to raise the necessary financing for a full-scale campaign. He must establish his name, which costs money, to obtain more money.

On the other hand, the incumbent finds a similar problem in that a well-established candidate often finds it difficult to convince supporters that he is in need of dollars. Senator Hugh Scott recalled a story that aptly demonstrates this difficulty. He was seeking primary support for his Senate race. It wasn't a serious primary, but he still had to run. He was leaving his office building in Philadelphia and ran into one of his well-to-do colleagues who said, "I am glad to hear you're running for the Senate. This fall I'll give you $5000." Senator Scott answered, "Can you make it $500 right now?"[40] Early dollars are important in any campaign, and the finance chairman must be an individual who has the ability to acquire this "seed money."

The Public Doesn't Support Campaigns

In general, the public at large doesn't financially support political campaigns. In a discussion on campaign financing, political consultant Allen Munro estimated that "less than five per cent of the public ordinarily contributes to a political campaign."[41] However, Clifton White observed that perhaps the main reason for this lack of interest is because individuals are not asked to contribute. He recalled the story of an acquaintance who never went into a cocktail lounge, a tavern, or a store without asking those present to donate to a particular campaign. He remarked that the gentleman was often rebuffed but that he had a fantastic overall record of raising funds.[42] This is, of course, not to say that the dollars will automatically roll in, but approaches on a personal level by peers seems to be the most effective fund-raising technique. Programs such as the Democratic Telethon supply millions of dollars to Democratic coffers, but the largest total dollars are raised outside such extravaganzas.

Fund raising is a tedious and thankless job. For every acceptance there are many individuals who object to being solicited.[43] During the last congressional race a finance committee held a cocktail hour to solicit donations for the candidate. When the audit was finally completed, it was discovered that the effort had made less than $200. During the follow-

[40] As told to F. Clifton White, ibid.

[41] Remarks by consultant Allan Munro on political organization and fund raising to Center for the Study of Practical Politics, Seattle, 1 October 1971.

[42] White et al., op. cit.

[43] Munro, op. cit.

up activities, several individuals remarked that they had been told that what was really important was a good turnout. One individual was particularly indignant and said he had already given $10. Unfortunately it takes thousands of such donations to run an individual campaign. The ability to attract this manner of financial support often begins with distinguishing the kinds of people who donate to campaigns?

Who Donates to a Political Campaign?

1. Those individuals who are issue-oriented; that is, they support the candidate's position and are willing to contribute to the "cause."
2. Dedicated persons who support the candidate or cause personally.
3. Regular political contributors to political activities on several levels.
4. Those individuals who hate the opposition and are willing to invest money to stop it.
5. Those persons who want a reward for their contribution. These, of course, can be political favors (for example, the milk-fund controversy) or merely a wish on the part of the donor to be considered as a "friend of importance."

What Are Effective Methods of Soliciting Funds?

Although such categories are convenient for discussion purposes, it is important to realize that a wide number of other forces, religion, socioeconomic position, and national events such as Watergate, may play an additional role. Thus, in approaching potential contributors, a variety of methods should be considered:

1. Direct mail solicitation (generally effective if it is used as part of an appeal by an individual in a peer group).
2. Fund-raising events, such as cocktail parties, dinners, and breakfasts.
3. Solicitation of professional, labor, and business groups.
4. Approaching all individuals who have contributed to similar candidates or causes in the past.
5. Solicitation of funds from major contributors.

The effective combination of these approaches will vary with the particular campaign. What works in one campaign may fail miserably in another.

Yet a successful fund raising effort is no guarantee of victory at the polls. A healthy campaign warchest expended in a campaign marked by poor timing and other characteristics of poor management will usually prove disastrous. Consequently, some major consulting firms demand complete authority over the organization structure as a prerequisite to the contracting of their services. They depend heavily on a combination of organization, timing, and technology to gain victory. As Doug Bailey of the consulting firm of Bailey, Deardourff and Bowen explained, businessmen who are the major contributors to campaigns are accustomed to paying high prices for media costs. As important as organization is, though, they would be unwilling "to contribute so much for organization."[44] Thus management firms organize *flashy* campaigns not only to attract the votes but *big-money* donations as well.[45]

The Campaign Plan

Even campaigns run from "under the hat of the candidate" need carefully planned campaign activities.[46] Usually this planning begins between the candidate and the individual he approaches to act as campaign manager. After general guidelines have been established regarding lines of authority, the real effort of organizing begins. There are probably as many campaign organizations as there are campaigns. "It's a little like football; there is no one system that is better. One team runs a single wing, another the T-formation. That doesn't mean that one is better, only that one is better for that particular team."[47] If the individual seeking support is well known, a good organization will help him expand his familiarity to a broad base. If he is an unknown, a well-run campaign organization is essential to demonstrate to the public that the candidate, in the words of one consultant, "lives, breathes, and thinks."

In discussing organizing a campaign, one party chairman observed that a planning group (steering committee) is one of the most necessary ingredients in systematically approaching the voter. "Planning the campaign is like playing three-dimensional chess: No one can see all the plays."[48] Thus the committee usually represents a number of individuals with expertise ranging from media and advertising to voting analysis and fund raising. All these activities are important ingredients for a successful electoral effort. The committee will decide the preliminary elements of the

[44]Coffey op. cit., p. 21.

[45]For a good discussion of the effectiveness of political media and to change attitudes of voters see Allen D. Gardner, "Political Ads: Do They Work?" *Wall Street Journal*, 1 February 1972, p. 10.

[46]Sorauf, op. cit., p. 248.

[47]Pritchard, op. cit.

[48]State Chairman Peter O'Donnell, Jr., Republican party of Texas, in *Ways to Win* (Washington, D.C.: Republican National Committee, 1968), pp. 17–22.

campaign and act throughout as a sounding board for the campaign manager. Initially, fund-raising priorities will probably dominate, because even in their earliest phases campaigns require dollars for building rentals and telephone deposits. Clifton White noted that, when he ran Senator Buckley's campaign in New York, they used the offices that had been occupied in 1968 by Robert F. Kennedy. The Kennedy campaign still owed rent; so, instead of requiring the normal deposit on the space, the owners had insisted they wanted the entire rent in advance. Additionally, the telephone company, with bills outstanding from Kennedy, required a $300 deposit for each telephone before installation—this figure was projected to include all telephones to be in service at the height of the campaign.[49] Thus, startup dollars and preliminary planning are the two key ingredients initially undertaken by the steering committee.

The scheduling of the campaign and construction of a long-range financial picture are the next responsibilities of this committee. One must remember that, before an accurate budget can be constructed and deadlines established, each activity must be scheduled. Such planning may appear at first glance to be nothing more than establishing a date for each milestone of the campaign, but the following example given by consultant Allan Munro will serve to demonstrate the difficulties and importance of such a project.

Scheduling a Campaign

The campaign has decided to use bulk mailing of endorsement cards to persuade the electorate to support a particular candidate. . . . They start planning with the primary election. . . . As an example, with endorsement cards the last activity is to deposit them in the post office for mailing. The following list demonstrates the effort necessary for a successfully scheduled event:

1. Materials to be included, such as photograph, printing, etc., must be collected.
2. Layout has to be approved for printing.
3. Endorsement cards must be printed.
4. Delivery of the cards to those individuals who are going to address them must take place.
5. It is necessary to contact the addressers that you are going to come and pick up the endorsement cards.
6. Collect the endorsement cards from the addressers.
7. The cards have to be zip-coded. Many individuals who address

[49]White et al., op. cit.

endorsement cards and letters for the candidate do not know how to find zip codes. Someone at campaign headquarters must do it.

8. The cards must be separated by zip codes.
9. To bulk mail, endorsement cards must be bound. That's going to take some time.
10. When do the endorsement cards go to the post office? If they are bulk-mailed out they can be held by the post office for up to 48 hours. The campaign wants these endorsement cards to reach the voters before they vote. Perhaps the week prior to the election. They must be delivered in plenty of time.
11. Delivery of the cards to the post office.[50]

We can see by the above examples that the scheduling of activities is not an easy chore. Any delay in accomplishing any step could mean added cost and even failure. In addition, fund-raising activities, coordinated by the finance chairman and the steering committee, must also be scheduled so that, when dollars are needed for reserving television time or mailing literature, the funds are available. The success of coordinating all these activities rests with the campaign manager or the firm directing the entire effort. But without the careful preplanning by the steering committee the job is almost impossible to accomplish.

Once scheduling has been completed, most campaigns then begin the extensive task of organizing the overall effort. Two basic organizational models usually used in campaigns include the functional model and the geographical model.

The Functional Model

The functional model associates workers by specific function (Figure 8.1). The significance of this approach is that it is particularly effective where volunteers constitute the major resource of the organization. Individuals recruited are given a particular task (say, doorbelling) and are not required to complete additional assignments. In today's society, where large numbers of individuals are but slightly interested in the political process, the functional model allows them to participate in a brief simple effort without consuming too much time.

The Geographical Model

The geographical model (Figure 8.2) has been traditionally used in the past for large statewide campaigns where the party or political machine of a particular candidate exercises considerable power. In this organization,

[50]From Munro, op. cit.

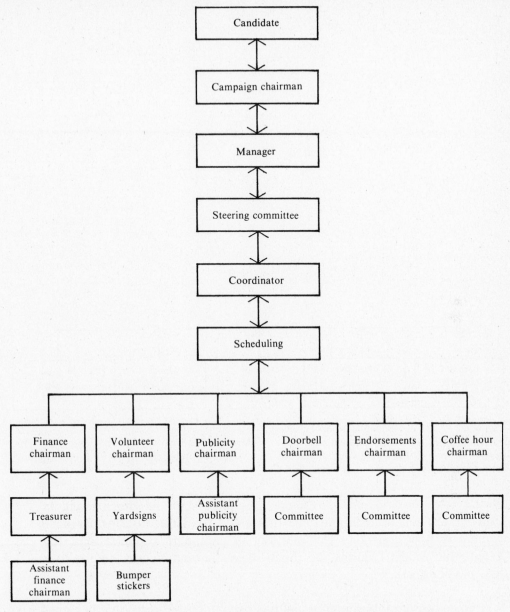

Figure 8.1. The functional model campaign organization. (The functional model establishes an individual to direct each task. No one person performs more than the assigned duties.)

each area of the electoral district (state, county, district, and so on) is divided into subsections under the control of a particular worker. These individuals could be county chairpersons, wardspersons, or volunteers. In these areas the individual directs all of the political activities. From doorbelling to fund raising. The responsibilities are extensive. As we have seen in our earlier discussion of parties, such organizations are becoming a thing

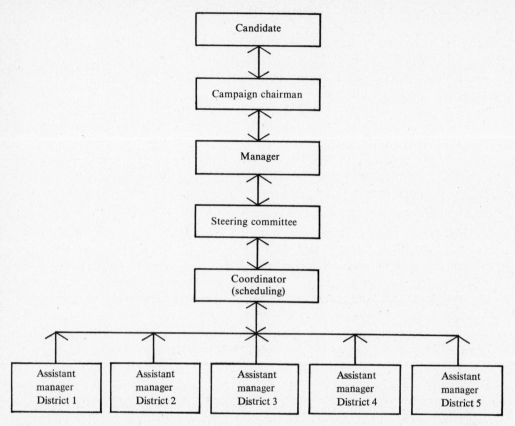

Figure 8.2. The geographical model campaign organization. (The geographical model assigns all responsibilities for campaigning in a particular region to one individual located in that geographic region. Responsibilities in district include finance, volunteer organization, publicity, doorbelling, endorsements, coffee hours, all other duties.)

of the past. In addition, patronage machines such as those found in Chicago are generally diminishing throughout the United States. Because volunteers now constitute the majority in campaign organizations, the geographic model requires too much diversification—often leading to a loss of volunteers.[51]

Once the organizational model has been adopted, recruiting becomes the main activity. It is difficult to explain the art of recruitment, because it involves a diversity of approaches. As we have seen in our discussion of voting behavior, the electorate responds on different levels of consciousness to different elections. Presidential races are high visibility elections; those for school boards are not. The number of individuals interested in participating in a political campaign fluctuates in much the same manner. In the depths of the Watergate tangle both Democrats and Republicans had

[51]Ibid.

difficulty in recruiting supporters. Most Americans seemed to be turned off by politics. Hopefully, as the political climate improves, Americans will began to reassert their faith in government and become more interested in the electoral process.

Volunteers

Probably the candidate and his immediate circle of friends are initially the best source of volunteers. As recruitment expands, the campaign manager must take those individuals who are responding favorably to the candidate and weld them into a functioning unit. He must make assignments, keeping in mind the political experience of a volunteer is his best guide. One consultant noted that "people are always itchy. A number of volunteers are people who emotionally need support at one time or another. They don't really have a problem. They find it difficult to go and do something— doorbelling, handing out materials, or whatever. Campaigning is an emotional experience. For some people it is very difficult. The manager must be there to lend them emotional support."[52]

However, once assignments have been made and the campaign is under way, the cardinal rule of the campaign is to follow the plan. This is often very difficult, especially when the opposition begins to deride your candidate. Volunteers are willing to be led into those *blind alleys*. But to be successful, the organization must be willing to follow its own strategy. In trying to establish and maintain its schedule many problems are found— crises seem to be everywhere, accelerating as the election nears. Yet the image of the candidate must remain cool and organized. One manager noted that "even if the building is on fire, my candidate will walk, not run."

In discussing aspects of campaign management and organization, it has not been our intention to give the student an outline for a political campaign. Campaign management, both professional and volunteer, is an expanding part of modern politics. What we have seen is what is practiced today. Over the years some roles have remained the same, while the players changed—the amateurs giving way to the professionals, political patronage to volunteers. But in America today there is a trend away from participatory democracy. Concluding his remarks on campaign management, consultant Allan Munro made some projections on American democracy. They deserve repeating:

What Does the Future Hold for American Democracy?

The style and approach to politics in America is changing rapidly. [The Watergate Affair], . . . coupled with a growing professional campaign in-

[52] Ibid.

dustry, all demonstrates this change. There seems to be a secular trend against citizen participation in politics. I am certain that many more participated in politics on an active basis in the 1940's than in the 1970's, and this downward trend seems to be accelerating. The number of Americans active in politics, as a percentage of the population, seems to drop every election. The efficacy of the traditional type of campaign organization, whether it be functional, geographical or one of the other possible highbreds, is declining. Traditional campaign organizations are less persuasive, reach fewer people, and are staffed by different types of individuals than they used to be; because there are not as many people involved in politics as in the earlier period. This means the influence of the media, particularly television, but also radio and newspapers, have increased. Some rather spectacular campaigns dramatically demonstrate the impact of this change.

Approximately three and one half weeks before the gubernatorial primary in Pennsylvania, a man named Milton Shapp would have received about three per cent of the democratic votes for governor according to a poll paid for by Shapp's organization. Between then and the primary election Mr. Shapp spent $1,400,000.00 primarily on television but also on radio and a great deal on direct mail. He won that primary. Similarly, up in Alaska, Senator Ernest Gruening, who was a very well respected elder statesman was leading in the polls very shortly before the primary. Mr. Mike Gravel, who is a present Senator from Alaska, spent an incredible amount of money on a half hour fully produced television presentation. The fact that he won handily provided the value of media in his campaign. In 1970, John Glenn, one of the first astronauts who was a national hero, or always thought he was judging by the amount of publicity he always received, suffered disastrously in the Ohio U.S. Senate primary race at the hands of Howard Metzenbaum. Why? Because Mr. Metzenbaum was a millionaire industrialist who spent nine hundred thousand to one million five hundred thousand dollars on television spots that were very effective and very dramatic.

Based on this and similar evidence, I am rapidly coming to the conclusion that the traditional style of political organization is disappearing. The sole purpose of today's organization, if the candidate is not independently wealthy, is to raise money. The campaign will be directed by professionals, publicity men, media specialists, advertising agencies, advance men, and the like.

I am not commenting on the morality of this. I am commenting on what I see happening in American politics. There are abuses that can come from this kind of transition. [We have seen some of them as the result of Watergate.] I am certain we can all visualize what some of these problems are, but I'm not really certain as to what kinds of regulations are needed to protect the public against these kinds of abuses. The present techniques in campaign disclosure will not, in most states, or at the national level, protect the public from these last-minute blitzes or outside money spent by "friends of the candidate" on his behalf but not as part of his regular campaign. Nor are they going to protect the public from the hypocritical candidate who sends letters to the Veterans of Foreign Wars advocating increasing Veterans' benefits, while at the same time sends letters to those groups who have opposed tax increases telling them he is against increased spending. Given the opportunity, a good organizer could direct a mail campaign and promise everybody everything and nobody would know, until after they had all voted. There might be an outcry after the election, but that's too bad. The individual is in office, and has two, three, or even six years in which to mend his political fences with the voters. That's the most important lesson to remember. "Crooked politicians" keep getting re-elected because recruiters are not interested in learning which candidates really represent them. In today's political world, the average voter cannot afford to ignore his political responsibility![53]

[53] Ibid.

9
The Image Builders

When style and charisma connotes the idea of contriving, of public relations, I don't buy it at all.

RICHARD M. NIXON

Richard Nixon had taped a set of one- and five-minute commercials at the Hotel Pierre on Monday morning, October 21. Frank Shakespeare was not happy with the way they were done. "The candidate was harassed," he said. "Tired and harassed."[1]

Shakespeare obtained backstage space at the theater on West Forty-fourth Street where the Merv Griffin Show was done, for Friday morning, October 25, and Richard Nixon agreed to do another set. . . .

Harry Treleaven got to the theater at ten after ten Friday morning. . . .

Richard Nixon entered the studio at ten-fifty. He went straight to an enclosed dressing room called the Green Room, where Ray Vojey, the quiet, blond makeup man, was waiting with his powders and cloths.

Nixon came out of the Green Room at eleven o'clock. There was a drop of three or four inches from the doorway to the floor of the stage. He did not see it and stumbled as he stepped out the door. He grinned, reflexively, and Frank Shakespeare led him to the set.

He took his position on the front of the heavy brown desk. He liked to lean against a desk, or sit on the edge of one, while he taped commercials, because he felt this made him seen informal. There were about twenty people, technicians and advisers, gathered in a semicircle around the cameras.

[1] Joe McGinnes, *The Selling of the President 1968* (New York: Trident, 1969), pp. 1–12, Copyright © 1969 by Joemac, Incorporated. Reprinted by permission of Trident Press, division of Simon & Schuster, Inc.

Richard Nixon looked at them and frowned.

"Now when we start," he said, "don't have anybody who is not directly involved in this in my range of vision. So I don't go shifting my eyes."

"Yes, sir. All right, clear the stage. Everybody who's not actually doing something get off the stage, please. Get off the stage." . . .

Richard Nixon turned back toward the cameras.

"Now when you give me the fifteen-second cue, give it to me right under the camera. So I don't shift my eyes."

"Right, sir."

Then Len Garment came out with some figures about the rising crime rate in Buffalo, which also happened to be an area where Nixon was falling far behind. It was felt at this time that the Buffalo margin . . . could be large enough to cost Nixon New York State. Len Garment explained that they would like him to do a special one-minute commercial for Buffalo, concentrating on the rise in crime. He showed Nixon his papers with the statistics.

"Are the figures higher there?" Nixon said. Len Garment told him they were—significantly. Nixon studied the papers for a moment and then handed them back. "All right," he said.

Then there were ready to start. Richard Nixon sat at the edge of the desk, arms folded, eyes fixed on the camera lens.

"Now let me know just a second or so before you start," he said, "so you don't catch me frozen"—he made a face—"like this."

"Yes, sir. Okay, we're ready now."

"You're going to start now?"

"Right now, sir. Here we go." The red light on camera one began to glow, the camera made a low, whirring sound, and the tape machine emitted three beeps to indicate it was operating.

The Last Few Days

"As we enter the last few days of this critical campaign," Richard Nixon said, "one issue on which the greatest difference exists between the two candidates is that of law and order in the United States. . . ."

He turned immediately to a technician.

"Let's try it once more," he said. "That was a little too long."

Frank Shakespeare said something from the side of the stage.

"Well, we won't use that one," Richard Nixon said. "Because I have another thought. I have to cut it just a little in the outset."

Frank Shakespeare said something else. The tape machine beeped three times.

"Yeah, I know, but we want to get another thought in at the last," Richard Nixon said.

Mike Stanislavsky stepped from behind a camera. "When you bring your head up and start talking, bring your head up and look at the camera for a moment . . ."

"Yeah." Richard Nixon nodded. . . .

"Okay, Mike?" a floor man asked.

Mike Stanislavsky turned. "Let's have quiet on the floor, please. There was a little noise during the last take. Stand by, please, here we go." He looked at Nixon. "When you're ready," he said.

"As we enter the last few days of this critical campaign," Richard Nixon said, "there's one issue on which the differences between the candidates is crystal clear. And that's the issue of law and order in the United States. . . . I pledge a new attorney general. I pledge an—" He stumbled here as the pledges bumped one against the other in his mind.

"Oh, start again," he said. "Can you just keep it rolling?"

There were three beeps from the tape machine.

"Quiet, please, here we go," Mike Stanislavsky said. "When you're ready."

Al Scott and Harry Treleaven were watching from a control room one flight below the stage.

"I wish he'd use a teleprompter," Treleaven said.

"That's been bugging me for a year," Scott said, "People think he's reading anyway." . . .

Three beeps.

"This is again one minute?" Richard Nixon asked.

"Okay, Mike?" a floor man asked.

"Right, one minute. Quiet on the floor. Here we go, please. Ready when you are, sir."

Richard Nixon looked at the camera with an expression of concern on his face. *"Are the figures higher there?"* he had asked. "In reading some recent FBI statistics, I found that Buffalo and Erie County was one of the areas in the nation in which we've had an appalling rise in crime. I think we can do something about it. But we can't do something about it if we continue the old leadership. . . . I pledge a new attorney general. We will wage an all-out war against organized crime all over this nation. We're going to make the cities of our country, the streets of our country, free from fear again. With your help on November fifth, the first civil right of every American, the right to be free from domestic violence, will again be a right that you will have."

That "first civil right" line had not come back to him until the final version of the first commercial. But it pleased him so, the way it marched out of his mouth, that he was reluctant to abandon it. It was as if an old friend had paid him a surprise visit this gloomy morning.

"*With a good public-relations team on the job, Senator, you'll come through as a smart guy who happens to be inarticulate, instead of a guy who doesn't know what the hell he's talking about.*"

Drawing by Whitney Darrow, Jr., © 1968 *The New Yorker Magazine,* Inc.

"Let's try it once more," Richard Nixon said.

"Damned good," Frank Shakespeare said.

There were three beeps from the tape machine.

"Well, we can even use that, but we'll try it again," Nixon said.

Shakespeare stepped forward. "If you do this, and you end it again, say, 'it will again be a right that you will have here in Buffalo,' so that you'll have Buffalo—"

Richard Nixon was nodding. "Uh-huh. That's right."

"Ready when you are, Mike," the floor man said.

"Okay? Quiet, please, here we go again." Mike Stanislavsky looked at Nixon. "Ready when you are."

"In reading some recent FBI statistics, I found. . . ."

The cameras stopped.

"I think that's good," Nixon said. "What was the time on that?"

"Forty-eight." . . .

Nixon again took his position on the edge of the desk. The tape machine beeped three times.

"Okay, Mike, we're ready."

"Okay, quiet on the floor, here we go again, please. Any time you're ready sir."

"The latest FBI figures indicate that Erie County and Buffalo are one of the areas in which the greatest rise in crime has occurred—No, let's start again. Just keep right on."

Three beeps.

"Okay," the floor man said.

"All right," Richard Nixon said.

"Any time you're ready," Mike Stanislavsky said.

Nixon began, "In reading the—" He closed his eyes and winced. "No," he said.

Three Beeps

Three beeps from the machine.

"All right," Nixon said. "In reading the latest FBI figures I found that the most appalling rise in crime—Uh-uh. No."

He shook his head again. There were three more beeps from the tape machine. He looked at the floor again, steadying himself.

"Once more, then this'll do it," he said.

"Okay. Quiet, please. Here we go. Whenever you're ready."

"In reading the most recent FBI figures, one of the most appalling rises in crime in the whole country occurred in Erie County and in Buffalo." Nixon was impatient now and plunged on despite that syntax. "I think we can do something about it. . . ."

He finished, delighted to be rid of the FBI statistics and the people of Buffalo and Erie County and their most appalling rise in crime.

"All right," he said. "That isn't important enough to do that often, but that's all right. But it's done now. That last one was a—" But his thought shifted suddenly.

"Now we'll do the southern one," he said.

"Tell me when you're ready," Mike Stanislavsky said.

Three beeps from the machine.

"This is another one-minute," Nixon said. . . .

Packaged and Sold

If Richard Nixon was packaged and sold to the public as 99 and 44/100ths percent pure, he was not alone in becoming the *product you can't live without.* After the 1970 election, the *Congressional Quarterly* commented,

"The outstanding political upsets of 1970 have been made by men of great wealth, presenting their politics to the voters on television and spending their way from obscurity to success in a matter of weeks."[2] Howard Metzenbaum's defeat of John Glenn in the Ohio Democratic primary was a case in point. Starting with a recognition factor of 15 percent compared with Glenn's 97 percent, Metzenbaum spent his way through nearly 1.8 million dollars and to victory. There was little separating of the two liberal candidates philosophically save the *morality* of *buying the election.* With clever and careful packaging, Joseph Napolitan Associates and filmmaker Charles Guggenheim had created and merchandized the Metzenbaum product. Whether or not this raised a question concerning the ethics of the situation seemed to be a moot point. When Napolitan was asked whether it was moral to *sell candidates*—because when they were elected they might not deliver what they promised—he remarked that that was government, and he didn't know anything about government. Getting people elected was his business. That ended on election day.[3]

Television Blitz

In California it was John V. Tunney who defeated Senator George Murphy by earmarking $1,300,000 for a television blitz in the top 10 California population areas on the eve of the election.[4] Commenting on this procedure, one political consultant noted that given the dollars he could get anyone elected through the use of the television blitz.[5]

While these examples seem to justify the growing alarm among many journalists, educators, and other concerned citizens that one day some unknown, unqualified but very rich individual will *buy* the presidency and land the United States in the proverbial "soup," considerable evidence seems to negate the fear. For instance, even before the 1972 election there were startling defeats among hopeful candidates whose campaigns were under the tutelage of the nation's leading media consultants. Charles Guggenheim ran eight media campaigns and lost three. Roger Ailes failed in two of his four efforts, while Harry Treleaven, of *Selling of the President* fame, attempted five such efforts, suffering four losses.[6]

[2]"Almanac," *Congressional Quarterly,* 1970.

[3]Mike Wallace interviewing Joseph Napolitan in "T.V. and Politics" (CBS White Paper). 1971.

[4]Michael C. Emery and Ted C. Smythe, *Readings in Mass Communication* (Dubuque, Iowa: W. C. Brown, 1972), p. 271.

[5]Allan Munro, address to the Center for the Study of Practical Politics, Seattle, 1 October 1971.

[6]James M. Perry, "Psst, Image Maker, You're Naive," *National Observer,* 16 November 1970.

Yes these failures reflected a changing public attitude toward the *image merchants* because of Watergate and the like. Perhaps most importantly, however, they reflected the inherent limitations of media itself, particularly television.

It cannot be denied that television has "altered our political process."

It has changed whom we elect, how we elect and even why we elect a particular person. Like many technological advances, the impact of political television has preceded the understanding of its meaning and its uses. The natural human reaction to a lack of understanding is fear, and that single emotion—fear—still overrides the attitude of too many people toward the political uses and power of television. . . .

Television Surpassed Newspapers as Source of News

[In] 1963 television surpassed newspapers as the people's major source of news. Television has been widening the gap ever since. [By the 70's] 60% of those polled said they relied on television as their *major* news source, and nearly one-third of the people said they relied on television as their *only* source of news. . . .

Keeping these figures in mind, consider that the . . . average news item in a TV newscast is covered in less than a minute. All of the facts of an earthquake, an invasion, or even a robbery next door cannot be seen or told in kinetic shorthand. Television may be the best means of communication devised by man, but it is not without limitations. Time is a major one. Does anyone really believe that local problems can be solved in 60 seconds and world problems can be solved in 60 minutes, as they appear to be on TV with time left over to capsulate tommorrow's problems? In a world charged with simultaneity—from instant breakfast to instant sex—we tend to want and expect instant solutions to all our problems. Television rarely, if ever, tells the whole story. It is imperative that we begin to understand what TV can and cannot do.

. . . [I presume] the candidate is credible, the media strategy good, and the money limitless. However, this isn't all it takes to get elected in America. . . .

In the thirty-five gubernatorial races of 1970, nineteen winners did indeed outspend their opponents on television and radio, but sixteen men who also outspent the opposition on the broadcasting media lost. . . .[7]

[7]For an interesting discussion of media costs reflected in dollars raised, see "Needy Candidates: Why Campaign Chests Are Low," *U.S. News & World Report,* 30 September 1974, pp. 57–58.

"I wish to God he'd bring his new TV image home with him!" (Broadcasting Magazine)

From *Campaign Insight*. By permission.

It is estimated that Richard Ottinger spent a million dollars in the 1970 New York primary alone. This was budgeted almost entirely for spot announcements of 60 seconds or less, which created an impressive state-wide identity profile for him. Going into the general election he was clearly the leader. Then he was faced with longer programs and televised debates, and he didn't look nearly so formidable in these as he did in his "canned" commercials. Credibility is still the most important factor in getting elected. No amount of money can buy it, nor can television create it.

. . . [T]he introduction of television into politics causes fear . . . because we fail to understand the *limits* of the medium. . . . [T]here has been much publicity about television distortion. If distortion exists in television, it is the reporters themselves and the editors responsible for selection of material who are responsible, and not the medium.

. . . [In 1971] CBS Washington Correspondent Roger Mudd said, "The inherent limitations in our medium . . . mean a dangerous concentration on action, usually showing violence rather than thought. And on happenings rather than issues, on shock rather than explanation. Our broadcasts have not improved," Mudd declared. "If anything they have declined." . . .

The television camera by itself does not distort. Distortion means exaggeration. TV magnifies but does not exaggerate. . . . [I]t is a close-up medium and a nervous twitch will be seen and interpreted by 40 million people, but exaggeration means to magnify *beyond* the limits of reality, and that the camera cannot do.

Less Money on Commercials

. . . [L]ess time and money [should be] spent on commercials, which represent the ultimate in selective editing, and less time spent with reporters telling viewers what they think or ought to think, and more time spent with the candidate himself on camera *live*. At least half of this time should be spent in an adversary situation. . . . [L]ive TV exposure of the candidate is the best way to give the public . . . [the] opportunity [to spot phonies].

However, because of the recent publicity about distortion, fear does exist. The next logical step is overreaction which leads to control or repression. . . . [F]air guidelines and some limitations are needed in the political television arena, but . . . the recent publicity surrounding campaign spending is overblown, . . . the righteous outcry of some would-be "limiters" is self-serving, . . . the so-called evils of television in the political process are exaggerated and oversimplified, and . . . the values and accomplishments of television in politics are seldom, if ever, pointed out to the general public.

. . . [In many] elections . . . the losing candidate lost primarily: 1) because somebody in his own party inadvertently killed his credibility on a key issue, or 2) because the candidate really didn't want to win, or 3) because the candidate failed to listen to his advisers, or 4) because the opponent was more credible, had a better media plan, even though he had less money, or 5) because somebody in his own party deliberately sabotaged him, or 6) because the volunteer organization failed to turn out the vote on Election Day, or 7) because the candidate's wife didn't want him to win, or 8) because a candidate, eight points ahead in the polls, dropped hopelessly behind after a one-hour television debate. These are just a few examples of how to lose an election even if the candidate, the money, and the media are in order.

A candidate must be credible. He must show a track record of success in something, if not politics, and he must indicate his position on some issues. . . . [T]here is too much emphasis on where a candidate stands and not enough on the direction in which he is moving. Is he leading the charge or reluctantly being dragged, kicking and screaming all the way? Is he consistent? Television cannot create credibility, but it does reflect credibility or the lack of it, thereby establishing or destroying some candidates. As long as we live in a free society where a candidate must face live television and the written press, and speak to issues publicly, . . . [there is] no fear that we will elect a monster in disguise.

. . . [T]he number of commercials shown on TV during a campaign should be limited. . . . [A]t least 35% of broadcast monies available to a candidate [should] be spent for the purchase of *program* time as distinguished from commercial time. . . . [S]tations [should] make several hours of prime time television available in statewide elections to major party candidates, free of charge. After all, these are the men we must rely on to govern this nation—men of vision who can lead and men of conscience who can act. We have a much better chance of finding those men within the intimate environment of live TV than we ever did by watching a candidate wave from the back of a train.

There has been much criticism recently of the media strategy used in political campaigns. . . . [But] trying to censor a campaign from the advertising viewpoint treats a symptom and neglects the cause. A candidate and his campaign management or consulting firm set the *ethical* level for the campaign—the public should be reminded of this!

There are . . . [few] capable campaign consulting firms in the country today. Most of these belong to the American Association of Political Consultants, . . . [an] organization that . . . [worked] out a voluntary ethical code covering truthfulness, fairness and accuracy to be followed by all campaign consultants. . . . [E]ach of these companies should register and should meet certain standards to qualify as a legitimate campaign consulting firm. A good portion of the responsibility for returning politics to an honorable profession rests in their hands. Are these companies necessary? The answer is yes. Getting elected is extremely complicated and a candidate needs professional help in fund-raising, polling, organization, research and media planning. No one will ever be elected to a major political office again without the use of television.

Money Is Needed to Get Elected

There is no doubt that money is needed to get elected today. However, it is important to keep the outcry against campaign spending in perspective. It is true, according to FCC records that all candidates and parties spent about $89,000,000 on radio and television in 1968. (This figure includes both time-buying and production expenses.)

So, $89,000,000 was spent to help us decide for whom to vote and to tell us something about each of the candidates and issues. However, last year Procter & Gamble, one of hundreds of television advertisers, spent $179,276,100 on TV advertising alone. Also, last year seven companies spent over $60,000,000 each to advertise products on TV. . . . 89 million dollars worth of television and radio for all political candidates, nationwide, during an entire presidential election year is dwarfed by comparison.

. . . [T]he British use of television in elections has some merits. While their total system would not work here, at least one element is particularly appealing: limiting the duration of the campaign to three weeks. Admittedly, three weeks would be much too brief a period for the United States but, on the other hand, the fatiguing situation of . . . seven semi-announced presidential candidates running around the country Monday-morning-quarterbacking 18 months before the national election—is going too far.

. . . [I]f all the news media quit trying to create false excitement by covering all potential presidential candidates in terms of a popularity poll, which is meaningless at such a stage, they would be taking a giant step forward in journalistic responsibility.

Television Has Failed

It is no secret that the television industry has largely failed in communicating its own intrinsic value to the public in many areas—particularly regarding politics. There is a negative attitude about television in politics, a creeping fear that somehow we are electing contrived images and not men. That simply is not true. It is to the voters' (and thus the country's) advantage to see and hear political candidates. Television has revived political discussion in this country on all levels—even in our grade schools. It has influenced more people to get involved in the political process than ever before. It is breaking down back-room bossism and will continue to do so. Television has made the viewers and thus the voters more knowledgeable on the basic social issues that face this nation. And it has been primarily responsible for influencing the business and political communities to do something about the environment.

. . . [T]here are still some inequities in the use of TV in politics. However, . . . we have a far better political communication system *with* television than without it. . . .[8]

Need to Know

Although the need to know and be informed is obviously necessary in any democratic society, the *packaging* of candidates is a questionable contribution to this goal. J. A. C. Brown noted in his work, *The Techniques of Persuasion,* that "nobody can create emotions which are not already there."[9] But playing on these emotions has become a multimillion-dollar business. The successful media consultant, while not distorting the candidate's image, certainly tries to eliminate, as much as possible, all that is unfavorable.[10] Perhaps Stephen Shadegg put it most succinctly when he

[8]From Roger Ailes, "Candidates + Money + Media = Votes," *Politeia* 1 (Winter 1972): 29–31.

[9]Quoted in Michael Rowan, "Candidates Aren't Packaged—You Are," *Politeia* 1 (Fall 1971): 7.

[10]Wallace, op. cit.

remarked that, "There is a market for ideas and concepts, just as there is a market for girdles and mink coats. . . . In politics the candidate is the product."[11]

Yet most ad men would agree that a *product* can only be managed to a certain point. "The agency has utterly no business in the area of . . . [the candidate's] position on issues and his platform."[12] "He's the expert on what is said. We're the experts on how it is said,"[13] seems to be a commonly held view.

However, Allen Toffler's discussion of the engineered message in *Future Shock* certainly applies to campaigning. For the engineered message, unlike other *coded messages,* such as verbal communications, is a planned, if you will, an *engineered* system of delivering massive amounts of data in a brief and concise fashion. Television news is probably one of the best examples. In a few seconds, the viewers learn of the fall of Haile Selassie of Ethiopia or the resignation of Richard Nixon as president of the United States. He is bombarded in staccato fashion until, as Toffler argues, his nervous system is loaded to dangerous levels.[14]

If, as evidence indicates, over 60 percent of Americans receive the majority of their information from television, then the political spot[15] takes on new dimensions. The viewer is not only accustomed to receiving most of his data from television but is also programmed to react positively: "You use Dial. Don't you wish everybody did?" Given this conditioning, the American public may very well be an open receptacle for political *pitchmen.*

Eisenhower hits the spot
One full General, that's a lot.
Feeling sluggish, feeling sick?
Take a dose of Ike and Dick.
Philip Morris, Lucky Strike,
Alka Seltzer, I like Ike.[16]

[11]Stephen D. Shadegg, *How to Win an Election: The Art of Political Victory* (New York: Taplinger, 1964), p. 169.

[12]John Posten (senior vice-president and director of planning at Fuller and Smith and Ross, former President Nixon's advertising agency), in Walter Troy Spencer, "The Agency of Political Packaging," *Television Magazine* 25 (August 1968): 82.

[13]Arnie Kopelman (vice-president and account supervisor of Doyle Dane Bernbach—Procter & Gamble, Heinz Ketchup, Hubert Humphrey), in ibid.

[14]Alvin Toffler, *Future Shock* (New York: Random House, 1970), pp. 145–148.

[15]Refers to 30- and 60-second political commercials usually designed to create a name recognition for a particular candidate.

[16]BBD&O poem in George Braziller, Inc., *Subverse: Rhymes for Our Times* by Marya Mannes, drawings by Robert Osborn; reprinted with the permission of the publisher. Copyright © 1959 by Marya Mannes and copyright © 1959 by Robert Osborn.

Yet the so-called *image merchants* hold that "the television camera by itself does not distort." Could it be that we have grossly erred in judging the medium or are they playing with our minds again? Is the real threat, if there is one, coming from those whose task it is to produce the image for public consumption?

The Image People[17]

The "image people" work with concepts like *charismatic, handsome, youthful*, etc. And they strive to keep their candidate *moving*—through shopping centers, old-age homes, schools, etc. They utilize visual information on television to communicate this image. Television is thus conceptualized as a vehicle for bringing the voters to the candidate, where they can see and experience his glorious image.

. . . [I]t is far more important to understand and affect the inner feelings of a voter in relation to a political candidate than to package an image that voters tend not to believe anyway. It would be more correct to say that the goal of a media adviser is to tie up the voter and deliver him to the candidate. So it is really the *voter* who is packaged by media, not the candidate. The voter is surrounded by media and dependent on it in his everyday functioning. The stimuli a candidate uses on the media thus surround the voter. They are part of his environment, his packaging.

In assessing the reactions of voters to candidates on television, it becomes very clear that a person sitting in his home watching a political figure on his TV set four or five feet away wants to feel that the candidate is talking to him. A politician who typically speaks to large audiences, in a grandiose style, must adjust his speech scale for television or radio. Though he may be part of an audience totaling ten or twenty million people, a TV viewer experiences the candidate as someone speaking in his home to one, two, or maybe five people gathered around the set.

Any situation in which a politician is filmed may potentially find its way to the television viewer or the radio listener. Thus a politician on the street, shouting over the volume of traffic to fifty or a hundred people, must understand that a home audience of two or three million listening to him that evening will be put off by his shouting. The home viewer's ear is, in effect, only four or five feet away from the politician's mouth. And there are no diesel trucks or air hammers in his living room. . . .

[17]From Tony Schwartz, "The Inside of the Outside," in *The Responsive Chord*, (Garden City, N.Y.: Doubleday/Anchor, 1973), pp. 80–105. Copyright © 1973 by Anthony Schwartz. Reprinted by permission of Doubleday & Co., Inc.

Many politicians in a recording situation will talk either to an imaginary vast audience spread across a wide geographic area, or *on behalf of themselves,* i.e., as if their position had been challenged by a reporter and they were defending it. A home listener is not interested in a politician who formally expresses a position. To the average voter, expressing-a-position-talk is what government officials do when they want to cover up something. A voter wants the candidate to talk *to* him, not *at* him; to use the medium not as a large public *address* system, but rather as a private *undress* system. Furthermore, many politicians tend to organize their thoughts for a home listener the way they might for a group of lawyers. But the logic of the positions they try to develop fails to impress the typical voter, who has one thought in the back of his mind whenever he listens to a politician: "How do I *feel* about him?"

Face-to-Face Audience

Traditionally, successful politicians are usually quite effective in tuning their speech for a face-to-face audience. They learn to interpret very subtle feedback from a crowd and adjust their style to maximize the impact. However, when they have to speak to a radio or TV home audience (non-face-to-face), they often give a mechanical rendering of their feelings. Rather than adjust for a more intimate relation to the listener, they project for a larger audience. . . .

It is much more important for a voter to feel a candidate than to see him. Despite all the myths to the contrary, a candidate's physical appearance alone does not win him many votes. But looks can lose votes. Generally, candidates tend to *look* dishonest, but *sound* honest. This visual handicap is magnified by the fact that most situations where a voter is likely to see the candidate are detrimental to his visual presentation of self. Television in particular is very difficult to structure for effective visual communication of a candidate. The candidate typically has no feeling of who is looking at him; he does not know which camera is on; and the lighting often puts him in a spotlight situation, not an interpersonal encounter. . . .

It is often argued that TV *wears out* a candidate. This is generally true, but only because most political advertisers use a *campaign* approach (in the old product advertising sense) in creating and running TV spots. . . . Since the commercials are produced so far in advance, they can only touch on general problems, not specific issues of the day. And since the public hears a candidate say the same irrelevant thing over and over, they get tired of him very quickly. . . .

There are, of course, certain themes and issues that may be central to an election. Commercials dealing with these problems can be repeated. However, they should be works of art, which grow with multiple viewings. . . .

"Candidate *wear-out*" can take two forms: saturation *wear-out* from too much exposure of the candidate, and "fuse blowout." Mario Procaccino, a candidate for mayor of New York City a while ago, blew out the receptivity fuses of people listening to him on radio, or listening and viewing on television. He was hotter than our personal media fuses could take. Every appearance on TV was like a performance before twenty thousand people at Madison Square Garden, without a microphone. He should be advised to run for a mayor of a city like Havana or Saigon, where people generally watch TV in public, some distance from the set.

Important announcements by a candidate (e.g., that he is running for office) present special media problems. The broadcaster may cut a twenty-minute speech to one minute for the evening news. His message is not only cut to 5 percent of its original length, it is edited by someone who does not have the candidate's interests in mind. It makes sense, therefore, to use a forty-five-to-fifty-second speech when announcing something important. . . .

[This] suggestion runs directly against the advice of many who say that political speeches and commercials should be longer. Somehow these people feel that a politician can more easily lie in ten seconds than in five minutes or one hour. However, . . . in the thirties . . . radio was hailed as a means to shorten the long-windedness of politicians. At that time people felt that politicians had developed a special way of deceiving the public through long circumlocutions. Radio was perceived as beneficial to the electorate since it would force politicians to speak to the point and avoid unnecessary platitudes or bombast.

. . . Eisenhower [did not need] . . . five minutes to say, "If elected, I will go to Korea." Similarly, Johnson did not require five minutes to announce that he would not seek reelection in 1968. Yet both these statements were quite clear, meaningful, and *truthful*. Time has nothing to do with clarity, truthfulness, or honesty. One can be clear or unclear, truthful or dishonest, in twenty seconds or two hours.

The Disclaimer

Another fascinating media problem is the disclaimer at the end of political spots. All political commercials are required to have a legal label at the end, stating who paid for the message. Naturally, there is a conflict

Editorial cartoon by Paul Conrad. Copyright, Los Angeles Times. Reprinted with permission.

between the candidate's interest in communicating an effective political message and the government's requirement of a label. The intent of the disclaimer is to frame the spot as a paid, partisan message. The problem for a media specialist is to minimize the negative effects of the label (from the candidate's point of view) without violating the law. . . .

See how the two versions might affect you:

(A) Political spot ends . . .

ANNOUNCER: "Paid for by the Senator Jones Campaign Committee."

(B) Political spot ends . . .

ANNOUNCER: "And that's why this message was brought to you by a lot of people who want Bob Jones in the Senate."

The 1971 San Francisco Alioto mayoralty campaign illustrates a very important principle in media campaigning. . . . [T]he early part of the campaign . . . emphasized Alioto's personal feelings about a wide range of social problems. These were very low-key spots designed to show voters that he was a man of deep feelings. Later in the campaign . . . [the] spots became highly competitive: counterpointing Alioto's specific stand on an issue with other candidates; building up his record and attacking the record of other candidates; and asking the voter to support him. . . . This same kind of commercial would have been all wrong at the beginning of the campaign. If we tell someone why he should vote for a candidate and ask him to do so, seven or eight weeks before the election, we are asking him to perform the impossible. He cannot vote until election day.

We Want the Voter to Think

In the early part of a campaign we simply want the voter to think about the candidate and the issues. As the campaign proceeds, we can focus on specifics, such as why someone should support the candidate or why a given problem is important to the voter. Only in the last weeks should we ask voters to come out for what Joe Napolitan calls the *one-day sale*. In this way we do not create frustration in a potential voter.

People tend to read ads for products they already own. The function of political advertising, then, may be characterized as organizing or confirming the feelings of two groups who already own (or believe in) many of the products (approaches to solving problems) a candidate is selling. The first group is the campaign workers and people who are planning to vote for the candidate. Their attitude can be reinforced by political advertising. The second group consists of those people who share certain of the candidate's feelings about social problems. Advertising can reveal the candidate's feelings to those who inherently share these beliefs. The realization of an identity between their feelings and the candidates can provide a strong motivation to vote for the candidate. (We should not overlook the fact that a voter has *four* ways to vote: for or against either two candidates.)

It is very hard to change fixed beliefs. Hence, political advertising is not likely to change strongly held attitudes or convince a conservative Republican to vote for a liberal Democrat. However, most political decisions result from an interaction of many feelings and attitudes, often covering a wide spectrum of social beliefs. For example, there are many people who express a generally negative attitude about a candidate, but agree with many of the positions he expresses. One such individual might be someone who traditionally votes for party X but shares party Y's feelings that the economy can be strengthened. If you can evoke these feelings deeply, you may be able to change his overt voting behavior. Traditionalists in political science call this person a ticket splitter.

Television is an ideal medium for surfacing feelings voters already have, and giving these feelings a direction by providing stimuli that may evoke the desired behavior. . . . [T]he best political commercials are similar to Rorschach patterns. They do not tell the viewer anything. They surface his feelings and provide a context for him to express these feelings.

The real question in political advertising is *how to surround the voter with the proper auditory and visual stimuli to evoke the reaction you want for him,* i.e., *his voting for a specific candidate.*

A commercial . . . in 1964 illustrates my point. The spot shows a little girl in a field counting petals on a daisy. As her count reaches ten, the visual motion is frozen and the viewer hears a countdown. When the countdown reaches zero, we see a nuclear explosion and hear President Johnson say, "These are the stakes, to make a world in which all God's children can live, or to go into the darkness. Either we must love each other or we must die." As the screen goes to black at the end, white lettering appears stating, "on November 3rd, Vote for President Johnson."

The *Daisy* spot was shown only once, on "Monday Night at the Movies," but it created a huge controversy. Many people, especially the Republicans, shouted that the spot accused Senator Goldwater of being trigger-happy. But *nowhere in the spot is Goldwater mentioned.* There is not even an indirect reference to Goldwater. Indeed, some unfamiliar with the political climate in 1964 and viewing the spot today will not perceive any allusion at all to Goldwater. Then why did it bring such a reaction in 1964? Well, Senator Goldwater had stated previously that he supported the use of of tactical atomic weapons. The commercial *evoked* a deep feeling in many people that Goldwater might actually use nuclear weapons. This mistrust was not in the *Daisy* spot. It was in the people who viewed the commercial. The stimuli of the film and sound evoked these feelings and allowed people to express what they inherently believed. . . .

Probably the smartest thing Goldwater could have done at the time was to agree with the attitude of the commercial and offer to help pay for running it. This would have undercut the sensational effect of it and possibly won him many votes.

Political advertising involves tuning in on attitudes and beliefs of the voter and then affecting these attitudes with the proper auditory and visual stimuli. If our research shows that most people feel one vice presidential candidate is clearly superior, we do not have to hit him over the head with this information in order to make it work for us. We might simply list their names on a card and ask, "Who is your choice to be a heartbeat away from the presidency?" In this way, you surface attitudes (held by many) that can produce the desired effect. Commercials that attempt to *tell* the listener something are inherently not as effective as those that attach to something that is already in him. We are not concerned with getting things *across* to people as much as *out* of people. Electronic media are particularly effective tools in this regard because they provide us with direct access to people's minds.

In situations where voters do not share the same feelings or have divergent views on a subject . . . stimuli [must be designed] that will be meaningful to the different groups within the audience, at the same time. For example, in a gubernatorial race . . . there [was] a large bloc of public school teachers who might vote for the candidate if he promised to increase their pay. At the same time, the general public objected to an increase in teachers' salaries, feeling that the quality of teaching was too low to merit higher wages. One solution to this conflict might involve having the candidate promise to "up-grade teachers." The teachers could interpret this as *upgrade salary,* while the general public might hear it as *upgrade quality*.

Structure Nonpaid Media

A major problem of political candidates is to structure the effects of nonpaid media, such as news, word of mouth, editorials, etc. A candidate gets more free time in a campaign than paid time. . . . If there is a lot of news about the candidate, and you do not feel it is accurately framed by the newscaster, station, or newspaper, you can put it in a proper frame by use of paid media.

. . . [A]n example outside the area of political campaigning—Con Edison, a large eastern power utility, is constantly receiving bad press because of power failures. However, the same people who hear this news have also heard, at other times, that Con Edison's repeated attempts to build new plants are rejected by the Public Service Commission because of objections by various groups. Con Edison could put those two pieces of news together in paid spots and thereby give the power failure a proper context, a reason for happening. Later, when a person hears of a new power failure, he is likely to associate it with news of plants being rejected. Paid media would have taught him to attach two pieces of information from his environment. In this way, Con Edison can make an ally, rather than an enemy, of the public.

Paid media can also be used to introduce new information into the environment, for later recall. An incumbent can take a position on a given problem and use paid media to convey his stance to the public. Later, when running for re-election, he can recall this position in his advertising. . . .

Do People Understand the Message?

Most advertising research investigates whether people understand the message told by a commercial, and if they retain it. Good political research seeks out attitudes in the environment and then judges a political spot by the way it affects these attitudes. . . . A political spot has meaning only to the extent that it affects behavior at the voting end. There is no way you can test a commercial in isolation to see how it will function. A political spot is broadcast into an environment rich with interaction: People are talking to friends about a candidate, reading and watching news, listening to other candidates' spots, etc. This is where a commercial must function, not in a theater testing environment. A person does not listen to a political spot in isolation and then decide whom he will support, based on this single input. Therefore, the commercials must function as part of the environment. They must interact with all the elements present in a person's environment and produce the desired behavioral effect. The people listening are actually part of the content of any commercial. Their feelings and beliefs interact with the commercial stimuli in creating any attitudinal changes. . . .

The political poll is a way to measure attitudes and concerns of people in the environment. It can provide raw data that are valuable only to someone who can analyze it honestly and critically. As an X ray, it is a great tool if it is read correctly. For instance, we often deal with a LOP factor—that is, a favorable response on a poll often means that the candidate is the Least Objectionable Politician. "Politician" is a negative word and tends to group with others, like "landlord," "tax collector," "meter maid," "salesman," etc., in the public's ear. If one accepts this view, the logical task of the media specialist is to make his candidate the least objectionable politician in the race. Many presidential campaigns have been organized with this specific task as the major goal.

Issues Are Relatively Unimportant

Research also reveals that issues are relatively unimportant. As long as pollsters ask voters whether the economy, defense spending, or transportation deserves the most attention, we can obtain only a list of the relative importance among various issues. But if issue-oriented questions are mixed with inquiries about personal qualities of the candidates in a single poll question, the relative unimportance of issues is revealed in a startling way. The following is the result of a poll taken in 1969 and 1970 by Michael Rowan in several states.

QUESTION: If you were to see a TV program about a candidate running for governor, what would you like to know or feel about him after seeing it?
Answers broke down this way:[18]

That he is honest, a man of conviction	47%
That he is a hard worker	27%
That he is an understanding, compassionate man	14%
That he is a capable, qualified person	9%
That he is a good person, warm	7%
That he is a leader, bold	5%
That he is a bright, intelligent man	4%
That he is a man who perceives the vital issues	3%
No response	8%

Consumed by Issues

No one should interpret this as meaning that people are not concerned about issues. All our research reveals that people are *consumed* by issues. The point here is that when it comes time to choose the person to be elected, voters are looking for the man best capable of dealing with the issues. Most of the problems he will face in office do not arise until after the election. Issues in the campaign are typically a list of past problems. Kevin White, mayor of Boston, puts this quite well: "I had no way of knowing that two months after I took office as mayor of Boston, that the biggest problem I would face would be getting fuel oil into the city to keep the people warm. That's not the kind of thing you can anticipate. What you

[18]The question was open-ended; that is, the nine groups of responses were not offered by the interviewer; they were coded after-the-fact and came directly and spontaneously from the respondents.

need in office is a man who can cope with situations as they arise, situations that no one ever thought of." . . . It is personal qualities like honesty or integrity that tell a voter whether the candidate will be able to handle problems when they arise in the future. Understanding this, the task of a media specialist is not to reveal a candidate's stand on issues, so much as to help communicate those personal qualities of a candidate that are likely to win votes.

Campaign Slogans

The campaign slogan, a carry-over of print's historical role in political campaigns, has little relevance in task-oriented political advertising. Print fostered a long-range *program* approach to campaigning. The time lead needed in organizing, producing, and distributing printed materials (e.g., pamphlets, billboard ads, posters, etc.) required a great deal of guesswork about the problems that would emerge during the campaign. The slogan was an attempt to focus on a central, overriding issue that would serve as a theme for the entire campaign.

The task-oriented use of electronic media enables the candidate to deal with campaign problems on a fire-fighting or guerrilla warfare basis— to tune media to needs (or calculate feedback), to go deep rather than broad. On a given day people may feel that the candidate is antilabor (e.g., the day after the president of the United Auto Workers attacked him in a speech), or that car safety is the most important issue facing the country (e.g., the day after General Motors announces it is recalling one million cars to correct defects). The long-range *program* campaign cannot deal with these specific problems that arise on a day-to-day basis. A task-oriented campaign can create, overnight, a commercial that relates to a problem that has just arisen. . . . The quicker we respond to a problem, the greater are our chances of achieving a desired effect. Also, this utilizes a principle McLuhan described . . . : "Instant information creates involvement in depth."

A task-oriented approach can also be applied to buying radio and TV time. It is important that . . . the specific audience for whom the spot will be most relevant [is reached]. Task-oriented time buying involves a careful analysis of the people who listen to radio or watch TV at various times. . . .

There are a host of considerations in time buying. An afternoon radio program with light music will attract more older people than a late-night rock program, and is therefore a better environment for placing a spot about Social Security. However, advertisers can buy time with a good deal more sophistication than simply correlating the demographic characteristics of a program's audience with the subject matter in a given spot. Advertisers can pinpoint the hours when people are driving to and from work in their cars (and the programs drivers listen to most), and affect them with the sound they sit in. These spots can be designed for car listening. The physical characteristics of sound can be equalized to maximize its impact in a car environment. Similarly, the advertiser can alter the characteristics of a spot if he knows it will be heard by people primarily in kitchens, or living rooms, or outdoors, or any other environment. . . .

Direct Spots

By directing . . . spots toward a highly selected local audience, it is often possible to give the feeling of a national campaign. For example, we can determine the radio stations congressmen and senators listen to in Washington, D.C., at what hours, and saturate those media environments with . . . spots. In this way, a relatively unknown person (or issue) may become a national political figure (or national issue) overnight. (Similarly, we have found that advertising exclusively on the op ed page of the New York *Times* may generate the feeling of a national campaign in the corporate environment.)

Task-oriented buying also permits us to match or counterpoint the mood of the commercial with the mood of the person listening to our spot. For example, the mood of a person listening to radio in the morning, as opposed to the afternoon or evening will be quite different. . . .

The Medium Is the Message

But for the citizen who is on the receiving end of this *efficient* and *extraordinary* procedure, the media itself might indeed become the message. Bombarded for nearly four hours a day by radio and television, exposed to newspapers and millions of magazines and paperback books, the average citizen may reach a point at which he *short circuits* the purveyors of corn flakes and candidates. In other words, with enough media saturation, the viewer-listener can become oblivious to the presence of media output. The media becomes so pervasive that the individual is to media as the fish is to water.[19]

One young matron, when asked by a neighbor why she left her television on all night, looked shocked and answered that she couldn't

---

[19]For a further discussion of this concept, see Marshall McLuhan, *Understanding Media: The Extensions of Man* (New York: McGraw-Hill, 1964).

(From *Campaign Insight*. By permission.)

have. She "hadn't even turned the damned thing on." She insisted that television served no useful purpose so she kept it turned off. Yet on closer examination, she realized that her four children had been watching television regularly, leaving it on until all hours of the night. She had grown so accustomed to its presence that she had failed to react to it at all.

Physicians relate that such instances are not unique in American society, and quickly recount cases of ear and eye damage resulting from loud radios and blurry television. Some psychiatrists note damage to the psyche, while others speculate on the tendency toward violence among those who spend many hours in front of the tube. At the same time educators argue for the benefits of "Sesame Street" and Big Bird. The problem is that, in the Orwellian world of twentieth-century America, too much media can serve to give the public a case of *electronic schizophrenia*.

A Day in New Hampshire

During a snowstorm on a Saturday morning a few weeks before the New Hampshire primary, Mary McGrory of the *Washington Star* followed two young McGovern canvassers up the stairs of a walk-up apartment in one of the French Canadian wards of Manchester. They sat at the kitchen table talking to the middle-aged housewife about Senator McGovern and his policies. The television set was on in the background. They asked what she thought was the most important issue this year.

"Oh, stopping the war up there," the housewife said, gesturing vaguely toward the television set.

"Well, that's what Senator McGovern is for. He wants to stop the war," the canvassers pointed out.

"He can't do that," she protested. "Only the President can do that."

"But Senator McGovern is running for President."

"Oh," the woman said, "I didn't know that."

How could she not have known? She did not live in a remote farmhouse beyond the White Mountains. She lived in the state's biggest city served by a widely read, if somewhat idiosyncratic, newspaper and by several television and radio stations. And McGovern had been actively campaigning in New Hampshire for over a year.

The incident was chastening . . . to anyone who confidently sets out to discuss the effect of television journalism on the electoral process.

It is so easy to assume that because there is a television set in practically every household in the land the information it pumps out will stick in the minds of the viewers. It is also easy to assume that because the millions are more securely "hooked" by television than by any other leisure activity . . . and that because a growing percentage of Americans depend on television to know what is going on in the world . . . the journalistic activities of the medium must have a colossal political effect.

That may be so. Certainly that is what all sorts of people—learned, qualified or not—have been assuming for years, and the literature of their speculation is prodigious. But it remains speculation. . . .

"[T]he real impact of the (television) medium on the American democratic process is still too sparsely documented or analyzed to justify sweeping conclusions." . . .

No One Knows What the Real Impact Is

That does not inhibit politicians who view the medium as one entity (entertainment, journalism and paid political advertising) from leaping to vivid, even exotic conclusions. Harley Staggers, [former] Chairman of the House Interstate and Foreign Commerce Committee, said during hearings . . . that the television networks "can ruin every President and every member of Congress." . . .

Clearly, whether television journalism is a decisive influence on our electoral processes or not, many important politicians *believe* it might be and act accordingly. That is one reality.

Another reality is a paradox. Despite all the attempts of politicians, especially during the Nixon years, to discredit and vilify television journalism, public trust and confidence in television as a source of information has actually grown—and grown, moreover, at the expense of public confidence in government and politicians. . . .

Since 1959, Burns Roper has been conducting regular national surveys to determine public attitudes toward television and the other media. He has found a remarkably steady growth in the percentage of Americans who say they get most of their news about what is going on in the world from television, rather than from radio, newspapers, or magazines. . . .

More interestingly, Roper's survey has traced the relative credibility of the media over the same period. His question has been: "If you got conflicting or different reports of the same news story from radio, television, the magazines and the newspapers, which of the four versions would you be most inclined to believe?"

Television Brings the News

In 1959, newspapers were the first choice with 32% and television second with 29%. But while newspaper credibility has continued to sink from that figure, television's has consistently gained. . . . [By the 1970s, nearly half of all Americans believed television to be the most credible purveyor of news.]

So, despite all the political attempts to discredit television journalism, despite all the theories about the American public instinctively and primitively wishing to punish the bringer of bad news, television is increasingly the medium people rely on for news and the medium in which they increasingly put their trust. . . .

That is where one should start in looking for the possible political effects of television journalism. By 1972, after a quarter-century of growth, television journalism is the most popular, and most highly trusted journalistic medium this country offers and it is seen to be fair. With those facts in mind, it should be an act of basic political common sense for politicians to accept television journalism as an open marketplace for their ideas and to stop trying to hold it up to public scorn. By approaching the medium constructively rather than destructively, politicians could have a considerable influence in making television journalism a lot better than it is.

Television Is Most Trivial

For there is another side of the picture. Television is clearly the most pervasive and vivid medium of political communication today. It is also the most trivial, superficial and, in a sense, irresponsible.

A certain degree of superficiality is inevitable in a mass medium. But there is no inherent limitation requiring television to rejoice in its present superficial treatment of news and public affairs. . . . [I]t does so because of its commercial greed. Television news "shows" (the vocabulary is significant) do not have to bewilder us with a multiplicity of brief, unback-grounded items; they do it to produce a show-business pace and to avoid straining the attention span of the average viewer. The medium does not require newsmen to laugh inanely with each other or to throw snowballs around the studio (as I recently saw them doing on a news program in Florida); they do it to make their shows more entertaining, to enhance the ratings, to attract advertisers.

Television Is Irresponsible

Television is irresponsible not when it does its journalistic duty but because it shirks that duty so often. Under the Communications Act of 1934, television is required to operate "in the public interest." Informational programming, programs about the real world as opposed to fictional, fantasy, escapist programs, are indisputably in the public interest. But although 60% of the American people say they depend on television to tell them about the real world, the industry permits them very limited glimpses. True, television occasionally performs expensive prodigies of journalism at moments of great public interest—space shots, summit meetings, political conventions. But the day-to-day events are treated cursorily at best, and from 7:30 to 11:00 P.M., commercial television continues to feed on a diet of mediocre fiction.

So, this is the context in which the search for political effects of television journalism should be made; a popular and trusted medium, embattled by . . . critics, the chief purveyor of political and other information to the American masses but on a relatively superficial level most of the time.

I believe that the context itself has a certain, though immeasurable, political effect. The level of public information and the motivation to seek information both have a bearing on political behavior. . . . If the medium on which the masses are dependent for information chooses to minimize its journalistic role, that presumably has an effect on the amount of information the public absorbs and on the quality of public understanding of the political issues of the day.

Moreover, although it cannot be documented, I suspect that millions of people do not perceive the informational programming television does offer as essentially different in tone or texture than the rest of what comes at them out of the box. Indeed, the journalistic side of television has been at pains for years to shape the form of its news programs so as to conform as nearly as possible to the patterns of entertainment programs: the commercial interruptions are as frequent and abrupt; there is the same premium on picture and action; newscasters, whether trained journalists or not, have the same qualities of glibness and charm as entertainment personalities; and a great effort is made to avoid straining the audience's intellectual attention span, already conditioned by the overall output of the medium over many years. Furthermore, many of the most popular fictional programs deal with subject matter that is relevant to the real world described in the news but deal with it in a romantic and often highly prejudiced manner. Two obvious examples are the plethora of fictional series dealing with medicine and police work. Both areas involve major areas of controversy in political life today—the quality of American health care and the effectiveness and legitimate extent of the police role. Yet, as frustrated writers of these serials have often complained, these programs reduce all such issues to a bland soup of reassurance in which virtually all doctors are selflessly dedicated miracle-workers and all policemen paragons of virtue and good citizenship. Since such programs vastly outweigh in quantity television's few journalistic attempts to examine these issues objectively, I assume the total impact of the medium is to give the unsophisticated viewer at least a distorted picture of reality. . . .

Impact of Television on Elections

With this context in mind, let us break down into categories what real effect on the electoral process television journalism could possibly have. I think there are four basic areas: the first two operating chiefly *between* election campaigns, the latter two principally as a result of actual campaigns.

Identifying Candidates. By bringing lesser-known personalities before the gaze of millions who do not follow politics intimately, television journalism may give such figures identity and credibility which are prerequisites for office-seeking. There is little doubt that television conveys an impression of personality and character far more vividly than all but the most inspired print journalism. Even viewers only casually interested in politics are liable after a certain amount of television exposure to feel they "know" a public figure far better than if they had merely read about him. Politicians aspiring for office, and their advisers, are anxious to get such exposure on news programs, especially those programs like *Face the Nation, Issues and Answers,* and *Meet the Press,* which show them in a setting reserved for "important" people. In this area, television behaves very much as newspapers do, the criteria for exposure being newsworthiness. At the national level that criterion can be very narrow, often confining the field to a small "club" of already famous people.

Choosing Issues. By the same criterion of newsworthiness, television journalists, like the newspapers, play a major role in setting the parameters of public debate on the issues. In the words of Dr. Ithiel de

Sola Pool, Chairman of the Political Science Department at M.I.T.: " . . . the media are doing exactly what they should be doing, news story by news story. They are recognizing the issues, identifying issues, and thereby making them issues. The power of TV is the immediacy, the rapidity, the overwhelming force that it has in doing this, in taking an event and immediately turning it into an issue on which sides are chosen."

There are ways, other than its vividness and immediacy, in which television works on issues differently than the better print media. Because of the time limitations it imposes on any news treatment, television is liable to present any issue very badly and thus oversimplify it. By its legal requirement to be fair, the industry feels the need often to present sides of an issue in something like mathematical balance. It may often seem that there are equal sides to every issue, pro and con, which is rarely the case. Television journalism may thus help to create artificial polarities in the public mind.

But where television is weakest is in devoting enough time and care in trying to explain the background complexities to issues.

Increasing Voter Turnout. The television industry, in earlier days, used to claim that its efforts had substantially increased voter turnout. This is one area that has been quite well studied and the findings have been negative or inconclusive. In one study William A. Glaser of Columbia University concluded that "newspaper reading may be more effective than television watching in affecting turnout and in affecting the fulfillment of intention to vote."

Affecting Election Results. It is probably futile to ask whether television journalism of and in itself can influence the way voters behave on any election day. There are always simply too many interacting variables: the coverage by other media; the competence and objectivity of the television station or network in question; the effectiveness and amount of paid television advertising by the candidates; the nature of the issues; the relative strengths of the candidates; their telegenic qualities; the success of their campaigns in attracting television news coverage of their activities and, finally, whether or not there are televised debates.

Television Bias Doesn't Affect Elections

I do not know of any campaign, local, state or national, in which it could be said that bias by a television station or network decisively affected the outcome of an election. Edith Efron's painstaking mathematical analysis of network coverage of the 1968 Presidential election in *The News Twisters* attempts to prove that the national networks were biased against

Richard Nixon. If they were, they were unsuccessful in swinging the election against him. While there may be some truth in the frequent charge that the network news departments contain a disproportionate number of so-called Eastern liberals, the news personnel are on the whole too cautious and too professional to be caught up in any conspiracy, conscious or not, to inject consistent bias into coverage of a campaign.

There are, however, some aspects of the manner in which television news works which, together with other forces might have an influence on a campaign. They are worth noting.

Television, for a variety of reasons, does less original reporting than the newspapers and this applies to politics as well to general news. Television tends to follow the pack; it is often reactive. It will cover stories after they have appeared in an influential newspaper or magazine. Television may thus have the effect of reinforcing the points that a print journalist has made and communicating them to a wider and different audience. If the print journalist has slanted the story, or told only part of it, a lazy or rushed television crew may do the same. This is far more likely to happen in the news departments of less competent local television stations than in the networks.

Television has a hunger for action which can be filmed. If a campaign were turning on complex economic issues, for example, voters would be less likely to hear those complexities on television than to see them in the press. If one candidate had an interest in attacking or oversimplifying the issues, and the other in making a complicated defense, the former candidate might benefit from television's tendency to reduce its nightly coverage to a couple of minutes of campaign action with a few snippets from the day's speeches. The . . . California primary contest between Senators McGovern and Humphrey is an example. The nightly news coverage tended to consist of brief snatches of rhetoric, of traded charges and counter charges. Humphrey's interest was clearly in raining fairly simplistic attacks on McGovern's highly complicated economic proposals—to depict them as wildly radical. McGovern was not adept at presenting his economic ideas clearly. Even in the televised debates, which went into far more detail, it was difficult for a voter to understand clearly what the two men were talking about. Fortunately perhaps for McGovern, the election actually appeared to turn on deeper questions of image and credibility.

Television Hungers for Filmable Material

There is another way in which television's hunger for filmable incidents can affect the course of a campaign. For several years now astute campaign managers have realized that what a candidate does on the stump may be far less effective than what he does on television, especially what he can manage to do on television news programs. There he is relieved of the expense of commercials, freed of the taint of image making, and he appears in a context of credibility. His campaign incidents thus have the aura of news. These managers have also discovered that local television stations need to "fill up" their one-hour evening news shows and can be fairly easily seduced into covering almost any incident which makes good pictures. Hence the arrival of the pseudo event as standard campaign procedure, a happening devised to attract television coverage in good time to be processed and edited for the evening news programs. In effect, television is asking the campaign "please fill this space." Campaign managers adept at that will benefit.

Senator Muskie's appearance on a flatbed truck in front of the *Manchester Union Leader* to berate its publisher, William Loeb, was such an event, although notoriously it backfired. Curiously, however, the political impact of Muskie's crying did not come through the television film but through print reporting. CBS had extremely good close-up shots of Muskie, his face half-averted, large flakes of snow falling on his shoulders, his voice constricted. But by itself, the film did not convey the story that the political reporters filed. In the film he looked rather upset. In print he broke down and wept.

There is yet another way in which the nature of television news allows manipulation during a campaign. Many local stations are willing, incredibly it seems, to let a candidate give them his own film or videotape coverage of himself campaigning. And the stations run it in their news programs!

All these mechanical realities are well known to the professionals who run political [campaigns] and, to the extent that these are exploited and television journalism manipulated, they may be having an effect on political process.

But I would like to conclude by speculating about an aspect of television that gets too little attention: who television really talks to.

Define the Floating Voter

For many years political scientists have attempted to define "the floating voter" and there is a widely accepted hypothesis about him. One part of the hypothesis is stated by Philip E. Converse of the Survey Research Center at the University of Michigan: "Not only is the electorate as a whole quite uninformed, but it is the least informed members within the electorate who seem to hold the critical balance of power, in the sense that alternations in governing party depend disproportionately on shifts in their sentiment . . . it is easy to take the stable vote for granted. What commands attention as the governor of party success at the polls, and hence administration and politics, is the changing vote. . . ."

Converse goes on to argue that as the flow of political information has increased in this century, especially through the "spoken media," voting trends show swings of increasing amplitude between the parties at the national level.

These observations hold really important implications for the political impact of television. The floating voter is a person with weak motivation to seek political information. The people with the highest motivation, [or] . . . with more stable partisan identity, seek the most information. Typically they fall into the section of the population with the most education and they rely predominantly on the print media.

While television network research has shown that the audience for their news programs represents something very close to a cross section of the entire population in socio-economic terms, that audience also contains a high proportion of people who read newspapers and magazines very little. So it is probable that the people who decide elections, the floating voters, are the same people who depend more or less exclusively on television for their political information.

Richard Scammon further defines them as the Lower Middle Class. Because they are relatively disinterested in politics and relatively uninformed, they make up their minds very late in a campaign. Media consultants imported increasingly into political campaigns during the 1960's brought with them from Madison Avenue the knowledge that the less people care about something, the more easily they believe what they are told about it. Putting together these facts about the weakly motivated floating voter, dependent on television, inclined to make a late decision trivially, provided the rationale for much of the so-called new media politics.

But the same facts may tell us something about the effect of television journalism. I wonder, in fact, whether television has not done a great deal to stir up in the electorate what it is fashionable this year to call "alienation." The . . . Harris survey on faith in institutions . . . and almost any attitude poll taken by candidates this year reveal widespread disenchantment with political institutions, deep mistrust of politicians as a breed and a conviction that government has consistently lied to the people. These attitudes are concentrated . . . in the same socio-economic group we have been discussing, the Lower Middle Class, the floating voter, the people dependent on television.

It is through television that they will have absorbed the traumas of the past decade. They will have vivid visual memories of riots, wars, assassinations and urgent Presidential appeals, glimpsed through the reassuring twilight of . . . *Bonanza* and *Marcus Welby*. Is it any wonder that they feel disconnected? Television has wooed them for a generation by concocting a womb-warm fantasy of America, a dream world of nice people, solving all problems in the wild west, or the hospitals or the Peyton Places of their lives and solving them *simply* with guns, or aspirins, or fists or laxatives or deodorants—but solving them.

Into Fantasyland
Television Keeps Bursting

Into this fantasyland, however, television journalists kept bursting with increasing frequency . . . like cold strangers breaking down the door, letting in the noise and stink of a dangerous and complicated world outside. Their bulletins were often brief with little to prepare you for the horrors they told of—our kids were fighting another war and *losing,* they were burning the flag, they were tearing up the universities, and they were shouting obscenities at the cops, and the taxes were going up and crime was going up and the blacks were all over the place and President Johnson and President Nixon kept breaking in and saying "believe me, it will be all right." But it didn't get all right. It just got worse. Yet every evening there was television trying to pretend that the good old America of . . . *I Love Lucy* was still there.

If anything was calculated to induce schizophrenia, this conditioning would. And television journalism did little to help people understand. The better educated people, whose college years had given them some sense of history and perspective were disturbed too, but they could go outside television to books, newspapers and magazines, for deeper explanations of what was happening to the country. The others were trapped and confused.

Every critic of television journalism has complained that where the industry fails most is in explaining the news, putting events into perspective, telling the "why." Yet the people who depend on television for their information need such perspective more than the others. It may well be that we are now reaping the harvest of that neglect.

People Trust Television

The people who depend on television trust it, as we noted earlier, but they look at the entire output of the medium, not just the pockets of news. Taken as a whole, that output has presented a disconnected and schizophrenic view of America. On the one hand the industry was trying to do its duty journalistically, on the other it was trying to be a more efficient vehicle for commercials. Given the nature of its devoted watchers, and their probable role as floating voters, it would be very surprising if television has not contributed substantially to the disorientation and volatility of the . . . election scene.[20]

Television's Split Personality

Consistent with this split personality of television, the word *qualified* best describes much of the available evidence of this medium on voter reaction. Robert Bower noted in *Television and the Public*[21] that information based on data gathered by the Bureau of Social Science Research in Washington, D.C., seems to substantiate a lukewarm appraisal. The television viewing public is seen as generally endorsing the format and journalistic roles of the media but being little persuaded, one way or the other, by the impact of media coverage of politics.

"Television does not tend to favor one faction over another in such a way as to suggest a partisan political influence during a campaign. . . . [Thus] to an amazing degree the perceived effects of television political coverage are spread evenly among the public."[22] That is to say, the impact of television may be of a very gradual nature, raising the political awareness of a heretofore apolitical segment of the population, but not influencing them to support any one particular party or faction. In part, this may help explain the drift of a significant portion of the population into the growing ranks of the Independents.

If television is bringing on a schizophrenic reaction because of its "Bionic Woman" versus "Sixty Minutes" coverage of American society, it may become even more important to try and understand whether or not political television advertising really has the desired political impact. A question which then becomes significant to the potential candidate and to the *image builder* is, Which approach is most successful in gaining new adherents to the *cause?* In 1972 the controlled press conference was engineered by the Nixon advisers to draw on the credibility of such programs as "Meet the Press" and "Face the Nation," while offering the candidate the opportunity to expand on his own philosophy. In Alaska, Mike Gravel employed the legitimacy of the documentary technique of

    [20]From Robert MacNeil, "Electronic Schizophrenia: Does Television Alienate Voters?" *Politeia* 1 (Summer 1972): 5–10.

    [21]Robert T. Bower, *Television and the Public* (New York: Holt, Rinehart, Winston, 1973).

    [22]Ibid., p. 128. Also see "Election Coverage '72: How Fair?" *Columbia Journalism Review* 11 (January–February 1973): 9–42.

Guggenheim to tell his political story. Both examples were clever and updated variations of the 60-second political spot first used in the 1952 Eisenhower campaign. But in the final analysis, how effective is television advertising? Does it change the course of history as Joe McGinnes's book, *The Selling of the President, 1968,* would have us believe?

Does Money Mean Victory?

In 1972 the media budget of Richard Nixon's presidential campaign was 4.4 million dollars. George McGovern spent 6.2 million dollars. For Nixon this was a cut of nearly two-thirds over his 12.6-million-dollar media expenditure in 1968. The reason was simple. Nixon didn't need the name identification that can be created through television, so he spent less. But would more exposure have turned the tide for McGovern? Could the "mystics of media," if given enough air-time and money, have sold McGovern to a majority of the American people. Obviously not.

So what? you say. The candidacy of George McGovern made 1972 a somewhat unique year for the presidential race. Nevertheless, the Gallup Poll demonstrated that between April 1972 and the election in November, Nixon's popularity ran between 53 and 62 percent. McGovern, on the other hand, stayed between 34 and 38 percent.[23] As one journalist quipped, "Senator McGovern was a kind of third-party candidate, and he came in third in a field of two. . . ."[24] Thus the impact of media on his campaign was slight. But can this be generalized in all presidential campaigns?

In 1968 from Labor Day to Election Day, Richard Nixon spent $12 million on advertising, mostly on television.

Hubert Humphrey spent $6 million.

George Wallace, running the most expensive third-party campaign in history, spent $3 million on advertising.

As an advertising professional and a sometime political consultant . . . I submit that the expenditure of this $21 million—an annual rate equivalent to the combined budgets of Coke, Pepsi and 7-Up—was marginally effective, at best. Political advertising in a presidential campaign, particularly the barrage of 20-, 30-, and 60-second commercials, is a highly overrated art. . . .

[23]Gallup Poll, *Washington Post,* 10 September 1972, p. A-3. Gallup Opinion Index, Report no. 89, November 1972, pp. 1–3.

[24]Shana Alexander (*Newsweek* journalist and CBS commentator), in *Crisis In Confidence: The Impact of Watergate,* ed. Donald W. Harward (Boston: Little, Brown, 1974), p. 43.

Does Television
Change Popularity?

Mr. Nixon's 43% popular vote on Election Day was identical to his showing in the public opinion polls the previous May. And during that time, his strength never varied significantly from the 42%–45% range. At best, you could say that the advertising held together his natural coalition and furthered some kind of defensive strategy that worked—barely.

Three weeks after our Humphrey commercials began, the polls had him at 28%—the low point of the campaign. Then, in a 30-minute program televised on Sept. 30 he moved a millimeter to the left of President Johnson on the Vietnam issue. Suddenly the polls improved, money came in, the campaign caught fire. It was not a Svengali-like ad man who turned the trick. It was a straight-to-the-camera speech by a candidate demonstrating (albeit too late) some guts and credibility.

Was even the Wallace campaign anomalous? In late September the Gallup Poll gave him 21% of the vote. Then he named Curtis LeMay his running-mate and proceeded to spend the bulk of his advertising money. On Election Day he polled less than 14%.

. . . Congress, to a chorus of hosannas from editorial writers and columnists, has . . . passed legislation to limit—somehow the word seems inappropriate—political advertising in presidential campaigns . . . [Proportional limits also apply to House and Senate candidates and to primary elections.]

The seminal thinkers in the press who have suggested that our next President might emerge from a Wheaties box have hailed the end of a grave threat to the Republic. What Congress has done, however, and what the press and the liberal lobbies think it has done, are two different things.

Congress, recognizing the extraordinary power of incumbency, has closed a few loopholes. . . . [but] has made it a lot harder for an insurgent candidate to win nomination for a House or Senate seat. The press, with its traditional distrust of television, has welcomed the bill almost without reservation. Meanwhile, the positions of both Congress and the press rest on the implicit assumption that political advertising is sheer magic.

All this attention devoted to political advertising is mildly interesting to the general public, and highly gratifying to those of us who dabble in politics. But, sad to say, most of what is written about political advertising is born of ignorance—not stupidity.

Hardly anyone has any real facts. In focusing on ethics and finances we've skipped over the pragmatic question of effectiveness. In a presidential general election, despite the lack of objective evidence, the tautology goes something like this: If advertising works most of the time, and television is an all-pervasive medium, then political television advertising must work most of the time.

Granted, political commercials (not programs, telethons, etc.) can make a candidate's name and face well-known; and they can, through sloganeering, focus on the basic appeal that distinguishes a candidate from his opponents. But, do our presidential candidates need "recognition"? Do they suffer from underexposure? Were Mr. Humphrey and Mr. Wallace drowned out by Mr. Nixon? No, I think the electorate was more than surfeited by daily media coverage. As for slogans, 1968 produced nothing better than "Nixon's the One," which ranked somewhere below "Phooey on Dewey" for catchiness. Mr. Nixon's working slogan for . . . [1972 was] "A good, honest President." Will the Madison Avenue boys never cease to top themselves?

Considering politicians' penchant for "accountability," why will we see so much political advertising this year if it's impossible to determine its value?

The answer, in part, is that the political marketplace has done nothing more than borrow the imprecise research techniques developed in the packaged goods world; and it is still impossible to isolate quantitatively the effectiveness of most consumer advertising. But we'll undoubtedly continue to be bombarded with political commercials for three reasons—at once less technical and more emotional.

First, political advertising is not illegal. And when you run for President this kind of negative logic is ineluctable.

A second reason political advertising is here to stay is that it has bred its own bureaucracy. Today's young, tough campaign manager did his apprenticeship in "media politics." He knows more about television and charisma than canvassing or precinct captains, and once the campaign gets serious he calls in a television expert. At this point the candidate, already depressed by the endemic confusion, is ready to believe that advertising can play a crucial role and, further, that it will lend focus to a foundering operation.

Most important, however, is the candidate's predisposition to believe that television has some special magic. It takes enormous ego to run for office, especially for President. In the quiet recesses of his soul no man can truly feel equipped for the job. Perhaps, he reasons, advertising will imbue him with the "look" of a President. Then—if elected—the job itself will ennoble him. (Consider Ed Muskie: In 1968 he looked to many like Abraham Lincoln incarnate. . . . [However], after his televised announcement speech, he was asked whether his language might not have been too tough. He answered by saying that the program could have used some "cosmetic" improvements. Instead of worrying about whether his speech had a political cutting edge, he was more concerned that his television crew had made him look mummified.)

Advertising in primaries is a different story, of course. The presidential primaries . . . are a . . . circus (with five or six featured rings). Voter interest is low, media coverage is limited, issues are localized and some candidates are relatively unknown.

So advertising is often important—especially to the underdog who has little time to get his name and story across. Still, television can't guarantee victory—even to the candidate who greatly outspends his opponents—

any more than heavy introductory advertising guarantees sales for a new toothpaste. . . .

In placing limitations on primary spending, Congress has deliberately made access to political office much more difficult. The legislation not only favors incumbents, but it shores up the waning power of the political clubhouse. Insurgent candidates often relied on advertising because they didn't have an army of bell-ringers from the patronage rolls. Now renegades will pose less of a threat to the regular party organization.

You Can Buy a Seat in Congress but Not the Presidency

Fear not. If you are very rich and very handsome, Daddy may still be able to buy you a seat in Congress. But buying the presidency just isn't in the cards—there are too many other variables more critical.

If wealth, good looks and sophisticated advertising could turn the trick, Nelson Rockefeller would have been in the White House long ago. He could handle Messrs. Goldberg, O'Connor, Morgenthau and Harriman in New York, but on the presidential trail he has been humbled on successive occasions by the sons of an Arizona haberdasher and a gas station owner from California.

Sooner or later either you must assume that the media men can manipulate the electorate, or you can take solace in the voters' ultimate intelligence. Most conventional wisdom holds with the manipulation theory, but it overlooks the distinction between advertising's pervasiveness and its power. I prefer to believe that in presidential elections the voters wisely and instinctively reject most issue-related appeals (they've been burned too often) and make a conscious visceral decision on the basis of trust. . . .[25]

What About Lesser Office?

If there is, as we have already seen, a question about the effectiveness of television advertising for presidental aspirants, what about lesser offices? There is no doubt that some of the billboards between the candidate's home and campaign headquarters may very well exist to reassure the candidate and his volunteers. Nor can anyone deny the pressures applied by young congressional campaign managers who were bred on media politics.

[25]From Allen D. Gardner, "Political Ads: Do They Work?" *Wall Street Journal*, 1 February 1972, p. 10.

Nevertheless, comparing presidential politics with congressional or other similar races is like comparing Jack Anderson with the home-town newspaper's political columnist. Both are ace journalists, but the similarity ends there. Likewise, the media needs of a presidential aspirant are in a different class than those of a congressman. Where name identification is necessary, then media can have spectacular successes. The Metzenbaum–Glenn race in Ohio, Gravel in Alaska, and Tunney in California are just a few examples.

But perhaps in the end the old-line political campaigner's remarks are as good as an evaluation of political advertising as any: "Politicians don't really know what combination of events are needed to win an election—so they stand back and use the shotgun technique. Some of what they do isn't necessary. Some of the money spent isn't needed. But in which area can a campaign cut expenses? It's better to hit them all, rather than risk losing because you guessed wrong." Was Nixon's victory in 1968 because advertising held his coalition together? Or did it create the coalition?[26] Such questions, generally unanswered, assure the continued success of the campaign consultant industry. For in today's complicated arena, a consultant may be what's needed to *get it all together,* even when the ingredients are already there. Consultant John Deardourff remarked that victory can be helped along by media, but if the candidate is not sincere or has no real issue, media won't make any difference.[27]

The Need for Sincerity

This belief in a need for sincerity and a person is perhaps the most noticeable result in the post-Watergate era. Sincerity and honesty are being demanded as prerequisites for candidates, even at the expense of such important issues as inflation and resource shortages. Today's candidate must convince the public that above all else he is credible and open. He cannot rely on issues or even experience to sell himself as the best alternative. In part, Ted Kennedy's withdrawal from considering the 1976 presidential race was a reaction to this new force. He even alluded to the fact that the Chappaquidick scandal had partly influenced his decision. Whether or not such a mood will continue indefinitely among the American electorate is, of course, problematical. But reforms passed and/or proposed in Congress and demanded by such growing powers as Common Cause, seem to indicate a continued interest by the public.

[26]The polls in the year preceding the 1968 election showed Nixon with a popularity of between 42 and 48 percent. In November 1968 the actual count gave him 43 percent of the popular vote.

[27]John Deardourff, in Perry, op cit.

People Want to Know
About the Candidate

"People will want to know what the candidate believes in before they want to know what's he's going to do about Interstate 75 . . . candidates . . . [should] first demonstrate to voters that they're honest people, make some value statements and hammer out the issues in print."

John Deardourff, a Washington consultant who works mostly with moderate Republicans, is thinking along the same lines. He is working with William C. Milliken, the Republican governor of Michigan, who is seeking a second full term.

When Milliken ran in 1970, his campaign stressed the specific issues and accomplishments of the two years Milliken then had spent in office. This year, Deardourff is advising Milliken to talk about his personal background—his legislative experience, his education, even his war record. Deardourff wants the human side of his candidate to come through first.

"I'm not sure it's at all unhealthy," said Deardourff. "During one term, a governor or senator will have to confront issues that nobody can predict at the moment. There ought to be more attention paid to the guy's background rather than to how he will vote on abortion."

I. Robert Goodman, a Baltimore consultant who also works with Republicans, believes the de-emphasis on issues simply reflects the profession's growing awareness of the things that have been influencing voters for a long time. "I think people have always voted for people," Goodman said. "According to surveys, they have always voted on honesty, competence and charisma, in that order. Many times issues are only used as a foil to express personal virtue. Our candidates have been expressing personal qualities since we've been in business."

One campaign that has been a major influence on consultants was the 1972 Senate race in Delaware. Democrat Joe Biden, a 29-year-old county councilman, who was almost unknown in the state when the campaign began, won a stunning victory over two-term incumbent Republican J. Caleb Boggs. Biden came out of that campaign saying that people voted for him because they trusted him, not because they agreed with him on specific issues.

Issues Don't Make
Much Difference

"I don't think issues mean a great deal about whether you win or lose," Biden said in a 1974 speech. "I think issues give you a chance to articulate your intellectual capacity. Issues are a vehicle by which voters determine your honesty and candor. I don't think a right or wrong answer on an issue makes up anyone's mind but the ideologues', and I distrust ideologues.''

The consultant who worked with Biden in 1972 was John Marttila of Boston. . . .

It is not clear how much of a role Marttila actually played in developing the ''sincerity first'' strategy for Biden in 1972. ''Nobody ran my campaign but me,'' Biden insisted, ''and ask John Marttila, who came in to run my campaign . . . I said, 'John, let me pay you $30,000 and don't interfere. The money will come back fourfold.' '' Biden explained that he found it hard to raise funds unless he could invoke the name of a nationally known consultant.

Whatever the origins of ''sincerity first'' in 1972, it is clear that Marttila and other consultants are convinced of its value . . .

''It showed everybody, . . . that if you get off your ass and recognize a voting audience that is frustrated because it doesn't have any access to the incumbent, you can overcome some very big odds.''

Former Rep. Nick Galifianakis (D 1967–73), running for the Senate in North Carolina, is sticking closely to the theme that issues are not what really counts. ''I think what you really have to demonstrate this time is that you care,'' Galifianakis said in a speech. ''I don't think it's vital that you know all the answers to all the issues. I think it is vital in order to restore confidence that you show you can handle the job and that you do care.''

Some political consultants are skeptical of a campaign year in which issues are secondary. ''I don't separate issues from personality,'' said Charles Guggenheim, a Washington film-maker for Democratic candidates. ''Candidates are in the business of issues. It's like trying to judge a lawyer who won't address himself to the law.''

Sanford Weiner, a California consultant who works for moderates and liberals of both parties, is even more blunt. ''Everyone is trying to put out the facade of honesty, purity and holiness,'' he said. ''The public is not going to buy that any more than they buy the other crap they put out. What they're looking for is a candidate who's credible on any issue he talks about. They know the great white knight isn't going to ride down the trail.''

If honesty is the desired effect . . . , personal contact is the method. . . .

Preach Personal Contact

But it is easier to preach personal contact than to establish it. Biden blanketed Delaware in person, but Delaware is barely larger than most House districts. Candidates running for governor or senator in most states

EVERYTHING IS GOING GREAT!
NOW ALL WE HAVE TO DO IS CHANGE HIS IMAGE.

Copyright © 1974, reprinted by permission of *Saturday Review/WORLD* and Evelyn Shafer.

. . . are confronted by the impossibility of meeting every voter they seek to convert.

Long-distance walks have worked because they have drawn television coverage, not because the candidates have met every voter in person. And most consultants agree that the tactic is too familiar now to generate the kind of news interest Sen. Lawton Chiles (D Fla.) received in 1970 when he popularized the tactic.

Some consultants are skeptical of the trend toward personal contact. "I think it's a little idealistic," said John Deardourff. "The hard reality of most elections," said Deardourff, "is that the constituency is too large for it. Almost every other form of campaign activity is a substitute for personal contact." . . .

Campaign Problems Guarantee the Use of Television

The problems inherent in conducting a personal campaign by canvassing or computer just about guarantee that television will be the main vehicle for whatever techniques of persuasion are dominant. . . .

Nothing illustrates that better than the thinking of Napolitan, who has always gone in heavily for television and is sometimes credited with inventing the pre-election media blitz.

In 1968, Napolitan helped win the Democratic Senate primary in Alaska for Mike Gravel by blanketing the state with a 30-minute film on Gravel the week before the election. Gravel leaped from obscurity to defeat Sen. Ernest Gruening (D 1959–69) and won the election in November.

Two years later, Napolitan was working for Maryland Gov. Marvin Mandel (D). Rumors persisted that R. Sargent Shriver, the former Peace Corps director, planned to return to Maryland and challenge Mandel in a Democratic primary. Napolitan used a barrage of early television commercials to create the impression that Mandel was invincible. Shriver stayed out.

Napolitan will be using television again . . . for Mandel and Gravel, among others, but he insists there will be few blitzes and little commercialism. "I think you will see a lot more of candidates speaking directly to the people on television," Napolitan said. He was working with Jerome Cavanagh, a Democratic gubernatorial candidate in Michigan, before Cavanagh's sudden withdrawal because of illness in April.

What they were planning was a series of five-minute television essays in which Cavanagh would address the voters in his own voice, while seated at a desk. It did not differ much from what candidates did on television in the early 1950s, before the medium became more sophisticated.

Very Low Key

"It's very low-key, eyeball-to-eyeball stuff," said Napolitan. "It takes it back to the beginning. Voters are more sophisticated. We used to do very sophisticated things on television, but now they're no longer new. How long can you get away with things? Something is only new once."

In 1966, Napolitan advertised Milton Shapp's campaign for governor of Pennsylvania with the slogan, "Shapp makes sense for Pennsylvania." One reason he cannot [presently] employ that approach for anyone . . . is that General Motors is using it to sell Chevrolets.

Deardourff, working on the Republican side with Gov. Milliken in the same race Cavanagh dropped out of, agrees that obvious commercialism is unlikely to work well. . . . Working with New York Gov. Nelson A. Rockefeller in 1966, Deardourff helped with a television campaign of slick cartoons designed to sell Rockefeller's re-election. "I don't think we could ever go back to those Rockefeller '66 commercials," said Deardourff. "We had animation, fish talking to each other, a road unwinding to Hawaii to show how many highways he had built."

"It's now up to the candidate to prove himself," Goodman commented. "The so-called imaging that is done is now only in terms of flattering camera angles and technical things."

Allen is also experimenting with a more direct approach to television. "The filming I've done so far," he said, "has accentuated direct eye contact with the voter. I still do it outdoors, because I like light. But very direct, simple rationale. . . . With most candidates I even try to have the candidate write the first draft of the essay, because he's almost like a newsman, trying to communicate his feelings to the people.''

Weiner said almost exactly the same thing. ''We're doing a lot of straight head-shot talking film, without people around, or the background stuff we used to used quite heavily. It's focusing on the face of the candidate, the eyes in particular.''

If the idea of direct contact sounds elementary, it is useful to remember that as late as 1970, most political television was not done this way. Consultants borrowed heavily from commercial advertising, often making 30- or 60-second spots in which a narrator, not the candidate himself, made the sales pitch. In some cases, the candidate did not appear at all.

Former Rep. Richard L. Ottinger (D N.Y. 1965–71) became a landmark figure in political television in 1970 when he won New York's Democratic Senate primary with a blitz of commercials that cost about $1-million. Produced by film-maker David Garth, Ottinger's commercials hammered at one simple phrase, ''Ottinger Delivers.'' . . .

But Ottinger faded badly in the general election campaign, and after he lost, observers noted that he suffered from the discrepancy between the fighting image Garth had built for him in the primary and the mild manner he later displayed in person.

The ''Ottinger syndrome'' quickly joined the vocabulary of political consultants. As Guggenheim put it, ''If a guy comes off differently in paid advertising than he does in the news, you're in trouble.''

If Ottinger's problems were one reason for consultants to turn away from outright commercialism, another was a study done after the 1970 election by Walter DeVries, a political scientist and a consultant in his own right. Questioning Michigan voters about the things that influenced their vote, DeVries found that television ads ranked 24th. Television news ranked first.

The solution, consultants reasoned in 1972, was to make their commercials look more like news and less like soap advertisements. That meant a move toward the kind of work Guggenheim had been doing for years—films of candidates moving and talking among the voters, with little script and no hard sell. It was the application of *cinema verité* to politics.

. . . [S]ome consultants are saying that even *cinema verité* must yield to the direct approach of the 1950s. Some argue that few voters make the distinction between *cinema verité* advertising and ''Ottinger Delivers'' advertising.

Public Wasn't Buying Spots

''We came to the conclusion at the end of last year,'' said Weiner, ''that the public wasn't believing the *cinema verité* kind of spot any more. The public was considering that as phony as the other kind.''

Guggenheim, who said he is disturbed by what he considers the faddish quality of the consulting profession, said he makes films based on what his clients are trying to express, rather than on what other consultants have decided is fashionable. "I'm always very suspicious . . . of people who say, 'Now we'll do this and now we'll do that, and now we'll sit someone behind a desk. . . .' The only good political advertisers are those who have gut feelings and value systems," Guggenheim said. "The ones who deal in formulas or styles or trends are fraudulent. Any candidate who takes that kind of advice is a fool." . . .

Consultants concede that many of them tend to sound alike at a given time. One reason may be the frequent meetings consultants hold to assess the state of their art and suggest new possibilities. After each major election there is a post mortem at which consultants offer theories about what worked and what did not. These sessions may determine the clichés of the next campaign.

After the 1970 election, consultants discussed the limited effect of media blitzes and the need to tone down the commercialism of their television advertising. One result was the "news look" of 1972. At the end of the 1972 campaign, consultants met to discuss the Biden upset and the year's other surprises. The consensus was that candidates who make a personal impression on the voters have an important advantage. That may be why sincerity and personal contact are familiar words. . . .[28]

Sincerity and the Personal Approach

If *sincerity* and *personal approach* are the bywords of the post-Watergate years, some consultants may be surprised if government and the public at large also look back to the simple sincerity of the 1950s to solve what they consider to be the "crap proliferation" put out by the Napolitans and Guggenheims.

Nicholas Johnson, one of the most outspoken members of the Federal Communications Commission in recent years, perhaps stated it best when he remarked that regulation in the *public interest,* the discussion of political issues, was not something that was alien to democratic societies. Indeed, other civilized countries controlled media to prevent just the type of political manipulation of the public interest as is done so successfully by the image merchants. He asserted that an effort to raise public awareness of politics and limit the impact of the image builders would not be so major a task as many suggest. Through the use of free air time and public discus-

[28]From "Campaign Consultants: Pushing Sincerity in 1974," *Congressional Quarterly: Weekly Report,* 4 May 1974, pp. 1105–1108.

sion of issues the general interest would be better served.[29] **This is not to say that Mr. Johnson advocates controlled media. Indeed, he firmly believes in the** *marketplace of ideas.* **But supporting the continuation of the market-place should be the aim of any regulatory agency whose responsibility is to safeguard freedom of expression. In this regard he feels there is a much greater danger to the exchange of ideas than that posed by the image merchants. These purveyors of** *instant success and charisma* **must face the public with their product as does Coca-Cola or Dial. The public's purchase of their product is measured in victory or defeat at the polls.**

However, there are dangerous, subtle forms of media manipulation that in the long run constitute the more serious threat to the public's decision-making ability.

Subtle Dangers Go Beyond
Television Con Men

Publishers and reporters are not alike in their ability, education, tolerance of diversity, and sense of responsibility. The hidden or overt pressures of advertisers have long been with us.

But one aspect of the problem is [clear] . . . the impact of *ownership* upon the content of the mass media. . . . There are a number of significant trends in the ownership of the media worth examining—local and regional monopolies, growing concentration of control of the most profitable and powerful television stations in the major markets, broadcasting-publishing combines, and so forth. But let's . . . look at the significance of media ownership by "conglomerate corporations"—holding companies that own, in addition to publishing and broadcasting enterprises, other major industrial corporations. . . .

Since the ITT-ABC case left the Commission[30] I have not ceased [to be] troubled by the issues it raised. . . . I ponder what the consequences might have been if ITT's apparent cynicism . . . had actually been able to harness the enormous social and propaganda power of a national television network to the service of a politically sensitive corporate conglomerate. . . .

I do not believe that most owners and managers of the mass media in the United States lack a sense of responsibility or lack of tolerance for a

[29]Mike Wallace interviewing Nicholas Johnson in "T.V. and Politics" (CBS White Paper), 1971.

[30]This case reached to the FCC in 1966 with the proposed merger of the American Broadcasting Co. and ITT. The discussion raised the serious question of the use of a major media network to subtly influence public opinion in favor of the interests of an economic conglomerate. While the case became moot because the merger proposed was cancelled, the questions raised were left unanswered.

diversity of views. I do not believe there is a small group of men who gather for breakfast every morning and decide what they will make the American people believe that day. . . .

On the other hand, one reason evidence is so hard to come by is that the media tend to give less publicity to their own abuses than, say, to those of politicians. The media operate as a check upon other institutional power centers in our country. There is, however, no check upon the media. Just as it is a mistake to overstate the existence and potential for abuse, so, in my judgment, is it a mistake to ignore the evidence that does exist.

In 1949, for example, it was reported that officials of the Trujillo regime in the Dominican Republic had paid $750,000 to officers of the Mutual Radio Network to gain favorable propaganda disguised as news. (Ownership of the Mutual Radio Network changed hands once again a few years later without any review whatsoever by the FCC of old or new owners. The FCC does not regulate networks, only stations, and Mutual owns none.) RCA was once charged with using an NBC station to serve unfairly its broader corporate interests, including the coverage of RCA activities as "news," which other newsmen considered unnewsworthy. There was speculation that after RCA acquired Random House, considerable pressure was put on the book publishing house's president, Bennett Cerf, to cease his Sunday evening service as a panelist on CBS's *What's My Line?* The Commission has occasionally found that individual stations have violated the "fairness doctrine" in advocating causes serving the station's economic self-interest, such as pay television.

Virtually every issue of the *Columbia Journalism Review* reports instances of such abuses by the print media. It has described a railroad-owned newspaper that refused to report railroad wrecks, a newspaper in debt to the Teamsters Union which gave exceedingly favorable coverage to Jimmy Hoffa, the repeated influence of the DuPont interest in the editorial functions of the Wilmington papers which it owned, and Anaconda Copper's use of its company-owned newspapers to support political candidates favorable to the company.

Edward P. Morgan left ABC to become the commentator on the short-lived Ford Foundation-funded Public Broadcasting Laboratory. (He has since returned to ABC.) Mr. Morgan has always been straightforward, and he used his final news broadcast before going to PBL to be reflective about broadcasting itself. "Let's face it," he said. "We in this trade use this power more frequently to fix a traffic ticket or get a ticket to a ball game than to keep the doors of an open society open and swinging. . . . The freest and most profitable press in the world, every major facet of it, not only ducks but pulls its punches to save a supermarket of commercialism or shield an ugly prejudice and is putting the life of the republic in jeopardy thereby."

Economic Self-Interest
Plays a Role

Economic self-interest *does* influence the content of the media, and as the media tend to fall into the control of corporate conglomerates, the areas of information and opinion affecting those economic interests become dangerously wide-ranging. What *is* happening to the ownership of American media today? What dangers does it pose? Taking a look at the structure of the media in the United States, I am not put at ease by what I see.

Most American communities have far less "dissemination of information from diverse and antagonistic sources" (to quote a famous description by the Supreme Court of the basic aim of the First Amendment) than is available nationally. Of the 1500 cities with daily newspapers, 96 percent are served by single-owner monopolies. Outside the top 50 to 200 markets there is a substantial dropping off in the number of competing radio and television signals. The FCC prohibits a single owner from controlling two AM radio, or two television, stations with overlapping signals. But it has only recently expressed any concern over common ownership of an AM radio station and an FM radio station and a television station in the same market. Indeed, such ownership is the rule rather than the exception and probably exists in your community. In more than 70 communities *all* media outlets are owned by a single newspaper-radio complex, and more than 90 communities are dominated by newspaper-television joint ownerships. Most stations are today acquired by purchase. And the FCC has, in part because of congressional pressure, rarely disapproved a purchase of a station by a newspaper.

There are few statewide or regional "monopolies"—although some situations come close. But in a majority of our states—the least populous—there are few enough newspapers and television stations to begin with, and they are usually under the control of a small group. And most politicians find today, as Congress warned in 1926, "woe be to those who dare to differ with them." Most of our politics is still state and local in scope. And increasingly, in many states and local communities, Congressmen and state and local officials are compelled to regard that handful of media owners (many of whom are out-of-state), rather than the electorate itself, as their effective constituency. Moreover, many mass media owners have a significant impact in more than one state. One case that came before the FCC, for example, involved an owner with AM-FM-TV combinations in Las Vegas and Reno, Nevada, along with four newspapers in that state, seven newspapers in Oklahoma, and two stations and two newspapers in Arkansas. Another involved ownership of ten stations in North Carolina and adjoining southern Virginia. You may never have heard of these owners, but I imagine the elected officials of their states return their phone calls promptly.

Monopolies Control the News

The principal national sources of news are the wire services, AP and UPI, and the broadcast networks. Each of the wire services serves on the order of 1200 newspapers and 3000 radio and television stations. Most local newspapers and radio stations offer little more than wire service copy as far as national and international news is concerned. To that extent one can take little heart for "diversity" from the oft-proffered statistics on proliferating radio stations (now over 6000) and the remaining daily newspapers (1700). The networks, though themselves heavily reliant upon the wire services to find out what's worth filing, are another potent force.

The weekly newsmagazine field is dominated by *Time, Newsweek,* and *U.S. News & World Report*. (The first two also control substantial broadcast, newspaper, and book or publishing outlets. *Time* is also in movies [MGM] and is hungry for three or four newspapers.) Thus, even though there are thousands of general and specialized periodicals and program sources with significant national or regional impact, and certainly no "monopoly" exists, it is still possible for a single individual or corporation to have vast national influence.

What we sometimes fail to realize, moreover, is the political significance of the fact that we have become a nation of cities. Nearly half of the American people live in the six largest states: California, New York, Illinois, Pennsylvania, Texas and Ohio. Those states, in turn, are substantially influenced (if not politically dominated) by their major population-industrial-financial-media centers, such as Los Angeles, New York City, Chicago, and Philadelphia—the nation's four largest metropolitan areas. Thus, to have a mjaor newspaper or television station influence in *one* of these cities is to have significant national power. And the number of interests with influence in *more* than one of these markets is startling.

Most of the top fifty television markets (which serve approximately 75 percent of the nation's television homes) have three competing commercial VHF (very high frequency) television stations. There are about 150 such VHF commercial stations in these markets. Less than 10 percent are today owned by entities that do not own other media interests. In 30 of the 50 markets at least one of the stations is owned by a major newspaper published in that market—a total of one-third of these 150 stations. (In Dallas–Fort Worth *each* of the network affiliates is owned by a local newspaper, and the fourth, an affiliated station, is owned by Oklahoma newspapers.) Moreover, half of the newspaper-owned stations are controlled by seven groups—groups that also publish magazines as popular and diverse as *Time, Newsweek, . . . , Parade, Harper's, TV Guide, Family Circle, Vogue, Good Housekeeping,* and *Popular Mechanics.* Twelve parties own more than one-third of all the major-market stations.

In addition to the vast national impact of their affiliates the three television networks each *own* VHF stations in all of the top three markets—New York, Los Angeles, and Chicago—and each has two more in other cities in the top ten. RKO and Metromedia each own stations in both New York City and Los Angeles. Metromedia also owns stations in Washington, D.C., and California's other major city, San Francisco—as well as Philadelphia, Baltimore, Cleveland, Kansas City, and Oakland. RKO also owns stations in Boston, San Francisco, Washington, Memphis, Hartford, and Windsor, Ontario—as well as the regional Yankee Network. Westinghouse owns stations in New York, Chicago, Philadelphia, *and* Pittsburgh, Pennsylvania, Boston, San Francisco, Baltimore, and Fort Wayne. These are but a few examples of today's media barons.

There are many implications of their power. Groups of stations are able to bargain with networks, advertisers, and talent in ways that put lesser stations at substantial economic disadvantage. Group ownership means, by definition, that few stations in major markets will be locally owned. (The FCC . . . approved the transfer of the last available station in San Francisco to the absentee ownership of Metromedia. The only commercial station locally owned today is controlled by the San Francisco *Chronicle.*) But the basic point is simply that the national political power involved in ownership of a group of major VHF television stations in, say, New York, Los Angeles, Philadelphia, and Washington, D.C., is greater than a democracy should unthinkingly repose in one man or corporation.

Increasing Purchase of Media by Conglomerates

For a variety of reasons, an increasing number of communications media are turning up on the organization charts of conglomerate companies. And the incredible profits generated by broadcast stations in the major markets (television broadcasters *average* a 90 to 100 percent return on tangible investment annually) have given FCC licenses, particularly owners of multiple television stations like the networks, Metromedia, Storer Broadcasting, and others, the extra capital with which to buy the New York Yankees (CBS), Random House, (RCA), or Northeast Airlines (Storer). Established or up-and-coming conglomerates regard communications acquisitions as prestigious, profitable, and often a useful or even a necessary complement to present operations and projected exploitation of technological change.

The national problem of conglomerate ownership of communications media was well illustrated by the ITT-ABC case. But the conglomerate problem need not involve something as large as ITT-ABC or RCA-NBC. Among the national group owners of television stations are General Tire (RKO), Avco, Westinghouse, Rust Craft, Chris Craft, Kaiser, and Kerr-McGee. The problem of *local* conglomerates was forcefully posed for the FCC in another case early in 1968. Howard Hughes, through Hughes Tool Company, wanted to acquire one of Las Vegas's three major television stations. He had recently acquired $125 million worth of Las Vegas real estate, including hotels, gambling casinos, and an airport. These investments supplemented 27,000 acres previously acquired. The Commission majority blithely approved the television acquisition without a hearing, overlooking FCC precedents which suggested that a closer examination was in order. In each of these instances the potential threat is similar to that in the ITT-ABC case—that personal economic interests may dominate or bias otherwise independent media.

The problem posed by conglomerate acquisitions of communications outlets is given by a special but very important twist by the pendency of sweeping technological changes which have already begun to unsettle the structure of the industry. . . .

General Sarnoff of RCA has hailed the appearance of "the knowledge of industry"—corporate casserole dishes blending radio and television stations, networks, and programming; films, movie houses, and record companies; newspaper, magazine, and book publishing; advertising agencies; sports or other entertainment companies; and teaching machines and other profitable appurtenances of the $50 billion plus "educational biz."

And everybody's in "cable television"—networks, books publishers, newspapers. Cable television is a system for building the best TV antenna in town and then wiring it into everybody's television set for a fee. It improves signal quality, increases the number of channels, and has proved popular. But the new technology is such that it has broadcasters and newspaper publishers worried. For the same cable that can bring off-the-air television into the home can also bring programming from the cable operator's studio, or an "electronic newspaper" printed in the home by a facsimile process. Books can be delivered (between libraries, or to the home) over "television" by using the station's signal during an invisible pause. So everybody's hedging their bets—including the telephone company. Indeed, about all the vested interests can agree upon is that none of them want us to have direct, satellite-to-home radio and television. But at this point it is not at all clear who will have his hands on the switch that controls what comes to the American people over their "telephone wire" a few years hence. . . .

Foolish to Try
to Restructure the Media

It would be foolish to expect any extensive restructuring of the media in the United States, even if it were considered desirable. Technological change can bring change in structure, but it is as likely to change to even greater concentration as to wider diversity. In the short run at least, economics seems to render essentially intractable such problems as local monopolies in daily newspapers, or the small number of outlets for national news through wire services, newsmagazines, and the television networks. Indeed, to a certain extent the very high technical quality of the performance rendered by these news-gathering organizations is aided by their concentration of resources into large units and the financial cushions of oligopoly profits.

Nevertheless, it seems clear to me that the risks of concentration are grave.

Chairman Philip Hart of the Senate Antitrust and Monopoly Subcommittee remarked by way of introduction to his antitrust subcommittee's . . . hearings about the newspaper industry, "The products of newspapers, opinion and information, are essential to the kind of society that we undertake to make successful here." If we are serious about the kind of society we have undertaken, it is clear to me that we simply must not tolerate concentration of media ownership—except where concentration creates actual countervailing social benefits. These benefits cannot be merely speculative. They must be identifiable, demonstrable, and genuinely weighty enough to offset the dangers inherent in concentration.

This guideline is a simple prescription. The problem is to design and build machinery to fit it. And to keep the machinery from rusting and rotting. And to replace it when it becomes obsolete.

America does have available governmental machinery which is capable of scotching undue accumulations of power over the mass media, at least in theory and to some extent in practice. The Department of Justice has authority under the anti-trust laws to break up combination which "restrain trade" or which "tend to lessen competition." These laws apply to the media as they do to any other industry. . . .

[But] only the FCC is directly empowered to keep media ownership patterns compatible with a democracy's need for diversified sources of opinion and information. . . .

The American people are indebted to the much maligned FCC for establishing these rules. Imagine, for example, what the structure of political power in this country might look like if two or three companies owned substantially all of the broadcast media in our major cities.

. . . It forces one to question whether government can ever realistically be expected to sustain a vigilant posture over an industry which controls the very access of government officials themselves to the electorate.

I fear that we have already reached the point in this country where the media, our greatest check on other accumulations of power, may themselves be beyond the reach of any other institution: the Congress, the President, or the Federal Communications Commission not to mention governors, mayors, state legislators, and city councilmen. Congressional hearings are begun and then quietly dropped. Whenever the FCC stirs fitfully as if in wakefulness, the broadcasting industry scurries up the Hill for a congressional bludgeon. And the fact that roughly 60 percent of all campaign expenses go to radio and television time gives but a glimmer of the power of broadcasting in the lives of Senators and Congressmen.

. . . And if we are unwilling to discuss this issue fully today we may find ourselves discussing none that matters very much tomorrow.[31]

---

[31]From Nicholas Johnson, *How to Talk Back to Your Television Set* (New York: Bantam Books, 1970), pp. 39–69.

10

Challenge of Decision Making: A Serious Game of Politics

Introduction

As you are no doubt aware, the style of this book has attempted to provide you with a significant departure from the traditional textbook approach to the study of American politics. The objective was to offer a *behind the scenes* insight of American political reality. In pursuit of this goal, we have extensively supplemented our own writing with the views and interpretations of professional political consultants, social scientists, journalists, and politicians.

As one old-line politician once told a campaign strategy committee, "There is nothing that can test the spirit of a man like the excitement and competition of politics and war. It can bring out the worst and best of you. The most impressive advantage of politics is that the chances of getting shot is minimal." This perspective was candidly attested to by Aaron Donner, Congressman Pike's campaign manager. He was in politics for more than public service. Donner's love of the challenge and excitement was inherent in the remark that the fun of campaign politics "is in being an amateur and figuring out how you're going to correct all the mistakes you've made."

The problem for most of us is that to arrive at the level of politics where the clash of political arms is most exhilarating, often takes many years of experience. Yet in the game of politics, one can never totally discount the role of chance. In a field where campaign decision makers are becoming increasingly younger, an individual in the right place, at the right time, can be thrust into a critical campaign position. The remainder of this book has been designed to offer you another option to gain an *insider's* perspective on politics.* Through the medium of a simulation game you can make the transition from reading and discussing the campaign process to actually experiencing the dilemma of these demands.

In the role of a candidate or member of the campaign steering committee you will acquire the *feeling* of campaign pressures and frustrations because you will no longer be the removed observer. As a consequence you are asked to interpret the information of the previous chapters and the data supplied in the Appendices, because it is *you* who must make the political decisions. The "Rules of the Game" (see below) partially structure this effort, as do the campaign laws for your own congressman. The excitement is provided by the participants themselves, as the decisions and actions of the simulation force them to compete with opposition campaigns for good media exposure.

Given the spontaneity arising from this approach, there is no answer book provided. Within the perimeter of the "Rules of the Game" almost anything can, and often does, happen. The success of you and your campaign is dependent on the combined resourcefulness, creativity, and judgment that you exhibit in the interactions of your own campaign and with the competing campaign(s) and media.

Though the wide acceptance of serious gaming as a learning device for political science courses is of a recent origin, the technique has a long and respectable lineage. The ultimate goal has been discovery, what it's *really like.* Whether the gaming is sponsored by the Department of Defense, a business corporation, or a political campaign, the goal is the same: discovery.

As for political simulations, approaches similar to this one have been executed for many years by noted leaders in the field of professional campaign management. In fact, they have considered simulation of the opposition's campaign to be of prime importance.[1] Today presidential

---

Note to the student: Because this chapter offers a learning device that necessitates your active involvement, we feel that it would be antithetical to provide one orientation to you and another to your instructor. Consequently we have decided to integrate any recommendations, advice, and rationale on the use of this learning medium into one message. As you read the following pages, you will note that the target of the message vacillates from you to your instructor. However, you will find it to your benefit to read everything, including those communications on which your instructor will make his or her decisions on the use of this gaming experience. Although your instructor must make the final decisions, you will gain by having a more comprehensive understanding of the game.

[1]Stanley Kelley, Jr., *Professional Public Relations and Political Power* (Baltimore: John Hopkins Press, 1966), p. 49.

campaigns invest considerable resources in computer simulations of their political adversaries' campaigns.[2]

Although the advantages of gaming to politicians and their consultants have been proven, educators have also begun to discover benefits of serious political games. When used as a learning tool, the immediate application of classroom skills to a real-world situation stimulates motivation. Therefore, an inherent quality of this approach is that students become willingly involved because the readings take on a sense of relevancy. This self-motivation characteristic was well documented by a pattern that consistently emerged during the three years we tested various approaches to campaign gaming with freshmen and sophomores. The initial student concern with grade criteria disappeared as they immersed themselves in pursuing the objectives of the simulation. This response was the result of the competitive nature of the game itself and the realization that an active role in the learning process could be fun. That's right, serious campaign gaming is actually fun!

Perhaps one of the most important considerations of the gaming program offered in this book is its flexibility and adaptability to a wide array of teaching styles and course contents. From the traditional American government courses to sophisticated political seminars, this game will provide a viable form of learning experience. The basic simulation model has been designed for completion during four 50-minute class sessions: strategy meeting of steering committees; news conferences; public forum speeches; and an evaluation of simulation experience. Consequently the minimal cost in terms of class sessions permits real consideration of campaign gaming in almost any course offering that pertains to American politics and government. As for class size, this simulation has been successfully used with varying numbers of participants. The campaign gaming model can be effectively adapted to several approaches—laboratory, modular, or retreat.*

If the laboratory approach is used, the instructor can specify that a certain day of each week will be set aside for campaign gaming. On the specified day, over a period of four weeks, participants will engage in simulation activities. The advantage of this scheduling approach is that it can be routinely integrated into the curriculum while extending the vitalizing characteristics of simulation for a longer period of time. Furthermore, the delay between game sessions will provide the participants more time for presimulation preparations.

The modular approach concentrates the campaign simulation activi-

[2]Ithie de Sola Pool et al., *Candidates' Issues and Strategies: A Computer Simulation of the 1960 and 1964 Presidential Elections* (Cambridge, Mass.: M.I.T. Press, 1965).

*Note to instructor: See Appendix B for recommended scheduling of these approaches in terms of varying length (semester, quarter, trimester, or retreat).

ties during a block of time, perhaps at the end of the course. The advantage of the modular technique is that the concentration of the gaming permits the participants to become more immersed in their campaign experience. Evidence indicates that there is a positive relationship between role immersion, motivation, and the resultant learning process.

The retreat technique is more dramatically removed from traditional educational confines, at least in appearance. Nonetheless, it simply converges the modular technique with an exciting adaption of the tried-'n'-true seminar approach. The retreat approach does, however, provide the opportunity to offer the campaign simulation experience as a mini-course under the auspices of traditional college catalog listings such as "directed studies," "special studies," and so on. The other *plus* of the retreat approach is that the isolation character of a retreat atmosphere maximizes the immersion of participants into the gaming experience. The students can actually *live* in a structured campaign atmosphere for a couple of days.

It is also of importance to emphasize that, with the exception of this book, the gaming model makes no assumptions on the political knowledge and/or experience of the participants. Thus, a class of freshmen in an introductory course in American government can effectively utilize this gaming program. On the other hand, even this basic gaming model can expand the understanding and insights of more advanced students. The reasons for this are significant. First, the great majority of students, regardless of their background in political science, are limited by the traditional academic style of readings, discussions and lectures. This is not to discount the value of traditional political science, but only to recognize the obvious limitations.

In fact, the second reason that more advanced students can enhance their political understanding *vis-à-vis* the gaming experience is because of their mastery of the factual and conceptual dimension of politics gained through traditional means. That is to say, advanced students will be more perceptive of the subtleties in this campaigning gaming program because of their academic background.

The campaign simulation is structured around the center of any campaign organization—the steering committee. The function of the steering committee is to chart the overall strategy and tactics of the campaign. To provide the expertise for this level of decision making, the membership includes representation from all major functional areas of the campaign: the candidate, the manager, and a chairperson to accept responsibilities in the areas of public opinion analysis, issue analysis and development, demographic analysis, voter turnout analysis, and media relations.

It is the overriding purpose of each campaign steering committee to calculate their decisions in a manner which best enhances the competitive advantage of their candidate over opposition candidate(s) for the office of congressman in the 17th Congressional District. To accomplish this objective, each steering committee must use the various data provided in the Appendices, in addition to drawing on perspectives offered earlier in this book.

Once the philosophical position of the candidate is determined, you must then compete for media coverage. This is where your media relations with the only significant newspaper in Metro City—*The Metro News*—becomes critical. For reasons that have never been adequately explained, the influence of the *Metro News* on voters is phenomenal. Some discount this influence by saying that the *Metro News* only appears critical because it endorses obvious winners. Nevertheless, no candidate for a major political office has won in the last 20 years that did not receive the editorial endorsement of this newspaper.

Thus you should have a general familiarity with at least the process of how the *Metro News* decides which candidates shall receive their editorial blessing. The decisions are made by the editorial board one week before election day. Earlier that same day the editor-in-chief of the *Metro News* (whose role is played by your instructor) meets with the political editor and political reporters (whose roles are played by fellow student participants) to discuss the assets and liabilities of candidates. The purpose of this discussion is to recommend endorsements to the editor-in-chief. Rumor has it that the editorial board listens intently when the editor-in-chief recommends specific candidates be endorsed by the *Metro News*.

From this brief overview it becomes clear that the simulation is organized around those decisions which relate to the overall strategy and tactics of the campaign process. The criterion of success is the effectiveness that each steering committee has in communicating their candidate's image and message to the voters via one mass medium. As with any workable simulation, several components of the real world have been abstracted. By isolating these elements and collapsing the time and space dimensions for the gaming participants, it becomes possible to approximate the experiences that are taking place in campaigning with a surprising degree of accuracy. Although the abstract level of all gaming models fall short of reality, they allow the participants to grapple with experiences that are *realistic*.

Campaign Tactics

Before proceeding to the "Rules of the Game," let us say a few words on tactics. Tactics are specific actions to accomplish the strategic objectives of the campaign. Some of the more common approaches in the *care and feeding* of the political campaign that could be used in this simulation include:

APPROACH	EXAMPLE
Attack	"In the 15 years of alleged public service, my opponent has failed to . . ."
Challenge opponent to debate	"The citizens of our community have a right to hear my opponent and myself confront each other on the real issues of this campaign. And I am most anxious, at any reasonable time or place to . . ."
Creating impressions	"No! The sexual indiscretions of my opponent will not be an issue in this campaign. The people want to hear positive alternatives, not another 'flim-flam' account of the personal life of . . ."
Creation of ad hoc committees	Committee of Young Attorneys for . . .
Making issue appeals to particular voter groups	Labor, elderly, and so on
Campaign on candidate's record	"At a time when some candidates are trying to create a new image for themselves, I am proud of what I have accomplished in my years of public service. . . ."
Announcement of group endorsements	"I am most appreciative of the endorsements of . . . but the final decision is yours—the voters of Metro City."
Asking the endorsement or active assistance of community or political leaders	A popular U.S. senator
Shifting responsibility	"If we look beyond the inferences of my opponent to the facts of the situation, we will discover . . ."

In selecting to use any of these tactics, it must be remembered that your candidate will be held accountable for any ethical implications of the tactical decisions of the steering committee.

Rules of the Game

As we have emphasized, campaign gaming is a dynamic medium to gain new insights into the decisions (and nondecisions) that create the ballyhoo of campaign politics. However, simulations are only successful if the gaming model is clearly developed and if precise instructions are provided to the participants. Thus the need to understand the perimeters of the simulation and the organizational procedures outlined below is imperative.

1. Evidence gathered during the pretesting of this simulation indicates that the most effective orientation to this gaming model is one that is provided early in the term. Early timing of the orientation not only allows the students to adjust their pregaming preparations to the scheduling approach, but it also affords an opportunity for delineating any adjustments to the basic simulation model. Furthermore, early introduction to a *foreign* learning process often converts initial apprehensions into stimulants for curiosity and interest among students. For these and other reasons, instructors have found it most convenient to integrate considerations of the simulation into the general orientation to the course.

2. Because this simulation was designed to permit its use with a broad spectrum of courses dealing with American government and/or politics, no special effort is necessary in selecting other books to mesh with gaming experience. As noted, the contents of this book offer adequate information for meaningful participation. However, reading the previous chapters of this book by two weeks or so prior to the first day of formal gaming activities (the strategy meeting of the steering committees) is strongly recommended. This gives the students an adequate *political* perspective in approaching pregaming preparation. In addition, it allows sufficient time to focus on this chapter and to apply pertinent data from the Appendixes.

3. Two weeks before the first day of formal gaming activities, a few minutes should be reserved to divide the class into two groups (or more if the gaming activities are to include minor parties) for each simulation. Each of these groups will be a campaign steering committee of the political party to which they are assigned. The number of participants in each steering committee should not exceed the size of a discussion group (10 to 15 persons) and may include as few as 5 persons. This latitude in the number of participants per steering committee allows adjustment to meeting the size of the class and the number of political parties in each simulation. If the class is very large, more than one simulation can take place concurrently. At this time 3 to 5 persons should be assigned the roles of *Metro News* reporters for each simulation.

4. During the interim between the creation of steering committees and the first in-class gaming activities, the members of each committee must review and scrutinize the data contained in this chapter and the Appendices. With this task completed, each steering committee can arrange one

or more informal meetings to make presimulation considerations, decisions, and actions, which include:

(a) selection of a candidate whose profile is consistent with the party image you wish to espouse while holding promise of being a competitively viable in the upcoming congressional race. (See Appendix A, Candidate Profiles.)*

(b) Put out an informational news release accompanied by a fact sheet on your candidate. (See Appendix C, Confidential Packet from Congressional Campaign Committee, Items 4 and 5, respectively, for news release format and sample candidate fact sheet.)

(c) Selection of a campaign manager and the delegation of the following functional responsibilities to steering committee members—public opinion analysis, media relations coordination, issue analysis and development, demographic analysis, voter turnout analysis. (See Appendix C for an orientation to Metro City, the 17th Congressional District, and specialized data.)

(d) Tentative selection of campaign issues and preliminary development of a stance on these issues. (See Appendix C, Confidential Material from Congressional Campaign Committee, Item 3, Issues and Issue Development.)

(e) Preliminary development of the overall strategy and theme of the campaign.

5. To keep lines of communication open, all news releases must be provided to at least the editor-in-chief and either the manager or media relations director of opposition campaign committee(s).

6. The campaign manager has the responsibility for directing the efforts of the steering committee and, consequently, the thrust of the campaign. When properly coordinated, the expertise of each steering committee member will meaningfully contribute to the success or failure of the campaign effort.

7. Whether or not the candidate can veto the decisions of the manager and/or the steering committee is a matter that must be grappled with by the participants of each committee.

8. In the pregaming period each political reporter can direct his professional efforts toward writing articles that give perspective on the editorial position of the *Metro News* (that is, editorials on a critical local issue, analysis of the impact of campaign reform laws, and the like). To facilitate communication, all news and editorial articles must be provided to the editor-in-chief and either the manager or media relations director of each campaign steering committee. (See Appendix C, Confidential Material from Congressional Campaign Committee, Item 3, for a listing of potential campaign issues.)

---

*Note to all participants: For purposes of this simulation, it shall be assumed that the candidate profile selected by each steering committee has been nominated in the primary election by the respective political party.

9. Media relations directors will find the pregaming period an excellent time to acquaint themselves with news reporters and prepare them for upcoming news releases. A good media relations director will establish a cooperative, if not cordial, relationship with media reporters early in the primary campaign. For purposes of this gaming experience, this must be accomplished before the in-class simulation sessions. Make a concerted effort to become friendly with reporters. See to it that they meet with your candidate in an informal manner. Determine their attitudes and opinions. If a particular reporter writes good articles, compliment the individual on the even-handed manner in which the subject was handled, etc. If you find a reporter who reflected favorably on your candidate, you may find it advantageous to provide this individual with an early press release or exclusive information.

10. All participants are expected to facilitate communication during in-class sessions by wearing a color-coded identification badge that identifies them by name, campaign role, and campaign steering committee.

In-Class Activities

Session #1. *Strategy Meeting of Steering Committee.* **The purposes of the first formal simulation session are to set the basic strategy of the campaign and to finalize the position of your candidate on the issues that have been selected. (See Appendix C, Confidential Material from Congressional Campaign Committee, Item 3.) Though the confidentiality of this meeting will justify the exclusion of reporters, you may wish to adjourn the meeting early enough to answer their questions before the end of the class session.**

Based on the conclusions of this strategy meeting you should send out an informational news release that focuses on a major issue of the campaign. The release should allude to the rationale for your candidate's position on this issue.

Session 2. *News Conference.* **All campaign committees will have their media relations director present a news release to the *Metro News* reporters before this gaming session begins. The news release will function to kick off the general election campaign of the candidates and should include any prepared remarks that your candidate will make at this news conference. The prepared remarks of each candidate should be no more than 3 to 5 minutes in length.**

The format of this news conference calls for the reporters to ask questions of each candidate immediately after their prepared remarks. *

---

*Note to reporters: It is your responsibility to be the *public watchdog* during this simulation. Thus you would be remiss in your duty to rely simply on campaign committee news releases for writing editorials and news stories. You must take an aggressive posture

In a 50-minute class session the maximum time allocation of the prepared remarks and the question-and-answer session for each major party candidate should not exceed 20 minutes. Consistent with the intent of this simulation to approximate realistically campaign-media relations, the minor-party candidate(s) shall have whatever portion of this gaming session that remains.

Session 3. *Bipartisan Public Forum.* Your candidate has accepted an invitation to speak at an all-day candidate's fair sponsored by the State University of Metro. This event has been extensively promoted and should draw a good crowd. Because RYI-TV is videotaping the speeches of congressional candidates for delayed broadcast, all congressional candidates will be allocated equal time at this forum—maximum 7 minutes each. News reporters will be present, and they usually have questions—at least for *serious* candidates. So your candidate should be prepared to answer a probing question or two. Your candidate should also be prepared to handle pointed questions from the opposition, for it is not uncommon to attempt to embarrass a political adversary at events of this nature. In fact, some candidates wait for exactly this type of an opportunity to challenge the opposition to a debate.

Session 4. *Evaluation of the Simulation Experience.* This session can prove to be the most valuable of the simulation, for it places the happenings of the gaming experience in perspective. The objective is to illuminate the subtleties of the learning that transpired as the gaming participants grappled with the realism of political decision making.*

The format of this session is a discussion led by a panel of political reporters. The focal point of the discussion will be why the *Metro News* endorsed one candidate and failed to endorse other candidate(s). It is imperative that the reporters are prepared to list specifically the factors that influenced the editorial position of their newspaper. It is recommended that the reporters summarily list and explain these influences before taking questions from members of the steering committees.

---

in searching out information. Only in this way can you provide the public with in-depth news analysis.

Do not hesitate to seek out independent sources of information. Examine the background of the candidates (see appendix A). If a candidate is evasive in a public statement ask pointed questions. Look for inconsistencies between a candidate's past record and campaign rhetoric. If you find a discrepancy, insist on an explanation. And finally, do not forget to use the Confidential Material from the Congressional Campaign Committee (Appendix C) provided to you by a friendly candidate.

*Note to editor-in-chief and reporters: The editor-in-chief will meet informally with political reporters at a mutually convenient time between Sessions 3 and 4 to discuss the endorsement of candidates by the *Metro News*. The editorial endorsements of the *Metro News* should be posted before Session 4.

APPENDIXES

APPENDIX A
Candidate Profiles

NAME:	James T. Newton
AGE:	35
MARITAL STATUS:	Married in 1971, no children
EDUCATION:	B.A. in political science, University of Michigan, 1962; L.L.B., Yale, 1964
OCCUPATION:	Attorney
ANNUAL INCOME:	$19,000
RELIGIOUS AFFILIATION:	Methodist
ETHNIC BACKGROUND:	Afro-American
MILITARY:	United States Navy, honorable discharge in 1968
HEALTH:	Excellent
APPEARANCE:	Handsome young man with athletic physique; played football in college; keeps in shape through exercise program; likes health foods
WIFE'S APPEARANCE:	Young and quite attractive; involved in several youth projects and is rather outspoken on civil rights

Personal Characteristics

As a man who intends to make his mark on society, Newton's social-professional-political schedule is of unbelievable proportion; but he thrives on it. He is a very personable individual who radiates an aura of self-confidence. Though sometimes frustrated by injustices in the black community, he has moderated the radicalism of his younger years in order to achieve effective political action. He is active in the Urban League, ACLU, and several youth groups, including Big Brothers, as well as UGN, Lions, and Rotary.

Political Background

Since his days as an undergraduate, Newton has been active in politics, serving in student offices and working as a campaign volunteer in several legislative races. In 1963 he joined the ranks of another breed of activists as a participant in Mississippi sit-in demonstrations and registration drives. After his discharge from the Navy, he returned to establishment-type political action.

In 1966, Newton was elected to the county committee of the party and served on the executive committee. He was later appointed to the party's state central committee. With his partisan base established, he ran successfully for the state legislature in 1968. As a state senator, he has exhibited leadership on the Social and Health Services Committee and the Urban Transportation Committee. Though not serving on the Elections and Constitution Committee, Newton has been most outspoken on the issue of open government and election reform.

NAME:	Dorene Jansen
AGE:	29
MARITAL STATUS:	Single
EDUCATION:	B.A., San Jose State College (now known as California State University at San Jose), 1965; M.A., special education, Columbia University, 1967; graduate study in psychology, Columbia University, 1967–68
OCCUPATION:	Director of psychological counseling, Metro City School District
ANNUAL INCOME:	$21,000
RELIGIOUS AFFILIATION:	None
ETHNIC BACKGROUND:	English
HEALTH:	Excellent
APPEARANCE:	Attractive

Personal Characteristics

Dorene Jansen may reject the feminist rhetoric, but her accomplishments stand as evidence that she will not allow sexual stereotyping to hinder her personal or professional life style. She has been referred to as pleasantly aggressive. During a few years in the Metro City school system she has converted her concern for disadvantaged students (retarded or psychologically troubled) into districtwide programs to assist these students. The program is well funded, is professionally staffed, and has widespread community support.

Political Background

Despite the demands of her administrative responsibilities, Dorene Jansen has been actively involved in the civic affairs of Metro City. Her activities began after the realization that community support was a prerequisite to jarring support for program ideas from the Board of Education. By early 1971 she had organized the Committee of Concerned Parents into a potent lobby force. Her political activities then spread to include leadership roles in school levy campaigns, the Committee for a Responsive City Council, and the Coalition for Campaign Reform. As chairman of the campaign reform group, her actions were most instrumental in the enactment of state legislation.

NAME:	Howard V. Hartman
AGE:	25
MARITAL STATUS:	Single
EDUCATION:	B.A., philosophy, State University of Metro, 1975; graduate study in philosophy, 1975 present
OCCUPATION:	Graduate student
ANNUAL INCOME:	$6,500
ETHNIC BACKGROUND:	German
MILITARY:	None
HEALTH:	Excellent
APPEARANCE:	Handsome young man; wardrobe vacillates from "proletariat" to "mod," depending on the occasion

Personal Characteristics

Hartman sees that the end to America's problems can only come with the downfall of the capitalist system and the end of our imperialism abroad. Capitalism and militarism place acquisition and power before human needs.

The Watergate and CIA exposés are only symptomatic of the pervasive corruption of our nation. The United States and its people are controlled by big business and a personal greed that is caused and perpetuated by a capitalist state.

Political Background

Hartman was active in the Student Mobilization Committee and was chairman of the Metro City Peace Coalition in 1971. In 1974 he made an unsuccessful bid for the governorship as a Socialist Worker Party candidate.

NAME:	Gerald R. Goldman
AGE:	51
MARITAL STATUS:	Married in 1952; divorced in 1960; remarried in 1962. Gerald, Jr., and Lisa, children of his first marriage and in his custody, are students at the University of California, Berkeley
EDUCATION:	B.S., University of Michigan, 1944; Ph.D., M.I.T., 1949.
OCCUPATION:	Professor of mathematics, State University of Metro
ANNUAL INCOME:	$20,000
RELIGIOUS AFFILIATION:	Jewish
ETHNIC BACKGROUND:	Slavic
MILITARY:	Army intelligence, honorable discharge, 1956
HEALTH:	Excellent
APPEARANCE:	Distinguished-looking man who looks at least 10 years younger than his actual age
WIFE'S APPEARANCE:	Looks about her age (44); pleasant person but generally very quiet

Personal Characteristics

Dr. Goldman possesses a brilliant mind and is most articulate. He is highly respected by friends, colleagues, and students. Because of the prestige received from his professional excellence, he exercises considerable influence in professional circles. Perhaps for this reason, in conjunction with his brilliant mind, he resents taking directions from anyone. As a man who advocates and practices efficiency, he is most impatient with the absence of long-range planning, with organizational bungling and with general incompetence.

Political Background

Dr. Goldman, after several years active partisan activity in the party, decided in 1959 to express his political concerns in city politics. After careful examination of the political setting, he declared his candidacy for the city council. After his successful bid for office in 1961, he served two terms but was surprisingly (at least to him) defeated in 1965. Since that time he has refrained from vying for elective office. However, he has remained politically active in local issue politics. In addition to his professional affiliations, Dr. Goldman has remained active in such organizations as Lions, Elks, and Kiwanis. He is also active in B'nai B'rith. Since 1965 he has given assistance to several congressional and state legislative candidates. In this role he has been particularly valuable in organizing demographic and similar voter analysis.

NAME:	Thomas J. Olson
AGE:	58
MARITAL STATUS:	Married in 1934. His son, John, has taken over his insurance business in upstate New York. Olson's younger son is an officer in the U.S. Navy.
EDUCATION:	Studied business administration at the University of Buffalo from 1930 to 1931
OCCUPATION:	Retired businessman, formerly a corporate real estate investment consultant
ANNUAL INCOME:	$35,000
RELIGIOUS AFFILIATION:	Lutheran
ETHNIC BACKGROUND:	Scandinavian
MILITARY:	Served in U.S. Army as corporal in World War II, honorable discharge in 1945
HEALTH:	With exception of sporadic discomfort from an ulcer, health generally good
APPEARANCE:	Relaxation of retirement has expressed itself in a slight paunch; well-dressed man with an occasional flare for the "now" look
WIFE'S APPEARANCE:	Looks younger than her husband although she is actually one year his senior; dresses well but has a tendency to be a bit of a snob

Personal Characteristics

Though Olson continues a relatively active social life, his time orientation to achievement has been somewhat frustrated after the first year of his inactivity. He sees himself as a self-made man; his successes are attributable to hard work, sacrifice, common sense, and a little luck. His business was started from scratch.

Political Background

Olson has never had time for the luxury of active political participation. Only recently has he begun to make somewhat modest political contributions to candidates whom he favors. However, he has different plans for the future. With the free time of his present position he feels that he has an obligation as a good American to express his concern through political leadership. Some individuals from his area have encouraged him in this thought.

APPENDIX **B**
Scheduling Recommendations

Modular Technique

	Quarter System	*Semester and Trimester System*
Fri.	Strategy meeting of steering committee	Strategy meeting of steering committee
Sat.		
Sun.		
Mon.	News conference	News conference
Tues.	Public forum speeches	
Wed.	Evaluation of simulation experience	Public forum speeches
Thurs.		
Fri.		Evaluation of simulation experience

Retreat Technique

First week of term   Orientation and assignment of readings
Midterm   Divide class into steering committees and assign political party.
Provide all students with class roster, which includes phone numbers and identification of steering committee or newspaper role assignments.
Discuss readings

Second week prior   Meeting to discuss readings and to remind students of
to retreat   pregaming activities

Retreat Schedule

Saturday	8:00–8:25 A.M.	Orientation
	8:30–8:55 A.M.	Coffee break
	9:00–12:30 P.M.	Strategy meeting of steering committees
	2:00–3:00 P.M.	News conference
	7:00–8:30 P.M.	Steering committee meetings
Sunday	9:30–11:00 A.M.	Public forum speeches
	11:00	Meeting of editor-in-chief and reporters
	12:00	Announcement of *Metro News* endorsements
	1:30	Evaluation of simulation experience

APPENDIX **C**

FOR THE EYES OF CAMPAIGN STAFF ONLY

METRO CITY

CHOICE COUNTRY FOR LIVING AND BUSINESS

Located where the mountains meet the sea. In clear view to the north are two snowcapped mountains. To the east are the beaches of Whalers Sound. A few minutes drive will take you to the serenity of Crystal Lake.

Metro City is a place of wide streets, appealing homes, modern shopping centers and excellent schools. In the last decade the city's population has multiplied sixfold in a pattern of carefully planned growth and now ranks among the most desirable places to reside in the state.

Metro City has also become the prestige address for the regional offices of many national firms. They occupy the spacious office buildings that have been constructed in recent years. Light industry is also encouraged and there are presently several strategically located industrial parks. Pepsi-Cola operates a large bottling plant. Mayfair's $25 million regional distribution center is located in Metro City. Examples of other major employers include Trafco Electronic, Framm Inc., Whalers Sound Power and Light, Northwest Car and Foundry, General Electric, and Metro State University. Also in close proximity are the aerospace industries in Felton and the maritime related industries to the south.

Metro City is the educational heartland of the state. Not only is the median educational level of our area the highest in the state; we take great pride in the quality of our educational institutions. State University of Metro is outstanding, as are our three community colleges and public school system.

METRO CITY
Incorporated 1955

20/20

1955 • 1975

POPULATION
68,958 • 575,000

BANK DEPOSITS
$63,711,000 • $2,295,092,000

POSTAL RECEIPTS
$1,053,360 • $25,155,000

ASSESSED VALUATION
$50,400,000 • $2,970,325,099

GROSS SALES
$288,000,000 • $5,272,351,200

BUILDING PERMITS
$27,180,000 • $248,273,955

HIGH SCHOOLS
4 • 12

JUNIOR HIGH SCHOOLS
12 • 24

ELEMENTARY SCHOOLS
19 • 61

Other schools: State University of Metro,
Community College—3,
private schools—14
Area: 225 square miles, 12,000 acres
elevation—168 feet
Climate: mean temperature, 46.4° min., 60°
max/mean annual precipitation,
34.10 inches
Churches and congregations: 113
Clubs and associations: 1100
Public libraries: 13
Memorial Hospital: 1300 beds
Transportation: rail Burlington Northern, Inc.
bus Metro Transit
Suburban Airporter
air Riker Air Field
Metro International
Airport

ON TWO INTERSTATES: 67 and 301

Come Visit with Us

The lodging and dining facilities of Metro City
make it an outstanding place for conventions
and conference groups alike. If you are looking
for a city to combine a little fun after the
business meeting, Metro City offers enough
diversity for every taste. Outdoor activities,
quality cultural events, or good night life—the
choice is yours.

For a new business location, Metro City
possesses the prime elements—a growing local
market, handsome executive offices, reasonably
priced land, and a cooperative local government.

Whatever your needs—a new home or place of
business, vacationing, convention, or browsing
in a specialty shop—you will find a friendly
welcome in Metro City. The Metro City
Chamber of Commerce is always ready to
answer your inquiries if you desire any further
information.

Chamber of Commerce
100 E. Main Street
Metro City, U.S.A.

From the Desk of
CONGRESSIONAL CAMPAIGN COMMITTEE CHAIRMAN

This material is representative of the new approach of your party to assist your campaign. In contrast with the past, we are experimenting with a localized information program for our candidates. Although the information is by no means exclusive in nature, we feel that it will save your campaign staff precious time in the coming months.

If at any time you believe that I or any of the specialists here in Washington can be of any help, feel free to call me.

APATHETICS KEY TO UPCOMING ELECTIONS!!
(Washington News Syndicate)
Washington—The victors in the November election may very well undermine both Democratic and Republican hopefuls. This newly revived and powerful political entity that raises its threatening head in the political arena this year is running no candidates. It is not a new political party. The membership is made up of those that have soured on what one network calls "Campaign American Style." In fact, many political analysts are saying that a significantly large percentage of Americans have been "turned off" by politics in general.

The state of affairs has grown to such proportions that even presidential elections are shaking fewer and fewer of the "potential" American electorate from their easychairs. Since the hotly contested Kennedy–Nixon race of 1960, when 59% of registered voters cast their ballot, voter turnout has sequentially dropped in every presidential election.

POLITICIANS BY ANY OTHER NAME?
(Knight News Service)
By Abe Zaidan*

The common theme of most politicians running for office this year is that they are not politicians. As it was explained to me the other day by a truck driver who is running for county commissioner, "I am very qualified for the job because I am not a politician," which is another way of paraphrasing Charles de Gaulle's "Politics is too important to leave in the hands of politicians." (My French isn't that good but it's close enough.)

Because of the problems in Washington these days, it is very hard to find anybody who will admit that he is a politician, a professional title that someday may go the way of undertakers and garbagemen (which translates roughly today as "morticians" and "sanitation workers").

But if one who has embarked on a career of politics is not a politician, then what is he? That has become one of the profound questions of this political year, and so far, no one has answered it to

*The Seattle Times, 16 April 1974

the satisfaction of the (public, voters, electorate, constituency—choose one).

One veteran officeholder has pondered the evolutionary conflicts of his profession deeply and has confessed that, in the final analysis, he remains a politician, for better or worse, "because I have learned to think in those terms since puberty. If I had been anything but a politician for the past 25 years, I could have never served in public office." Indeed, he may be right. There is a certain inconsistency in people aspiring to political office who scorn the title of politician. And a certain innocence, too.

The road to political office is littered with the carcasses of nonpoliticians whose hearts were pure and techniques were disastrous. They might as well have announced their candidacy for quarterback of the Miami Dolphins, where professional football players get paid for being professional football players, and if you don't know how to play the game, you are likely to be carried off the field in several pieces.

The characteristic flaw in nonpoliticians is that they have trouble raising campaign money, put their billboards in

418

the wrong places, spend their evenings talking to a few friends and wear their campaign buttons under their lapels.

There is nothing morally wrong with these political figures. In fact, they are usually refreshing.

But in the end, it's the street-smart seasoned politician who wins on election day. And even for nonpoliticians, . . . winning is the name of the game. Or what's a nonpolitical campaign for?

UNIVERSITY OF METRO TO HOST CANDIDATES' FAIR
(Metro News Service)
Political Americana will be theme of the all-day candidates' fair at the State University of Metro on October 27. Candidates for all political offices in the state, as well as congressional seats and ballot issue spokespersons have been invited to attend.

Underlying the hoopla of the bunting, ballons and entertainment, "the objective of this nonpartisan forum is to provide the voters with information on candidates and issues," according to David Flax, director of the event. Flax went on to point out the unique advantage to the voter of the nonpartisan nature of the event. "To become informed," he explained, "the voter does not have to attend a dozen partisan rallies to follow competing political hopefuls."

If the university's candidates' fair of two years ago is any criteria, large numbers of voters agree with this viewpoint. To the surprise of many political observers,

close to 10,000 from all walks of life attended the last event of this type. The excitement of competition may be another attraction. One man at the last candidates' fair commented, "It's just like a wrestling match where the candidates verbally beat each other on the head."

THE FUTURE OF METRO CITY
(Metro News Service)
Metro 2000, a city-sponsored project to guide our city into the future, is pouring forth a wealth of information on numerous facets of our present life style.

The subcommittee on recreational, cultural, and leisure activities is a case in point. Although the objective of this subcommittee is to facilitate greater opportunities for future participation in these aspects of life, they have collected data on such matters as the organizations to which the people of greater Metro presently belong. This is the pattern that has emerged, expressed as a percentage of total population:

Religious	55
Social	26
School	23
Charitable	21
Labor union	16
Professional	14
Civic	14
Fraternal	14
Veterans	12
Political	12
Sports	11
Business	10
Arts or cultural	9
Fan or boosters club	7
Ethnic	3

The question that has been raised by several conservative groups opposed to Metro 2000

is: "What is the value of these statistics besides the fact that they are interesting?"

Roberta Long, chairperson of the subcommittee, heatedly remarked at a meeting last night that "Our group seemed to be plagued by shortsighted citizens with an eighteenth-century viewpoint of society." In a calmer tone she went on to explain, "the meaning of their research is found in the social interaction patterns that organization affiliations reveal." "Organization membership," she argues, "reflects the diverse value priorities of our community. Only by determining the present value orientation of Metro City can we project the atmosphere that will be necessary for a healthy community in the future."

INFLATION CRUEL BURDEN FOR ELDERLY
(Metro City News)
A special task force of the American Association of Elderly called the answers offered by a HEW representative "totally inadequate." The task force, chaired by William Blaus, is investigating the hardships caused by the current two-digit inflation on the elderly of the nation.

According to Blaus, "our findings today have documented the extent and severity that the rate of inflation has imposed on a class of citizen who must survive on a fixed income." Another member of the task force, Joan Freedman, expressed the plight of the elderly more emphatically when she referred to elderly citizens living on a fixed income as an "economic and political caste."

When one listens to the testimony of a widowed woman of 81 years who must survive on a Social Security check of $186, the concern of the task force becomes vividly clear. After Mrs. Ethel Ross pays for rent, utilities, and other miscellaneous necessities, the issue is not one of eating properly. The issue is minimizing hunger.

CITY OFFICIALS GET PAY BOOST

(Metro City News Service)
The Metro City Council voted, 7–0, today to boost the salaries of city department heads and elected officials by 12 percent. The salary increase would be retroactive to July 1.

At the same session the council directed the Personnel Department to investigate the feasibility of developing an "executive compensation program" that would provide lesser salary increases for city executives and officials in the future. The "executive compensation program" idea was suggested originally by Councilman John Heath. "Since officials may not be feeling the bite of inflation as much as rank-and-file city employees, we must investigate the possibility of giving them less substantial pay increases in the future."

The Council approved 12 percent wage increases for rank-and-file city employees earlier this month.

The selection of campaign issues involves more than simply identifying the public policy orientations of the candidate. The issues, if properly selected and developed, serve to distinguish the candidate among the multitude of other candidates competing for the public eye. Because public attention to political matters is limited at best, major campaign issues must necessarily be few in number.

It is also because of relative apathy of citizens toward politics that candidates use the tactic of direct attack on a campaign opponent. This tactic sometimes involves confronting the opposition on a significant issue. On other occasions the substance of the attack may be an attention-getter to focus public attention on the adversary or even on the race itself. For example, in a recent campaign that was all but being ignored by the general public, one candidate charged that "the office of city attorney had become a hereditary position. For 50 years the top assistant to the city attorney has become the city attorney when his boss resigned." The facts of the charge were true but not significant to the real issues of the campaign.

With these considerations in mind, select three of the following issues as the major issues for the campaign of your candidate:

- Wage and price controls
- Law and order
- Nationalization of the oil industry
- National health care program
- Consumer protection
- Mandatory school busing
- Food as a viable diplomatic weapon
- Conservation of national resources
- Foreign aid
- Open government and campaign reform
- Penal system reform

The development of any issue is influenced by the generality or specificity of the policy area under consideration, for example, foreign aid versus a national health care program. Nonetheless, all issues must be converted from their relative abstractness into a candidate's position that is in language easily understood by the voters. And, of course, the issue position must be communicated in a way that the benefits for the candidate's constituency and constituency groups are obvious. In issue development it must be remembered that "constituency" must be defined in terms of voters, not potential voters. This means that the candidate's issue position must be scrutinized by the steering committee in the light of voter turnout projections, public opinion surveys, and the location of opinion groupings in relation to demographic factors.

Some campaign managers have found it advantageous to test the electoral viability of issues by directing persons charged with issue analysis responsibilities to develop pro-con arguments on all issues that exhibit reasonable appeal to the constituency. This advocacy approach avoids bypassing issue positions that could hold voter appeal for significant group(s) in the constituency.*

CONTACT: Bill Freel   April 19, 1974
        457-8000   FOR IMMEDIATE RELEASE

Gayle Brewster, a Democrat and former ABC newswoman, announced her candidacy for the State Senate today. She has already received the full endorsement of Phillip Rossmart, who is vacating the seat. "Gayle Brewster will make an outstanding legislator," he noted.

"The tone of my campaign will stress the urgent need to return honesty, openness and candor in California politics," Brewster stated at an early morning breakfast meeting. The breakfast—a fund raiser—was attended by some 75 persons to . . .

Sample Candidate Information Sheet

INFORMATION SHEET ON: Donald M. Trimble
                          Candidate for the U.S. House of Representatives
                          21st Congressional District, New York

Personal Background

Age 33, born 13 July 1941
Married, Maria Angela Pecatti, 3 August 1963
Two children, Jack 6, Christina 4

Don was raised on a farm in the Yakima valley in eastern Wasington. As a youth he helped to finance his education, from age 13 on, with regular summer employment on farms. His ancestors were midwestern farmers who settled in eastern Washington around the turn of the century.

*In terms of simulation activity, the comprehensive nature of the advocacy approach to issue development demands the attention of several steering committee members, particularly in the pregaming period.

Note to students: The "contact" person indicated at the top left corner is the media

Education

New York City
  University   Don earned a bachelor of science degree in history. Married
                during the last of his undergraduate years, Don and Maria both
                attended classes while holding part-time jobs to earn their
                entire support.
                Don continued his education training and earned a law degree.
  Yale

---

relations director. The purpose of this format item is to provide the media with a specific individual to contact if further information or clarification is desired.

The purpose of the date and desired release time is obvious if one considers how many news releases arrive on the desk of a reporter in any one day. In this particular example, it informs the reporter that it is today's news, at least *if* the subject matter of the release is newsworthy.

Newsworthiness is a relative term. Its determination often rests on the newsworthiness of one happening in relation to competing news. With this in mind, a release must address a matter of significance. The news significance of a candidate's statement, to exemplify, is considerably enhanced if it was presented to a group of 500 cheering supporters.

With regard to the content of a news release, it should contain the five essentials of a news story: who, what, where, when, and why. In fact, a weakness of the above sample news release is that these elements are not contained in the first paragraph. When this is accomplished in the lead paragraph, the remainder of the release will function to give the details of these five elements in decreasing order of importance.

The writing style of a good news story is characterized by concise sentences and short paragraphs. Direct quotes of the candidate and other significant individuals add interest, not to mention the objective of using the candidate's name as often as feasible. Remember that the purpose of campaign media relations is to expose the candidate's name in relation to matters pertinent to voters in as many news stories that you can get printed. Thus, keep the news releases reasonably short—one or two pages maximum. If the release runs more than one page, indicate "(more)" at the bottom of the first page, and, in the upper left corner of the second page, type: Gayle Brewster for State Senate Release Add 1

And finally, all news releases should be typewritten, double spaced, and on one side of the paper.

Note to students: As you see, the purpose of a candidate information sheet is to give the reader the background of the candidate at a glance. The format used above is one of many ways to accomplish this end.

If the above sample information sheet were to be completed, if would outline Mr. Trimble's professional background and accomplishments. Then attention would turn to governmental and political background. It is also important to include the professional, civic, and religious affiliations of the candidate. The concluding section would concisely present the philosophical position of the candidate.

Voter Turnout in the 17th Congressional District (Population: 469,107)

Percent Voting in Last	Presidential	Congressional	Local
Cities	69	51	55
Suburbs	76	59	58
Towns	76	60	53
Rural	74	63	60
18 to 29 years	54	23	32
30 to 49 years	81	68	66
50 years and over	80	75	68
Men	74	58	58
Women	72	58	56
Eighth grade	65	60	55
High school	69	55	55
College	83	60	59
White Protestant	76	61	58
White Catholic	75	60	58
Jew	86	74	63
White	75	59	57
Black	58	47	53
Union Member	72	64*	**
Under $5,000	59	54	47
$5,000 to $9,999	69	48	51
$10,000 to $14,999	78	60	61
$15,000 and over	87	70	67
Republican	83	74*	**
Democrat	73	67*	**
Independent	72	65*	**

*Data supplemented from local sources.

**Data not available.

SOURCE: These data were acquired by the Congressional Campaign Committee from a 1973 study sponsored by Senator Edmund Muskie's Sub-Committee on Intergovernmental Relations entitled *Confidence and Concern: Citizens View American Government*. Although the data were collected in a nationwide survey by Louis Harris and Associates, it is directly applicable to your campaign. In 1974 a Metro City survey research firm determined that Metro City was a microcosm of the national picture on voter turnout and on several other aspects of voter behavior.

**Demographic Characteristics
of the 17th Congressional District**

Characteristic	Percent
Professional, managerial	38
Skilled labor	22
White collar	32
Manual labor	8
Union members	24
Nonunion members	53
Men	54
Women	46
Eighth grade	6
High school	35
College	56
18 to 29 years	20
30 to 49 years	48
50 and over	22
Under $5,000	6
$5,000 to $9,999	20
$10,000 to $14,999	35
$15,000 to $19,999	23
$20,000 and over	16